Cultural Entanglement in the Pre-Independence Arab World

Cultural Entanglement in the Pre-Independence Arab World

Arts, Thought and Literature

Edited by
Anthony Gorman and Sarah Irving

I.B.TAURIS
LONDON • NEW YORK • OXFORD • NEW DELHI • SYDNEY

I.B. TAURIS
Bloomsbury Publishing Plc
50 Bedford Square, London, WC1B 3DP, UK
1385 Broadway, New York, NY 10018, USA
29 Earlsfort Terrace, Dublin 2, Ireland

First published in Great Britain 2021
This paperback edition published in 2022

Cover design: Adriana Brioso
Cover image © Stella and Alexis Dimou

A catalogue record for this book is available from the British Library.

A catalog record for this book is available from the Library of Congress.

ISBN: HB: 978-1-7883-1955-3
PB: 978-0-7556-3540-5
ePDF: 978-0-7556-0632-0
eBook: 978-0-7556-0630-6

Typeset by Newgen KnowledgeWorks Pvt., Ltd, Chennai, India

To find out more about our authors and books visit www.bloomsbury.com
and sign up for our newsletters.

Contents

Figures

Contributors

Hussam R. Ahmed is Assistant Professor in History at Maynooth University, Ireland. He was formerly a postdoctoral fellow in the Prince Alwaleed Bin Talal Centre of Islamic Studies at the University of Cambridge. His research interests focus on the social and cultural history of the modern Middle East. He has published on the Arab Nahda and Egyptian institutions of culture and education in the twentieth century. His forthcoming book (2021) is a social biography of the iconic intellectual and educator Taha Hussein (1889–1973) and his role in building Egyptian institutions of education and culture in the first half of the twentieth century.

Sarah H. Awad is Assistant Professor in General Psychology at Aalborg University, Denmark. She received her PhD in cultural psychology from Aalborg University and her MSc in social and cultural psychology from the London School of Economics and Political Science, UK. Her research interests are in visual methodologies and the analysis of public images and their influence on identity, collective memory and politics within a society. Her most recent books include *Street Art of Resistance* with Brady Wagoner (2017) and *The Psychology of Imagination* with Brady Wagoner and Ignacio Brescó de Luna (2017).

Ami Ayalon is Professor Emeritus of Middle Eastern History at Tel Aviv University, Israel. His scholarly interest focuses on the cultural history of Arabic-speaking societies in modern times, primarily language modernization, history of the Arab press and the history of printing and reading in the Middle East. His most recent book is *The Arabic Print Revolution: Cultural Production and Mass Readership* (2016).

Elena Chiti is Associate Professor at Stockholm University. A cultural historian of modern Egypt, she holds a PhD from Aix-Marseille Université. She is interested in cultural productions as sources to explore identity-making in times of social and political turmoil. From this perspective, she has studied Alexandrian literary circles between the late nineteenth and the first third of the twentieth centuries, aiming to go beyond the cliché of 'cosmopolitan Alexandria'. Since 2011, she has applied the same perspective to the present and to popular culture, to explore the postepoch that follows the Arab revolutions.

Raphael Cormack is a visiting scholar at Columbia University. His research focuses on Egyptian theatre and popular culture at the beginning of the twentieth century. He recently edited a collection of contemporary Egyptian short stories, *The Book of Cairo* (2019).

Joy Amina Garnett is a visual artist and writer from New York. Her work has been shown at the FLAG Art Foundation and MoMA–PS1 (New York), the Milwaukee Art Museum and the Witte Zaal (Ghent, Belgium), and has been published in *Virilio and Visual Culture* (2013) and *The Artists' and Writers' Cookbook* (2016). She is working on an illustrated family memoir of Egypt, a short excerpt of which appears in *Rusted Radishes* (2019).

Anthony Gorman is Senior Lecturer in Islamic and Middle Eastern Studies at the University of Edinburgh. He is the author of *Historians, State and Politics in Twentieth Century Egypt* (2003) and co-editor (with Marilyn Booth) of *The Long 1890s in Egypt* (2014), (with Sossie Kasbarian) of *Diasporas of the Modern Middle East* (2015) and (with Didier Monciaud) of *The Press in the Middle East and North Africa, 1850–1950* (2018). He continues to work on a history of the Middle Eastern prison, the anarchist movement in the Eastern Mediterranean before 1914 and the resident foreign presence in modern Egypt.

Sarah Irving is a Leverhulme Early Career Fellow at Edge Hill University. She was awarded her PhD in Islamic and Middle Eastern Studies by the University of Edinburgh in 2018 and has published on Mandate and Late Ottoman Palestinian history and on representations of Arab-Jewish romance in Arabic novels in journals including *Jerusalem Quarterly*, *Contemporary Levant* and the *Journal of Middle East Women's Studies*. She is the author of several non-academic titles on Palestine and is currently completing a book manuscript on women's labour in Late Ottoman Palestine.

Idriss Jebari is Assistant Professor in Middle Eastern Studies at Trinity College, Dublin. His research interests cover North African critical thought in post-1967 Arab intellectual history. He has published on notable figures such as Abdallah Laroui, Hichem Djaït, Abdelkebir Khatibi and Mohamed Abed al-Jabri. He is currently working on a monograph that will address North Africa's contemporary intellectual history between Europe and the Arab Levant.

Alia Mossallam is a EUME postdoctoral fellow at the Alexander von Humboldt Foundation and Visiting Scholar at the Lautarchiv, Humboldt University of Berlin. She is interested in exploring moments of popular mobilization and popular political expression in Egyptian history through songs. Her work has focused on popular histories of the Nasserist era and, lately, experiences of Egyptian workers in the First World War. Her latest publications include 'Strikes, Riots and Laughter: Al-Himamiyya Village's Experience of the 1918 Revolt', and she is working on the manuscript 'Damming the Nile: (hi)Stories of Submersion and Liberation during the Building of the Aswan High Dam'.

Yasmine Nachabe Taan is Associate Professor in Art and Design Practice and Theory at the Lebanese American University, Lebanon. Her research interest focuses on gender representation in photographs of the Middle East and North Africa region and on compiling and analyzing the work of prominent Arab designers, illustrators and typographers of the 1960s and 1970s. As a curator and an art and design critic, she publishes essays, reviews and articles on a range of art and design related topics. Her most recent publication is entitled *Saloua Raouda Choucair: Modern Arab Design: An Exploration of Abstraction across Materials and Functions* (2019).

Acknowledgements

The initial impetus for this volume came from a workshop titled 'Cultures of Diversity, Arts and Cultural Life in Arab Societies before Independence', held at the University of Edinburgh in December 2015. The occasion was sponsored by the Centre for the Advanced Study of the Arab World (CASAW) and was funded through the generous support of the Language-Based Area Studies (LBAS), an initiative of Research Councils UK led by the Economic and Social Research Council. The event brought together a collection of scholars from Europe, the Middle East and the United States who presented a series of stimulating papers that form the basis of this book. We wish to express our thanks to all attendees for their participation, including those who were not able to contribute to this volume, as well as Rebecca Wolfe for her energetic research support and Marie McPherson for her administrative dexterity. We also wish to thank the publisher, and a number of readers, both anonymous and those known to us, for their role in the preparation of the final text.

Note on Transliteration

In transliterating Arabic this volume generally follows the International Journal of Middle East Studies system. There are, however, some exceptions to this rule: personal names where a specific spelling was preferred and used by the individual in question or has become recognized as the norm over time; and transliterations of colloquial Arabic (*ammiyya*), where authors have used styles of transliteration which they feel best evoke the sounds and cadences of particular forms of the language. For ease of reading, diacritical marks have not been used, except to indicate the letters ayn and hamza. Capitalization in transliterated Arabic sentences and book or journal titles occurs only in the first word and personal names.

Greek bibliographic references have been presented in Greek script with an English translation.

Introduction

Anthony Gorman and Sarah Irving

During the advance of Commonwealth troops into Palestine in 1917, men of the Egyptian Labour Corps who carried materiel, dug trenches and laid railway tracks would sing the mournful words of 'Ya 'aziz 'aini'. This well-known song, with its roots in the peasant folklore of Upper Egypt, had already been adopted by the celebrated singer Naʿima al-Masriyya in recordings with the revolutionary songwriter Sayyid Darwish. As the conscripted Egyptian workers chanted the song, it was memorized by British soldiers who, even if they understood none of the words, recognized in it a shared sense of longing for home and for an end to the bloody conflict. And, once many of the British soldiers had moved on or been demobilized, the song took on new meanings of resistance back in Egypt for working men who were not released to go home and continued to labour for the colonial authorities. The story of this song and its shift in meaning for working and middle-class Egyptians and for the colonizing British exemplify how the contributions to this volume see cultural productions – music, theatre, literature, translation, photography and caricature – as entangled phenomena, enmeshed in complex social relations of power and meaning.

In seeking to explore this diversity and in resisting essentialist views of Arab culture, Muslims, 'Peoples of the East' or colonial victimhood, this volume employs the language of entanglement and an underlying appreciation of complexity and its potential richness and depth to consider how the Mashriq and Maghrib in the first half of the twentieth century, despite political challenges and impending ferment, played host to a myriad of interlinked cultural formations. Reflecting on the interconnectedness of these societies, their cultural production and transnational links and *entanglement*, the collection explores how the interaction between Arabic and non-Arabic cultural and intellectual practices, as well as influences from imperial Europe and the Islamic East, at various times and in diverse spaces inspired creative tensions which challenge binary views of East-West relations and standard imperialist-colonial frameworks. In this sense, it offers a collective critique of established modernizing conceptions of cultural development on the one hand, and nationalist, nativist frameworks based on the values of a specific political project and unitary ideas of national identity and culture on the other. Its contributors consider, at heart, the mobility of ideas and cultural practices, and question how different groups and individuals, often in asymmetrical relations of economic and political power, make ideas, languages and cultural manifestations their own.

The Arab world and cultural pluralism

Between 1850 and 1950, the Arab world underwent a period of great transformation as the Ottoman Empire, dominant in the region for centuries, yielded to European power and influence. Beginning with the invasion of Algiers in 1830, the region came steadily under direct European control, with the sweep of French authority across North Africa from Morocco to Tunisia, the British occupation of Egypt in 1882 and the Italian invasion of Libya just before the First World War. With the Ottoman defeat in 1918, and the subsequent dismemberment of empire, much of the Mashriq came to be administered as League of Nations mandates with the Maghrib under French and Italian colonial rule. In the decade or so after the Second World War, a more genuine independence came on the back of ideological appeals to local and Arab nationalism, manifested in radical thought and institutionalized in organizations such as the Arab League.

The conventional term 'the Arab world' needs some elucidation. While a convenient shorthand to refer to the majority Arabic-speaking regions, it can imply a uniformity that conceals the very considerable heterogeneity in its social and cultural character. Even during the long period of Ottoman rule, the Arab world encompassed a great diversity of languages, cultural traditions, customs, art forms and artistic practices. European influence then occupation across the region brought with it even greater complexity. With faster, more extensive systems of communication and transport, along with expanding access to education, came the potential for more intensive interaction at different levels of society. People speaking, writing and singing different languages, or employing diverse dialects and registers of the same language, encountered one another more often and in quicker succession; local norms and customs met other ways of being and doing. With formal independence came a call for the establishment of national institutions as part of the decolonizing process, one demanded by political impetus but which came at the cost of full recognition of the pluralist nature of the region.

Cultural and intellectual life in the Arab world in the century before independence was framed by a number of critical developments that included the expanding scope of state responsibility, the greater engagement of civil society, the emergence of new genres of cultural expression and the changing profile of intellectuals and other cultural practitioners. Each of these played a significant role in the formation, character and practice of the cultural field.

Characteristic of the emerging modern state in the Arab world has been the state's increasing involvement in promoting and supporting certain cultural activities, institutions and practices. The establishment of the Madrasat al-Alsun (School of Languages) by Muhammad Ali in Cairo in 1835 was early recognition of the need to engage with the knowledge and literature of other cultures, particularly manifest in the translation movement.[1] As the ambition and authority of governments increased, so did state responsibilities expand to establish and support educational and cultural institutions, schools, libraries and arts institutes. Certain branches of the arts, such as opera and theatre, were favoured with royal patronage. After 1918, the creation of different agencies and organizations, such as the Department of Antiquities of Palestine or branches of the British Council, provided additional opportunities for collaboration in cultural work/activities. The convening of the first International Congress of Arab Music in Cairo in 1932, which drew attendees from across the Arab world and beyond, testified to the aspirations of a city to the status of an international cultural centre.

Beyond the circles of government, civil organizations would also play a critical part in educational and cultural affairs. Learned societies, such as the Institut Égyptien (later Institute d'Égypte) (est. 1859) or the Palestine Oriental Society (est. 1920) were set up, often with some official patronage and a membership notable as much for its social as its academic distinction, to provide a forum for the discussion and dissemination of work across a wide range of literary and scientific subjects. Less elite associations of artists, intellectuals and littérateurs, each with its own purpose and audience, served as crucibles of critical thought, artistic creativity and social identity. Literary salons and cultural clubs brought together intellectuals and dilettantes; ideas were transmitted in print and conversation, in mutually intelligible languages and in translation; personal connections and networks were forged. Across the Arab world at large, both Arab and other communities established local organizations, arranged activities and sponsored publications that demonstrated their engagement in this general cultural dynamism.

The press would emerge as a critical vehicle in which culture was both expressed and commented on. Embraced first by political authorities in Egypt and Lebanon in the first half of the nineteenth century, by 1900 a vibrant and privately owned local press had established itself as a significant actor in the public space and cultural landscape. Arabic periodicals, exemplified in specialized cultural and scientific journals such as *al-Muqtataf* (est. 1876, Beirut and Cairo) and *al-Hilal* (est. 1892, Cairo) served as powerful catalysts for cultural appraisal and renewal. In subsequent decades, the proliferation of titles, genres, languages and readerships supported an environment in which cultural entwinements and their productive tensions arose. In interwar Egypt, cultural reviews such as *La Semaine égyptienne* (est. 1927) served elite multilingual readerships.

The multicultural character of late Ottoman societies allowed for complex routes of dissemination and influence. As the majority spoken language, Arabic enjoyed a distinctive status across the region, but other Middle Eastern and Mediterranean communities – Armenians, Greeks, Kurds, Jews, Berbers and Turks – maintained and developed their own literary traditions and cultural practices, neither wholly segregated nor integrated with the others. Rising European influence promoted the spread of French, English and Italian not just as languages of colonial authority but as vocabularies of commerce, law and social distinction. In this milieu, bilingualism and multilingualism were not uncommon, and at times even routine, especially in port cities such as Alexandria, Beirut, Tangiers and Jaffa, or centres of pilgrimage, diplomacy and scholarship, as Jerusalem or Cairo, where merchants, itinerant labourers, sailors, diplomats, missionaries and scholars met and mixed. This polyglottal milieu and the babel of signs crowding the streetscape embodied the entwined and entangled relationship of a fertile cultural dynamism.

Increasing popular literacy accelerated these developments, if unevenly across different ethnic and religious communities, classes and genders. At the beginning of the twentieth century, literacy in Arabic-speaking societies was generally low: in Egypt in 1907, for example, it stood at 7 per cent of the general population, with male literacy at 13 per cent and at 1 per cent for women. However, among different communities, such as the Italians, Greeks and Jews, it could be above 50 per cent.[2] Literacy slowly improved as the century progressed; the state became more involved in education while private associations, especially missionary bodies, continued to serve as important enablers of cultural expression, particularly in Egypt and Greater Syria.[3]

The written word was received in more complex ways than simply the reading of the literate and was also transmitted via community and family members who read texts to wider audiences, or through other graphic presentation, by illustrations and caricatures. While social divisions undoubtedly influenced the range, accessibility and frequency of cultural practices, the delineations were often vaguer and more dynamic than has been recognized. Some traditional cultural forms are an important reminder of this. Folk songs, for example, were best remembered by women in the villages. Other cultural forms were more accessible even if at times more elite practices. Theatre in the Arab world began as a popular medium, with acting performances, shadow-plays and puppetry travelling around towns and villages, sometimes with religious but often secular purposes, or hybrid forms of singing, dancing and acting which catered for male audiences in the main cities. More 'serious' theatre was primarily a phenomenon of the late nineteenth century.

Certain forms of cultural expression, even if they owed something to European influence, demonstrated an interplay between local and foreign practice. In the figurative arts, the pioneering caricatures of Ya'qub Sannu' (1839–1912), likely inspired during his time in Italy, laid the foundation of an artistic genre in Egypt that was maintained into the interwar period by the Spanish cartoonist Juan Sintes, the Armenian-Egyptian Alexander Saroukhan and later Egyptians Muhammad Rakha and Salah Jahin, to become an established feature of national press culture.[4] Egyptian painters, such as Muhammad Naji, Mahmud Sa'id, and in Lebanon, Daoud Corm, who often received their training either locally from resident European teachers or abroad, were pioneering artists but not simply of a national tradition (as they might later be cast).[5] They were part of a wider spectrum of cultural practitioners that included others less well known, such as Giorgis Dimou, whose work reflected the Egyptian environment in which he lived.[6] A vibrant engagement of local practice with internationalist perspective came together in Art et Liberté, the Egyptian surrealist movement of the 1930s.[7] In Palestine, painting developed as an elite practice during the nineteenth century but even earlier had taken on popular forms, such as the Jerusalem school of icon painting, which was influenced by the growing photographic industry and increasing demand from pilgrims and tourists to the Holy Land, and reached its apogee in the work of Niqula Sayigh (d.1942).[8] Comparable trajectories can be found in other artistic fields, such as sculpture, where the Egyptian Mahmud Mukhtar and Iraqi Jawad Salim, both former students in Paris, would later gain great national acclaim in their respective countries.

Part of this expanding canvas of artistic expression was precipitated by technological innovation. The arrival of photography in the middle of the nineteenth century, first in Cairo and a decade later in Beirut, created new practitioners, audiences and consumers. The role of members of various ethnic communities as local photographers was a notable feature of its introduction, but developments in camera technology made the profession less specialized and more accessible over time.[9] The extent to which technical, aesthetic and social changes were entwined is witnessed, for example, in the large number of Armenians who entered the photographic profession in Palestine, their presence the result of waves of violence against their communities across the Ottoman Empire.[10] The arrival of cinema and the recording industry to the Middle East around the same time provided yet other genres of cultural performance and production. The dynamics of these interactions varied. The flow of technological innovation may have been mostly eastward but its local practice was not predetermined but conjugated by existing traditions, social structures and specific context.

These changes in the role of the state, the nature of civil participation and new forms of cultural expression transformed the social standing and professional status of the intellectual, artist and performer. At the beginning of the nineteenth century, intellectuals and cultural practitioners in the Arab world were principally educated in religious learning and the traditional arts. The practice of sending student missions to Europe in the 1820s, adopted by both Egypt and Istanbul, provided an avenue of professional opportunity for young Arabs/Ottomans to become trained as translators, scholars and bureaucrats.[11] This policy was continued into the twentieth century, often in the form of state-funded scholarships. In certain roles the religious scholar ceded ground to the journalist, cultural commentator and secular public intellectual.[12] The emergence of new fields and genres of cultural production, especially in the press, brought greater prospects and public visibility for a wider spectrum of practitioners.

The cultural ferment created in this environment arose out of an uneasy tension between the conditions of colonialism and of indigenous traditions. The former held up the vaunted claims of the 'civilizing' project and its promotion of modernist cultural forms along with its strategic sponsorship of minority communities, partly to undermine nationalist movements that were themselves players in a complex and contested landscape of local identity. Yet while the colonial and semi-colonial order maintained a regime of legal obstacles, social hierarchies, power differentials and interferences that were its hallmark, the uneven and at times inconsistent character of these administrations engendered porous cultural boundaries which allowed for inversions, transgressive connections and subaltern resistance to the formal titular order. Personal networks, work relationships and collaboration were forged sometimes in spite of these divisions. The national identities and ideologies of Arab nationalism, still coalescing and yet to assert themselves, fuelled cultural activism and creativity.

By the late colonial-early independence era, the acceptable parameters of cultural expression had begun to narrow. Partly driven by the anti-colonial imperative of the nationalist movement and the departure or public elision of some non-Arab populations, newly independent Arab governments came to see culture as an explicit instrument of state policy and an engine of national renewal. Programmes of cultural decolonization and even 'cultural revolution' were launched as part of ambitious political agendas; National Charters (e.g. Egypt 1962, Algeria 1976) set out visions of both the past and future of the imagined, reinstated national community.[13] Most pronounced in the radical Arab republics where bureaucracies were assembled in ministries of education or of culture to pursue a specific agenda (Egypt, 1958; Tunisia, 1961; Syria, 1976), the state now became the employer not only of cultural bureaucrats and state educators but also of many artists, poets, novelists and other intellectuals, to whom it offered security of tenure in return for an ideologically acceptable output.[14] Regulation of the press, already a familiar feature of colonial administrations, was enthusiastically employed with further restrictions on ownership (in some cases ending in nationalization) and greater use of censorship, with inevitable consequences for cultural freedom of expression.

The commitment to the construction of an Arab culture and view of history, conceived either as a modernist project or as a return to an authentic national personality, now became a regular refrain, at times applied pointedly to language policy, especially in Algeria where Arabization became a mantra of the nationalist movement or in Lebanon where identification with French culture took on specific partisan overtones. While such policies did not always meet their stated aims, they were generally successful in establishing the state as the central player of the cultural establishment and in eliding or reframing the presence of some of these elements deemed symbols or products of the colonial order and therefore inconsistent with the new national identity.

Contested paradigms

Scholarship on cultural production and change in the Arab world in the century or so before independence has been dominated by three main paradigms: the colonial-national narrative, the cosmopolitan society and the Nahdawi perspective. Each invoke a central principle of cultural production within a structure of social and political relations that determine the dynamics and hierarchy of different cultural forces and their agents.

The colonial-national paradigm regards the period as one principally determined by the conflict between European colonialism and local-national responses and resistance, played out in the political and economic fields as well as the cultural arena. Culture production is evaluated from the imperialist perspective by reference to the *mission civilisatrice* and, with the rise of a nationalist movement, can take on an explicitly political dimension in which local traditions and practices seek to assert or reassert themselves against colonial strictures. In the postcolonial era, the dominant narrative becomes the affirmation of authentic, local values as part of the assertion of national identity and the nation-building process in contrast to the foreign, alien values of the colonial period.[15] This interpretation relies on clear definitions and boundaries, of distinctions between the national and the foreign, with implications for what is native and authentic, and what is imported and imposed. In this dichotomy, the complexity of the presence of other ethnic and religious groups, often viewed as allies or beneficiaries of one side or the other, is at best underplayed and at times disregarded.

In contrast to the binary of the colonial-national framework, cosmopolitanism, either as an empirical description or a conceptual category, has been called on to encapsulate the underlying impulse of multilingual, multiethnic and multifaith societies of the Arab world. Invoked especially in urban contexts, the cosmopolitan society has served as a potent literary trope, often cast in a nostalgic idiom that has sought to capture and articulate the nature of the open and pluralist society.[16] Attractive because of its universalist claims and its endorsement in the accounts of many memoirists, the image of cosmopolitan Alexandria, Baghdad and Middle Eastern cities has been faulted for its lack of analytical rigour and its often elitist Eurocentric and non-Muslim bias. Its tendency to obscure the workings of power and privilege within these settings and its failure to recognize the political and social underpinnings of a multicultural society, often complicit with a hierarchical colonial order that benefitted communities of specific faiths or originating from imperial states, has attracted particular criticism. Literary portrayals particularly have been critiqued for their orientalist images, and like-minded scholarly accounts for their neglect of the ways in which class and perceptions of race restricted access to cultural circles and expression.[17]

If cosmopolitanism is often associated with a wistful and sentimental perspective of the colonial period, the discourse of the Nahda (literally 'awakening') as the core of cultural and intellectual life in the Arab world has been framed in more progressive terms. Defined as a period of reform or revival beginning in the mid-nineteenth century and continuing into the twentieth, particularly evident in Cairo, Alexandria and Beirut, the Nahda relies on an idiom of rebirth of the Arab past inspired by the challenge of ideas and practices from Europe.[18] While discussion and debate on its nature and even timing continues, the Nahdawi perspective has come to occupy a strong presence in the scholarly literature and been particularly successful in projecting a picture of cultural dynamism and mission. Its principal agent is the Arab intellectual and its primary form the full spectrum of Arabic literature. In a more specifically political sense, it is attached to the seminal writings of George Antonius and others from the late 1930s that have proved enduring points of reference with the emerging Arab nationalist movement.[19]

The Nahdawi approach provides an attractive discourse by which to explain the outburst of creative vitality in the Arab world inspired by contact with the West but expressed within the idiom of local cultural forms and traditions.[20] However, it also carries certain limitations and embedded values. If the cosmopolitan perspective may overlook cultural and other barriers between different groups, the Nahda narrative tied as it is closely to Arabic language and culture runs the risk of failing to recognize the pluralist character of Arab societies and the significant interaction between different social and intellectual non-Arab communities.[21] Further, while some Arab nationalists, such as Satiʿ al-Husri, defined Arabness as a matter of language and history, which allowed for some variation in what constituted Arab/ic culture (often in an effort to forge a coherent identity in the wake of colonially imposed political rule, economic exploitation and cultural hierarchies), others hewed to more rigid lines, looking to essentialized visions sustained by an idealized distant past or romanticized peasantry. Some even adopted nativist notions of identity where cultural variation was thought of as a manifestation of underlying differences of blood and descent in which the only *authentic* cultural creator was one tied to a specific image of the nation.[22]

Cultural entanglement

In engaging with the cultural vitality of the self-styled Arab world, we endeavour to avoid the binary character of colonial and national discourse, the nostalgic and idealistic ballast of cosmopolitanism, and the limiting cultural specificity of Nahdawi studies. Rather, we seek to explore this asymmetrical pattern of relations between different cultural references in a way that implicitly critiques notions of authenticity or the idealized pluralism of cosmopolitanism and thus recognize the interrelational quality of cultural practices set in a specific context.

The idea of entanglement provides an effective idiom in which to analyse this pattern of interaction and offers ways of understanding cultural and social relations without implied political judgements and normative associations.[23] It fully acknowledges the role of the haphazard and contingent in cultural lives, and permits ideas of transmission and influence on scales ranging from the local to the global and within or between cultural and social groupings. It also allows for multiple forms of social interaction to be understood as entangled threads within an overall process, combining acts of accommodation, negotiation and creative interaction with more forceful dynamics of domination and resistance.

As a concept, however, entanglement needs to be deployed with some caution. It is not merely a matter of random interactions between different political, social and economic forces to produce a cultural kaleidoscope. The interplay between different cultural sources should neither ignore the critical role of power relations and structural factors, whether of class, ethnicity or gender, nor be subsumed under a standard banner of, for example, colonialism and subaltern domination. Rather, it should divine ways in which social and cultural relations may emerge that crystallize different aspects of the idea of encounter and diversity, and of distinct value judgements. Each case has its own dynamics and idiom. The relative hierarchies of power should thus be read specifically rather than asked to conform to a generalized theme.

In exploring this concept of entanglement in the context of the pre-independence Arab world, the collection engages with a time of great confrontation and engagement on many different levels. Emerging from the late Ottoman period at the beginning of the twentieth century, the diverse Arab world sought to articulate different perspectives and dimensions of its society, culture and self. Already pluralist in terms of its religious character, ethnicity and language in the imperial Ottoman order, the collision between this and the encroachment of European political and economic influence complicated the milieu but also opened up new channels of transmissions, local, international and transcultural. The shift from the hierarchical diversity of the colonial period to the essentialist simplicity of the nation, captured and constrained, offers fertile ground in which to explore these themes. In focusing on the turbulent but vibrant period leading up to independence in the Arabic-speaking world, this volume foregrounds themes of the interaction between cultural production and colonialism, and the tensions – sometimes productive, sometimes conflictual – which the colonial environment brought to the writers, artists and performers with whose work these studies engage.

One of the effects of this decentring of the main narrative from Arab(ic) culture in the pre-independence period is a critique of the idea of authenticity as the domain of a specific ethnic, national or cultural group. Authenticity is instead viewed as a concept which itself is a product of the European Enlightenment, bound up with its focus on the individual and on the author or creator as separate from society, not embedded in his (*sic*) social, political and economic surroundings.[24] Indeed, authenticity has been pinpointed as an essentializing device by which women and other non-hegemonic figures within a culture can be marginalized and silenced.[25] Instead, cultural outputs are encountered as contingent, produced in a specific historical time and place, and informed or inspired by, reacting to or in tension with, the workings of others.

Specific themes and questions

In the studies presented here, these processes of entanglement are played out in distinct ways in different media and through diverse channels of transmission: through reading and the drawing of caricatures; translating of texts and production of theatrical scripts; performing songs and plays. The individual chapters appear in broadly chronological order to offer a selective but coherent trajectory of entanglement over the colonial-early independence period in the Arab world. The emphasis given to Egypt and the Levant reflects the research interests of the contributors but also points to the seminal role that the Eastern Mediterranean played over this period. Nonetheless, we argue that the dynamics of cultural entanglement as conceived here can be seen at work elsewhere across the Arab world, as illustrated by the last chapter where the ideological logic of the nationalist project in Algeria clashed with the liberal utility of the colonial legacy.[26]

In adopting the general framework of entanglement to characterize a pattern of cultural interaction, the individual studies collectively engage with a range of more specific and interlocking themes concerning language production and transmission, cultural boundaries and artistic forms, personalized narratives and critiques of authenticity, and cultural pluralism.

The interplay between languages in a pluralist environment and particularly the role of non-Arabic languages in the multilingual Arab world in creating new cultural forms or fields is a common concern. Individual chapters take up different aspects of this phenomenon: how the French language in Egypt can be seen as an arm of colonial influence but also be appropriated and reconfigured to serve as a vehicle of local elite culture (Hussam Ahmed); how the English translation of an original Ottoman text served as a medium of collaboration between an Arab and Jewish scholar (Sarah Irving); and the development of a local Arabist tradition among Egyptian Greek scholars based on language teaching, translation and commentary that emerged in the interwar period (Anthony Gorman).

The porous nature of the boundaries between different 'cultures' serves as a persistent concern. The discussion of francophone cultural salons in interwar Cairo and Alexandria depicts Egyptians who celebrated their intimate connection with French culture yet regarded themselves as Egyptian and deeply invested in the politics, economics and culture of the country (Ahmed). An examination of French-language texts by Egyptian-based authors more critically addresses attitudes to cultural pluralism (Elena Chiti), while an analysis of the adaptation of *Oedipus Rex* to the Egyptian stage allows space for a spectrum of relations that can be viewed as part of a global dialogue and not simply characterized as an imperial-colonial relationship (Raphael Cormack).

Some contributions focus on the new and expanding forms of cultural transmission and practice. The phenomenon of Arabic reading as an important medium through which transnational and cross-cultural communication occurred leads the collection (Ami Ayalon). Elsewhere, we find songs with their roots in rural Egypt carried by forced labourers to Sinai and Palestine, and thence to Britain by British soldiers (Alia Mossallam). New theatre forms serve as a vehicle for the exploration of aesthetic debates in an account of a stage performance in Cairo in 1912 (Cormack), while an examination of political caricature in Egyptian periodicals in the 1930s (Sarah Awad) and of photography in mandate Lebanon (Yasmine Taan) highlight the developing character and utility of innovative forms of social image.

A number of contributions mine the personal dimension of entanglement by tracing individual trajectories in a specific context and foregrounding it in the extent to which friendship, liking, collegiality and respect – or their reverse – impacted on the movement and articulation of ideas and aesthetics. Joy Garnett offers a personal account of her grandfather, poet, apiarist and cultural critic, Ahmed Zaki Abushâdy, who expressed some of these complementary and contradictory influences in posing himself as a genuine transnational figure. The collaboration between a Palestinian Arab, Stephan Hanna Stephan, and a Galician Jew, Leo Mayer, colleagues in the library of the Department of Antiquities in Palestine, sustains a professional relationship overlapping in matters ranging from their German educations to views of Palestinian nationhood (Irving). Panos Patrikios, a progressive intellectual and Greek Arabist, exemplifies a mode of intercultural communication during the interwar period in Egypt (Gorman), while a woman photographer in Lebanon during the mandate period, Marie al-Khazen, offers an intriguing discussion of self-depiction (Taan). In his own work of self-representation, Malek Bennabi constructs a personal trajectory grounded in the ambiguities and contradictions of an Algerian life (Idriss Jebari).

Art forms challenged notions of authenticity and probed the extent to which peoples under colonialism had the agency to reshape ideas, narratives and technologies that might be assumed to be objects of oppression. Both the graphic and performative arts, in the form of caricature (Awad) and theatre (Cormack), are explored in how they were taken up and adapted to the Egyptian context. The exploration of the historicity of the term 'cosmopolitan', the stability of its meaning and the issue of anachronism and nostalgia in its more sentimental contemporary uses (Chiti) contrasts with the imagery of depictions of the authentic Egyptian character, while a discussion showing how female practitioners of the new art of photography, themselves manipulated and subverted notions of authenticity, orientalism and cosmopolitanism as used by colonial artists, offers very different implications (Taan).

Finally, an analysis of the work of Malek Bennabi provides an illustrative case of the tension between the call of Arab authenticity and of colonial influence, between nativism and liberal formation in the context of independent Algeria (Jebari).

Conclusion

Cultural life in the Arabic-speaking world in the century before independence was multidirectional, fluid and complex with implications of multiple ideas, identities and sources which can only be disentangled with great difficulty, and rarely without damage and loss. In highlighting this aspect of interaction and change across various fields of cultural expression, this collection adds richness, depth and complexity to our understanding of its character and dynamics, and suggests ways in which the monolithic images of 'Arabic' and more broadly 'Middle Eastern' cultures, arts and the influences which shaped them might be better understood. In exploring these different entanglements, these case studies offer an important insight into not only the creative potential of intercultural connections but also the critical importance of the political context that facilitated or obstructed their exercise, whether the political pressures of late 1930s Palestine, the relative openness of polyglot interwar Egypt or the tensions of newly independent Algeria.

The search for cultural authenticity and the rejection of values deemed foreign, alien or imposed continues to exercise its sway in the Arab world (and elsewhere), most recently in claims made of Islamic culture. In presenting these detailed studies of cultural production and interaction in the late colonial Middle East, this volume seeks to illustrate the expression of the arts as a product of contingency and, in drawing attention to the dynamic processes of cultural interaction, to challenge assumptions about authenticity and colonial or national essence. This is not to deny the force of local traditions or the exploitative nature of foreign imposition and expropriation, but it endeavours to point out the existence of examples of creative engagement that contrast with some of the stereotypes parlayed to justify political programmes. It is this multidimensional and dynamic process that is most characteristic of cultural expression in the Arab world rather than conceptions of fixed traditions and static cultures. As the singing soldiers of First World War Egypt show, the parsing of their experiences through the idea of entanglement allows bringing together cultural, political and economic actors, forces of colonialism and resistance, and indigenous and overseas voices. In doing so, the chapters in this volume bring to the fore the richness, vitality and complexity of culture across the Arabic-speaking world during this turbulent period.

Notes

1 Baker (ed.), *Routledge Encyclopedia of Translation Studies*, 322.

2 Reid, *Cairo University*, 113; for figures on different communities, see Tignor, *State, Private Enterprise*, Tables A.1–2. Mandate Palestine offered similar contrasts with c. 72% of Christian men and c. 3% of Muslim women literate, see Ayalon, *Reading Palestine*, 16–17.

3 In Egypt, general literacy had only reached 25% in 1950 (37% male; 13% female), Reid, *Cairo University*, 113.

4 The status of Alexander Saroukhan in the history of Egyptian caricature continues to be celebrated: see '"Saroukhan Comes Back": Int'l Caricature Competition Focusing on Egypt's Famed Cartoonist Reveals Winning Works', Ahram Online, 26 March 2019, http://english.ahram.org.eg/NewsContent/5/25/328888/Arts--Culture/Visual-Art/Saroukhan-Comes-Back-Intl-caricature-competition-f.aspx (accessed 2 April 2020). Sintes seems less well-remembered.

5 Kane, *Politics of Art in Modern Egypt*, 13–15.

6 Born in Cairo of Greek parentage, Giorgis Dimou (1911–2004) was active in the 1930s as an artist and wood engraver, see Dimou, *Charaktika*.

7 Bardaouil and Fellrath, *Art et Liberté*, 16–53.

8 Ari, 'Spiritual Capital', 61–3.

9 Sheehi, *Arab Imago*, 27–36, 57–64.

10 Ankori, *Palestinian Art*, 36.

11 Brummett, *Image and Imperialism*, 78–80; Gürkan, 'France', 224–5.

12 See Hamzah, *Making of the Arab Intellectual*, 90–127.

13 On the Algerian cultural revolution, see McDougall, *A History of Algeria*, 260–1, 266–70.

14 E.g., on the cultivation of state intellectuals and government support of artists in postwar Iraq, see Bashkin, *Other Iraq*, 89–93, 240.

15 Kane, *Politics of Art in Modern Egypt*.

16 Haag, *Alexandria, City of Memory*; Meijer, *Cosmopolitanism, Identity and Authenticity*.

17 E.g., Fahmy, 'For Cavafy, with Love and Squalor'; Hanley, 'Grieving Cosmopolitanism in Middle East Studies'; as well as Chiti in this volume.

18 Albert Hourani's *Arabic Thought in the Liberal Age 1789–1939* (1962) was an early statement of this thesis; for more recent studies, see Patel, *The Arab Nahdah*; and Hanssen and Weiss, *Arabic Thought beyond the Liberal Age*.

19 See Hamzah, *Making of the Arab Intellectual*, 1–19. For an interpretation of a socialist Nahda, see Khuri-Makdisi, *Eastern Mediterranean and the Making of Global Radicalism*.

20 See the Introduction to Allen, *Essays in Arabic Literary Biography 1850–1950*, vol. 3.

21 For a discussion on the centrality of the Arabic language in the Nahda, see Hanssen and Weiss, *Arabic Thought beyond the Liberal Age*, 14–18.

22 See, e.g., the discussion by Idriss Jebari in this volume.

23 The term 'entangled'/'entanglement' has been employed in a number of recent works, e.g., Bauer and Norton, 'Introduction: Entangled Trajectories'; and Firges et al., *Well-Connected Domains: Towards an Entangled Ottoman History*.

24 Handler, 'Authenticity', 2.

25 See, for instance, Emily Lee's arguments regarding the role of discourses of authenticity and essentialism in relation to women of colour in the United States

and to the works of postcolonial theorists Uma Narayan and Gayatri Spivak: Lee, 'Question of Authenticity', 258 *passim*; and also Monahan, 'Conservation of Authenticity', 37–9.

26 See, e.g., the chapter here by Jebari on Algeria. Other examples of this trend are Spencer Scoville's study of Palestinian translator and litterateur Khalil Baydas; Eric Calderwood's analysis of the interactions between Moroccan history writing, the Nahda and nationalist figures from the Mashriq, and Spanish nationalist nostalgia for Andalucia; and Jonathan Gribetz's exploration of contacts between Zionist and Ottoman Palestinian scholars and parliamentarians (see bibliography).

Bibliography

Allen, Roger, ed. *Essays in Arabic Literary Biography 1850–1950*, vol. 3. Wiesbaden: Harrassowitz Verlag, 2010.

Ankori, Gannit. *Palestinian Art*. London: Reaktion Books, 2013.

Ari, Nisa. 'Spiritual Capital and the Copy: Painting, Photography, and the Production of the Image in Early Twentieth-Century Palestine'. *Arab Studies Journal* 25, no. 2 (2017): 60–99.

Ayalon, Ami. *Reading Palestine, Printing and Literacy, 1900–1948*. Austin: University of Texas Press, 2004.

Baker, Mona, ed. *Routledge Encyclopedia of Translation Studies*. London: Routledge, 1998.

Bardaouil, Sam, and Till Fellrath, eds. *Art et Liberté, Rupture, War and Surrealism in Egypt (1938–1948)*. Paris: Skira, 2016.

Bashkin, Orit. *The Other Iraq, Pluralism and Culture in Hashemite Iraq*. Stanford, CA: Stanford University Press, 2009.

Bauer, Ralph, and Marcy Norton. 'Introduction: Entangled Trajectories: Indigenous and European Histories'. *Colonial Latin American Review* 26, no. 1 (2017): 1–17.

Brummett, Palmira. *Image and Imperialism in the Ottoman Revolutionary Press, 1908–1911*. Albany: SUNY Press, 2000.

Calderwood, Eric. *Colonial al-Andalus: Spain and the Making of Modern Moroccan Culture*. Cambridge, MA: Harvard University Press, 2018.

Dimou, Giorgis G. *Charaktika/ Skedia/Keimena/ Epistoles*. Athens: MIET, 2004.

Fahmy, Khaled. 'For Cavafy, with Love and Squalor: Some Critical Notes on the History and Historiography of Modern Alexandria'. In *Alexandria, Real and Imagined*, edited by Anthony Hirst and Michael Silk, 263–80. London: Ashgate, 2004.

Firges, Pascal W., Tobias P. Graf, Christian Roth and Gülay Tulasoğlu, eds. *Well-Connected Domains: Towards an Entangled Ottoman History*. Leiden: Brill, 2014.

Gribetz, Jonathan. *Defining Neighbors: Religion, Race, and the Early Zionist-Arab Encounter*. Princeton: Princeton University Press, 2016.

Gürkan, Emrah Safa. 'France'. In *Encyclopedia of the Ottoman Empire*, ed. Gábor Ágoston and Bruce Masters, 221–5. New York: Facts on File, 2009.

Haag, Michael. *Alexandria, City of Memory*. New Haven, CT: Yale University Press, 2012.

Hamzah, Dyala, ed. *The Making of the Arab Intellectual, Empire, Public Sphere and the Colonial Coordinates of Selfhood*. London: Routledge, 2013.

Handler, Richard. 'Authenticity'. *Anthropology Today* 2, no. 1 (February 1986): 2–4.

Hanley, Will. 'Grieving Cosmopolitanism in Middle East Studies'. *History Compass* 6, no. 5 (2008): 1346–67.

Hanssen, Jens, and Max Weiss, eds. *Arabic Thought beyond the Liberal Age: Towards an Intellectual History of the Nahda*. Cambridge: Cambridge University Press, 2016.
Kane, Patrick. *The Politics of Art in Modern Egypt, Aesthetics, Ideology and Nation-Building*. London: I.B. Tauris, 2013.
Khuri-Makdisi, Ilham. *The Eastern Mediterranean and the Making of Global Radicalism, 1860–1914*. Berkeley: University of California Press, 2013.
Lee, Emily. 'The Epistemology of the Question of Authenticity, in Place of Strategic Essentialism'. *Hypatia* 26, no. 2 (Spring 2011): 258–79.
McDougall, James. *A History of Algeria*. Cambridge: Cambridge University Press, 2017.
Meijer, Roel, ed. *Cosmopolitanism, Identity and Authenticity in the Middle East*. Richmond, UK: Curzon, 1999.
Monahan, Michael. 'The Conservation of Authenticity: Political Commitment and Racial Reality'. *Philosophia Africana* 8, no. 1 (March 2005): 37–50.
Patel, Abdulrazzak. *The Arab Nahdah: The Making of the Intellectual and Humanist Movement*. Edinburgh: Edinburgh University Press, 2013.
Reid, Donald Malcolm. *Cairo University and the Making of Modern Egypt*. Cambridge: Cambridge University Press, 1990.
Scoville, Spencer. 'Reconsidering Nahdawi Translation: Bringing Pushkin to Palestine'. *The Translator* 21, no. 2 (2015): 223–36.
Sheehi, Stephen. *The Arab Imago: A Social History of Portrait Photography, 1860–1910*. Princeton: Princeton University Press, 2016.
Tignor, Robert. *State, Private Enterprise, and Economic Change in Egypt, 1918–1952*. Princeton: Princeton University Press, 1984.

1

The emergence of mass readership in Arab societies

Ami Ayalon

Imagine travelling by time machine to one of the central Arab-Ottoman cities – Cairo, Alexandria or Beirut – and landing there, say, in the year 1914. Coming out of the machine, we would find ourselves in a highly textual environment, quite like the one in our own hometown, with streets and buildings covered by writings of every kind: street name signs, shop and business name plates, commercial adverts, posters bearing public announcements, personal notices, graffiti and more. The sight would suggest that reading, perhaps also writing, is a standard device of public communication in this place. Our eyes would meet printing presses, bookshops and newspaper vendors, and we would learn of a vast number of printed texts in circulation, including newspapers, journals, pamphlets and books in every conceivable category, from 'do it yourself' guides to tracts of pious counselling. We would also notice that printed items, such as money bills and tram tickets, change hands among people as a matter of routine. Many people, we would realize, rely on reading to navigate in the city and manage their affairs in it. If we care to ask, some of them will tell us that they communicate in writing with partners in near and far provinces, in private letters or over the pages of periodical publications. At the point in time when we visit the place, all such sights are essentially new. If we take our magic machine some four or five decades further back, we would find none of them in that same city: no commercial boards (a handful in foreign idioms might be an exception), no newspaper sellers, hardly a printing press, very few books and an infinitesimal circle of readers. What we witnessed in 1914 was a novel reality, a scene in its infancy.

Prior to the advent of printing in the Middle East, Arabic-speaking societies had adhered to an order whereby reading and writing were designed for limited purposes handled by specific groups; they were not a means of popular communication. Writing was employed in preserving and transmitting the community's spiritual and legal legacy, tasks that were carried out by *ᶜulama'*; in government and administration, the domain of officials and scribes; and in scholarly and literary endeavour, the realm of a few intellectuals who engaged in various fields of knowledge, from chronicle writing to philosophical deliberation and from scientific exploration to poetry. Here and there, people beyond these categories also read and wrote.[1] Taken together, all of these made up a thin layer of society. Exactly how thin it is hard to say, but there can be no doubting their negligible share of the whole. As reading and writing were not considered essential skills for everybody, the bulk of society outside that limited circle was basically illiterate. The community saw nothing problematic in this division and regarded it as the normal order of things. Various needs that would later come to be served by writing and reading were handled by spoken means. Channels of oral communication functioned well throughout the pre-modern history of these societies: conveying messages from rulers to the ruled, circulating information within the community, running people's day-to-day affairs and a rainbow of leisure activities, based as they were on listening rather than reading. This sketch of the cultural scene is, admittedly, rather simplified, and there were exceptions of various kinds in different times and places. But in its general contours it seems to be valid. That such an order worked well for many generations also explains, to a large extent, Middle Eastern society's absence of interest in printing for several centuries after Gutenberg.[2]

The scene we encountered in our imaginary 1914 visit to the area reflected a departure from these time-honoured norms and signalled the dawn of a new phase. The emergence of mass reading was a part of the historic change known as 'the Arab *Nahda*' – the intellectual-cultural 'awakening' in the Ottoman-Arab lands, which began around the mid-nineteenth century and bore implications of great magnitude for the region's social, cultural and political life.[3] The *Nahda* has been a focus of much scholarly attention in recent years,[4] but important aspects of it have received less attention than others. Among the lesser-studied developments have been the emergence of a printing and publishing industry, the formation of a large-scale distribution infrastructure to support that industry and the rise of a popular reading public trained in drawing wisdom from printed texts. In the process, new kinds of writings in unprecedented quantities came to fulfil multiple roles in personal and communal life, and people became used to benefitting from and eventually depending on them.

In this chapter, I propose to explore one facet of this manifold development: the emergence of mass-reading audiences in the Middle East. I shall focus on the region's population whose language of speaking, and then of writing and reading, was Arabic, which included predominantly Muslim and Christian Arabs. It is important, however, to bear in mind the presence of religious and ethnic groups (Jews, Armenians) who were affected by the entry of printing in ways unlike those experienced by Muslims and Christians. Different cultural outlooks and educational backgrounds, and long-time exposure to imported printed works in their respective idioms, placed these minority groups in a distinct position with regard to consuming printed products. Reading, both before and after the adoption of printing, evolved differently in these communities, and it deserves to be studied separately. Considering reading in Arab societies below, then, we should keep in mind that the overall regional scene was more diverse and more colourful than that which is sketched here. In the same vein, we should also keep in mind that comparable developments took place in other parts of the Middle East and the Islamic lands at about the same time, where other languages were spoken and read. The story presented below bears many of the traits that typified the emergence of mass reading across those expansive regions.

A profitable way to explore the change would be by looking at it from two different perspectives: one focusing on society's immediate reaction to the entry of printing and the other on the longer-term process of forming a mass readership. In the former, centring mainly on the Ottoman part of the period (roughly the half-century up to the First World War), the probe should be addressed to those segments of society that were already proficient readers or were in the process of acquiring the skills for that, who quickly moved to profit from the large quantities of printed works that began to pour out of the proliferating presses. These members of the community's educated groups, including the small but expanding circles of graduates of the new schooling projects, formed the modest market that was in place to absorb the products of the nascent industry. The other, longer-term course likewise had its roots in that early period, but its unfolding was perforce slow and lasted for many decades thereafter. In it, the rest of society – or at least the greater part of it – was trained through organized education in using reading to many ends. We will look at this process in the second part of this chapter, by examining an illustrative case from Palestine during the interwar period. The short- and long-term phases together were parts of a transition from predominant illiteracy to popular reading, a historic development that entailed multiple social and cultural difficulties and had far-reaching repercussions.

Short-term changes

The nineteenth century was a time of change unprecedented in scope and pace in Ottoman history. Shifts in the global balance of power, alien infringements through endless channels, rapid technological developments and reforms by rulers in response to these challenges all transformed realities in the areas under Ottoman rule in many ways and modified the long-familiar scene that met the eye almost everywhere. The changes grew in tempo as the end of the century drew near. A person born around mid-century in a large urban area of the Arabic-speaking lands would, by the time they had reached middle age, witness a physical environment quite unlike that which they had known in their youth: major transportation projects, such as roads and railways, steam navigation and the Suez Canal; new means of communication, such as postal services, telegraph and telephone; new urban neighbourhoods, public facilities and services; and a growing presence of foreigners, from diplomats and missionaries to merchants and tourists. Such dynamic turns increased the local population's need for information that would map the kaleidoscopic scene and make sense of the new sounds, views and rules. This thirst for news and enlightenment was a key factor in the emergence of the phenomenon with which we are concerned here.

With the thirst came the means to quench it: printing and publishing, which appeared in the region among many other innovations. Some sporadic ventures of small consequence in earlier periods aside,[5] printing as a major means of text production was adopted in the Arab provinces only during the nineteenth century, first in Egypt and then in Lebanon.[6] State, institutional and private presses popped up and printed books, booklets and, more important for our discussion, periodical publications: newspapers, reporting past events and those that were anticipated in the region and elsewhere; and journals, which examined the changes at more length, discussed their significance and debated possible responses. Making vigorous strides during the last third of the century, the Arabic press fulfilled another important role besides imparting news and views: it served as an interactive platform for exploring the urgent questions of the day for concerned readers. A typical journal of the formative period – for example, *al-Muqtataf*, *al-Hilal*, *al-Diya'* – would carry instructive pieces that would cast light on different aspects of the changes, receive and respond to readers' queries, and facilitate the written exchange of ideas among readers across the region. Largely prompted by a need for orientation, consuming these publications instilled the habit of drawing enlightenment from printed texts. Journals also promoted the sale of other products of the young printing industry, books and booklets of many types, classical and modern, pious and mundane, scholarly and literary. While handwritten books had been few and usually expensive, printing made large parts of the rich written heritage in Arabic accessible and affordable both to those who had acquired books in the past and to those who had not. Periodicals addressed the urgent needs of the time; books gratified the educated and curious and enriched their collections. Printing also made simple the production of modest-scope publications, most typically humble pamphlets of religious guidance, which were easily diffused on a large scale.[7]

The learned segment of society, those who had been literate when these initiatives were launched, immediately displayed interest in the new products and signalled a demand for them. For historical reasons that are all too obvious, production was centred mainly in Cairo/Alexandria and in Beirut (with a third, more modest centre in Istanbul). The entire area from Morocco to the Persian border represented a single market for Arabic writings, as it had during the preprinting era. Educated people throughout this area ordered books from the publishing centres in the region (and from outside it) through the expanding postal services, or bought them in bookshops that opened in their neighbourhoods; and subscribed to journals and newspapers, directly or through agents the papers appointed in many places. Readers often responded in writing to what they had read, addressed inquiries to the editors and commented on each other's ideas. As the century drew to a close, an established and active clientele for printed Arabic works was in place, and growing.

What was the size of the consumer market for printed Arabic at that point? As is so often the case, the quantitative side of these developments is problematic, to say the least. Indeed, we might never know how big the potential or actual Arab readership was at any point along the process, or in any part of the region. The evidence we have is partial, speculative and often indirect. It includes some rough data on the scope of printing ventures and the amount of printed items that were produced during the period, which may give us a clue to the general scale of the market. Thus, we have a certain notion of the spread of printing presses, barely existent in the region prior to the nineteenth century but proliferating there after mid-century. By 1900, Egypt alone had some 150 of them, and dozens of others had opened in Lebanon and elsewhere.[8] Similarly, there are loose assessments regarding the number of Arabic books printed from the early nineteenth century to 1914, which together amount to an estimated fifteen thousand Arabic titles in about ten million copies overall.[9] There is also information on the number of Arabic periodical publications and rough estimations of their circulation: over 1,300 had appeared in the region by 1914, the great majority in Egypt and Lebanon, whose circulation had reached around 120,000 copies by that year, according to one sensible evaluation.[10]

The usefulness of such figures in assessing the scope of reading is, however, limited. Even if we know the number of copies that were printed of all items or of specific titles, we have no way of knowing how many of these copies were bought, let alone actually read. In the same vein, even if we carefully count the readers who sent queries and comments to journal editors – several thousand overall by 1914 – there is no telling what their share was of the entire readership. As we shall see below, appraising the scope of newspaper reading entails still more complications, due to the popular habit of reading in groups. Nonetheless, the data on production and circulation is not entirely without value. They do indicate that the consuming public was constantly and vigorously increasing, and permit us to offer this assessment: readers of Arabic texts throughout the region, comprising a couple of thousands around the mid-nineteenth century, increased to several tens of thousands – apparently no more than a hundred thousand – around the end of the century. With the accelerated spread of the practice thereafter, they probably reached a few hundred thousand by the eve of the First World War and would encompass millions thereafter. Any attempt to be more specific would be foolhardy.

The expansion of popular consumption stemmed from ongoing exposure to the novel products through multiplying diffusion conduits and from the gradual rise in literacy thanks to public and private schooling enterprises, a development to be considered in the next section. As with all big historic changes, the formation of reading audiences did not occur evenly across the region and its various social sectors but affected certain parts more than others. For reasons that need no elaboration, readers first appeared in urban rather than rural areas, in major cities rather than smaller ones, and in places close to the Egyptian and Lebanese production centres more than in the remoter periphery. For equally obvious reasons, popular reading evolved as a predominantly (though not exclusively) male phenomenon: boys/men made up the bulk of the student body during the early stages of educational reform – as they had since time immemorial – and hence the greater part of the emerging reading public. Women would join later on.[11] Yet another important characteristic of the budding readership was the presence of a large number of Christians, far beyond their relative share in the population. Maronite, Greek Orthodox, Greek Catholic, Copt and other Arabic-speaking Christian communities had long given learning a high priority, both because of social and political considerations designed to improve their minority status and due to a religious belief (firmer in certain denominations than in others) that literacy led to self-salvation.[12] There were disparities of several kinds between various Christian groups, but for the most part they were equipped for the new practice better than their Muslim neighbours and more receptive to the cultural messages coming from Europe. Finally, another mark of the new readership, already at the inception stage, was its gradually declining average age, owing to the continuous joining of young graduates of educational projects, an important point to which we shall return later on. Urbanites, primarily Egyptians and Lebanese, mostly men, typically members of non-Muslim minorities, and progressively getting younger – these were the main attributes of the Arabic readership during the initial phase of the printing age in the Middle East.

Reading, a human activity that seldom leaves a record, is a tricky subject for historical exploration. More than the quantitative aspects, it is the nature of the practice itself, its mode, purpose and impact on the reader, that are difficult to reconstruct. First-hand testimonies on reading in the Middle East are few, even rare, but we do have enough clues in the sources to recover at least a general image of the experience. For example, journal articles in which veteran readers advised neophytes on the proper ways to read, frequent in the press of the early years, shed light on the conventions and modes of the practice: choose your materials perceptively and avoid useless or harmful stuff; read deliberately and critically, and reread the more valuable texts; take notes of the materials read so you can return to them as necessary; and, on the functional level, make sure lighting is adequate and your physical posture is comfortable so as not to fatigue your eyes and body.[13] Such basic directives were often presented in response to readers' requests for guidance.[14] They revealed not just the novelty of the activity but also the practical dilemmas evoked by the new pursuit and the puzzlement that accompanied it in its initial phase.

We also have more direct statements on reading. Memoirs and autobiographies occasionally feature descriptions of their authors' experience with written texts, usually in their youth, expressing their tenderfoot fascination with the new horizons they discovered and sometimes casting light on the logistical difficulties that were involved. Such, for instance, is an account by one Yusuf al-Hakim, a youth in Latakia in the 1880s, who was introduced to the practice as a school student. He recalled how he came to 'prefer reading of useful books during school breaks' to any other activity. Rather than playing with his friends, he used to read in his 'small room, which was lit by a gas lamp that threw light on the desk'. More such testimonies suggest that al-Hakim's experience was typical of the entry of many into the circle: a small room, a gas (or kerosene) lamp, the reader's solitude and the contrast between them and their peers – these are recurrent features in descriptions that come down to us.[15] So was the young age of the reader, as we shall see below.

More evidence illuminates a somewhat different mode of the practice: reading aloud in groups, usually in the public domain and normally involving light reading materials, such as newspapers. This was a distinctive mark of the transition from popular illiteracy to popular reading. Printed news – the kind of reading material most in demand – was accessible to anyone with reading skills and an urge to know what was happening. The urge, however, was more widespread than the ability to read independently. For those who were more eager than able to access the written news on their own (and for those who did have the necessary skills but could not afford to buy their own copy), there was an age-old solution in the local tradition: collective reading, in which a single educated person with one copy of a text enlightened a circle of listeners. The ritual, long familiar from situations such as storytelling sessions and listening in groups to town crier announcements, was now naturally extended to public newspaper reading, thus markedly increasing the size of the public exposed to the written messages. Local and foreign observers report such group readings, usually depicting 'someone surrounded by a crowd and reading aloud from one or more of these newspapers'.[16] In this routine, the literacy of a few, or of a single person, was converted into 'collective literacy' so to speak, making the text at hand accessible to all those who were present. It may be argued that those who received the written contents through their ears rather than their eyes cannot be considered 'readers', strictly speaking. In the narrow literal sense of that noun, this is probably true; but in a broader, more practical sense, they may well be regarded as a part of the public that accessed printed texts – at least printed news – through the mediation of the few educated among them. Forming a large, concentric circle around the small one of schooled readers, these 'readers by listening' represented a quantity manyfold bigger than those obtaining printed knowledge directly. The phenomenon, common in urban places already in the early phase of the change in the Middle East, would expand later on and persist wherever sizeable sections of society were still illiterate.

The sight with which we opened this discussion – written signs, banners, placards and the like in urban public places – mirrored the beginning of change in the society's attitude to reading and writing, from prevalent disregard to conscious interest. The emergence of Arab readership on a modest scale during the *Nahda* would later evolve into an extensive process that would eventually transform the cultural scene completely: the long-term training in reading of the bulk of society.

The long-term process

The Arab reading public during the early *Nahda*, if markedly bigger than the pool of readers in earlier times and growing, formed a tiny minority of society. Alongside members of the old literate classes, this public comprised graduates of the educational projects launched in Egypt by Muhammad ᶜAli, Ismaᶜil and their successors; schools run by foreign missions and local religious organizations in Lebanon, Egypt and elsewhere; and those which the Ottoman government and some private entrepreneurs (e.g. Butrus al-Bustani in Beirut, Khalil al-Sakakini in Jerusalem) set up during the last half-century of Ottoman rule. Their total number made up a small group. To members of society's traditionally literate segment, entering the world of printing did not really signify a dramatic change: their reading in the new era was different in scope, pace and contents but not in the very praxis of deriving knowledge from written works. To others, products of the modern schooling systems, the change was truly profound, even revolutionary. This last category of newcomers to the practice pioneered the cultural transformation that would later sweep most of society. By 1914, the trend appeared to be irreversible.

An illiterate society's road to literacy is ever long and winding. Time-honoured conventions need to be abandoned or altered. The benefits to be gained from the change are not always clear to everyone (e.g. to rural populations); at times they are deemed redundant (or even undesirable, as so often with regard to women). Turning written texts into vehicles of interpersonal communication and self-enlightenment involves a conceptual metamorphosis and requires tremendous resources. Arab societies, which began this long journey in the nineteenth century, continued it throughout much of the twentieth. These, we will remember, were fateful times in the region, marked by recurrent political instability and economic tensions which often hindered the cultural process.

If mapping the reader market during the initial phase was possible only in a very sketchy way, assessing it for the longer term is still more problematic. The highly diverse populations, the disparities between social sectors and occupational groups within each community, the divergent paces of technological progress across the region, all render an attempt at such an appraisal impractical. We probably have to make do with no more than the crude assumption that post-First World War Arab societies were moving towards greater literacy almost everywhere. With the recurrent political dramas in the region during the interwar years, the appetite for news and information – a prime incentive for reading – remained as high as before, or higher. The local publishing industry, modest in size during the last Ottoman decades, now progressed more vigorously and put ever-greater quantities of affordable printed products at the public's disposal. And the governments of the newly carved states invested considerable resources in schooling, which expanded society's educated layer. Needless to say, this was not a hurried process. Rather, it was checked by obstacles of every kind: pervasive indigence, organizational difficulties and the public clinging to norms which slowed down the shift to reading habits. Unfolding slowly, the change occurred at varying speeds in the region's different parts and among the various social sections. But if slow, the share of the literate segments in Arab societies continued to climb constantly: in Lebanon, it rose from an estimated 50 per cent in 1914 to around 60 per cent in 1932 and 80 per cent by mid-century; in Egypt, from 8 per cent in 1917 to 18 per cent in 1937 and 23 per cent in 1947; in Syria, from 37 per cent in 1932 to about 60 per cent by mid-century; and in Arab Palestine, from 19 per cent in 1931 to 27 per cent in 1941.[17]

The change impacted sections of the population that had not engaged in reading in the past. One such sector was village dwellers, the majority of the region's populace, inhabitants of areas where both schooling and printed publications were slow to arrive. The spread of educational projects into the countryside would draw them bit by bit into the circle, slowly narrowing the gulf between urban and rural communities throughout the region. Thus, we are told, an itinerant book peddler used to visit an Upper-Egyptian village periodically in the early twentieth century and sell or lend its dwellers books of every taste, from Qur'an exegesis to Sherlock Holmes in Arabic.[18] Another sector of new readers was women, that half of society which initially had been represented in the readership only very marginally. With the change in women's status in some parts of the region during the twentieth century and the concomitant progress in girls' education, their presence in the reading publics began to increase. More women read, wrote articles and even novels, and published journals by and for members of their gender.[19] This, too, was a protracted process: a century after it had begun, women were still a minority among Arab readers almost everywhere.

Children and youth were yet another sector to engage in the practice as newcomers. Their joining was a development of major import, in a way perhaps the most significant aspect of the Arab cultural transformation. It would be worth our while to consider it somewhat more closely.

The natural route to the cultural change passed through society's bottom tiers, the training of children in institutions that imparted reading and other skills. Such a scheme would make the reading public expand at the lower stratum of the age pyramid, something that would constantly bring down its average age, as already noted. Teaching adults beyond that age, as a subsidiary complement to the training of youth, could be implemented only haphazardly and with limited effects. As a result, the older generation, uneducated for the most part when the process began, was left outside the expanding circle of skilled people. In grand historic terms, this could be regarded as a temporary phase that should come to an end once literacy had become prevalent across society. But the process was slow, lasting for many decades, during which the younger generation was benefitting from acquired abilities their parents lacked. Such remoulding of certain parts of society to the exclusion of others had momentous implications for intergenerational relations and for the community's life routine at large. These implications, however crucial, must be left for another study. Here we will only examine the process itself and some of its characteristics. A convenient way to probe it would be by looking into a typical case study: the personal experience of a representative product of the change, the Palestinian-born author Jabra Ibrahim Jabra, as he depicted it in his literary autobiography, *al-Bi'r al-ula*, 'The First Well'.[20]

Jabra Ibrahim Jabra (1920–1994), a novelist, poet, translator and painter, grew up in Bethlehem and Jerusalem during the 1920s and 1930s. After graduating from school, he went on to study English literature at Cambridge, then returned to Palestine in 1946 and worked as an English teacher. In 1948, he moved to Iraq, where he became one of the leading Arab writers of the twentieth century, authoring and translating scores of novels and other books. *Al-Bi'r al-ula* is a charming account of his Palestinian childhood and a vibrant portrayal of the country's material and cultural realities during that time.

Jabra was, in more ways than one, an embodiment of the new generation that made up the better part of the Arab readership in the post-First World War Middle East. His parents were illiterate despite being both Christian (Syrian Orthodox) and city dwellers. On his first day in school, he related, returning home around noon he found his unschooled grandmother in the backyard:

> She looked at the shadow which the almond tree cast on the house wall and said:
> – Why have you returned so early?
> – But it is noon time.
> – No, my dear. The shadow has not yet reached this stone – and she pointed to a stone protruding out of the wall – do you think I don't know when noon is?

The next day, back from school again, the proud pupil Jabra approached his mother and showed her his copybook with the first Arabic letters he had scribbled in his class. 'How do you expect me to read your copybook when I don't know how to read!' she exclaimed.[21] His father, a simple labourer who barely managed to feed his indigent family, was likewise uneducated, yet he vowed to keep his children in school 'so long as I have pulse in my veins and breath in my chest … Do you want to be illiterate like me when you grow up?' he scolded his son, who voiced his desire once to withdraw from his studies.[22]

The untutored parents remained behind, tasking their children with getting an education so they could move themselves and society towards a better life. A poverty-stricken family such as Jabra's – as were a great many in the area – would cut into its tightly rationed resources so their children could remain in the system. The schools themselves, the main vehicle of change, had to overcome formidable obstacles. In post-First World War Palestine, they struggled with a range of inescapable infancy diseases: deficient infrastructure, insufficient staff, wanting equipment, incomplete curriculum, loose working regulations and, not least, the need to train a population that was often less than ready for the change and not always cooperative. In the Bethlehem National School which Jabra attended in his third and fourth grades,

> the class was not a homogeneous group but a blend of shapes, ages, clothing, and dialects. Some of the boys in my class were my age; others were older and may have been fourteen years old, or even more. Some were tall and had a coarse manly voice. Some of them wore gowns (*qunbaz*) while others wore shorts or trousers. Some wore shoes and long socks, others wore shoes without socks, and still others were barefoot, their feet dusty and their legs soiled. There were those who wore a fez (*tarbush*), a cap (*taqiyya*), a head covering (*kufiyya*) with an *ᶜiqal* to hold it in place, or casquette … The kids in school spoke in different dialects, but all were understood. There were dialects of Bethlehem, Bayt Sahur, Bayt Jala, Hebron, Bayt Faghur, and Bani Taᶜmar. In addition, some of the kids were Christian and some Muslim. The Christians, who were the majority, included Greek Orthodox, Latins, Syriacs, Catholics, and Armenians – a great human jumble.[23]

The school, then, was a funnel that assembled a crowd of pupils as diverse as could conceivably be and channelled them all towards literacy and education. In Jabra's portrayal, it was an untidy system: children entered school on their parents' whims, were placed in classes according to the headmaster's fleeting impression of their capabilities and sometimes left the system when they chose to do so (this, in many ways, was reminiscent of the old, very loose *kuttab* system).[24] These weaknesses of the early phase inevitably slowed down the machine designed to carry society down the road to literacy.

Jabra, an outstanding student with a unique sensitivity for things literary, describes in lively colours the wonder of entering into the world of reading. For him, the adventure was first inspired by his elder brother Yusuf, before he himself began attending school:

> One evening he sat me next to him, opened his English book, and read to me the story of Aladdin and the Lamp. We were sitting on the straw mat, thumbing through the pages of the *New Method Readers* in the light of the oil lamp, and our imagination flying from our dim lamp (*al-lamba*) to Aladdin's magic lamp (*misbah*) which, whenever he rubbed it, made a genie appear who performed miracles for him.

I said:'I want to enter the National School like you', believing that by doing so I would obtain Aladdin's lamp.
He said:'They will not accept you now, because the first term has almost ended. You must wait until the beginning of the next school year'.
So I was left waiting.[25]

Brother Yusuf was likewise a gifted and curious youth and an avid reader. At age 12 he would 'read books he came upon or journals sold in the market, persuading the vendor to let him read articles in them before they were sold'. Leaving school to work as an apprentice in a carpenter's shop to supplement the family's income, he 'would hold the saw in one hand, and books and journals in the other'.[26] Saving from his meagre resources in order to buy books, often second-hand, Yusuf built a modest collection which he kept in a special 'treasure box' that he built for the purpose. Among these books were anthologies of the great Arabic classics, from Abu al-Faraj to al-Ghazali, literary translations such as Robinson Crusoe, popular eposes such as stories of ᶜAntar and the Bani Hilal, and more.[27] The collection later passed to his younger brother, who was ceaselessly thrilled with the treasures he discovered in it. He tells us at length about some of them, which he could now read for himself. One item in the box was a 'bunch of yellow pages my brother had bound together with pins' which, it turned out, included parts of *Alf Layla wa-Layla*, a staple text for lovers of reading and storytellers' audiences. Jabra relates how his brother came to possess this book, a simple but illuminating episode that in many ways epitomizes the society's entry into the new era of books and reading. Having left school, Yusuf worked for a while as a helping hand in the grocery shop of the Armenian Khukaz:

> Every few days, Khukaz would bring a pile of old magazines and copybooks, from which he would tear out sheets to wrap the sold goods. One day, my brother was using two worn-out books, tearing pages from them one by one and putting on them a piece of halva, a quantity of olives, pickles, or a slice of fish, then weighing and wrapping it. He noticed strange pictures on some of the pages, and when reading the text underneath them he realized they were long stories. Examining them more carefully he discovered they were serialized by nights, and guessed they had to be the 'One Thousand and One Nights', of which we had read selections in the *Majani al-adab* reader. It was Saturday, the weekly market day, and the clients, villagers and Bedouins, were crowding at the shop's doors. Khukaz and Yusuf were cutting pages and wrapping what they sold as fast as they could. At the appropriate moment, Yusuf took advantage of the Armenian's inattention and hid the two collections of yellow pages under another heap of magazines and newspapers. At the end of the day he returned home with his booty, or what remained of it, and began reading it with profound delight. He then added it to his books which he subsequently collected in the small box.[28]

Widening their horizons, the inquisitive Jabra brothers were also widening the gap between themselves and the older generation, a gap that would continue to affect social relations throughout Arab societies for another two or three generations. As we have seen, efforts were made to reduce the effects of this gulf in specific matters, most typically in communicating urgent information, which alleviated the problem somewhat. Children played a central role in these efforts: equipped with skills their parents did not have, they became chief mediators of written contents to the illiterate sections of society. Jabra tells us how, during his early childhood, he used to hear *Alf Layla wa-Layla* stories from his uneducated father, who related them from memory. Once capable of accessing these stories on his own, the son saw himself as duty-bound to read them for himself so he could then 'tell them to my father when he returns from work in the evening' – a striking change of roles and means.[29] In Jerusalem, where Jabra moved with his parents, an uneducated labourer used to come to the courtyard near the Church of the Holy Sepulchre on Sundays, carrying a copy of a local newspaper, 'hand it to one of the youth in the yard who would appear to be literate, and ask him to read out the headlines and some of the passages, especially editorials … When running into me or my brother, he would ask us to read for him pieces the others had not read.'[30] In another episode, Jabra's training became handy when he helped two adult women who lived in the neighbourhood, 'both of them illiterate even though their appearance seemed to suggest otherwise'. At their request, he read and reread for them a letter they had received, and then drafted a response to it on their behalf, phrasing some of it in elegant rhymed prose.[31]

Finally, one more instance of Jabra, the educated child in the world of illiterate adults, involving another Jerusalem neighbour, Musa al-Khuri the stonecutter:

> He said to me one day: 'Do you know … what the wish of my life is?'
> And before I had a chance to guess, he added: 'To learn how to read …'
> I said: 'So, why don't you learn how to read?'
> He said:'I am afraid they would say about me: after he became old he joined the *kuttab*.'
> I said: 'First, you are still young. Second, I am ready to teach you, if you accept me [as your guide].'
> He could not believe his ears and asked: 'Really? Do you think you can teach me how to read a newspaper at least?'
> I said: 'Let's try. And let's begin from today. Where is your newspaper?'
> From that day on I began to teach him how to read. … As we were making some progress in reading and I asked him to study at night, he began to express fatigue and said: 'You know … I return [home] exhausted after dressing stones all day, with no energy left in me to focus on anything. Besides, you know, my eyes are not in the best of shape.'
>
> I accepted and lowered my expectations, and he was content with his acquired ability to read the major headlines of his favorite newspaper. He would sometimes try to read the editorial as best he could, grasping it in his own way, perhaps more by inference and reading between the lines than by getting the sense of whole sentences. But the important thing was that he now read the

newspaper. He read it to himself or to his family without relying on help from others.[32]

The captivating memories of young Jabra – the magic of reading, the entry into a territory out of reach for his elders, the new social responsibilities his training entailed for him – all characterized the experience of a society becoming gradually educated. Such aspects of the change are echoed in other extant personal testimonies of the process. Children led the way to the community's assimilation of the novel medium not only at the centre, where most educational institutions were set up, but also in the rural periphery, where their building advanced more sluggishly. In the village of Musha (Egypt, Asyut province) in the post-First World War years, it was the teenage Sayyid Qutb who, along with his school-aged friends, was 'the best customer' of the local book dealer, and whose humble book collection earned him repute in the largely illiterate village.[33] The gradual entry of Arab women into the reading circle, too, was mediated by the younger generation: 'The daughters and granddaughters', a foreign visitor to Egypt observed, 'read … the news of the world' to 'women of the older day'.[34] The people 'of the older day', as we have seen, did not necessarily remain unenlightened and uninformed. Rather, they often reached the knowledge they desired with the help of their juniors or through the 'collective literacy' option which was based on the proficiency of few. If unusually ambitious, like Musa the stonecutter, members of that stratum would strive, and sometimes manage, to attain independent reading abilities. But the principal road leading to mass reading passed via the training of the young, a sure if drawn-out course.

Scholars of book history in the West have described the advent of printing there as a major 'revolution' in human history. Others have questioned the applicability of this term, arguing that the historic role played by printing had been more modest than that; the issue remains a matter of unresolved controversy.[35] Be that as it may in the Western context, the Middle Eastern version of that development, telescoped as it was into a far shorter period, was certainly more dramatic than that which had unfolded in Europe. When Arabs began printing, issuing journals and circulating the products of their presses, functional models of all of these had already been at work in Europe, available for borrowing; there was no need to wait for a paced evolution. The formation of Arab reading publics, an important part of the process, began by small steps in the late nineteenth century, expanded more briskly after the turn of the century and grew exponentially after the First World War. During its early phase, which involved the community's thin layer of literates, a consumer circle of printed texts emerged as dynamically as their production. In the subsequent phase, however, as reading came to be embraced on a massive popular scale, the process turned considerably slower. Indeed, it became the most protracted aspect of the Arab entry into the world of printing. This was inevitable, given the low point of departure – near-complete popular illiteracy, the masses that had to be trained and the formidable material and conceptual hurdles to be overcome. Still, if slower than the assimilation of printing itself, the Arab mass adoption of reading habits marked a major turn in the region's cultural history. In that sense, calling it 'revolutionary' might not be too far-fetched.

Notes

1 E.g. Sajdi's study on the 'nouveau literates' in *The Barber of Damascus*. See also the discussion of literacy (rather, 'literacies') in pre-nineteenth-century Egypt, in Yousef, *Composing Egypt*, 14–20, 25–8.
2 See discussion of this point in Ayalon, *Arabic Print Revolution*, 1–17.
3 'The Arab *Nahda*' is a loose concept with a range of meanings. Used narrowly, it refers to the changes in Arabic thought, literature and language of the late nineteenth century. Sometimes it also embraces the broader sociocultural shifts entailed by these changes; and in a still wider sense, it denotes the popular demand for political freedom and rights which stemmed from the cultural ferment. In the present study, the term refers to changes in the intellectual and cultural spheres. For further discussion of the notion, see Patel, *Arab Nahdah*, 12–35.
4 See e.g. Patel, *Arab Nahdah*; Zachs and Halevi, *Gendering Culture in Greater Syria*; and list of works quoted in Booth, *Classes of Ladies*, 370 n. 25.
5 An elaborate account in Schwartz, 'Meaningful Mediums', 30–53.
6 Mostly Beirut and a couple of other places in the Mount Lebanon region, an area which, for convenience, I will refer to as Lebanon.
7 See discussion in Ayalon, *Arabic Print Revolution*, 69–96.
8 Nusayr, *Harakat nashr*, 399–459, lists 149 presses in Egypt up to 1900. For Lebanon, see details (apparently incomplete) in Shaykhu, *Ta'rikh fann*, 43–149.
9 Nusayr, who conducted an extensive (but less than complete) study of books published in Egypt until 1900, traced a little over ten thousand of them in an estimated seven million copies; Nusayr, *Harakat nashr*, 53–98. Most of these copies, however, were school texts and army guidebooks. Shaykhu, *Ta'rikh fann*, 43–149, offers a partial list of over 1,500 books printed in Lebanon during that period, whose total print-run was likely around one million. More books and booklets were no doubt printed in the region, which were not included in these two surveys.
10 Newspaper lists in Tarrazi, *Ta'rikh al-sihafa*. For the cited circulation evaluation, see Malul, *ᶜItonut*. Malul was a Palestine-born Jew who lived for many years in Egypt. As a writer and journalist, he was intimately involved in the Arabic press and contributed extensively to Egyptian and Palestinian newspapers during the first half of the twentieth century.
11 See discussion in Yousef, *Composing Egypt*, 49–75.
12 As a study by Heyberger has shown, among Christians in Syria and Lebanon, reading had become popular already in the seventeenth and eighteenth centuries. Heyberger, 'Livres et pratiques'.
13 E.g. *al-Muqtataf* 1 September 1876, 205–7; 1 April 1890, 492; 1 September 1894, 793–7; 1 March 1903; 256–8; 1 May 1904, 452; 1 December 1904, 1097–8; 1 June 1906, 496; 1 October 1913, 352; *al-Hilal* 1 December 1896, 262.
14 See the sources quoted in note 13 above, as well as: *al-Muqtataf* 1 May 1916, 509; 1 August 1918, 194; 1 June 1924, 107; 1 December 1924, 577–8; *al-Diya'* 15 May 1899, 529–32.
15 Al-Hakim, *Dhikrayat al-Hakim*, 108. For similar examples, see: Zaydan, *Mudhakkirat*, 33–6; Qutb, *Tifl*, 110–14; Shaᶜrawi, *Harem Years*, 39–41; Jabra, *Bi'r*, 113, 136–44.
16 Sharubim, *Kafi fi ta'rikh*, vol. 5, book 1, part 2, 660, quoted in Fahmy, *Ordinary Egyptians*, 35. For similar instances, see: Rae, 'Egyptian Newspaper', 214; Crabitès,

'Journalism', 1050; Aburish, *Children of Bethany*, 41–2, 45–6; Hurani, *Watan*, 267; *al-Bilad al-Sa*ᶜ*udiyya* (Mecca) 30 January 1947, 3.

17 Ayalon, *The Press*, 141–4; Yousef, *Composing Egypt*, 18–20, 28–33. Data taken from official censuses and estimates. They should be treated cautiously, as indicators of scale and tendency rather than as precise figures.
18 Qutb, *Tifl*, 110–14.
19 Baron, *Women's Awakening*, 80–100; Booth, *May Her Likes*, chapter 4; Zachs and Halevi, *Gendering of Culture in Greater Syria*, 16–41, 111, *passim*.
20 English translation by Issa Boullata, *The First Well*. All quoted passages here are my translations from the Arabic version.
21 Jabra, *Bi'r*, 29, 31.
22 Ibid., 128–9.
23 Ibid., 119–20.
24 Ibid., especially chapters 12 and 13. For a discussion of *kuttab*, see Ayalon, *Reading Palestine*, 26–32.
25 Jabra, *Bi'r*, 113.
26 Ibid., 113, 115.
27 Ibid., 136–8.
28 Ibid., 142.
29 Ibid., 138.
30 Ibid., 176. Similar accounts come from different parts of the region. See, e.g. Sharubim, *Kafi fi ta'rikh*, vol. 4, 258–9; al-Khuri, 'Mudhakkirat kahin', 64; Darwaza, *Mudhakkirat*, 160; al-Dabbagh, *Hadith al-sawma*ᶜ*a*, 117; al-Arsuzi, *Mu'allafat kamila*, 296.
31 Jabra, *Bi'r*, 174–5.
32 Ibid., 176–7.
33 Qutb, *Tifl*, 110–14.
34 Cooper, *Women*, 241.
35 See e.g. the exchange between Elizabeth Eisenstein and Adrian Johns in 'AHR Forum', 87–128; Eisenstein, *Printing Revolution*, 'Afterword'.

Bibliography

Journals

*al-Bilad al-Sa*ᶜ*udiyya* (Mecca)
al-Diya' (Cairo)
al-Hilal (Cairo)
al-Muqtataf (Beirut/Cairo)

Published works

Aburish, Said K. *Children of Bethany: The Story of a Palestinian Family*. London: I.B. Tauris, 1988.

al-Arsuzi, Zaki. *al-Mu'allafat al-kamila*, vol. 4. Damascus: Matabiᶜ al-idara al-siyasiyya li'l-jaysh wa'l-quwwat al-musallaha, 1972.

Ayalon, Ami. *The Arabic Print Revolution: Cultural Production and Mass Readership*. Cambridge: Cambridge University Press, 2016.

Ayalon, Ami. *The Press in the Arab Middle East: A History*. New York: Oxford University Press, 1995.

Ayalon, Ami. *Reading Palestine: Printing and Literacy 1900–1948*. Austin: University of Texas Press, 2004.

Baron, Beth. *The Women's Awakening in Egypt: Culture, Society and the Press*. New Haven, CT: Yale University Press, 1994.

Booth, Marilyn. *Classes of Ladies of Cloistered Spaces: Writing Feminist History through Biography in Fin-de-Siècle Egypt*. Edinburgh: Edinburgh University Press, 2015.

Booth, Marilyn. *May Her Likes Be Multiplied: Biography and Gender Politics in Egypt*. Berkeley: University of California Press, 2001.

Cooper, Elizabeth. *The Women of Egypt*. New York: F. A. Stokes, 1914.

Crabitès, Piérre. 'Journalism along the Nile'. *Asia* 27 (1927): 992–1052.

al-Dabbagh, Ibrahim. *Hadith al-sawmaᶜa: rasa'il fi al-adab wa'l-fukaha wa'l-naqd wa'l-falsafa*. Jaffa: Maktabat al-tahir ikhwan, n.d.

Darwaza, Muhammad ᶜIzzat. *Mudhakkirat 1305–1404/1887–1984*, vol. 1. Beirut: Dar al-gharb al-islami, 1993.

Eisenstein, Elizabeth L. *The Printing Revolution in Early Modern Europe*, 2nd edn. Cambridge: Cambridge University Press, 2005.

Eisenstein, Elizabeth, Adrian Johns and Anthony Grafton. 'AHR Forum: How Revolutionary Was the Print Revolution?' *American Historical Review* 107, no. 1 (February 2002): 84–128.

Fahmy, Ziad. *Ordinary Egyptians*. Stanford: Stanford University Press, 2011.

al-Hakim, Yusuf. *Dhikrayat al-hakim: suriya wa'l-ᶜahd al-ᶜuthmani*. Beirut: al-Matbaᶜa al-kathulikiyya, 1966.

Heyberger, Bernard. 'Livres et pratiques de la lecture chez les chrétiens (Syrie, Liban) XVIIe-XVIIIe siècles'. *Revue des mondes musulmans et de la Méditerrannée* 87–8 (1999): 209–23.

al-Hurani, Faysal. *al-Watan fi al-dhakira: durub al-manfaᶜ*. Damascus: Dar kanᶜan li'l-dirasat wa'l-nashr, 1994.

Jabra, Jabra Ibrahim. *al-Bi'r al-ula*. London: Riyyad al-rayyis li'l-kutub wa'l-nashr, 1987.

al-Khuri, Niqula. 'Mudhakkirat kahin al-quds al-khuri niqula al-khuri, birzayt 1885-bayrut 1954'. *Dirasat ᶜArabiyya* 30, nos 5–6 (1994): 62–76.

Malul, Nissim. 'ha-ᶜItonut ha-ᶜaravit'. *ha-Shiloaḥ* 31 (1914): 447–9.

Nusayr, ᶜAyida Ibrahim. *Harakat nashr al-kutub fi misr fi al-qarn al-tasiᶜ ᶜashr*. Cairo: al-Hay'a al-misriyya al-ᶜamma li'l-kitab, 1994.

Patel, Abdulrazzak. *The Arab Nahdah: The Making of the Intellectual and the Humanist Movement*. Edinburgh: Edinburgh University Press, 2013.

Qutb, Sayyid. *Tifl min al-qarya; hayat Sayyid Qutb bi-qalamihi*. Beirut: Dar al-hikma, 196-?

Rae, Fraser W. 'The Egyptian Newspaper Press'. *The Nineteenth Century* 32 (1892): 213–23.

Sajdi, Dana. *The Barber of Damascus: Nouveau Literacy in the Eighteenth Century Ottoman Levant*. Palo Alto, CA: Stanford University Press, 2013.

Schwartz, Kathryn Anne. 'Meaningful Mediums: A Material and Intellectual History of Manuscript and Print Production in Nineteenth Century Ottoman Cairo'. PhD dissertation, Harvard University, 2015.

Shaᶜrawi, Huda. *Harem Years: The Memoirs of an Egyptian Feminist 1879–1924*. Translated by Margot Badran. New York: Feminist Press at the City University of New York, 1987.

Sharubim. Mikha'il. *al-Kafi fi ta'rikh misr al-qadim wa'l-hadith*, vols 4 and 5. Bulaq: al-Matbaᶜa al-kubra al-amiriyya, 1900.
Shaykhu, Luis. *Ta'rikh fann al-tibaᶜa fi al-mashriq*. Beirut: Dar al-mashriq, 1995.
di Tarrazi, Filib. *Ta'rikh al-sihafa al-ᶜarabiyya*, vol. 4. Beirut: al-Matbaᶜa al-adabiyya, 1933.
Yousef, Hoda. *Composing Egypt: Reading, Writing, and the Emergence of a Modern Nation, 1870–1930*. Palo Alto, CA: Stanford University Press, 2016.
Zachs, Fruma, and Sharon Halevi. *Gendering Culture in Greater Syria: Intellectuals and Ideology in the Late Ottoman Period*. London: I.B. Tauris, 2015.
Zaydan, Jurji. *Mudhakkirat*. Edited by Salah al-Din al-Munajjid. Beirut: Dar al-kitab al-jadid, 1968.

2

Who's afraid of musical theatre? George Abyad's 1912 *Oedipus Rex*

Raphael Cormack

On 21 March 1912, George Abyad's troupe of actors performed the first Arabic translation of *Oedipus Rex*.[1] It was the first in a series of three theatrical productions that also included Shakespeare's *Othello* and Casimir Delavigne's *Louis XI*. Sophocles' play tells the story of Oedipus' attempts to find the killer of Laius, the previous king. The murderer's presence in Thebes has led to divine pollution, which is causing a plague. After his long search, Oedipus finds that he himself is the killer, that Laius was his own father and that he is now married, until now unwittingly, to his mother Jocasta. The play ends with Jocasta dead and Oedipus, the once great king, violently blinding himself.

In Cairo, a mood of anticipation preceded the performance. Posters went up in the city, informing people of the details:

> The capital was all hustle and bustle. The people in the cafes talked about nothing else but Abyad and you could hear the student say to his friend in front of school, 'Are you buying tickets for the first show or the second?'[2]

The next day, a correspondent for *al-Ahram* newspaper reported:

> Truly, I have never seen a night at the Opera [the name of Cairo's main theatre] like last night. There was a large crowd of our elite, upper classes, intellectuals and writers; the ones who could get tickets. There was also a large crowd of people looking for tickets but who could not find a place.[3]

Among the throngs of spectators were dignitaries from Egypt's Ottoman elite and further afield, including Khedive 'Abbas Hilmi II, the future King 'Abdallah of Jordan, Egypt's ministers of education and of works and war, and Husayn Rushdi Pasha, the foreign minister.[4]

This run of plays in the prestigious Cairo Opera is now seen as a landmark moment in the history of Egypt's then-nascent theatre tradition. For his contemporaries, George Abyad, the head of the troupe, had done something revolutionary. The prominent theatre critic and playwright Muhammad Taymur, writing in the late 1910s, placed Abyad at the start of a new era of Arabic theatre that 'truly expanded the art of acting'.[5] *Al-Ahram*'s reviewer stated that the performance was a step towards 'an improvement in Egyptian acting so that it competes with European acting' – something he said that the Egyptian people had been demanding for years. *Al-Jarida* concurred that 'the general opinion agreed on the point that that night Arabic drama had taken a long step forwards'. The Khedive was singled out for particular praise in *al-Hilal* for funding Abyad's studies in Paris. The review directly connected Egypt's ruler to the success of this new endeavour and implicitly cast the performance as his own achievement, claiming that 'history will remember the favour of his highness, as he was the first to raise up the art of Arabic acting on intellectual principles'.[6]

Long after its first performance, this Arabic translation of *Oedipus Rex* by the prominent author and journalist Farah Antun continued to influence writers and theatre practitioners. Writer, academic and critic Taha Husayn claimed that 'I never tasted the beauty of true acting except when I witnessed [*shahadtu*] George Abyad acting the story of *Oedipus Rex* and his other plays'.[7] As a child, Tawfiq al-Hakim, later one of Egypt's most prominent playwrights, memorized Abyad's speeches as Oedipus and recited them to his classmates. Najib al-Rihani, who went on to become a famous actor and troupe leader, travelled to Cairo in his holidays from work in a sugar factory just to attend the theatre. In his memoirs he tells how he would irritate his co-worker – a dentist by the name of Dr Guda – by reciting extended passages from, among other works, *Oedipus Rex*.[8]

Despite its important place in the historiography of Arabic theatre, one aspect of this play's significance has been misunderstood. Modern critics have assumed that it contained no singing, but this was not the case.[9] There is good reason for this assumption. Sameh Hanna has pointed out 'the absence of any mention of singing and comic scenes from newspaper advertisements of Abyad's performances'. Hanna explained that *Oedipus Rex* was seen as an attempt to move Egyptian drama away from its roots in musical theatre, often seen as vulgar and populist, towards a new kind of theatre, reliant on the spoken word and not on songs.[10]

However, from contemporary reviews, a more complex picture of this first performance emerges. Abyad's version of *Oedipus Rex* did, in fact, include music and songs. A review in *al-Ahram* praises 'the actors, the *singers*, the dancers and the musicians' and later says that 'the acting opened with a sorrowful tune which complemented the plot thanks to the skill of 'Abd al-Hamid, the group's musician'. The reviewer even mentions the odd contradiction between the happy smiles of the dancers and the sorrow of Oedipus.[11]

The act of expunging these songs from memories of the play reveals some of the most important tensions and concerns of early-twentieth-century Egyptian theatre. An attempt to understand this selective memory elucidates some of the most important formal, stylistic and cultural questions being debated on the early-twentieth-century Egyptian stage and reveal much about what Egyptian writers and critics thought theatre should look like, what it was for and what role it could play in Egyptian society. Drama of this kind, as a genre, was still seen as a recent import into the Egyptian cultural world and contemporary commentators were often unsure how to react to it and what kind of influence it was having on the audiences. Singing became a key battleground in the development of the form.

The fact that this production was of *Oedipus Rex*, the Arabic translation of an ancient Greek text performed in the Arab world, and a play that was at the centre of global debates, is also instructive in expanding the questions raised in Egypt to interrogate a wider, transnational moment of performance modernism.[12] This classic of ancient Greek drama can be used to look at some of the most important cultural questions of early-twentieth-century Egypt: performance aesthetics and popular engagement with the arts. It allows us to see the transnational connections that tied Egyptian theatre to global artistic movements in unexpected ways, showing the complexity of influences that helped shape this early theatrical tradition.

Musical theatre in the early twentieth century

It is fortunate that the first performance of this play coincided with a rise in the prominence of theatre criticism in the press. When coverage of the theatre began in the late nineteenth century, it was mostly limited to brief notices announcing performances and praising them in glowing terms, often before they had even been performed. The early twentieth century saw more in-depth discussion of theatre and plays in the Egyptian media, and the 1912 *Oedipus Rex* was one of the first plays to be discussed in detail across different publications.

It was not until the mid-1920s that specialist magazines for theatre reviews started to appear in Egypt, such as *al-Tiyatru* (1924–5) and 'Abd al-Majid Hilmi's *al-Masrah*, launched on 9 November 1925. However, in the 1900s and 1910s, journalists in Egypt began to write articles (often unsigned) about performances or the theatre in general with much more frequency and greater depth. Several papers, of which *al-Ahram* was one of the more prominent, carried articles that offered general discussions of this new art form. It is not clear that any Arabic newspapers had particular aesthetic alignments when it came to theatre, as they did with politics, nor did they yet have permanent theatre critics on their staff.

Nonetheless, certain themes were starting to generate particular discussion. One of the most important debates was about the place of music in the theatre (other common themes included the necessity of funding for Arabic theatre and the promotion of Arabic-authored plays). Singing, and its role in the Egyptian theatre, was not a minor stylistic concern; it was emblematic of the most important questions that were being asked of drama. Despite its huge popularity, many critics were fiercely opposed to singing on stage. Theatre, in the eyes of many critics, was not only for entertainment but also for moral and social improvement.

In the late nineteenth and early twentieth centuries, Egyptian audiences wanted to hear singing when they went to the theatre and a singer was a vital part of any theatrical troupe. These included stars like 'Abduh al-Hamuli and Muhammad 'Uthman, 'the two pillars of the renaissance [of] musical modernization that started in the nineteenth century',[13] as well as lesser-known singers about whom little is now known, such as Murad Rumanu, Hasan Salih and Ibrahim Ahmad.[14] Several women also played important and well-received parts. Almaz, who is still remembered as one of the most significant singers of the age, rose to fame until she married fellow singer 'Abduh al-Hamuli, who apparently did not view this as a respectable profession for his wife and forced her to stop performing.[15] Newspaper notices of the time refer to female singers, but details of their lives are hard to find and they were often referred to by their stage names alone, including Malikat al-Surur, Kawkab, Layla and al-'Alima.[16]

Despite their popularity, these singers had many critics in the press, who argued that song was not a part of 'true' theatre. Opinion pieces claimed from various interconnected positions that singers posed a danger to their audiences, through the power they wielded over spectators or their seductive, siren-like qualities. One particular source of uneasiness was the proximity of theatres to their immoral counterpart, the music hall. This was partly literal. Around the Azbakiyya district of Cairo, where many of the theatres (including the Opera) stood, singers performed in *cafés chantants* or smaller musical halls; the brothels of Clot Bey Street and Wish al-Birka were close by. It is hard to find descriptions of these places that are not tinged with disapproval or moral panic.[17] One article by a critic named Fakhr al-Din, published in 1910 in *al-Mahrusa*, complained that the area was full of

> theatres for singing and cafes for balladry, where (female) singers sing and delight the ears with their sentimental tunes and where women give performances, which would not be performed were it not for people's love of watching things that can only be seen in secret or under the cover of dark night. Passers-by can see all of these things but they do not see any theatres for acting in its [correct] meaning or in name.[18]

Journalists worried that the presence of singing in theatrical plays made it hard to separate respectable drama from its morally questionable counterpart.

There were other criticisms of the art form, beyond moral concerns. Singing in a traditional Egyptian style was regarded as unrefined and inappropriate for artistic connoisseurs. It is striking how often the singing in theatres is compared to rural or folk art (by implication, not suitable for the urbane theatregoer). This is very clear in Muhammad al-Muwaylihi's famous *maqama*, *Hadith 'Isa ibn Hisham* ('What 'Isa Ibn Hisham Told Us'), in which a Pasha from the time of Muhammad Ali is resurrected in turn-of-the-century Cairo. Guided by 'Isa ibn Hisham, the Pasha samples modern life, giving his generally unflattering opinions on the state of modern Egypt. Al-Muwaylihi himself was an elite Egyptian nationalist, and part of his aim in writing this book was to show how low Egypt had fallen under British occupation. He is hostile to Cairo's recent corruptions like bars and night clubs but, as a man from a wealthy, highly educated background, is also suspicious of 'lower-class' culture.[19]

Near the end of his tour, 'Isa takes the Pasha to a theatre, where the reader is told that

> a group of actresses and actors appeared, chanting and singing in an unbearable fashion, a spectacle against which human nature revolted. They were using obscure and unintelligible language and sounded like camel drivers in the waterless desert or people attending a funeral.[20]

The narrator's scorn for the musical element of the theatre is undisguised. In particular, his imagery stresses that this mode of performance is out of place in the refined setting of a theatre. His invocation of camels is a deliberately jarring image, contrasting uncomfortably with the supposed elegance of the surroundings.

The narrator moves on quickly from this to repeat that the theatre is supposed to be a place where audiences are trained in good morals and behaviour. He explains the cultivation and benefits that theatres can bring to society:

> This place isn't a dance hall [*marqas*] or a playhouse [*mal'ab*]. This is a theatre [*tiyatru*], something that westerners acknowledge as having educational and corrective qualities. It encourages virtues, exposes evil traits, and portrays the deeds of former generations so that people can be educated and learn lessons from them.[21]

Despite the narrator's pleading, the Pasha sees none of these positives. In his eyes, it is a den of iniquity, not a place of self-improvement:

> What I've seen here is just a repeat of what I've observed in the dance hall – drinking wine, flirting with women, portraying amorous situations in a highly suggestive manner, one that's designed solely to arouse people's passions, make things more accessible and easy, and stir up lustful emotions.[22]

This view of the theatre as a place to educate the audience in correct behaviour is one of the guiding principles of theatre critics from the mid-nineteenth century. Rifa'a Rafi' al-Tahtawi, one of the first Egyptians to write about the phenomenon of theatre that he saw in Paris, described how 'people take from it amazing examples, for they see in it good and bad acts and see the former praised and the latter criticized. So, the French say that it develops people's morals and refines them.'[23]

This attitude was typical of arguments for the moral improvement of the masses. In Egypt, writers also sometimes made a connection with the Quranic injunction of *al-amr bil-ma'ruf wa-l-nahi 'an al-munkar* ('Commanding what is approved and forbidding what is disapproved'). An article by an unnamed critic in *al-Mu'ayyad*, for instance, commended how one play 'provided [the audience] with examples of noble character traits, warned them off corruption and commanded what is approved and forbade what is disapproved'.[24]

It was uncommon, though, for negative opinions about singing in the theatre to be given specific religious justification. The aversion to song in theatre was just as likely to come from the rising 'effendi' bourgeoisie, with secular educations rather than the traditional religious training of al-Azhar. This new generation was developing a culture of its own that was 'refined', serious and literary.[25] New trends combined worries about the moral degradation that they saw as rooted in 'popular' culture with a patronizing disdain for 'traditional' art forms, from folk tales to epic ballads, including singing.[26] These two prejudices united into a general suspicion of 'popular' or 'low' culture, broadly speaking.[27]

The *Nahda* (the period of cultural 'awakening' in the nineteenth- and twentieth-century Arab world) was a time when intellectuals were debating how to form the ideal 'Egyptian subject' in a colonial context.[28] Writing in the press and in 'high' culture was often explicitly aimed at building a strong, coherent and principled Egyptian nation and citizen. There was space for considerable disagreement and debate within this world of letters. However, the theatre, with its singing and its focus on entertainment, stood dangerously outside of the accepted framework for discussing these issues.

Entertainment or edification?

Criticism of singing cannot be assigned to snobbery alone. There was something about the medium that was fundamentally threatening to the *Nahda* project. The case of Salama Higazi, undoubtedly the most popular stage singer of the time, helps to highlight these tensions. Born in Alexandria in 1852, Higazi began singing as a child, reciting the call to prayer in local mosques and sitting for hours in Sufi singing circles, listening intently to the sheikhs. He was trained in a traditional religious style of singing by respected teachers such as Kamil al-Hariri, a prominent Alexandrian singer, and Khalil Mihrim, known as the man who taught Yusuf al-Manyalawi (one of the most popular recording artists of the early twentieth century).[29] Higazi is said to have been suspicious of acting when he was young, perhaps on religious grounds. However, some members of Yusuf Khayat's troupe saw him singing at his sister's wedding and were so impressed that they wanted to enlist him in their company. He resisted at first but was eventually convinced to lay aside his concerns and bring his voice to the theatre. He soon became one of the greats of the period.[30]

Higazi was not a vaudeville singer and would have been out of place in the dance halls that scandalized the press. His style of singing was refined and classical,[31] but he was still the target of critical attacks. Farah Antun, who translated the text of *Oedipus Rex* into Arabic, had been active in the Egyptian cultural world since the late nineteenth century. In 1899, he set up the magazine *al-Jami'a*, which became an important mouthpiece for his brand of secular modernity, which stressed the importance of both Arabic traditions and Western thought, simultaneously arguing for the place of minority communities in the region while criticizing the clerical structures within them. In its pages he presented his side of a famous debate with Muhammad 'Abduh (who wrote his responses in *al-Manar*) on secularism in the Arab world, debated through the writings of Ibn Rushd.[32]

In 1900, Antun also used the paper to critique Higazi's popularity among Egyptian theatregoers. In one article, he wrote, 'We have heard many people say that Shaykh Salama Higazi has killed the art of theatre in Egypt. They say this because the audience do not go to the theatre to hear the plays but to hear his songs.'[33] Critics increasingly felt that, rather than being part of it, singing distracted from the real business of acting and from the educational, improving elements of theatre.[34]

Attacks on singing in theatre, and on Higazi in particular, increased as the first decade of the twentieth century went on. One unsigned article in *al-Akhbar* blamed Higazi's singing for what it described as the undeveloped state of Egyptian theatre:

> Yes, some writers have translated parts of Shakespeare, Corneille, and Hugo but these translations are only written to make Salama Higazi distort them with his bad acting or sing some poems in them and nothing more.[35]

In 1910, *al-Hilal* published a long article on the state of Arabic acting. The journal, established in Cairo in 1892 by the Lebanese writer and intellectual Jurji Zaydan, had become a home for 'refined' and improving content aimed at the new Egyptian and Arab middle classes. In his article on the theatre, Zaydan, a prolific writer himself and author of several well-researched historical novels, criticized people's belief that singing had to be a part of acting. He put the blame on Lebanese theatrical pioneer Marun al-Naqqash, credited as the first person, in 1847, to produce Arabic theatre, for favouring the genre of opera:

> People thought [in the early days of theatre] (and this is still widespread now) that acting was not really acting unless it was interspersed with singing parts. This opinion came about because the founder of acting [Marun al-Naqqash], God rest his soul, when he wanted to translate this art into Arabic, he preferred musical plays, or what the Europeans call Opera, wanting people to turn up even if it was for the sake of hearing singing ... So the first examples of acting that Arabic speakers knew were plays mixed with singing and they continued in this fashion even for plays which were not Operas before.[36]

The pre-First World War theatrical world was dominated by rival troupes vying to win audiences. Among the biggest contests was that between Lebanese impresario Iskandar Farah, whose troupe was one of the largest in Egypt, and Higazi, who had been singer in Farah's troupe but quit after an argument with the leader in 1905.[37] Each of the men went on to form their own acting company and Zaydan lamented,

> Farah Effendi wanted to return acting to its basis so he made the [word missing, perhaps 'foundation of'] his new troupe without singing [*bila ghina'*]. His reception amongst the literati was good but the audience did not find in it what they found in other plays so Salama Higazi's troupe won that competition.[38]

This opposition to singing, even the relatively high-class, skilled and respectable singing of Higazi, is inseparable from prevailing views about the role of theatre in early-twentieth-century Egypt. Its goal, as al-Muwaylihi argued, was to create virtuous subjects who learned from the action on stage, either as a warning to avoid or a model to emulate. Theatre, where different classes gather together and have their own interpretations of the action on stage, always has the potential to be a radical form of expression. However, in early-twentieth-century Egypt, the role of the audience was to watch and be educated. Ilham Khuri-Makdisi, discussing the theatre of this period, says that '[its] features, though radical, were at the same time quintessentially bourgeois. The new system would maintain class distinctions even more strictly than those upheld by the previous social system.'[39]

Farah Antun's writing about the theatre exemplifies this attitude. People could not be trusted to know what was good for them and could be deceived by things they found entertaining. This is how he described one visit to the theatre:

> When we went to the acting of some plays and saw the licentiousness and profanity in them which the listener recoiled from, we did nothing but hope that no young man or woman would hear this rubbish. Unfortunately, young men and women, like other men and women, pay great attention to this rubbish in plays and they laugh and cackle not thinking that they are being corrupted by the poison of vice in the souls without realizing. It surprises us that the government in Egypt does not think of putting a stop to the prevailing moral chaos on Egyptian stages. For among the plays that are put on these stages, especially the comic ones, there are things that no ear should hear and that no eye should see.[40]

Just like novels and cultural journals, theatre became increasingly concerned with 'refinement' (*taraqqi*). This was, as Lucie Ryzova's *The Age of the Efendiyya* argues, one of the key words that signified *effendi* literary ideals.[41] One particularly clear example of this came in 1908 when 'the elite of the young literati of Cairo' set up a group 'for the refinement of Arabic acting' (*taraqqi al-tamthil al-ʿarabi*).[42] A critic called 'Fuʾad' of *al-Akhbar* went to the opening night of this new project and wrote a notice, which, despite his obvious mockery, shows the goals of their literary mission:

> One of the literati got up and gave a speech … and the speech was no shorter than two acts of the play, God give him strength … and among what he said – God gave us a blessing with abundance of his words – that the name of the group alone was enough to bring us to its aid. For it was a group for refinement [*taraqqi*] – and we are in great need of refinement – and then there is the word 'Arabic' in it and, my my, there's nothing better than this word.[43]

Farah Antun's reaction against singing and his belief in the improving power of the theatre were not coincidental. The popularity of singing in the theatre was symbolic of the emphasis on emotional content instead of the educational mission that many thought the theatre should promote. The word used for singing (*tarab*), which can mean pleasure or rapture, emphasizes its detachment from the intellect. Singing, in its appeal to emotions and feelings, works against the civilizational project of the theatre, as envisioned by contemporary writers and critics. It creates reactions in the audiences which are dangerously hard to predict or control, making them difficult to shape in the correct way.[44]

George Abyad's *Oedipus Rex* in context

George Abyad's 1912 Arabic version of *Oedipus Rex* offers a particularly revealing and instructive example of how these clashes were enacted in early-twentieth-century Egypt. In order fully to tease out the issues at stake in this landmark play – and to explain why a performance *with* singing has come to be remembered as a performance *without* singing – it is necessary to turn to the history of the production itself. Both the play and Abyad's journey to performing it situate this Egyptian production of Sophocles' tragedy in dialogue with a wider modernist movement, mirroring the debates about performance that were prevalent at the time and adding new dimensions.

Abyad was born in Beirut in 1880 but moved to Alexandria in his early childhood and became part of a large community of Syrians and Lebanese living in Egypt. In the early twentieth century, he performed before the Khedive 'Abbas al-Hilmi II, who was, it is said, so impressed that in 1904 he sent this part-time actor and employee of the Egyptian railways to Paris to perfect his art. He studied, unofficially, with Eugène Silvain, the Comédie Française legend and famous lover of classical drama who was in his fifties when Abyad met him. After several years in France, during which he attended and performed in plays, Abyad returned to Egypt in 1910 with a French troupe performing plays in French. Even then he said that his real ambition was to perform plays in Arabic for the Arabic-speaking people of Egypt. In 1912, he realized this aim, staging *Oedipus Rex*, alongside *Othello* and *Louis XI*.[45]

Being in Paris would have exposed Abyad to the modernist debates on form happening in Europe and beyond. A study of the performance of classical plays, such as *Oedipus Rex*, in the early twentieth century proves to be a particularly useful way of exploring the aesthetic conflicts simultaneously playing out in Europe and in Egypt. The clearest example is the famous production of Strauss's *Elektra* in London in 1910. Strauss's experimental musical score and unrefined performance style shocked the press. The final scenes presented Elektra feverishly dancing herself to death while her brother murders their mother. Many critics were scandalized. Their reactions bear a striking similarity to the debates about singing happening in the Egyptian theatre.

The performance is discussed at length by Simon Goldhill, who collects the reviews, most of which were extremely hostile. '*The Daily Express* summed it up with the memorable headline', Goldhill concludes, '"DECADENT, NOT CLASSIC."'[46] Others attacked Strauss's music and the dancing in particular. *The Spectator*, for instance, accused Elektra's 'nameless dance' of being 'a long sequence of those reptilian contortions and convulsions extremely popular at the modern music-halls under the title of Apache dance, Vampire dance, or some such lurid designation'.[47] Here the British reviewer threw accusations that would have been at home in the Egyptian press: the opera would be better suited to a music hall. It was not refined music but a 'vulgar din'.[48]

This performance was a snapshot of the controversies in European drama in the period. Unrestrained, modernist works like *Elektra* or Albert Jarry's grotesque *Ubu Roi* openly challenged conservative, refined theatrical trends. Two sides had emerged, and by studying with Silvain, Abyad was putting himself in a specific camp: the classic, not decadent. Silvain himself had a very classical approach to acting, focused heavily on the declamation, diction and poetry of the text. According to one contemporary account,

> Mr Silvain's class is very literary, literary because the professor loves literature and he strives to make his students share this taste. He loves poetry, he loves it for

> itself: he likes it out loud [*en auditif*]. To hear him one would think that he is listening to himself and that he would never forgive it if he allowed one syllable to be lost – even a silent one – or if he did not give, in the harmony of voice, the exact and subtle impression of the cadence of the poetry. He has remained classical: he will remain classical [*il est resté classique: il restera classique*].[49]

This education clearly had a considerable influence on Abyad, who appears to have followed his mentor's taste for poetry 'en auditif' and focus on the importance of the voice. When Abyad was advertising for his troupe to perform in 1912, he proclaimed, 'Filip Efendi Makhluf is in charge of teaching the actors and training them in proper declamation [*Sihhat al-ilqa'*] in the Arabic language.'[50] When it came to performing Oedipus, Abyad was the poetic, declamatory actor in the style of Silvain and the Comédie Française. Muhammed Taymur even went as far as to say, a few years after the first performance of *Oedipus Rex*, that 'many people say that [Abyad] is a copy of Silvain made smaller for the spectators and that he moves in the same way as Silvain in everything, even in the roles which are not suited to Silvain's nature'.[51]

However, it was not only Silvain who influenced Abyad in France. During his studies, Abyad went to shows at the Comédie and other theatres of Paris.[52] Back in Egypt, people were used to seeing European theatre. Many of the most important French and Italian actors came to Egypt, including the great French actress Sarah Bernhardt, the Italian actor and playwright Ermete Novelli, and Jean Mounet-Sully. Egyptians did not see themselves merely as passive receivers of European drama but as part of a wider theatrical culture. Muhammad Fadil's biography of Higazi describes a scene in which Bernhardt saw him act and was so moved that she stood up in her box and shouted praise to the performers, exclaiming, 'The genius of the East is more zealous and productive than that in Western countries.' Fadil also reports that Mounet-Sully told several people, including George Abyad, that he learnt how to play Hamlet from Salama Higazi.[53]

One performance that Abyad was likely to have attended was that of Jules Lacroix's *Oedipe Roi* starring the great French actor Jean Mounet-Sully. Mounet-Sully performed the play every year that Abyad was in Paris and eleven times in 1908 alone.[54] When Abyad took *Oedipus Rex* to Egypt, he had Farah Antun translate it into Arabic from the same Lacroix text that Mounet-Sully had used in his version.[55] He also took cues from its performance. It is said that during Abyad's Paris rehearsals in 1910, Mounet-Sulley sat incognito in the stalls. After the rehearsal he revealed himself to Abyad and declared, 'After having seen you acting this role I am relaxed about its fate on the Egyptian stage and I congratulate you.'[56] Photos of Abyad's performance show that the stage design and particularly costumes were almost identical to Mounet-Sully's production.[57]

Abyad's *Oedipus Rex*, at least partly inspired by the Mounet-Sully performance and using an Arabic translation of Lacroix's French, again located him on a particular side of the debates: the controlled, 'classical' side. In Fiona Macintosh's study of *Oedipus Rex* in production, she singles out Mounet-Sully's version as one of the most important and influential. She shows that his staging of Lacroix's text, written in formal neoclassical rhymed alexandrines, and his acting style, using a 'sculptural' technique which constructed the actor as a pristine object of beauty but not one necessarily full of life, were hugely influential at the turn of the century.[58]

Macintosh sets Max Reinhardt's revolutionary 1910 *Oedipus Rex*, premiered in September in Munich, in total opposition to Mounet-Sully. Reinhardt's play was more like Strauss's *Elektra*, full of sounds and music and inspired by the cabarets of Europe. He crowded the stage, using 'large numbers of extras as scenery',[59] an innovation in stagecraft that soon came to the Covent Garden Theatre in London, starting on 15 January 1912. One review said that 'the audience was spellbound by the climax of horrors in the final passages'.[60] *Variety* called it 'daring and different'.[61] Another critic dubbed the play 'a theatrical revolution'.[62]

The contest between these two styles of performance (Strauss/Reinhardt versus Mounet-Sully/Silvain) can best be explained with reference to Friedrich Nietzsche's hugely influential *The Birth of Tragedy*, in which he distinguishes in tragic art between the Apolline and Dionysiac. Apollo, for Nietzsche, represented rationality and clear thinking, most clearly demonstrated in the art of sculpture. Dionysus was wild, drunken and irrational, and found his expression in music. 'To both of their artistic deities, Apollo and Dionysus, is linked our knowledge that in the Greek world there existed a tremendous opposition, in terms of origin and goals, between the Apollonian [Apolline] art of the sculptor and the imageless Dionysian [Dionysiac] art of music', he wrote.[63] Dionysus presided over festivals where 'the wildest beasts of nature were unleashed ... to the point of creating an abominable mixture of sensuality and cruelty'. Apollo, meanwhile, 'stood tall and proud among [the Greeks] and ... warded off this grotesque barbaric Dionysian force'.[64] For Nietzsche, Greek tragedy was informed by the tension between these two forces.

First published in 1872, *The Birth of Tragedy* became extremely influential in artistic circles and formed the basis for many of the theatrical experiments of this period. Mounet-Sully had an Apolline, sculptural view of tragedy 'with its individuation, restraint and formal beauty'; Reinhardt's new production had space for 'life-enhancing/death-dealing Dionysiac music, with its collective, intoxicating, rapturous and murky depths'.[65] In the European context, it is not 'singing' that is seen as dangerously appealing to the emotions but 'music' more generally, whether it be in Strauss's *Elektra* or Reinhardt's *Oedipus Rex*.[66]

Abyad's performance of *Oedipus Rex* was negotiating similar terrain, inspired by similar issues. The performance makes most sense when seen as part of global discussions about theatre. Abyad, who was familiar with developing performance styles in Europe and in Egypt, was able to bring a version of *Oedipus Rex* to the Egyptian stage that both included singing and situated him on the more austere, conservative side of the dramatic divide. Managing to bring different sides of the debate together, he commissioned Salama Higazi to write songs for the version of *Oedipus Rex* translated by Farah Antun, who had earlier accused the singer of killing the art of theatre in Egypt and who worried about the effect that singing had on the audience. He attempted, with some success, both to maintain the hugely popular musical part of Egyptian drama and not to offend the aesthetic sensibilities of the critics.[67]

After the first performance of *Oedipus Rex*, Abyad and Higazi began to work together more and in 1914 merged into a single troupe, officially combining their apparently contradictory styles of performance.[68] This double troupe performed *Oedipus Rex* a number of times during its two-year life, and although Higazi, due to his failing health, never acted in the play, leaving Abyad in the dramatic centre as Oedipus, he did sing between acts.[69]

Abyad's success in incorporating singing into his refined production reveals much of what was behind the criticism that journalists and intellectuals levelled at the genre. The aversion to the medium in Egypt was about more than music. Although critics did not use explicitly Nietzschean vocabulary, they were responding to the same worries as critics in Europe. It was the 'Dionysiac' elements of music and song that worried them – the unrestrained, irrational power of singing to produce dangerous emotions in the audience (coupled with the perceived moral laxity of the venues at which it could be seen). This moral and emotional weakness could have serious consequences for the health of the emerging Egyptian nation.

The different ways that Abyad's production limited the seductive power of singing confirm the basis of this concern. First, the setting, Cairo's elite Opera House, was far from the bawdy music halls and *cafés chantants*, low-life clients and licentious performers which populated the seedier parts of Azbakiyya. The audience, including the highest stratum of society, meant that the atmosphere on opening night could hardly seem vulgar or déclassé. Second, Abyad defused the potentially dangerous elements of singing by setting them in isolated sections of the play and not having them bleed into the rest of the action. In this he was helped by the nature of the original *Oedipus Rex*. Previously, in Egyptian theatre, singing parts had not been separated from the action of the play. Actors would simply burst into song at moments of emotion or heightened drama. In Sophocles' *Oedipus Rex*, there were already choral odes that had their place in the action. Salama Higazi's songs in Abyad's play did not translate the choruses of the Greek tragedy, but they did come in the same distinct places. Thus, the production reined in the negative influence of singing on the audience, drawing a ring around the musical sections and letting the rest of the play rely on 'acting'.

In his review in *al-Hilal*, Jurji Zaydan commented on this feature and praised 'the lack of singing interfering in the acting [*al-'adul 'an idkhal al-ghina' fi-l-tamthil*]'.[70] It is ambiguous sentences like this that have led people to remember *Oedipus Rex* as a play without songs, though the wording does not strictly say so. This was a strategy that may have been suggested to Abyad by the nature of *Oedipus Rex* itself, as a Greek tragedy with spaces for songs, but he continued to do it in other works that were not based on this genre. When he performed *Louis XI* and *Othello*, songs were also said to have come 'at the appropriate place in the action'.[71] Abyad did not eliminate singing, but opposition to the form had never really been about singing per se. He managed to tread a line that both pleased the enemies of singing and included songs by the most celebrated singer of the time.

It is important, of course, not to overstate the lasting legacy of this one performance. Debates about the place of singing in the theatre did not end here. However, this first example of *Oedipus Rex* in Arabic in Egypt continued to be performed on and off until 1949 and was greatly appreciated by important writers and theatre-makers, including Taha Husayn, Tawfiq al-Hakim and Najib al-Rihani. It also offered an important building block for the formation of an Egyptian tradition of plays dealing with

Oedipus by writers such as Tawfiq al-Hakim, who first saw Abyad's version of the play at school and made his own version, *Oedipus the King*, in 1949; 'Ali Ahmad Bakathir, who produced a 1949 version called *The Tragedy of Oedipus* shortly after al-Hakim; and 'Ali Salim, whose 1970 *Comedy of Oedipus* dealt with the political situation at the end of the Nasserite period.[72]

Above all, this performance is important because Abyad demonstrated in it one way to navigate the complexities of Egyptian theatre at the time and elucidated what lay behind many of the theatrical debates among Egyptian critics. By situating this play alongside other performances of classical drama across Europe, it is possible to see that Egypt was participating in wider, global formal controversies and theatrical movements. There were contextual differences; the focus on singing in Egypt is not replicated everywhere else. Also the relationship to tradition is figured differently. In France, for instance, actors like Silvain could appeal to tradition to justify their aesthetic decisions. In Egypt, it was Higazi who was seen as the representative of 'traditional' singing and Abyad who was attempting to move theatre in a new direction. In an obituary of Higazi in the *Revue du Caire* in 1917, the author compared the two artists: 'Shakyh Salama persisted in the same tradition, whereas Abyad sought to innovate.'[73]

There were both connections and differences in debates around performance in Egypt and Europe. There was, however, a uniting concern in these transnational controversies, which can be best expressed as an attempt at control. Whether it is the clash between the 'wild' Dionysiac and 'ordered' Apolline or that between the role of theatre to improve popular morality and the irrational pleasure that singing evokes, the camps were built on similar foundations. Egyptian intellectuals in the early twentieth century debated what it meant to be a virtuous and productive political subject in the state. The growing nationalist movement was trying to form the 'Egyptian people' into a well-functioning polity, and they saw theatre as part of this education. Singing, and the dangerously emotional reaction that it provoked, was a threat to this mission. Certain elements in the press, inspired by bourgeois ideals of respectability, self-improvement and moral rectitude, therefore launched attacks on the public's love of singers and lack of interest in 'proper' theatre.

Abyad, in his 1912 *Oedipus Rex*, offered a model that managed to incorporate singing into a kind of theatre that could also please the more high-minded critics. By giving the songs their own sections and setting them in the context of a classical Greek tragedy performed in the Khedival Opera House, he managed to bring the threat they posed under control. The praise that this musical play received across the press shows that it was not singing in itself which was looked upon with suspicion but the danger it posed to the idea that theatre (and literature more broadly) was designed primarily for moral and social improvement.

Notes

This chapter is based on work included in my thesis (Cormack, 'Oedipus on the Nile', PhD, Edinburgh). The ideas have been developed with the generous advice and suggestions of participants at the conference and, in particular, the editors of this collection.

1 Translated into Arabic by Farah Antun. I have not found a printed text in any library nor have I seen any mention of it. When Muhammad Yusuf Najm republished Farah Antun's plays, he did not include this one.
2 Taymur, *Hayatuna al-tamthiliyya*, Pt. 2, 131–2.
3 *Al-Ahram* 22 March 1912, 2.
4 *Al-Jarida* 23 March 1912, 5.
5 Taymur, *Hayatuna al-tamthiliyya*, 24: 'Irtaqa fann al-tamthil irtiqaʾan.' This division of the progression of Arabic theatre through different stages (based on Taymur) can also be found in Barbour, 'The Arabic Theatre in Egypt', 179. The title highlights the words *fanni* and *raqi*, both commonly used to describe 'artistic' theatre.
6 *Al-Ahram* 22 March 1912, 2; *Al-Jarida* 23 March 1912, 5; *Al-Hilal* 1 April 1912, 437.
7 Letter to Suʿad Abyad from 1965 reproduced as the epigram of Abyad, *Jurj Abyad*.
8 Al-Rihani, *Mudhakkirat Najib al-Rihani*, 29.
9 Litvin, in a broader discussion of singing in the theatre (*Hamlet's Arab Journey*, 67) also mentions Abyad's attempt 'to present "serious" theatre, with no singing' and gives *Oedipus* as one example. (Other plays by Abyad, such as *Othello*, seem to have appeared without singing).
10 Hanna, 'Decommercialising Shakespeare', 34–5, though, in note 30, he does clarify that in the second season of plays after this performance, Abyad was 'in the position of having to use some of the elements of commercial theatre which he had previously refrained from, such as music and dance'.
11 *Al-Ahram* 27 March 1912, 2. My emphasis.
12 Other classically themed plays had been performed before, such as Voltaire's *Oedipe* in 1900 and 1905. However, this was the first translation of an original Greek tragedy (done through an intermediary French translation).
13 Foundation for Arab Music Archiving and Research: Muhammad Uthman, http://www.amar-foundation.org/muhammad-uthman/ (accessed 16 September 2018).
14 For al-Hamuli, Rumanu and ʿUthman, see Sadgrove, *Egyptian Theatre in the Nineteenth Century*, 155–7. For Salih, see e.g. *al-Muqattam* 23 April 1895, and for Ahmad, see e.g. *al-Surur* 17 March 1894 or *al-Muqattam* 14 October 1893. References to Egyptian newspapers without page numbers come from a series of anthologies of articles from the historical Egyptian press edited by al-Markaz al-Qawmi li-l-Masrah in Cairo, entitled *Silsilat Tawthiq al-Masrah al-Misri*, which began in 1997 and is still releasing new volumes.
15 On Almaz and her troubled marriage to al-Hamuli, see Booth, *Classes of Ladies of Cloistered Spaces*, 294–8.
16 For Malikat al-Surur, see: *Misr* 12 January 1898 or *al-Akhbar* 20 November 1897; Kawkab: *al-Surur* 21 and 28 March 1894; Layla: *al-Muqattam* 20 October 1891; al-ʿAlima: *al-Ahram* 29 February 1892.
17 Prestel, *Emotional Cities*, 123–32, describes the late-nineteenth-century reactions to the numerous new bars in the area, another thing that contributed to associations between music halls and moral decay.
18 *Al-Mahrusa* 26 January 1910.
19 Al-Muwaylihi, *ʿIsa Ibn Hisham*, includes a translation by Roger Allen. A new edition released by the Library of Arabic Literature in 2015 publishes, for the first time, the original text as published in Misbah al-Sharq without alterations. It also includes a short biographical introduction about al-Muwaylihi.

20 Al-Muwaylihi, *'Isa Ibn Hisham*, 164–5.
21 Ibid., 166–7.
22 Ibid., 168–9.
23 Al-Tahtawi, *Takhlis al-ibriz*, 133.
24 *Al-Mu'ayyid* 27 May 1907.
25 Ryzova, *The Age of the Efendiyya*, summarizes the formation and ideals of this new class.
26 See e.g. Selim, *The Novel and the Rural Imaginary*, 12: 'Intellectuals understood popular, oral narrativity as the antithesis of modern narrative, repeatedly attacking the former as both a cause and a symptom of the corruption of the masses.'
27 See Fahmy, *Ordinary Egyptians*, e.g. 128–31, on the relationship between Bourdieu's ideas of 'taste' and Egyptian theatrical criticism of the early twentieth century.
28 Omar, 'Arabic Thought in the Liberal Cage', offers a useful discussion of the quest to form Egyptian subjecthood in intellectual and political circles.
29 See the AMAR foundation biography of Higazi: http://www.amar-foundation.org/salama-higazi/ (accessed 16 September 2018).
30 This life story draws on Fadil, *al-Shaykh Salama Ḥijazi*, 10–26. The book is based on the author's own research and recollections as well as interviews with people who knew Higazi and the family.
31 I thank Frédéric Lagrange for stressing the difference between Higazi and less highly trained singers of the period.
32 Reid, *The Odyssey of Farah Antun*, 63–97.
33 *Al-Jami'a* March 1, 1900, 571.
34 At one point, Higazi himself tried to act a version of Hamlet without singing. The audience were angry and chanted for another act with singing, so Higazi was forced to have Ahmad Shawqi write songs for the performance. The earliest instance of this story is in Fadil, *al-Shaykh Salama Hijazi*, 40–1.
35 *Al-Akhbar* 22 January 1909.
36 *Al-Hilal* 1 May 1910, 464–72. Quotation from p. 471.
37 The terms of the argument are a little unclear but seem to have involved money, rather than artistic differences.
38 *Al- Hilal* 1 May 1910, 471–2. The 'blank' is where the text has printed incorrectly, leaving *–iyyāt* at the end of a word. It may be an important word missing as it seems strange to say that there was no singing in Farah's productions, since he had Ahmad al-Shami as a singer in his troupe (see e.g. *Misr* 17 May 1906) and frequently performed the Opera L'Africaine in Arabic which was 'full of songs' (*al-Muqattam* 19 May 1906). Perhaps he meant that the troupe did not focus on the singing as Higazi did.
39 Khuri-Makdisi, *The Eastern Mediterranean*, 60–93. Quotation on p. 91. Theatres as spaces could be used in many ways. Gorman, 'Anarchists in Education', discusses a radical 'university for all' launched in a theatre in Alexandria, though its later meetings were held elsewhere.
40 *Al-Jami'a* 1 March 1900, 568–9.
41 Ryzova, *The Age of the Efendiyya*, 7.
42 *Al-Mu'ayyad* 11 July 1908.
43 *Al-Akhbar* 14 July 1908.
44 The dangerous power of emotion over rationality (*'aql*) is discussed in Prestel, *Emotional Cities* (which helped solidify some of the ideas in this chapter). However, reservations about music go back at least as far as Plato, *Republic* 424c–d. In Tom Griffith's translation of *Republic*, Socrates claims that '[people] should beware of new

forms of music, which are likely to affect the whole system of education. Changes in styles of music are always politically revolutionary … It's certainly a place where breaking rules can easily become a habit without anyone realising' (117). See also Burnyeat, *Culture and Society in Plato's Republic.*

45 Abyad's life story is told in Abyad, *Jurj Abyad*. Full of rich detail, it does not have references and a number of details are open to question. For his entry into theatre and meeting the Khedive, see pp. 55–74. For his time in France and triumphant return to Egypt and performance of Oedipus in Arabic, see pp. 75–127. On his dream to perform in Arabic: *Le Matin* 16 March 1910, 4.

46 Goldhill, 'Blood from the Shadows', quotation from p. 138.

47 *The Spectator* 12 March 1910, 20.

48 *The Nation* 26 February 1910, 843.

49 *La Nouvelle Revue* February 1902, 47.

50 *Al-Akhbar* 25 August 1911. See also Hanna, 'Decommercialising Shakespeare', esp. 34–5.

51 Taymur, *Hayatuna al-tamthiliyya*, 141–2.

52 Abyad, *Jurj Abyad*, 83, 100.

53 Fadil, *Salama Hijazi*, 50–1. These stories are very hard to verify but at least show that Egyptian theatre practitioners saw themselves in an equal dialogue with French counterparts. *Al-Ahram* 17 April 1899 mentions Novelli's tour in Egypt.

54 For more details of plays performed at the Comédie Française, see Joannides's documentations under the title *Comédie Française* followed by a year, e.g., Joannides, *Comédie Française* 1908.

55 Najm, 'Masrah al-Shaykh Salama Hijazi'. On p. 81, Najm states that Abyad's *Oedipus Rex* was translated from Lacroix but gives no reference. For a more detailed exposition of the links between Lacroix's text and Antun's translation, see Cormack, 'Oedipus on the Nile', 57–61.

56 *Al-Ahram* 1 March 1949.

57 Photos of one performance of the play are on display at the National Centre for Theatre in Zamalek, but I have not been able to reproduce them.

58 Macintosh, *Sophocles: Oedipus Tyrannus*, 81–95.

59 Esslin, 'Max Reinhardt: "High Priest of Theatricality"'.

60 *New York Tribune* 16 January 1912, 7.

61 *Variety* 20 January 1912, 4.

62 *Current Literature* (New York) 52 (1912): 337.

63 Nietzsche (trans. Smith), *Birth of Tragedy*, 19.

64 Ibid., 24–5.

65 Macintosh, *Sophocles: Oedipus Tyrannus*, 102–12.

66 Ibid. On the British performance of *Oedipus* in 1912, see 112–23. On Reinhardt's *Oedipus Rex*, see also Taxidou, *Modernism and Performance*, 158–62, and Hall and Macintosh, *Greek Tragedy*, 538–42.

67 Fadil, *Salama Hijazi*, 312. Higazi himself did not perform in the 1912 Oedipus, though there was music and seemingly a chorus of singers, but it seems likely that Higazi wrote the songs. However, in subsequent years, as the play became a staple of Abyad's troupe and the songs become well known, Higazi began to sing them himself. By 1914, Higazi was performing the songs from *Oedipus* in his own shows.

68 Najm, 'Masrah al-Shaykh Salama Hijazi', 72–6. Their unification was likely spearheaded by 'Abd al-Raziq al-'Inayat who owned both troupes. On him, see Fadil, *Salama Hijazi*, 56–7.

69 For performances of the play, see Najm, 'Masrah al-Shaykh Salama Hijazi', 128–35; Najm says *Oedipus Rex* was performed on 12 December 1914; 10 April, 5 May and 24 December 1915; and 11 February and 10 March 1916.
70 *Al-Hilal* 1 April 1912, 437. It is perhaps this that M. M. Badawi refers to in *Modern Arabic Drama* when he writes that Abyad 'produced plays without the intrusion of singing' (65).
71 Al-Hifni, *al-Shaykh Salama Hijazi*, 190.
72 English translations are available in Carlson, *The Arab Oedipus*.
73 Cited in *Correspondance d'Orient* 10 November 1917, 279.

Bibliography

Abyad, Su'd. *Jurj Abyad: ayyam lan yusdal ʿalayha al-sitar*. Cairo: Dar al-Maʿarif, 1970.
Foundation for Arab Music Archiving & Research. Accessed 15 June 2020. https://www.amar-foundation.org/.
Amin, Dina. 'Egyptian Theater: Reconstructing Performance Spaces'. *Arab Studies Journal* 14, no. 2 (2006): 78–100.
Amine, Khalid, and Marvin Carlson. *The Theatres of Morocco, Algeria, and Tunisia: Performance Traditions of the Maghreb*. New York: Palgrave Macmillan, 2011.
Badawi, M. M. *Modern Arabic Drama in Egypt*. Cambridge: Cambridge University Press, 1988.
Bakathir, ʿAla Ahmad. *Ma ʾsat Udib* [The Tragedy of *Oedipus]*. Cairo: Dar al-Kitab alʿArabi, 1949.
Barbour, Nevill. 'The Arabic Theatre in Egypt'. *Bulletin of the School of Oriental Studies, University of London* 8, no. 1 (1935): 173–87.
Booth, Marilyn. *Classes of Ladies of Cloistered Spaces*. Edinburgh: Edinburgh University Press, 2015.
Burnyeat, Miles. 'Culture and Society in Plato's Republic'. In *The Tanner Lectures of Human Values*, edited by G. B. Peterson, 217–324. Salt Lake City: Utah University Press, 1999.
Cachia, Pierre. *Popular Narrative Ballads of Modern Egypt*. Oxford: Oxford University Press, 1989.
Carlson, Marvin. *The Arab Oedipus: Four Plays from Egypt and Syria*. New York: Martin E. Segal Theatre Center Publications, 2005.
Cormack, Raphael. 'Oedipus on the Nile: Translations and Adaptations of Sophocles' Oedipus Tyrannos in Egypt 1900–1970'. PhD dissertation, University of Edinburgh, 2017.
Esslin, Martin. 'Max Reinhardt: "High Priest of Theatricality"'. *Drama Review* 21, no. 2 (1977): 3–24.
Fadil, Muhammad. *al-Shaykh Salama Hijazi*. Damanhur: al-Umma, 1932.
Fahmy, Ziad. *Ordinary Egyptians: Creating the Modern Nation through Popular Culture*. Stanford: Stanford University Press, 2011.
Fathallah, Izis. *Salama Hijazi*. Cairo: Dar al-Shuruq, 2002.
Goldhill, Simon. 'Blood from the Shadows: Strauss' Disgusting, Degenerate "Elektra"'. In *Who Needs Greek: Contests in the Cultural History of Hellenism*, edited by Simon Goldhill, 108–77. Cambridge: Cambridge University Press, 2002.
Gorman, Anthony. 'Anarchists in Education: The Free Popular University in Egypt (1901)'. *Middle Eastern Studies* 41, no. 3 (2005): 303–20.
Hall, Edith, and Fiona Macintosh. *Greek Tragedy and the British Theatre, 1660–1914*. Oxford: Oxford University Press, 2005.

Hanna, Sameh. 'Decommercialising Shakespeare: Mutran's Translation of "Othello"'. *Critical Survey* 19, no. 3 (2007): 27–54.
al-Hakim, Tawfiq. *al-Malik Udib* [Oedipus the King]. Cairo: Maktabat al-Adab, 1977.
al-Hifni, Mahmud Ahmad. *al-Shaykh Salama Hijazi*. Cairo: Dar al-Katib al-'Arabi, 1968.
Joannides, Alexandre. *Comédie Française: 1908*. Paris: Plon-Nourrit, 1909.
Khuri-Makdisi, Ilham. *The Eastern Mediterranean and the Making of Global Radicalism, 1860–1914*. Berkeley: University of California Press, 2010.
Lagrange, Frédéric. *Musiques D'Égypte*. Paris: Actes Sud, 1996.
Litvin, Margaret. *Hamlet's Arab Journey: Shakespeare's Prince and Nasser's Ghost*. Princeton: Princeton University Press, 2011.
Macintosh, Fiona. *Sophocles: Oedipus Tyrannus*. Cambridge: Cambridge University Press, 2009.
Al-Markaz al-Qawmi li-l-Masrah. *Silsilat Tawthiq al-Masrah al-Misri*. Cairo: Wizarat al-Thaqafa, 1997–.
Mustafa, Muhammad Yusuf. 'Antecedents of Modern Arabic Drama'. PhD dissertation, University of Cambrige, 1967.
al-Muwaylihi, Muhammad. *Hadith 'Isa ibn Hisham: aw fatra min al-zaman* [What 'Isa Ibn Hisham Told Us: Or a Period of Time]. Parallel text translated by Roger Allen. 2 vols. New York: New York University Press, 2015.
Najm, Muhammad Yasuf. 'Masrah al-Shaykh Salama Hijazi fi tawr al-istiqlal'. *Majallat al-abhath (American University of Beirut)* 26 (1973–77): 57–139.
Nietzsche, Friedrich. *The Birth of Tragedy*. Translated by Douglas Smith. Oxford: Oxford University Press, 2000.
Omar, Hussein. 'Arabic Thought in the Liberal Cage'. In *Islam After Liberalism*, edited by Faisal Devji and Zaheer Kazmi, 17–45. Oxford: Oxford University Press, 2017.
Plato. *The Republic*. Translated by Tom Griffith. Cambridge: Cambridge University Press, 2007.
Prestel, Joseph Ben. *Emotional Cities: Debates on Urban Change in Berlin and Cairo: 1860–1910*. Oxford: Oxford University Press, 2017.
Racy, Ali Jihad. *Making Music in the Arab World: The Culture and Artistry of Ṭarab*. Cambridge: Cambridge University Press, 2003.
Reid, Donald Malcolm. *The Odyssey of Farah Antun: A Syrian Christian's Quest for Secularism*. Minneapolis, MN: Bibliotheca Islamica, 1975.
al-Rihani, Najib. *Mudhakkirat Najib al-Rihani*. Cairo: Kalimat, 2011.
Ryzova, Lucie. *The Age of the Efendiyya: Passages to Modernity in National-Colonial Egypt*. Oxford: Oxford University Press, 2014.
Sadgrove, Philip. *Egyptian Theatre in the Nineteenth Century*. Berkshire: Ithaca Press, 1996.
Salim, 'Ali. *Kumidya Udib: aw anta illi 'atalt al-wahsh [The Comedy of Oedipus: Or You're the One Who Killed the Beast]*. Cairo: Maktabat Madbuli, 1986 (first edition, Cairo: Dar al-hilal, 1970).
Selim, Samah. *The Novel and the Rural Imaginary in Egypt, 1880–1985*. New York: Routledge, 2004.
al-Tahtawi, Rifa'a Rafi'. *Takhlis al-ibriz fi talkhis Bariz*. Cairo: Kalimat, 2013.
Taxidou, Olga. *Modernism and Performance: Jarry to Brecht*. Basingstoke: Palgrave Macmillan, 2007.
Taymur, Muhammad. *Mu'allafat Muhammad Taymur: hayatuna al-tamthiliyya: al-juz' al-thani*. Cairo: al-I'timad, 1922.

3

‘Ya ʿaziz ʿaini ana bidi arawwah baladi …’: Voyages of an Egyptian tune – from estrangement at home to longing on the fronts of the First World War

Alia Mossallam

Caught between East and West

> East and West have come under the dominion of the crown
> They who rule the waves are now ruling the earth
> They make their planes fly like the prophet on his celestial journey
> Next they have us going on a pilgrimage to London
> You say the fellows who live in Paris are gentlemen
> While the Arabs in the colonies are the animals
> Why is it you’re Parisians and we’re Africans?
> Now show us what you’re going to do about the Germans![1]

Mustafa Amin’s voice is drenched with sarcasm as it comes through the muffled tones of the digitized recording, originally created in 1920 (though sung since 1916).[2] Much like his contemporary, the singer and composer Sayyid Darwish, the popular Alexandrian singer’s repertoire reflects the grievances of different segments of the Alexandrian population during and after the First World War. [3] Unlike Darwish, however, his songs were not connected with the plight of any particular nationalist party such as the Wafd and thus are less well known (less recorded and less remembered) in historical memory.

The same could be said about the experience of the First World War in Egypt, to which the above song refers. Outshone by the sensational historiography of the 1919 revolution, and the contemporary narrativization of the war as a feat contributed to by the Egyptian military,[4] little is known about the effects of the First World War on Egyptians, whether on the home or war fronts. In this song in particular, Mustafa Amin reflects sentiments that prevailed in Egypt when it became a British protectorate following the Ottoman Empire’s entry into the war. The status of ‘British protectorate’ entailed the censorship and political repression of martial law, the requisitioning of food and livestock from the countryside to feed the imperial army and, ultimately, the conscription of hundreds of thousands of Egyptian peasants into the Egyptian Labour Corps (ELC).

Records indicate that between ten thousand and up to 1.5 million Egyptian men between the ages of 17 and 35 were drafted to serve in Sinai, Beirut, Calais and Palestine during the First World War. This represents up to a third of the male population of that age at the time.[5] Many never returned, and lie buried in unmarked graves without receiving the burial rites of their respective faiths.[6] But their voices continue to roam various archives, echoing through the gramophone or trapped in police reports and image catalogues in British, French and Australian military collections. These are voices out of place, whether on account of the language in which they are written or the circumstances of their involvement in the war.

This chapter investigates the experience of Egyptians caught up in a war they did not perceive as their own, more specifically the ELC sent to the fronts between 1916 and 1918. One hundred years after the event, I search through songs echoing in popular memory, and documented in musical and military archives, to reveal traces of these experiences.

When I say echoes, I do not only mean the unclear sounds and notes that come through the recordings but rather that these voices are taken out of context, possessing the 'truncated mediated quality of voices whose speakers remain unknowable'.[7] According to Gayatri Spivak, an echo's voice is 'stable-yet-unstable, same-yet-different, and non-originary'.[8] This use of Spivak's ideas is inspired by Annette Hoffman's work using the notion of echoes to understand the voice recordings of West African soldiers and Labour Corps members imprisoned in Europe during the First World War.[9] We hear the voices of those who experienced the event mediated through other voices (their captors, singers who sing their songs, etc.), echoing, fragmented and out of their original context. Although not the original voice, the persistence of songs through various media from the same period still tells of the experiences of war and possesses an almost haunting quality.

The second theme this chapter tackles is methodology. How, one hundred years later, can we trace voices that lie buried under one hundred years of silence, re-narrativized and neglected?[10] I trace these voices through imperial archives, documenting songs sung by the members of the ELC on various fronts or recorded by singers who rose to fame with the onset of the record industry, singing in Cairo of the grievances of the war, and songs that persist in popular memory. Each of these sources raises questions as to the politics and techniques of their accessibility, and of what their echoes may silence or muffle of the original experiences.

I have chosen to read one particular song that appears consistently through each of the above-mentioned sources: 'Ya ʿaziz ʿaini' ('O apple of my eye'). The first version of this song (*c.*1913–15) comes through the voice of Naʿima al-Masriyya, a pioneering artist in the record industry who sang both in Asyut (from where many workers were taken, according to recruitment records) and in Cairo at the onset of the war (1913–16). The second version documents it as a work song sung by the ELC on the front in Palestine and recorded in the diaries of British lieutenant Ernest Kendrick Venables in 1917. The third is documented in the British Foreign Office archives as it is overheard in 'native quarters' by workers returned from the war to their Upper Egyptian villages in 1918.

'Ya ʿaziz ʿaini' is a popular song (of folkloric origin) that predates these recordings and documentations from 1915 to 1918. That is, the song already carries within its lyrics experiences of estrangement and loss (most probably through conscription) from earlier periods. They are elements of an 'intimate language'[11] – a language that carries within it the embryos of a particular experience, evoking that experience whenever it is sung, whether to remind, mobilize or comfort.

Through tracing various versions of the song, this chapter charts a constellation of relations between the songs and those who sang them, where they were sung and the experiences they present, between the past and the present where they linger. This constellation gives a sense of the experience of the war at the time and how these past experiences echo into the present. It discusses the nature of a song – evolving over time, collecting more experiences with time and changing in content, while maintaining the same refrain and emotional essence in its formulaic structure (in this case, estrangement). The song becomes an intimate language that instantly resonates among people with a shared history, a way of expressing emotion and articulating it collectively at any given moment. The chapter thus tackles the intimate experience of war, read through one song found in various sources between 1915 and 1918. Each version, keeping the same refrain, articulates a different aspect of the experience, while also highlighting a different use for the song. The main question then becomes: What can these mediated voices tell us about the war? What essence of these experiences do the echoes carry? And in tracing the song from city to city and archive to archive, what can be unravelled of the politics of the First World War and the geography of the workers' travels?

I. 'Sway back and forth between us …' Naʿima al-Masriyya – Asyut/Alexandria, 1915

O apple of my eye, I want to go back home!	يا عزيز عيني وأنا بدّي أروّح بلدي،
O apple of my eye I want to go back home	آه يا عزيز عيني وأنا بدّي أروّح بلدي
O apple of my eye, your absence is beyond me	آه يا عزيز عيني بُعدك على عيني
(repeat)	(مكرر)

My darling arose ready to depart,	صابح مسافر وداخل ليه يودعني
and he came to bid me farewell	بكى وبلّ المحارم قلت ليه يعني
He wept, drenching his handkerchief, and I asked	هو البُكا صنعتك ولّا دلع يعني
'Why do you do this?'	لا هو البكا صنعتي ولا هو دلع يعني
'Is crying your sport, or are you teasing me?'	لولا كلام العوازل مُر يوجعني
'Crying is neither my sport nor am I teasing you'	آه يا عزيز عيني بُعدك على عيني

The talk of the jealous ones is bitter and painful
O, apple of my eye, how I feel sorry for myself.
O apple of my eye, I want to go back home

يا عزيز عيني وأنا بدّي أروّح بلدي ...

O morning star, sway back and forth between us, send
my love to those who have captivated my soul
I have the cure for all ills, but none for my soul
My aches are so strong, I can't get a hold of myself

يا نجمة الصبح طلّي وارجعي وروحي
وسلمّيلي على اللي عندهم روحي
......أنا من صداعي وأنا التفيت على روحي

A good evening to you, oh flower of the nation
we are the ones who suffer while they are as they are
while others meet your fancy, embittered we become
May God ease your path, and may He grant us patience
O apple of my eye, your absence is beyond me

مسيت بالخير يا فلة على أمة
إحنا اللي ذقنا العذاب ودول زي ما همّ
إن كان غيرنا حِلي وإحنا اللي مرّرنا
الله يهوّن عليك وإحنا يصبّرنا
آه يا عزيز عيني بُعدك على عيني

This version of the song, sung by Naʿima al-Masriyya and composed by Sayyid Darwish, was recorded by Mechian record company[12] between 1913 and 1915 and is the longest version of the song that I have found documented from this time period.[13] The song is densely layered in content – every stanza persists separately in folk songs or a *mawwal*[14] deeply embedded in the Upper Egyptian folk repertoire and still sung today. It is also layered in format – the song 'sways back and forth' between the experience of those who were sent to war in the refrain ('O apple of my eye, I want to go back home') and the bitterness of those left behind, or longing for those who are gone in the song's content (in other popular versions, the refrain continues with 'My home, my home, and the authorities have taken my son'). The song in its compilation plucks at chords of estrangement experienced in Upper Egypt prior to and during the First World War.

In this section, I piece together the fragmented histories of Naʿima al-Masriyya's struggle as a singer, the record industry in Egypt during the First World War and Sayyid Darwish's composition, highlighting the significance of the song which appears repeatedly in British Foreign Office and Imperial War Museum archives as sung by workers on the front.

Born Zaynab al-Migharbilin in Cairo in 1892, Naʿima al-Masriyya was one of the first Egyptian Muslim women to perform onstage as a *mutriba* (artist) rather than an *ʿalma* 'of ill-repute, promoting an intricate image of sophistication and gentle debauchery'.[15] This new title was afforded her by the circumstances of the war, which changed the social and cultural contexts of singing, creating a commercial recording industry with opportunities for female artists, and performance spaces that opened earlier due to the curfew, making them accessible to both female singers and audiences.[16] Naʿima was one of the first female artists to write her own music and open and manage her own performance space (al-Hambra, *c.*1922), thus gaining economic independence through her craft.

According to the Naʿima Project,[17] al-Masriyya sang in Asyut between 1913 and 1916, and it was during these years that she made her first recordings with Sayyid Darwish.[18] The singer and the revolutionary composer had a close relationship in which Darwish would return to Naiʿima for her feedback on his own compositions, aside from composing her songs.[19] Naʿima's residence in Asyut in the two years before 'Ya ʿaziz ʿaini' was recorded explains how she accessed those stanzas of the song that originate in Upper Egyptian folklore. Their lyrics persist today in Upper Egyptian songs in the *hakawati* (storytelling) and *mawawil* (improvised) forms in Upper Egypt. They are still sung in gatherings, weddings and *mawalid* in the region by famous popular artists such as Farsh wa Ghatta.[20] These lyrics exist as elements of a folk repertoire familiar to Upper Egyptian audiences and to which they react.[21] Each stanza of the above song can be traced to songs that are either spiritual in nature, reflecting a mystical longing for a creator, or a longing for someone who has travelled. Many elements, such as 'A beautiful evening to you, oh flower of the nation' or 'O star of the evening sway back and forth' persist in songs from light-hearted *mawawil* to songs that erupt into ritualistic *dhikr* in festive events such as *mawalid* (religious festivals celebrating the birth of the prophet or Sufi saints).[22]

The fact that Naʿima's song comprises many other songs that existed in Upper Egypt at the time can be attributed to many factors. The first and easiest to claim is the nature of the songs that attracted the record industry at the time. On the introduction of phonographs to Egypt in the early twentieth century (probably 1903),[23] musical composition usually entailed editing existing songs to a shorter and more commercially viable format, the *taqtuqa*, a standard practice for the industry at the time. According to Racy, the commercial recording of songs was the first instance in which they were changed from long, improvised forms that depended on their audience's interaction and engagement to short, static forms that were both recordable for a singer singing into a phonograph speaker and commercially viable.[24] It is thus likely that Naʿima was already singing the popular *mawawil* (or *mawwal* – perhaps it was one song before exploding into fragments) as they were known to local audiences before it was shortened for recording purposes.

Another element that may have contributed to the form is Darwish and Naʿima's political inclinations. Many of Darwish's songs leading up to the 1919 revolution and until his death in 1922 reflect the politics of his discontented audiences.[25] During Saʿd Zaghlul's deportation and exile on account of his leading role in the revolution, Naʿima sang 'Ya balah Zaghlul', a song in praise of the leader disguised as an ode to the dates of the same name.[26] In addition to indicating her support of Zaghlul and the revolution, the song stands in brave defiance of a law that prohibited the mention of Zaghlul's name.

In the light of Naʿima's political audacity that appears through songs later in her career, and of Darwish's attempts to depict the plight of various segments of society in his songs, could this song have reflected the sentiment of those left behind during the war? It is possible, though impossible to prove. Having been in Asyut during the first years of the war, Naʿima may have witnessed people being taken away by force, as related in memoirs of political thinker Salama Musa's description of events in Minya and the judge Ismat Sayf al-Dawla's descriptions of Asyut.[27] If she did witness these events, her documentation of the many lyrical expressions of those left behind may have been intentional; if not, perhaps it is the popularity of these songs at the time that imposed themselves on the singer and the composer's repertoire – whether for performance or recording. The question remains as to why the song continued to be sung by Upper Egyptian peasants and workers on the various fronts of war. And how does it persist until now (the last version was recorded in 2005)[28] with a strong sense of estrangement whose content and direction changes over the eras?

Frédéric Lagrange claims that the 'genius' of Sayyid Darwish, his virtue as a popular singer, is indicated not merely by the millions who listened to his recordings at the time they were sung but by how long they have persisted.[29] Fadi 'Abdallah also claims that it is the need to create music for the theatre that made Darwish's songs accessible and singable by any person with theatrical drive.[30] Similarily, in helping to understand how a song persists through history, Susan Slymovics describes the 'energy' with which oral folk literature persists as 'constructed out of conventional epithetic features and repeated narrative archetypes. ... Such literature acquires a significant amount of its energy and its interest from its ability to bring present and past into active conjunction.'[31] Slyomovics's work refers to the Upper Egyptian 'Hilali epic' that reinvents itself to tell the stories of various political moments through its narrative frame.[32] In the case of 'Ya 'aziz 'aini', what the song continues to relate or recreate in its different versions, with the same formulaic form or frame, is the sense of estrangement. It is that experience of estrangement that the song so evocatively captures that explains its persistence.

Few of Na'ima's records and little about her career can be found through record markets and archives; what we have instead is a family history project that brings parts of her experience to light.[33] Na'ima's rise to fame did not come without personal cost, especially as a pioneer carving out new space for her art in Egyptian society. Perhaps it is on account of this cost that there are almost no radio or television recordings of her, in contrast with many of her contemporaries (such as Munira al-Mahdiyya),[34] among whom her art stood apart. With what we can piece together from stories and songs, however, along with the recording date (1915), the dates of Na'ima's work in Asyut (1913–16) and Sayyid Darwish's composition styles is that the song was being sung in the wake of the war and both the singer and composer encountered it in Asyut, a city where large numbers of peasants were conscripted. It can also be asserted that the song echoes previous experiences of conscription or estrangement.[35] What can be inferred, therefore, is the possibility of the song being very popular at the time (and indeed being recorded, distributed and persisting until today in recorded form) and that its very compilation was politically driven – in relation to the experiences of the First World War. What is explored below is how it continued to throb through workers' everyday lives throughout the war, giving us a glimpse of a new experience of the conflict in each instance.

II. 'Darling, light of my eyes, I want to go home ...' – Railway workers – Jaffa, 1917

Native songs were an abidingly quaint feature of life and work, and no doubt unwittingly they were an echo of servicemen's feelings in any army, in any war.

> Top favourite was certainly; 'Kam lehloh, kam yom?' – how many nights, how many days? – have we still to serve? A similar sentiment was expressed by 'Y 'azeez ya ehni, ana bidi arawah beladee! – Darling, light of my eyes, I want to go home.[36]

This version of the song appears in the memoirs of British lieutenant Venables, who oversaw the ELC while posted at El Arish, Rafah, Jaffa and Gaza between 1917 and 1919. Egyptian workers were used to perform manual labour, including constructing pipelines and railway lines, loading and unloading construction materials, and even carrying army huts on their shoulders to the front. Other dangerous tasks included carrying wounded soldiers away from the front lines to nearby roads.[37]

Because these troops were inexperienced and untrained to be soldiers, however, large numbers suffered injury, disease and death. The casualties were inflicted by more than just overwork. During the battle for Gaza, for example, the British Army used the ELC as night-time decoys in constantly moving boats to fool the Ottoman Army.[38] They were also assigned with clearing the battlefields of unexploded shells and grenades.[39] Or, in the words of Venables himself:

> Some nights were distinctly lively or deadly, though we were lucky in being placed on sand dunes a little removed from the military centre as the target of the moment. It was by no means exhilarating to hear bombs crashing and machine-gun bullets zipping into the ground, but it was a duteous comfort to the men as they lay here and there on the sand when their officer strolled about among them, assuring them it was all right, no need to be frightened; a cheerful lie often to be repeated in the future – while close by some camels were being let out to problematical safety, too obtuse to notice others being blown to pieces. Next morning it was joyless to count the prostrate figures of other ELC companies' men who had been killed as they waited squatting by the railway track in the main camp, literally and dreadfully without knowing what hit them, still enfolded in the dun blanket which had become their shroud.[40]

These sorts of 'cheerful lies' appear elsewhere in Venables's memoirs where, for reasons of convenience to the British army, workers were asked to stay near their work stations, only to come under fire. Still, throughout the account, there are assertions that the 'Egyptians were willing helpers of British troops' and references to their occasional singing as a 'quaint feature of work' which contributed to this construction of what Venables refers to as 'Happy singing Egyptians'.[41]

The songs featured frequently in Venables's memoirs and other documentations of the war. In a 1939 article on the history of military anthems in the periodical *al-Risala*, 'Abd al-Latif al-Nashar describes the 'volunteered' ELC as singing 'Ya ʿaziz ʿaini' as they were marched out of their villages on their way to war. In the article, he talks about the importance of military anthems throughout history and the consequential formation of a *'lagnat al-alhaan'* (committee of tunes) in military institutions. He highlights how popular 'Ya ʿaziz ʿaini' was among the recruited, possibly due to the extent to which people felt it represented them and their wartime experiences, and its place in the history of conscription.[42]

In Venables's memoirs, a similar description of singing appears when men are taken to war:

> Departure of a levy was an occasion of despondent disarray: the recruited men walking along together escorted by native police, who were hard pressed to restrain the crowd of women and other relatives following their menfolk to the railway station, wailing and waving mournful arms as the train of open trucks moved northward, bearing its human load irresolute between the grief of parting and doubts as to unknown troubles ahead. Sometimes they would break into song, as if to cheer themselves up, and wave home-sewn flags as the train passed other villages.[43]

'Ya ʿaziz ʿaini', however, appears mainly as a work song, used by both Egyptian and British troops. The song is sung by Egyptian troops in more than one format. Again, the 'frame' of the refrain of *ya 'aziz 'aini ana bidi arawwah baladi; Baladi ya baladi wel sulta khadit waladi*, evoking the experience of both those taken and those left behind, is used consistently, but the content changes with situation and context, as 'alternative lines could be added from choice or imagination … wording could be adapted to the aptness of the moment'.[44] In some cases, for example, the song is used in a confrontational way, with complaints about work elaborated upon to the tune of the song. Lyrics were tied to the motion of the *faas* (adze) and often presented a warning from one worker to another of an officer spying on them or passing by. Throughout the memoir, disguised jokes at the expense of Venables and other overseers appear, overheard during work, in the barracks or through the songs, thus making an intimate language of these repeated songs sung by workers from different villages, creating a space for defiance in a heavily supervised context.

The songs thus continued to evolve through the war, during work and while marching. Their popularity meant that even the 'British Tommies' caught on to them. *Kam Leyla wa kam yom* appears along with 'Ya ʿaziz ʿaini' as sung by British troops during their marches. They were largely integrated into longer English songs making fun of the ELC. In one of his diary entries, however, Venables describes being at a railway station in London, ten years after the war, and hearing a British railway worker hum the tune of the Egyptian song he had come to know so well. Recognizing the tune, and realizing that the worker must have been 'nostalgic to the Egyptian sun', he stepped behind him and sang along to his humming in an act of camaraderie.[45] Such is the power of the tune, perhaps not as composed by Sayyid Darwish, nor the persistent popularity of Upper Egyptian folklore, but on account of its embodiment of the circumstances and longings of war.

III. 'O! You who have fallen victims to your desire…': Qantara, 1918

O my love! I wish to go back home
O! you who have fallen victims to your desire,

Go to the military authorities;
They will take off your clothes and give you a uniform
They take you to the mountain, while
Your father and mother's heart are full of grief
My home, my home! The military authorities have taken my son
My home, my home! The military authorities have ruined my home
O! my dear I wish to go back home
When they wrote my name, it was against my will
They took me by surprise (or by force as I was in the fields)
The train has shrieked the signal to start,
It cried saying: 'where are you going?'
Is it one year or two that you will be away?[46]

This version of the song appears in the British Foreign Office Archives within a report on compulsory labour recruitment during the war. This particular document, titled 'Complaints of Men Returned from the ELC', documents the song as 'becoming very popular in native quarters' in Egypt. The whole report was produced in response to growing discontent among Egyptian peasants upon their return from war, manifested in crimes against recruitment officials. Its significance lies in the light it sheds on the question of 'why they went to the war' and the debate surrounding the forced volunteerism imposed by the British Army and the Egyptian administration. It was also used in the context of a growing movement communicating the experience of the war to local communities upon return.

The lyrics 'O! you who have fallen victim to your desire' indicate, despite the hardships, a desire among some men to sign up. The same song includes details of being taken from the fields to war, just as the report it is part of and most of the documents in this file in the British archives make an argument for the peasants' continued wish to go to war, although the song and growing dissent against the recruitment administration indicate otherwise. The report is part of a larger file containing correspondence and reports between the Ministry of Interior and the High Commissioner that discuss different means and methods for attracting villagers to the Labour Corps.[47] These were 'volunteerism', 'forced labour', 'reservists' and 'conscripts',[48] while British military authorities argued the need to keep up manpower given that initial techniques had yielded insufficient volunteers. These discussions continue through 1917 with indications that the preferred method would be volunteering and, when large numbers were needed, forced recruitment.

In May 1918, accounts started to appear in this folder reporting violence committed against figures of Egyptian authority responsible for recruitment, such as the local *'umad* (village headmen), and British military authorities. Although no explicit decision was made to carry out forcible recruitment prior to this, one of the reports declares that these moments of violence can only be a reaction to 'coerced volunteerism'.[49] An elaborate mechanism was developed by the British authorities to recruit workers for a war that was neither strictly run by British authorities nor by their Egyptian subordinates alone, thus opening up opportunities for abuses at both ends. This system of recruitment comprised two levels of colonial authority, state and local, and was referred to in many songs of the period as 'El Sulta' ('the authorities'). The term for 'volunteering' also came to mean something different, as, for example, in Ismat Sayf al-Dawla's memoir, where village peasants returned from war start spreading the word that people should resist being 'volunteered' for service. Similarly, in Foreign Office records, one person is arrested on the charge of telling people to 'resist volunteering'.[50]

The third version of 'Ya ʿaziz ʿaini' therefore illustrates the complexities of volunteering and coercion, while referring to what the war meant to those who served in it. In this song, the description of workers being 'victims of their own desire' captures this. The temptations to go to war were many and not all labourers were 'forced'. Some volunteered out of a need for money or obligation towards the *'umda*, but according to reports in the archive, these were few.[51] Upon experiencing the war, however, and realizing the ranges of horror from the cold weather with inadequate clothing to disease, harsh working conditions and lack of access to religious burials, they started mobilizing in opposition.

The temptations of recruitment also appear in a song sung and composed by Sayyid Darwish in 1918, 'Salma ya salama'. Much like 'Ya ʿaziz ʿaini', the song's refrain, *Salma ya salama ruhna wa gayna bil salama* ('Safe and sound, oh safe and sound, we went and made it back, safe and sound') can be found in songs (with different lyrics) recorded as early as 1904 and later sung by singers like Fairuz, Dalida and other contemporary artists. The First World War version tells the experience thus:

> Safe and sound, oh safe and sound, we went and made it back, safe and sound
> *Sulta* or not, at least we have something to show for it all,
> We've saved up our pay and are coming home
> We've seen the guns and we've seen the war
> and we've seen the dynamite
> with our own eyes
> There's only one lord and we only live once
> We went and made it back
> And we're no worse off
> Safe and sound, oh safe and sound.[52]

Despite the horrors of war and dynamite, and the *sulta*, 'we've saved up our pay and are coming home' with the conclusion that all that matters is that the singer has made it back, safe and sound.[53]

Elsewhere, al-Nashar elaborates on the verses of songs that became like slogans.[54] One of these, *Yalli ramaak al hawwa, hawwid 'ala al kumbu; Yi'alaʿuk al-halahil, wi-yilabisuk il-baltu* could very well be from the above version of 'Ya aziz ʿaini': 'O you who have fallen victim to your desires, go to the military authorities, they will take your clothes [here 'tatters'] and give you a uniform.' The prospect of going to war may have, at least at first, offered the prospect of new garments.

The second stanza of the same song, however, tells a different story, of being taken from the fields and of one's name being written down by force – possibly on the contracts included in the archives to make an argument for voluntary subscription.

In a similar instance, workers are overheard performing short skits of incidents in which they are made to sign the contracts by force. These were probably all means of raising resistance to recruitment by letting each other know the oppression behind the experience. This notion of those who returned initiating campaigns to discourage others from 'volunteering' comes across in memoirs of the war[55] and eventually led to the peasant uprising that started in the summer of 1918 and paved the way for the 1919 revolution.

IV. Conclusion – 'Amongst my family, my people, yet still estranged at home'

O apple of my eye, how I wish to go back home,
I went to sleep one night and arose without a home,
O apple of my eye how I wish to go back home,
my home, my home, and what has become of my home,
Amidst family and friends, yet still estranged at home,
Uncle passing by, don't surrender to my oppression,
My heart has departed and not returned, in search of my home
O apple of my eye, how I wish to go back home,
These are not your eyes, nor are these your hands
rather than fearing for you, I live in fear of you, my home.

يا عزيز عيني أنا بدّي أروّح بلدي
ليلة نمت فيها وصحيت ما لقيتش بلدي
يا عزيز عيني أنا بدّي أروّح بلدي
بلدي يا بلدي ويا عيني على بلدي
بين أهلي وناسي وبقيت غريب في بلدي
عمي ياللي ماشي ظلمي ما ترضاشي
سافر قلبي وماجاشي بيدوّر على بلدي
يا عزيز عيني أنا بدّي أروّح بلدي
ده مش لون عِنيكي ولا ديَّتْ إيديكي
بدال ماخاف عليكي بخاف منّك يا بلدي

This version of the song was written by poet Ayman Hilmi to commemorate the burning down of a theatre in Beni Suef in 2005, killing all those who were trapped inside.[56] It was first sung by a street theatre band and then recorded by singers Nagham and Mariam Salih, whose father died in the fire. The estrangement in this version of the song refers to the growing sense of estrangement and disenchantment at home, in the years leading up to the 2011 revolution.

The word *baladi* in all of the above versions literally translates as 'country'. However, I have preferred, like other translators whose versions I use, 'home', since in both the songs and memoirs, estrangement refers to leaving the village, not the geographic country, and also because the notion of *baladi* in Arabic translates to the sense of belonging to or relationship with a geographical space rather than the space itself (whether a village, city or country). In other songs and stories from the war, for most peasants, leaving the village for another place in Egypt or beyond is 'leaving home'.

There are many reasons why this song may persist into the future. Lagrange and 'Abdallah argue that Darwish's compositional genius lies in his ability to adapt to any ideological and aesthetic reference. I would add that, perhaps beyond Darwish, as is the case with 'Salma ya salama', the sense of estrangement that the song expresses is so strong, it lends itself to estrangements in different contexts. Thus, the longing and estrangement evoked by 'Ya ʿaziz ʿaini' persist despite the main experience behind them, the First World War, disappearing from wider popular memory. Although the song contains two voices – the estranged at war and those left behind – perhaps its genius is that it reflects the estrangement of the second group. Perhaps, as in Mariam Salih's version, it reflects not just the plight of those *away* at war but also those on the home front, oppressed by the war, stripped of their families and resources, and knowing the risks to which they themselves are exposed.

What I have tried to do in this chapter is read closely into these songs, profoundly 'fluid' in nature, in three of the fixed forms in which they have been captured in the moment that interests us. This is in opposition to the nature of the song itself, as it continues to persist since that moment and existed possibly even before it to sing of other estrangements. I have tried in each instance to understand what messages and sentiments the versions of 'Ya 'aziz 'aini' carried and contained, and what the format they are documented in tells of the war period as well. These include the recorded voice of an avant-garde politicized female artist, Mariam Salih, and the countervoices in the British archives. In each case I try to probe the song, to listen, not only to what the lyrics say, but also to what the person singing them meant to tell us beyond the moment in which it was sung.

Attempting to decipher Naʿima al Masriyya's version of 'Ya ʿaziz ʿaini' as a process can also be taken as a metaphor for my attempts to understand the social, cultural and emotional experiences of the ELC in those long years so far from home. It took a year to decipher the lyrics of the damaged record, only to find that they exist in the repertoire of popular (almost revered) Upper Egyptian singing cultures. I looked into Naʿima's own experience as a politically engaged singer and an entrepreneur, and that too gives insight into her own experience of the war and why she might have chosen to sing these songs. Finding the song was a first level of excavation, given Naʿima's scarce repertoire, requiring a trip to archives in Beirut. The second level of excavation was understanding the lyrics themselves, and the third was finding the contexts they originated from – creating a constellation that linked Naʿima's singing to Upper Egyptian voices, her own voice as an echo of others.

In London, exploring reports written one hundred years ago, the same song appears in a foreign language that I immediately recognize as a tune I already know. The lyrics in the text provide a profound experience of the complexity of having gone to war, of being 'victims of their own desire', while still expressing oppression in their experiences at war. This song does what scholars such as Anderson strive to do now by showing that conscription techniques were not binary; the question is not whether they were 'forced' or 'volunteered', each implying passivity and lack of agency on the part of the conscripted.[57] They did both. They went out of the desire for money (as in 'Salma ya salama') or for adventure; and they rose against the British imperialist and Egyptian administrators – the 'Sulta' – when they realized what the stakes were.

What this song – these songs – insert into the experience of war is desire, fear, abandonment, estrangement (on the part of those who left and those left behind) and loss. Their timelessness – the fact that they were probably sung before this moment and continue to be sung into the present – blurs boundaries of time and space. Experiences on the Western Front at Calais pour into the songs sung on the front in

Palestine and those sung at home (in 'native quarters') warning others of the perils of going to war or the importance of 'resisting volunteering'. Their exact sources may seem invisible, their origins obscure, and the attempt to assign the coordinates of time and place to them is slippery and elusive. They refuse to succumb to the fantasy of the real ('what really happened to them on the front') or the authentic ('the single real version of the song').

What I have tried to do is open up these songs and chart relations between them in their different geographies, building up biographies of the experiences of the workers of war and how these experiences ricochet through a wider community. By inevitably being at the centre of this constellation – inevitably since I only recognized the songs translated in the Foreign Office archives because I already knew them – I also indicate how events may fall upon history, but traces of such rupturing experiences are built into communal repertoires through the songs communities sing and the stories they tell.

Although the facts of the war, such as the number of Labour Corps members who died on the home and war fronts, are difficult to ascertain, the biographies of the singers, archivists and recorders, the dates and geographies of the documentations, the contexts of the archives, are the beginning of a trail that raises more questions, more testimonies of forgotten experiences and more evidence of atrocities, through fragmented archives and persistent voices.

Notes

1 Mustafa, 'Al-Sharq wa al-gharb'; translation by Katharine Halls.
2 I am grateful for countless conversations with Mustafa Sa'id and Zaynab Magdi which started when I began the research in 2014 for Laila Soliman's play 'Hawwa al-Hurriyya'. This is where the song and many of the First World War stories were discovered. I am also grateful to Britta Lange for reading and commenting on earlier drafts, and Heba Farid and Salwa Farid for filling in gaps on Na'ima al-Masriyya's life and inspiring most of the research relating to her.
3 Mustafa Amin sang a range of songs that reflect the grievances of societal groups such as *al-'arbagiyya* (the horse carriage drivers), *al-dagalin* (the soothsayers) and *al-zar* (exorcists); these are more like improvised *udabatiyya* performances from the First World War and the 1920s. The Arab Music Archiving and Research (AMAR) Foundation provided generous access to these records, with additional information from former director Mustafa Sa'id. Little biographical information is available on Mustafa Amin.
4 For more on debates about the Egyptian military authorities' celebration of Egypt's fictitious contribution to the war and resultant silencing of the trials of the ELC, see Fahmy's articles disputing the military narratives: 'al-Ihtifal bil la shay' ('The Celebration of Nothing') and 'al-Jaysh al-misri fil harb al-'alamiyya al-'ula ('The Egyptian Army in WWI').
5 An exact figure is not clear; annual (and sometimes monthly) figures exist in FCO archives for 1917 and 1918 but a whole figure is never indicated. Scholars point to between 'hundreds of thousands' (Anderson, 'The Egyptian Labor Corp', 5–24) to 1.5 million (Schulze, 'Colonization and Resistance', 185).
6 Ruiz, 'Photography and the Egyptian Labor Corps', 61–6.

7 Hoffman, 'Echoes of the Great War', 12.

8 Spivak, 'Echo', 27. Here Spivak refers to the excavating of feminist voices in the archive through Ovid's tale of Echo. In Hoffman's own words,

> in Ovid's Metamorphoses, the nymph Echo (vocalis nymphe), is punished by the goddess Juno for distracting her with beguiling talk (or stories) while Juno's husband, Jupiter, delights in other nymphs. The sanction, or say, measure against distracting talk, for Echo is her disablement: the loss of the ability to speak. From then on, she may only repeat an abbreviated and therefore distorted version of someone else's words. Her voice transforms into a disembodied, dislocated sound effect: an echo. (Hoffman, 'Echoes of the Great War', 13)

9 Hoffman describes these recordings as

> not 'voices' but as echoes, that is, as mediated, often effaced reverberations of accounts of the self and the war. The notion of echo … grapples with issues of extraction, attenuation, limitation, distance and distortion, or outright effacement, that is the result of the form and the mediation of those speech acts, the belatedness of listening to them, as well as, the gaps in meaning and intelligibility the recordings entail. ('Echoes of the Great War', 13)

While Hoffman works with recordings of songs by West African prisoners, possibly sung under duress, my case study is the opposite. These songs have been documented (not recorded) while people were singing them (supposedly) at work or in festive occasions – thus more of a stolen moment of wilful expression. Still the intention on the part of both singer and recordist cannot be ascertained.

10 The politics of the participation and experience of Egyptian peasants in the First World War has largely been ignored, with the exception of: Anderson, 'The Egyptian Labor Corps'; Ruiz, 'Photography and the Egyptian Labor Corps'; Goldberg, 'Peasants in Revolt'; and Schulze, 'Colonization and Resistance'. This chapter contributes to this growing body of work by focusing on the experiences of the Labour Corps and their politics through songs; while also contributing to the literature exploring the experiences of the Labour Corps and lower-ranking soldiers of the British and French armies during the war through various extractions of their own words (songs, poetry, letters, etc.). This includes: Lange, 'Poste Restante'; Lange, 'South Asian Soldiers'; Hoffman, 'Echoes of the Great War'; Hoffman and Mnyaka, 'Hearing Voices in the Archives'; Santanu, 'The Singing Subaltern'; and Omissi, *Indian Voices of the Great War*.

11 By an 'intimate language' I refer to poems, idioms, sayings and other intimate forms of language that encapsulate the struggles and emotional experiences of communities. They become how these communities remember events, how they present and re-present themselves to and among themselves. This language creates a history and repertoire of feelings that remind communities of their shared past and binds them together. With time, as the events fade into history, evoking these abstracted lyrics remind members of the essence of the experience if not the event itself; in that sense it becomes a 'coded language'. These forms of language become important for understanding popular politics and the intimate experiences behind metapolitical events. For more on how I define and use this concept of 'intimate languages', see Mossallam, '"Hekāyāt Sha'b." Nasserism, Popular Politics and Songs in Egypt. 1956–1974'.

12 A small record company in Cairo owned and operated by Egyptian-Armenian Setrak Mechian. Being economically independent meant being able to record during the First World War when recording engineers of foreign companies were no longer available in Cairo, and to salvage and popularize recordings that may have otherwise been forgotten, albeit in moderate quality. Racy, 'Record Industry', 43.
13 Based on interviews with Mustafa Sa'id, then director musical archivist at AMAR Foundation, audio recording accessed January 2017.
14 For more on this folk music form, see Cachia, 'The Egyptian "Mawwāl" '; and Sa'id, 'The Mawwāl'.
15 In the last third of the nineteenth century, female professional singers in Egypt were called *'awalim* and usually performed in the private sphere, essentially for other women, with an all-female limited *takht* (instrumental ensemble) (Lagrange, 'Women in the Singing Business', 228).
16 For the effect of the war on woman in the singing industry, see Fahmy, *Ordinary Egyptians*; Lagrange, 'Women in the Singing Business'; Baron and Niki, 'Artists and Entrepreneurs'; Racy, 'Arabian Music'; Racy, 'Record Industry'.
17 A project by her great-granddaughter Heba Farid who pieced together the details of Na'ima's journey through personal documents, family stories and newspaper and a bibliography of magazine articles written about Na'ima (Azimi, 'A Life Reconstructed').
18 al-Muilhi, 'Fi al-mir'aa: Na'ima al-Masriyya'; al-Muilhi; 'al-Sayyida Na'ima al-Masriyya'; 'Mutribatna fi al-mir'aa: Na'ima al-Masriyya'.
19 Born in Alexandria in 1892, composer Sayyid Darwish's career started in Egyptian coffee shops and developed into composing for the musical theatre, which thrived during and after the war. Darwish revolutionized the musical industry at the time by developing catchy tunes for songs of a political nature. Most of his songs are remembered and sung in political contexts until this day. Darwish revered Na'ima's musical ear and sought her feedback on his compositions (Baron and Niki, 'Artists and Entrepreneurs', 296; Fahmy, *Ordinary Egyptians*, 114).
20 For more on the singers Ahmad al-Brin and al-'Aguz, see Nada, 'Ahmad Brin'; Frishkopf, 'Inshad Dini and Aghani Diniyya in Twentieth Century Egypt'.
21 Inclusion of elements from a folk repertoire – such as these lyrics here – usually serve to grab the audience's attention through lyrics they can sing along to. Other examples of this are 'calls' at the beginnings of popular songs in Suez that allude to calls from the days of digging the Canal – the audience sing along and become attentive to the start of the show. My sense, therefore, given how these lyrics continue to appear in Upper Egyptian songs of different formats, is that even in the early twentieth century they already existed as *'irth sha'bi'* (popular heritage).
22 On deciphering the lyrics, I typed them into search engines and found recordings ranging from productions in the 1950s and 1960s to simple mobile recordings of intimate gatherings and festive events in mosques in Upper Egypt.
23 Racy, 'Record Industry', 25.
24 In Egypt commissioning was incompatible with the structure and aesthetics of the pre-First World War *wasla* (vocal-instrumental suite), a compound genre that relied heavily on spontaneous creativity. Instead, the attention of the commissioned composers shifted to the short *taqtuqa*. Traditionally associated with female professional musicians, this type of song was precomposed strophic and metric, and had an amorous text in colloquial Arabic; see Racy, 'Arabian Music', 49.

25 For more on Darwish's repertoire and the songs' representations, see Lagrange, 'Women in the Singing Business'; 'Abdallah, 'Asatir Sayyid Darwish'.
26 For lyrics of the song and on the conditions of censorship, see Fahmy, *Ordinary Egyptians*, 162, 216–17.
27 Musa, *Tarbiyyat Salama Musa*, 112; Sayf al-Dawla, *Mashayikh Jabal al-Badari*. Sayf al-Dawla was a son of the village who moved to Cairo to study at university and later became a renowned judge, ideologue and writer in the 1950s.
28 Salih, *Ya 'aziz 'aini*.
29 Lagrange, "Ala 'ad al layl ma yatawwil'.
30 'Abdallah, 'Asatir Sayyid Darwish'.
31 Slyomovics, 'Arabic Folk Literature and Political Expression', 184.
32 An epic folk tale that tells the story of the tribe of Beni Hilal and their journey from Najd (Arabia) to Tunisia via Egypt. The events took place in the eleventh century, but it continues to be sung in Upper Egypt; see Slyomovics, *The Merchant of Art*.
33 http://www.naima-project.org; Azimi, 'A Life Reconstructed'.
34 For Munira al-Mahdiyya (1884–1965), see Fahmy, *Ordinary Egyptians*, 112.
35 The oldest version I have found was collected by Heinrich Schaefer during excavations in Abu Sir, 1901, by Upper Egyptian workers (possibly from Beni Suef); Schaefer, *The Songs of an Egyptian Peasant*, 49.
36 Venables memoirs IWM EKV/2, 8.
37 Ruiz, 'Photography and the Egyptian Labour Corps', 57.
38 Ibid.
39 Ibid., 56.
40 Venables memoirs IWM EKV/2, III, 2.
41 Ruiz, 'Photography and the Egyptian Labour Corps', 59.
42 al-Nashar, 'Al-Thaqafa al-'askariyya wa anashid al-jaysh'.
43 Venables files IWMEKV/2, VIII, 4.
44 Venables memoirs IWM EKV II, 6.
45 Venables memoirs IWM EKV III, 7.
46 FO 141/797/1/2689/135, Complaints of Men Returned from the ELC, 11 August 1918.
47 FO 141/797/1/313, Complaints of Men Returned from the L.C., 11 August 1918.
48 FO 141/797/1/10, 1 May 1916.
49 FO 141/797/1. See especially telegrammes from various provinces to the Ministry of Interior and reports communicated about these incidents from the Ministry of Interior to the High Commissioner.
50 FO 141/797/1/7652, which details an incident in Kafr El Sarem Village where a 'Sidi Ahmed Shaaban' was arrested for telling people 'Do not accept and do not fear anything, but strike anyone who proposes to you to volunteer, etc.'
51 Anderson, 'The Egyptian Labor Corps', 19; Tawwaf, *Egypt 1919*, 9.
52 Translated by Katharine Halls.
53 Promised/documented rates were significantly higher than agricultural rates, ranging from triple to one hundred times the amount. For figures and comparisons, see Goldberg, 'Peasants in Revolt'; Schulze, 'Colonization and Resistance'.
54 al-Nashar, 'Al-Thaqafa al-'askariyya', 2269.
55 Saif al-Dawla, *Mashayikh Jabal Al-Badari*.
56 See interview with Ayman Hilmi; Al-Nasrawi, 'Ughinyet Ya 'aziz Aini - Mariam Salih'.
57 Anderson, 'The Egyptian Labor Corps', 9.

Bibliography

Archives

The National Archives (Kew).

FO 141/797 Foreign Office and Foreign and Commonwealth Office: Embassy and Consulates, Egypt: General Correspondence, 1916–22.

Imperial War Museum.

Venables, Ernest Kendrick. 'They Also Served: The Story of the ELC in Sinai and Palestine'. Unpublished Memoir 1916–19 held at the Imperial War Museum Department of Documents. London..

Songs

al-Masriyya, Naʿima. 'Ya ʿaziz ʿaini'. Alexandria: Mechian, 1915. 27 cm. Record number 2-483 1-483. Composition by Sayyid Darwish.

Amin, Mustafa. 'Al-Sharq wal gharb'. Alexandria: Odeon, 1921. 27 cm. Record number X45962 1/2. Composition by Bayram al-Tunisi. (Sung in Alexandria since 1916.)

Salih, Mariam. 'Ya ʿaziz ʿaini'. Cairo, Egypt, 2005. Lyrics and composition by Ayman Hilmi. https://ayman1970.wordpress.com/2011/12/17/أغنية-يا-عزيز-عيني-أنا-بدي-أروح-بلدي-أي/.

Secondary works

'Abdallah, Fadi. 'Asatir Sayyid Darwish. Hiwar maʿa Fadi 'Abdallah'. *Ma'azif* 29 June 2017. Accessed 16 June 2020. https://ma3azef.com/أساطير-سيد-درويش-حوار.

Anderson, Kyle. 'The Egyptian Labor Corps: Workers, Peasants, and the State in World War I'. *International Journal of Middle East Studies* 49, no. 1 (February 2017): 5–24.

Azimi, Negar. 'A Life Reconstructed. A Lost Musical Legacy Finds Its Voice in Cairo'. *Bidoun*, Fall 2004. https://bidoun.org/articles/a-life-reconstructed.

Cachia, Pierre. 'The Egyptian "Mawwāl": Its Ancestry, Its Development, and Its Present Forms'. *Journal of Arabic Literature* 8 (1977): 77–103.

Danielson, Virginia. 'Artists and Entrepreneurs: Female Singers in Cairo in the 1920s'. In *Women in Middle Eastern History. Shifting Boundaries in Sex and Gender*, edited by Beth Baron and Nikki Keddie, 293–309. New Haven, CT: Yale University Press, 1991.

Fahmy, Khaled. '"Al-Ihtifal Bil La Shai"' (The Celebration of Nothing)"'. *Khaled Fahmy* (blog), 16 November 2016. https://khaledfahmy.org/ar/2016/11/16/الاحتفال-باللاشئ.

Fahmy, Khaled. 'Al-Jaysh al-misri fil-harb al-ʿalamiyya al-ʿula" (The Egyptian Army in World War I)'. *Khaled Fahmy* (blog), 14 November 2015. https://khaledfahmy.org/ar/2015/11/14/الجيش-المصري-في-الحرب-العالمية-الأولى.

Fahmy, Ziad. *Ordinary Egyptians: Creating the Modern Nation through Popular Culture, 1870–1919.* Cairo: American University in Cairo Press, 2011.

Frishkopf, Michael. 'Inshad Dini and Aghani Diniyya in Twentieth Century Egypt: A Review of Styles, Genres, and Available Recordings'. *East Studies Association Bulletin* 34, no. 2 (Winter 2000): 167–83.

Goldberg, Ellis. 'Peasants in Revolt: Egypt 1919'. *International Journal of Middle East Studies* 24, no. 2 (1992): 261–80.

Hoffman, Anette. 'Echoes of the Great War: The Recordings of African Prisoners in the First World War'. *Open Arts Journal* 3 (October 2014): 7–23.

Hoffman, Anette, and Phindezwa Mnyaka. 'Hearing Voices in the Archives'. *Social Dynamics* 41, no. 1 (December 2014): 141–65.

Lagrange, Frédéric. "Ala 'ad al layl ma yatawwil. Sayyid Darwish wal-tirka al-masha". *Ma'azif* 17 March 2017. Accessed 16 June 2020. https://ma3azef.com/سيد-درويش-تركة/.

Lagrange, Frédéric. 'Women in the Singing Business, Women in Songs'. *History Compass* 7, no. 1 (2009): 226–50.

Lange, Britta. 'Poste Restante, and Messages in Bottles: Sound Recordings of Indian Prisoners in the First World War'. *Social Dynamics: A Journal of African Studies* 41, no. 1 (January 2015): 1–19.

Lange, Britta. 'South Asian Soldiers and German Academics: Anthropological, Linguistic and Musicological Field Studies in Prison Camps'. In *When the War Began We Heard of Several Kings. South Asian Prisoners in World War I Germany*, edited by Roy Fraziska, Heike Liebau and Ahuja Ravi, 149–84. New Delhi: Social Science Press, 2011.

Mossallam, Alia. '"Hekāyāt Sha'b." Nasserism, Popular Politics and Songs in Egypt. 1956–1974'. PhD thesis. London School of Economics and Political Sciences, London, 2012. LSE thesis online: https://core.ac.uk/download/pdf/16390657.pdf.

al-Muilhi, Muhammad al-Sayyid. 'Fi al-mir'aa: Na'ima al-Masriyya'. *Al-Majalla al-Musiqiyya* 3 January 1939, 690–2.

al-Muilhi, Muhammad al-Sayyid. 'al-Sayyida Na'ima al-Masriyya'. *Ruz al-Yusuf* 24 November 1927, 20.

al-Muilhi, Muhammad al-Sayyid. 'Mutribatna fi al-mir'aa: Na'ima al-Masriyya'. *Al-Kawakib* 15 August 1932, 4.

Musa, Salama. *Tarbiyyat Salama Musa*. 4th edn. Cairo: al-Hay'a al-misriyya al-'amma lil-kitab, n.d.

Nada, Ahmad. 'Ahmad Brin: Al-sab' aladhi isthmal assa al-ayyam'. *Ma'azif* 8 August 2015. Accessed 16 June 2020. https://ma3azef.com/أحمد-برين-السبع-اللي-استحمل-قسى-الأيام/.

al-Nashar, 'Abd al-Latif. 'Al-Thaqafa al-'askariyya'. *al-Risala* 336 (11 December 1939): 2268–70.

al-Nashar, 'Abd al-Latif. 'Al-Thaqafa al-'askariyya wa anashid al-jaysh'. *al-Risala* 224 (27 November 1939): 2154–5.

al-Nasrawi, Abir. 'Ughinyet ya 'aziz 'aini - Mariam Salih', 14 May 2015. https://www.mc-doualiya.com/programs/histoire-chanson-mcd/20150514-ياعزيز-عيني-نغم-صالح-مصر.

Omissi, David. *Indian Voices of the Great War: Soldiers' Letters, 1914–1918*. Basingstoke: Palgrave Macmillan, 1999.

Racy, Ali Jihad. 'Arabian Music and the Effects of Commercial Recording'. *World of Music* 20, no. 1 (1978): 47–58.

Racy, Ali Jihad. 'Record Industry and Egyptian Traditional Music 1904–1932'. *Ethnomusicology* 20, no. 1 (January 1976): 23–48.

Ruiz, Mario. 'Photography and the Egyptian Labor Corps in Wartime Palestine 1917–1918'. *Jerusalem Quarterly* 56 (2014): 52–66.

Sa'id, Mustafa. 'The Mawwāl'. *Foundation for Arab Music Archiving and Research*, 2013. http://www.amar-foundation.org/013-the-mawwal/.

Sayf al-Dawla, 'Ismat. *Mashayikh Jabal al-Badari: Al-juz' al-thani min mudhakirat qarya*. Cairo: Dar al-Hilal, 1996.

Santanu, Das. 'The Singing Subaltern'. *Parallax* 17, no. 3 (n.d.): 4–18.

Schaefer, Heinrich. *The Songs of an Egyptian Peasant. Translated by Frances Hart Breasted*. Leipzig: J.C. Hinrichs, 1904.

Schulze, Reinhard. C. 'Colonization and Resistance. The Egyptian Peasant Rebellion of 1919'. In *Peasants and Politics in the Modern Middle East*, edited by Farhad Kazemi and John Waterbury, 171–202. Miami: Florida International University Press, 1991.
Slyomovics, Susan. 'Arabic Folk Literature and Political Expression'. *Arab Studies Quarterly* 8, no. 2 (1986): 178–85.
Slyomovics, Susan. *The Merchant of Art: An Egyptian Hilali Oral Epic Poet in Performance*. Berkeley: University of California Press, 1985.
Spivak, Gayatri Chakravorty. 'Echo'. *New Literary History* 24 (1993): 17–43.
Tawwaf. *Egypt 1919. Being a Narrative of Certain Incidents of the Rising in Upper Egypt*. Alexandria: Whitehead, n.d. From the private papers of F. M. Edwards, Middle East Centre Archive, St Antony's College, Oxford University. D.T. 107.81.

4

What did cosmopolitan mean? An approach through Alexandrian francophone literary milieus (1880–1940)

Elena Chiti

According to a widespread commonplace, the city of Alexandria is a powerful symbol of cosmopolitanism. Moreover, cosmopolitanism is itself reified. Seen as an inherently positive attitude, it is intended to be a synonym for tolerance and openness to the world, embodied in the capacity of going beyond national horizons to meet universal values. Today the adjective *cosmopolitan* seems to be automatically associated with Alexandria, as if it summarizes the city's history up to the first half of the twentieth century, and as if this epoch was more significant than the present. In many cases, the expression *cosmopolitan Alexandria* is used as a term of periodization, like Ptolemaic Alexandria.[1] Nevertheless, unlike Ptolemaic, cosmopolitan is not a mere chronological reference. It embodies a value judgement and a nostalgic vision according to which Alexandria should remain as cosmopolitan as it supposedly once was. On 10 September 2012, for example, Egyptian writer Gamal Ghitani wrote against a book burning carried out in Alexandria by members of the Muslim Brotherhood. To emphasize his condemnation, he stated that this 'brutal, barbaric, fascist (*waḥshī, barbarī, fāshī*) act' shamed the nature of the city itself. Alexandria could not be the site of sectarian division, after being 'a place of encounter for religions and cultures from Antiquity until the twentieth century or, more precisely, until the mid-twentieth century, when the great Greek poet Cavafy and the Italian Ungaretti were among its inhabitants and the British writers Forster and Durrell settled there'.[2]

'Cosmopolitan Alexandria': From analytical category to research object

The image of a cosmopolitan city that draws a lesson of tolerance from its own history – or, more precisely, from a particular part of it – is the overwhelming cliché on Alexandria. It seems to be a European literary cliché, as its main cultural references are literary and European,[3] but it is so pervasive that it has shaped and risks shaping historical research. As late as 2004, Egyptian historian Khaled Fahmy urged his colleagues to put this cliché aside and open the way to explorations of Alexandria freed from this ideological bias. He showed that the truism of *cosmopolitan Alexandria* marked the equivalence between European presence and Alexandrian tolerance, veiling the history of the Arab majority and, more generally, the ordinary life of the Alexandrian lower classes during the colonial epoch.[4] Since then, the perspective of historians has considerably shifted and these once-neglected fields have come to attract wider attention.[5]

Nevertheless, a lacuna persists: cosmopolitan may have been discarded by some as a misleading framework for reading historical reality, but it has not been read as part of the historical reality itself. This is the purpose of the present contribution, which abandons cosmopolitan as an analytical category while approaching it as a research object. What did cosmopolitan mean in Alexandria in the five decades – from the late nineteenth century to the first half of the twentieth – that are seen today as a cosmopolitan epoch, and in the circles – literary and Europe-oriented – that are mentioned today as models of cosmopolitanism? Was cosmopolitan *Alexandria* already a cliché or, in other words, a representation collectively shared,[6] at least in these literary milieus? Was the positive perception of a multinational urban environment as widespread as it now is among men and women who produced literary texts in Alexandria at the time?

In order to answer these questions, this chapter approaches the topic from within, through the Alexandrian literature of the time.[7] In fact, the so-called cosmopolitan epoch, between the late nineteenth century and the 1940s, is also the colonial epoch. It represents a crucial phase of transition in the Arab world, since the decline of the Ottoman Empire coincides with European economic, political and cultural penetration, triggering the growth of organized nationalist movements. The Egyptian city with the highest number of foreign residents, Alexandria offers an ideal ground to study the notion of cosmopolitan as a shifting category, built up by actors and linked to this confrontation between Ottoman, nationalist and European horizons.

The Alexandrian cultural landscape can be explored through residents of the city who published literary texts during this period. They have been identified by examining lists of publications compiled by typographers, library catalogues, archives of cultural associations, anthologies and newspapers of the time, and, finally, gathering information from some of their descendants.[8] A quantitative approach shaped the selection, which did not privilege canonized authors but rather tried to reconstruct the Alexandrian literary scene through a socio-historical investigation.[9] The authors were not seen as scattered individuals but replaced as much as possible in their field, linking the personal to a collective dimension, in order to analyse literature as an aspect of the society and, as such, a source for history. The exploration allowed the identification of the names of around seventy authors active in Alexandria between the late nineteenth century and the 1940s who published in Arabic, French, Italian or English.[10] Among them, however, the production of fifty-three authors only could be found, adding textual to extra-textual elements.

These fifty-three authors, men and women, can all be considered amateurs. None of them made a living out of literature. Some of them did not need to work. The fortunes of their families, engaged in international or local business, gave them resources enough to live, and literary writing was a leisure they practiced along with other cultural activities, such as painting or music. The majority, however, were civil servants, students or teachers, but also members of liberal professions. Many sat on the boards of francophone or Arabic newspapers, at a time when the journalist had a twofold status, between intellectual and professional, and was undergoing significant change.[11] A few members of the poorer class – shopkeepers, barbers, manual workers – also turned to literary writing, in Arabic or Italian, in some cases as autodidacts. Thirty-one out of fifty-three authors used French, exclusively or not, as a literary language. Indeed, French was the language of cultural prestige in Alexandria at the time. It was mastered by people of different origins coming from Europe or the Levant, or born in Egypt and educated in francophone schools or raised in francophone environments,[12] as discussed in Hussam Ahmed's chapter in this volume.

This contribution will focus on francophone literary sources, aiming to study the meaning of 'cosmopolitan' in Alexandrian francophone literary milieus.[13] While applying a linguistic limitation, no aesthetic criteria oriented the selection. All the available works have been taken into account, whether known or unknown, celebrated or neglected, without regard to their subjects, genres and styles, and read as historical sources.[14] The first part of this study will be devoted to a historical overview of the uses and the meanings of the word *cosmopolite* in Alexandrian francophone literary sources. The horizon will then be broadened, moving from the word to the range of concepts associated with it, in order to underline the cultural evolution of the word in Alexandrian francophone milieus and, eventually, to compare it to a general European trend.

What did 'cosmopolitan' mean in French?

Composed of the Greek words *kósmos* ('world') and *polítês* ('citizen'), the term *cosmopolite* defines a 'person who, refusing the limits of a nation, claims to be a citizen of the world' or 'travels through the world without being fixed, by taste or necessity'.[15] This trajectory implies, materially or ideally, a crossing of borders, crowned with a sort of paradoxical balance, since the cosmopolitan is expected to feel everywhere as if he is in his own city. The studies that investigate the history of the concept in Europe traditionally trace it back to Ancient Greece, outlining a linear development from its emergence in Antiquity to its use in modern times.[16] However, the continuity thus established does not take into account the rupture represented by the colonial epoch. Indeed, the term *cosmopolite* seems to appear, in French, in the sixteenth century, before being used as an abstract noun, *cosmopolitisme*, during the nineteenth century. Both phases are linked to French colonial expansion.

One of the first uses of the word *cosmopolite* attested in French is in the volume *De la République des Turcs* ('The Republic of the Turks'), published in 1560 by Guillaume Postel.[17] This cleric and scholar, passionate about Oriental languages, intended to document Ottoman customs and laws for the benefit of the Dauphin of France, the son of King Henry II. In his dedication, Postel explains that knowledge of the culture and religion of the Ottoman Empire is necessary in order to subjugate it. The book makes a plea for gradual subjugation carried out through reason, rather than by force, and Postel sees in the *cosmopolite* an agent 'for universal peace': someone who is able to play, thanks to his experience as a cultivated traveller, the role of mediator between two civilizations.

However, it is difficult to deny the expansionary purpose of cosmopolitan mediation, designed to lead to diplomatic control and, ultimately, to political domination. This design is in tune with the times. During the sixteenth century, France and the Sublime Porte engaged in constant negotiations. The balance of power between the two was regularly tested by the diplomatic game unfolding behind commercial agreements, whether Capitulations, granting privileges to all French subjects, or commandments, benefitting specific individuals.[18] Recalling that commandments gradually supplanted Capitulations during the seventeenth century, historian Géraud Poumarède stresses that this transition accompanied the evolution of the French presence in the Ottoman territories.[19] Limited and insecure in the sixteenth century, in need of general agreements such as the Capitulations, French penetration became much deeper from the seventeenth century leading to the establishment of consular representations.

At the same time, the term *cosmopolite*, once of limited diffusion, was spreading in French and other European languages. In 1784, Immanuel Kant published his *Idea for a Universal History with a Cosmopolitan Aim*,[20] outlining a human evolution that may recall Postel's perspective. While wishing a future world governed by a universal civil community, Kant conceives it as an extension of European influence to the other continents. By praising the European political order as the crowning of Greek history through Enlightenment philosophy, Kant states that 'our' part of the world will at some point be called to give laws to all others. Although achieved through reason and not weapons, this cosmopolitan peace is, once more, pacification under the aegis of a dominant power. In this context, *cosmopolite* gave rise to the abstract noun *cosmopolitisme* during the nineteenth and twentieth centuries when, according to the Académie française, words bearing the suffix *-isme* were created to designate currents of thought, in the vast movement of ideas that accompanied the two centuries.[21] Given these historical premises, it would be reductive not to link cosmopolitanism to another *-ism* construction, such as colonialism, which seems to accompany its cultural evolution. Although this link will not predetermine the analysis, the purpose of which is to reconstruct the meaning of *cosmopolite* in Alexandrian francophone literature, the historical context will not be neglected.[22]

'A cosmopolitan city' (1907)

In Alexandrian francophone literature of the so-called 'cosmopolitan epoch', the link between cosmopolitan and colonial, although not explicit, shaped a vision that has had a lasting impact on the European image of the city. The term *cosmopolite* appeared in 1907 in a work written by an Italian archaeologist, Evaristo Breccia (1876–1967, Figure 4.1). Appointed the director of Alexandria's Graeco-Roman Museum, which he ran from 1904 until 1932, Breccia wrote a guide in French to both the Museum and the city, under the patronage of Alexandria Municipality.[23] Its literary style was

Figure 4.1 Evaristo Breccia in Egypt with his wife (Breccia Archives, University of Pisa).

probably the key to its success in Alexandria and beyond. Republished in a longer version in 1914, and translated into English in 1922, the book served as the basis for E. M. Forster's *Alexandria: A History and a Guide*, published the same year. Moreover, the latter was itself one of the main references of Lawrence Durrell's *The Alexandria Quartet*, issued between 1957 and 1960, the broad diffusion of which strongly contributed to propagating the cliché of 'cosmopolitan Alexandria'.[24]

The first chapter of Breccia's guide, devoted to the modern city ('La Ville Moderne'), starts with the following claim:

> As for the elements and nationalities that compose the Modern City, it is true to say, *mutatis mutandis*, that the conditions of the Greco-Roman epoch are closely paralleled; once more Alexandria can be defined as a cosmopolitan city.
>
> ('Pour les éléments et les nationalités qui la composent, il est vrai de dire, *mutatis mutandis*, que les conditions de l'époque gréco-romaine s'y répètent, car, aujourd'hui même, on peut définir Alexandrie une ville cosmopolite.')[25]

In the absence of a clear definition, the word *cosmopolite* relies on a tautology: the modern city is seen as cosmopolitan because it recalls the Hellenistic and the Roman city, which is labelled as cosmopolitan because it recalls the modern city. Only on the following page does the guide present, if not a definition, a set of attributes associated with a cosmopolitan way of life: a 'variety of races, languages, religions and manners' peacefully coexisting in the same city, as well as 'tolerance and mutual respect', and even 'hospitality', as the main markers of social relations.[26]

This vision of cosmopolitan life as social harmony is not historically rooted. In Hellenistic Alexandria, access to full citizenship was restricted and a rigid hierarchy regulated the relationships between different groups.[27] Riots were not uncommon, even if they have received little attention from the scholars of Ptolemaic Egypt.[28] They continued, for centuries, under the Roman occupation of Alexandria, unveiling the shift in the balance of power between pagans and Christians, as well as the tension it aroused in a city whose topography was shaped by intercommunal boundaries.[29] As for Breccia's times, Robert Ilbert talks about 'spaces of contiguity', such as streets, schools and clubs, marked by social and cultural divides, in which Alexandrians of different origins lived alongside one another, rather than living together.[30]

In fact, Breccia did not provide a socio-historical analysis but rather shaped a noble heritage for the foreign residents of Alexandria of his own epoch. Moving through a series of semantic shifts, he used the term *Gréco-romain* to mean *cosmopolite* and the term *cosmopolite* as a marker of universal values of peace and tolerance.[31] From this perspective, the Europeans of Breccia's time came to be the legitimate inheritors of the Greeks and Romans who made Alexandria the cradle of universal values in the past. A European presence in Alexandria appeared then culturally and morally rooted,[32] if not a historical necessity for the sake of the city and its development, supposedly jeopardized by the Arab population.[33] The ambivalence of Breccia's universality, implicitly identified with colonial Europe, clearly emerges in the guide. Breccia refers to the Arab conquest of Alexandria as a blank gap between Ptolemies and Europeans: 'In the place where Ptolemaic Alexandria had lived its life of magnificence, splendour and glory, ruin and death reigned supreme for long centuries.'[34] In his view, ruin and death were only driven away by sovereign Muhammad Ali (1805–1848), who opened Egypt again to the Europeans.

'A cosmopolitan name' (1913)

Some years later, the term *cosmopolite* acquired a different meaning in a novel by Jean-Léon Thuile. The Thuile brothers – Henri (1885–1960), poet, and Jean-Léon (1887–1970), novelist – were two French engineers living in Mex, on the western margins of Alexandria. Their home (Figure 4.2) housed a wide collection of books open to their acquaintances and, during the 1910s, a locally renowned literary circle.[35] While Henri is not an unknown figure, at least for experts of francophone Egyptian literature,[36] Jean-Léon has been totally neglected. Considered as lacking artistic value, his novels are extremely difficult to find, in French or foreign libraries.[37] One of them – taken for lost[38] but available at the Rare Books and Special Collection Library of the American University in Cairo (Max Debbane Collection) – is a valuable source to historicize the evolution of the term *cosmopolite* in the Alexandrian francophone milieus.

The novel *L'Eudémoniste* ('The Eudaemonist') was written in Alexandria and published in Paris in 1913.[39] It presents itself as the biography of a real person,

Figure 4.2 The Thuiles' house at Mex, Alexandria (*Henri Thuile, L'homme, l'œuvre, les témoignages. Numéro spécial de L'Égypte nouvelle*, 11 April 1925).

depicted as a wise man in search of true, absolute happiness. Shaped by this purpose, his existence becomes a sort of ascetic journey, through different stages. Initially, the hero tries to find happiness in sport and bodily well-being, then in sexual life, later in philosophy or religion. Eventually, discovering that real happiness is out of reach in this world, he commits suicide. The process of liberation from earthly existence to attain a limitless, absolute state of self-achievement is called 'cosmopolitan'. The word appears just once, at the beginning of the book, but it embodies the whole journey of the hero:

> He led his existence under a cosmopolitan name. But I will not take into account what can be extraneous to him, like the homeland of his fathers and his atavisms. … As soon as he became aware of his own individuality, he tried to challenge as much as he could anything not directly belonging to him. He considered himself too peculiar to accept any other's heritage.
>
> ('Son existence signa un nom cosmopolite. Mais je ne m'occuperai pas de ce qui peut lui être étranger, de la patrie de ses pères et de ses atavismes. … Dès qu'il prit conscience de son individualité, il chercha à contrarier le plus possible ce qui ne lui appartenait pas en propre. Il s'estimait en effet trop personnel, pour ne pas repousser l'héritage d'autrui.')[40]

Thuile explains that nothing subsists of the hero's past and it is therefore unnecessary to talk about his family or background, and even to reveal his identity. His cosmopolitan name is, in fact, the lack of any nameable dimension. Contrary to Breccia's universality, it can be seen as the individual path that leads to a consciously embraced nothingness. Such an ascetic choice is also defined as 'Stoic', and the reader finds, at the beginning of the novel, a brief description of the Stoic wise man: someone who can rely on himself and keep calm under the worst circumstances, while simple mortals lose control of their emotions 'for a dead dog or a broken vase'. [41] Like Evaristo Breccia, Jean-Léon Thuile goes back to the Greek heritage to give the word *cosmopolite* a meaning, but the references he draws from it are profoundly different from Breccia's.

'A cosmopolitan race' (1927)

A further occurrence of the word *cosmopolite* can be found in the work of Nizza (1904?–1953?), pseudonym of Marguerite Croisier-Goubran. An Alexandrian poet of Swiss origin, married to an Egyptian, Nizza published her work in the local francophone press. In 1927 and 1928, her short poems, under the general title of *Brindilles* ('Twigs'), appeared in the cultural weekly magazine *La Semaine égyptienne*. One of them contains the following lines:

> The biggest wealth is in a cradle
> Money comes from a cosmopolitan race
> There is a single kind: mankind.
>
> ('La plus grande richesse est au fond d'un berceau
> L'argent vient d'une race cosmopolite
> Il y a un seul genre: le genre humain.')[42]

The scarce biographical elements on Nizza,[43] as well as the aphoristic structure of all her poems, do not allow a grounded interpretation. It is plausible that the expression *race cosmopolite* indicates the Jews, given the frequency of this stereotype in the anti-Semitic propaganda of the 1920s and 1930s, not to mention its association with the cliché of money. In any case, what clearly stands out here is the opposition between cosmopolitan and human. Unlike Breccia's characterization, Nizza's 'cosmopolitan' is not a synonym for universal. The term linked to universality, in her poem, is *mankind* ('le genre humain'), while *cosmopolitan* refers to a specific part of it, depicted in a negative light. Accompanied by the word *race*, it emerges as a group deprived of homeland, of ties and, consequently, of loyalty, naturally inclined to make money because it places its own economic interest above the interests of humanity.

'The cosmopolitan life of beaches and the fusion of races' (1932)

The term *cosmopolite* takes on a different meaning in a novel entitled *La gamme alexandrine* ('The Alexandrian Repertory'), published in Cairo in 1932.[44] Its author,

Figure 4.3 A young Émile Gerteiny (seated left), with his parents and two sisters, Egypt (Courtesy of Alfred Gerteiny).

Émile J. Gerteiny (1902–1973, Figure 4.3), has since the 1930s been overlooked in the anthologies of Egyptian francophone literature. He was born into a Greek Catholic family, of an Armenian mother. Residents of Aleppo, the Gerteinys moved to Beirut in 1905, fearing a new outbreak of violence against Armenians after the assassination attempt on Sultan Abdülhamid II carried out by the Armenian Revolutionary

Federation.[45] Subsequently, they left Beirut for Egypt where some family members settled in Cairo, while others chose Alexandria.

Émile did not see Alexandria in a positive light. The word *cosmopolite* appears several times in his novel, always in relation to the city and always in a derogatory sense. At the core of the book is a mixed marriage that turns into a nightmare, marked by growing emotional distress that leads to hatred and violence. The groom is a rich and well-educated young Egyptian Muslim, while the bride is a French lower-class girl from Corsica. The unfortunate couple serves as a pretext for describing a wider category, labelled as cosmopolitan Alexandrian youth: 'little folk, shop or bank workers, shameless and penniless, of mixed origins, overstocked with acute idiocies, puffed up with stupid pride, deprived of real culture.'[46] They take part in the 'cosmopolitan hubbub'[47] of a vulgar party ending up in an orgy and, in spite of limited education, 'speak all the languages, because of the cosmopolitan life of beaches and the fusion of races'. [48] Women attract particular attention, as 'representatives of all the classes of Alexandrian cosmopolitan society': 'young girls already women from the age of puberty', who have sex for immoral pleasure or economic gain, form 'the other side of a society of shady pedigree'.[49]

The book does not simply condemn this society as a whole or according to gender lines. It lists the nationalities of its members, distinguishing them from the rest of Alexandria's foreign residents. In fact, it does not label as 'cosmopolitan' every non-Egyptian or non-Arab living in the city, but only the 'Greeks, Italians, Jews, Syrians'.[50] It highlights the feeling of superiority shown by the French bride while faced with Egyptian women and 'their kind, Italian, Jewish, Syrian girls'. *Cosmopolite* is, in the book, 'a jumble of human mud continuously vomited up by the other Mediterranean seaports'.[51] It refers to Mediterranean immigrants of various origins and multiple trajectories, belonging to the middle and lower classes, who sought their fortunes in Alexandria for both its flourishing industry and its illegal trades.

From four occurrences to a diachronic overview, an exploration of scarceness

The occurrences of the word *cosmopolite* analysed here are not just a few selected examples. They are the *only* cases in which the term appears in thousands of pages, produced by fifty-three authors living in Alexandria between the end of the nineteenth century and the 1940s, among whom thirty-one wrote, exclusively or not, in French.[52] It is clearly apparent that, in the francophone literary production of the so-called cosmopolitan period, the adjective *cosmopolite* was extremely rare and not yet reified. As for the abstract noun *cosmopolitisme*, it appears only once and in italics, as a neologism or, at least, an unusual term: Evaristo Breccia employs it to define a characteristic of Hellenistic art, namely, a development starting from several cities, in the absence of one main centre of influence.[53]

In spite of their rarity, these occurrences are sufficient to show the wide range of meanings the word *cosmopolite* was capable of denoting in Alexandria at the time: from a marker of positive universal values in Breccia to a nihilistic end of earthly limitations in Thuile; from a label for those deprived of homeland in Nizza to the derogatory sense of Gerteiny's cosmopolitan, linked to blurring of boundaries and, as a result, to moral confusion. Moreover, Gerteiny's cosmopolitan corresponds to the Mediterranean, through the stigmatization of workers' mobility in the areas of Mediterranean emigration: Corsica and southern France, Italy, Malta, Greece and the Syro-Lebanese territories.

The shift from the socio-economic evaluation of working classes to a mistrust expressed in moral terms, with a concern for public order, is not limited to literature. Post-Ottoman administrations similarly seemed to associate security risks with a set of territories, nationalities and social categories. Working on the so-called Register of the Undesirables of the Egyptian Consulate in Smyrna, dating back to 1926, Edhem Eldem sheds light on this understudied aspect of Mediterranean migration, far from the current positive, inclusive cliché of cosmopolitanism.[54] The consular record, a list of people who were denied access to Egypt, is a collection of profiles of Russians, Greeks, Italians, Maltese, Syro-Lebanese and French citizens from Corsica or southern France. It includes men listed as pickpockets or petty traffickers, women accused of being prostitutes or brothel-keepers, but also unemployed persons or manual workers with suspicious political views ('anarchists', 'Bolsheviks'). Many of them correspond, through their nationality and background, to the Mediterranean 'jumble of human mud' that Gerteiny despised. The migrants that Egypt, officially self-governing since 1922, tried to keep out of its territory were not simply stigmatized in terms of social marginality or illegal activities. Their transnational trajectories were also rejected in an epoch that followed the Great War and the fall of empires, in which the Mediterranean world was reshaped by post-Ottoman nation states and much less porous boundaries stood between them.[55] People whose paths did not fit in with the times were regarded as potential troublemakers and became objects of suspicion.

From the word to the concept, through an Alexandrian casino

The wide range of meanings found for the word *cosmopolite* suggests that, at least until the 1930s, the term was not a truism in Alexandrian francophone milieus. Nevertheless, its scarcity does not allow the formulation of grounded hypotheses about its historical evolution. Is there a cultural shift from Breccia's idealization of the cosmopolitan city, and Thuile's celebration of the cosmopolitan man, to Nizza's and Gerteiny's depiction of cosmopolitan groups as elements of perturbation? This question leads us to broaden the analysis, by shifting the attention from the term *cosmopolite*, linked to a specific etymon, to the concepts that can be included in its semantic field. Without limiting the selection to a predetermined range of notions, the focus can be on the descriptions of population mixing, cultural diversity and multiple belongings that emerge in the same Alexandrian literary sources.[56] Did these concepts acquire, in the Alexandrian

Figure 4.4 The veranda at Casino San Stefano (Édouard de Lagarenne, *L'Égypte fantaisiste*, Alexandria: Imprimerie de la correspondance égyptienne, 1897)

francophone literature of the 1920s and 1930s, a negative connotation they did not have during the pre-First World War era?

A closer look at this literature seems to confirm they did: French texts,[57] written by Alexandrian residents of different origins, show unprecedented deprecation of mixed environments and ways of life. A detailed enumeration of documents and results would go far beyond the limits of this contribution.[58] However, this process can be observed through the change of perception of a physical place in Alexandria, namely the Casino San Stefano (Figure 4.4).[59] Built in the 1880s, Casino San Stefano was a casino, hotel and restaurant designed by Boghos Nubar Pasha, son of former Egyptian prime minister Nubar Pasha. Fascinated by the casinos of the Norman and Belgian Rivieras, which he discovered during his studies in Paris, Boghos Nubar Pasha tried to recreate their atmosphere on Alexandria's eastern shore, an area shaped, since the end of the nineteenth century, by the projects of the Alexandria Municipality. Once it became the terminus of the tramway running from Ramleh central station, Casino San Stefano grew into one of the most renowned gathering places in town, patronized by the urban elite as well as by members of European royal families. In 1897, Édouard de Lagarenne (?–1901), a French journalist and author living in Alexandria, described the Casino as follows:

> Magic golden hive, Babel in miniature,
> Where joy rings out, whose pure healthy air
> Vibrates from big swarms of every people!
> Thinkers, you who talk about Unity in the future,
> Would this not be its present living picture?

In the same sunbeam Heaven seems to enlighten
The children of Shem, Ham and Japheth.
Our joyous, open heart gets accustomed
To confuse, in spite of language and culture,
The followers of Jesus, Moses and Muhammad.[60]

From a haven of peace, where gambling and drinking are transfigured into acts for achieving human harmony, Casino San Stefano shifts to a different image under the pen of Alexandrian authors three decades later. For Émile Gerteiny, Casino San Stefano is, along with the beach of Sidi Bishr, one of the symbols of a dangerous fusion of races, which inevitably leads to moral corruption. Unlike the image of de Lagarenne, Gerteiny's Casino is not a socially pacified refuge for Alexandrian high society and bourgeoisie. Its clientele is represented by the infamous 'cosmopolitan' youth, who spend the days 'in the miserable neighbourhoods of the city, deep in narrow foul-smelling lanes',[61] before going out at night in search of doubtful leisure and easy social promotion. For Georges Orfali (?–?),[62] an Alexandrian francophone author, the Casino is a place of perdition, because of the blurring of ethnic and social boundaries it encourages. In his novel *Secret de Princesse* ('Secret of a Princess'),[63] published in 1934, he follows three generations of women whose fate is determined by the moral dissolution linked to the Casino. Angèle, a beautiful, penniless young dancer, meets a member of the Egyptian royal family and becomes his mistress. The Prince abandons her as soon as she gets pregnant and, to keep his own reputation unstained, he pays a certain André to marry her and play the father's role. Gisèle, the child of sin, grows up a beautiful young lady, until she is seduced by her own stepfather André, giving birth to a second-generation child of sin. Raymond, a good man, falls in love with Gisèle, but after her initial refusal, due to an overwhelming sense of guilt, he finds comfort in Angèle's arms. This intricate chain only ends when Gisèle and Raymond distance themselves from the Casino, symbol of a life dedicated to easy money and dubious entertainment, in which 'the torturing voice of flesh triumphed over any other voice'.[64] For Fausta Cialente (1898–1994), an Italian author who lived in Alexandria from 1921 until 1947, Casino San Stefano is also one of the negative symbols of the city. She mentions it in several of her works and, while illegitimate sex is not at its core, a sense of moral condemnation is still present. Described as a place where idle people of different kinds gather for superficial reasons, instead of employing their time in fruitful activities, the Casino comes to embody the soul of a community of lazy foreigners, cut off from the world they live in and incapable of devoting themselves to its improvement.

The same vision is shared by Alec Scouffi (1886–1932), an Alexandria-born author of Greek origins, who lived between Egypt and France. While set in Nice and not in Alexandria, his 1932 novel *Navire à l'ancre*[65] ('Ship at Anchor') depicts the local casino in a similar way to the previous descriptions of Casino San Stefano. Without using the term *cosmopolite*, Scouffi strongly condemns Casino de Nice as a hotspot for men and women coming from France, Italy, England, Russia and America, brought together by the common passion for easy money, gambling and sex. Whereas women are described as a 'crazy army of polyglot adventurers',[66] ready to sell themselves with no scruples, the men they attract are no more than the debris of the Great War, who learned atheism and nihilism in the trenches. Far from being a sign of universal harmony, the mixing of populations is seen as an 'international caravanserai usually hosting opposite races, eager to harm each other'.[67] Along with the casinos, it is the reputation of their clientele which is irremediably stained. Once recognized as members of a transnational elite, at ease with different languages and cultures, these men and women are now depicted as dangerous agents of conflict, for crossing boundaries is perceived as a potential treason against the nation.

From Alexandria to Europe, post-Great War cosmopolitanism as dilettantism in life

As is the case for literature, in the 1920s and 1930s, the Egyptian francophone press stigmatized the categories of people who had multiple belongings and transnational trajectories. The term *cosmopolite* was often used to indicate a 'European aristocracy',[68] seen as a privileged group that neglected the interests of the masses, preferring international prestige over the improvement of living conditions for the poorer class of each country. Similar criticism targeted the 'intellectualistic attitude' of European national elites, accused of having dragged their countries into the Great War and careless about its cost in lives for the lower classes.

This is more than an Alexandrian or even an Egyptian trend. In 1918, Thomas Mann published in Berlin his *Reflections of a Nonpolitical Man*, in which he outlined the cultural factors he saw at the origin of the Great War. In his book, he advocated a 'German cosmopolitanism', which had to be national and patriotic, while harshly blaming the cosmopolitanism perceived as a 'non-pacified Esperanto world', marked by 'polyglot facility' and 'sophisticated dilettantism'.[69] The aspects of this second kind of cosmopolitanism, which is for Mann highly detrimental to the flourishing of nations, closely parallel the unwritten rules of etiquette that shaped European residents' savoir-vivre in Alexandria. Paolo Terni, an Alexandria-born Italian author,[70] recalls them in these terms:

> One had to declare oneself to be at the same time – for instance – Italian (in a highly ironic way) and Alexandrian, even if not native, not home-grown, fully in line with the accepted and beloved model, that is French (Proustian), but with British attitude and a real gift as a speaker, polyglot even if mischievous, abundant in quotes. In general – while being passionate about arts and literature – one's own *hortus conclusus* had to appear as the result of a fortuitous interest, slightly technical, without the least pedantry or haughtiness.[71]

Seen as the capacity to manoeuvre among languages and national ties, cosmopolitanism is here associated with dilettantism, namely the practice, as occasional as it is superficial, of several artistic disciplines, without specializing in any of them. The equivalence comes from a vision of cosmopolitanism as an upper-class inclination, spread across Europe since the end of the nineteenth century. In his 1883 *Essais de psychologie contemporaine*, Paul Bourget, a prominent French intellectual at the time, described both dilettantism and cosmopolitanism as notable characteristics of fin-de-siècle culture, inspired by French literary models and diffused across Europe.[72] Along with European cities, Eurocentric Alexandrian milieus also absorbed this culture: their members acted as francophone cosmopolitan amateur artists, mimicking the way of life of the high society, spent in pleasant travels and occasional cultural activities, and freed from the material concerns of the lower classes.

With the outbreak of the Great War and the fall of empires in its aftermath, mimicking European high society was no longer the fashion to follow. If the habit remained in bourgeois milieus, sometimes as a nostalgic attitude, it could now, as it was in Europe, be the target of moral disapproval:

> Jeanne Arcache belongs, through her father, to an ancient Syrian family and, through her mother, to an old family of Provence. Of Egyptian nationality, she was born and raised in Alexandria. She has often travelled to Syria, France, Italy, Switzerland, Germany and Holland. This *cosmopolitanism* did not prevent her from pursuing literary and musical studies or acquiring a deep knowledge of five or six foreign languages.[73]

Beyond a simple parallel, and by a significant semantic shift, cosmopolitanism comes to be a form of dilettantism in life: an unforgivable frivolity towards national belonging, which must now be unequivocal.

Conclusion

The terms *cosmopolite* and *cosmopolitisme* are extremely rare in Alexandrian francophone literary sources between the late nineteenth century and the 1940s. The abstract noun *cosmopolitisme* appears only once, in Evaristo Breccia's work. Breccia writes it in italics, treating it as an unusual term, if not a neologism, which is a further sign of its lack of standardization. As for the adjective *cosmopolite*, in spite of its scarce occurrence, its meanings are varied and differently connoted. Put together, scarceness and internal dissimilarity suggest that 'cosmopolitan Alexandria' was not a shared commonplace in Alexandria at the time. In other words, the cliché of 'cosmopolitan Alexandria' was not yet shaped in what is called, today, 'cosmopolitan Alexandria'.

In the five decades seen as its heyday, and in the European literary milieus seen as its cradle, *cosmopolitan* was not overwhelmingly used to define the Alexandrian urban environment and way of life. When the word was employed, it was not in a uniform manner and not even with the same positive connotation attached today to the leitmotiv of 'cosmopolitan Alexandria'. A marker of human universal values for Evaristo Breccia (1907), 'cosmopolitan' referred for Jean-Léon Thuile (1913) to the nihilistic strength of a single individual struggling against the human world and its worthlessness. Under Nizza's pen (1927), 'cosmopolitan' designated a people with no homeland, and no national allegiance, most likely associated with the Jews, whereas Émile J. Gerteiny (1932) described the 'cosmopolitan life of beaches' in Alexandria as the immoral result of a 'fusion of races'. The same multinational urban environment defined as 'cosmopolitan' could be seen in two opposite ways: as a haven of tolerance and social harmony inherited from the Hellenistic world, in Breccia, or a chaotic hubbub of filth and immorality produced by poverty and immigration from around the Mediterranean, in Gerteiny.

This last derogatory view is wider than the word *cosmopolite* itself. In the Alexandrian francophone literary sources of the 1930s, a general mistrust, if not sharp condemnation, accompanied descriptions of mixing of populations, multinational environments and transnational trajectories. Once a symbol of harmonious interaction between religions and cultures, Casino San Stefano turned into the sign of the social and moral chaos characterizing mixed spaces. Along with the Casino, its clientele lost their prestige. The members of Alexandrian high bourgeoisie, once imitated for their polyglot ability and cultural sophistication, were now considered to be frivolous individuals, as incapable of showing allegiance to one nation as they were of devoting themselves to one single discipline.

Associated and even confused with dilettantism, cosmopolitanism acquired a negative connotation, in Egypt as in Europe. In the aftermath of the Great War, national belonging became more prized and the people who moved across geographical, cultural and linguistic boundaries appeared as potentially dangerous. The present, inclusive cliché of 'cosmopolitan Alexandria', seen as a model of peaceful encounter between people of different nationalities, exclusively relies on Breccia's legacy, while it veils a far more complex evolution of the word 'cosmopolitan' in Alexandria.

Notes

I am grateful to Anthony Gorman, Sarah Irving and the colleagues who took part in the workshop 'Cultures of Diversity', held in Edinburgh in December 2015, for their valuable comments during the discussion. Ami Ayalon, Frédéric Abécassis, Alfred Gerteiny and Einar Wigen read previous versions of this contribution and provided helpful feedback. I also thank CEAlex for its support during my stay in Alexandria.

1 The examples of this tendency are too numerous to be discussed in detail. In autobiographies written since the 1990s by members of the Alexandrian diaspora, we frequently find statements such as 'the era of Cosmopolitan Alexandria had finally come to an end', as in Ismail, *East of the Sun*, 12. This perspective is also widespread in travel guides, explaining that 'the half-century between 1882 and 1936 was the heyday of cosmopolitan Alexandria', as in Haag, *Egypt*, 443. This guide, as many others, distinguishes between the ancient cosmopolitan Alexandria, associated with the Hellenistic epoch, and the 'Modern Cosmopolitan Alexandria', whose rise and fall are indicated by Haag. Even scholarly works do not escape this pattern. In some cases they do not even clarify the terms of this periodization, as if labels such as 'cosmopolitan Alexandria', 'golden age' or 'great epoch' of Alexandria were self-evident. For instance, the expression 'an Alexandrian of the great epoch' ('un Alexandrin de la grande époque') appears in a book on the Dominicans in Egypt, as if it could be unequivocally understood: cf. Avon, *Les Frères prêcheurs en Orient*, 289.

2 Ghitani, 'Maḥraqat al-kutub', emphasis mine; all translations in this chapter are mine.

3 Halim, *Alexandrian Cosmopolitanism*.

4 Fahmy, 'For Cavafy'; 'Towards a Social History', 263–80 and 281–306.
5 See, e.g., Hanley, 'Foreignness and Localness' and *Identifying with Nationality*; Khuri-Makdisi, *The Eastern Mediterranean*.
6 Amossy and Herschberg-Pierrot, *Stéréotypes et clichés*. See also Koselleck, *Futures Past*.
7 Works that appeared after this time, such as Durrell's *The Alexandria Quartet* (1957–60), are not considered here since they lack the informative potential to address the questions raised. For a discussion of Durrell's *Quartet* and its dominance in shaping the vision of Alexandria, see Halim, *Alexandrian Cosmopolitanism*, 179–225.
8 These data are taken from my PhD dissertation, which studied Alexandrian literary milieus between the late nineteenth century and the 1940s, in order to contribute to a better understanding of the construction of categories of belonging in the Arab world in a phase of transition. A field of confrontation between cultural and political horizons, Alexandria offered an ideal ground to study the notions of Ottoman, Arab, foreign, Egyptian, local, national, cosmopolitan as shifting categories, built up by actors. See Chiti, 'Écrire à Alexandrie (1879–1940)'.
9 I follow here Moretti's recommendation to submit literary texts to a historical, quantitative approach. See Moretti, *Graphs, Maps, Trees*.
10 Greek language sources are not dealt with.
11 Temimi, 'From Intellectual to Professional', 207–34.
12 Gérard, 'Le choix culturel', 253–84.
13 For a first reflection on 'cosmopolitanism' in Alexandrian Arabic sources, going beyond the literal translation of the European word, see Chiti, 'Et si la Grande Guerre commençait en 1911?', 153–71.
14 For a fuller discussion of this methodology, see Jouhaud, Ribard and Schapira, *Histoire Littérature Témoignage*.
15 The definitions are taken from the dictionary *Le Trésor de la langue française*: http://www.le-tresor-de-la-langue.fr/definition/cosmopolite.
16 Coulmas, *Les Citoyens du monde*.
17 Postel, *De la République des Turcs*. I thank Edhem Eldem for the enriching discussion on the topic. See also Eldem, 'Istanbul as a Cosmopolitan City', 212–30.
18 See 'Capitulations / Imtiyāzāt', *Encyclopaedia of Islam, Second Edition*: http://referenceworks.brillonline.com/entries/encyclopaedia-of-islam-2-Glossary-and-Index-of-Terms/imtiyazat-SIM_gi_01774.
19 Poumarède, 'Négocier près la Sublime Porte', 71–85.
20 See Oksenberg Rorty and Schmidt, *Kant's Idea for a Universal History*.
21 See the Académie française entry 'Construction en –isme': http://www.academie-francaise.fr/construction-en-isme.
22 For a reflection on the links between colonialism and cosmopolitanism in Egypt, see also Starr, *Remembering Cosmopolitan Egypt*, 1–10.
23 Municipalité d'Alexandrie, *Guide de la ville*.
24 Halim, *Alexandrian Cosmopolitanism*, 120–78 and 179–225.
25 The name of Evaristo Breccia does not appear on the cover of the first edition: Municipalité d'Alexandrie, *Guide de la ville*, 1. The same quote can be found in the second edition, in which Breccia is mentioned as the author, Evaristo Breccia, *Alexandrea ad Ægyptum*.
26 Breccia, *Alexandrea ad Ægyptum*, 2.
27 Empereur, 'Le rêve d'une ville cosmopolite', 23–33.

28 See Fischer-Bovet, *Army and Society in Ptolemaic Egypt*, 94. For an analysis starting from a specific riot, see Barry, 'The Crowd of Ptolemaic Alexandria', 415–31. For a general perspective, see Collins and Manning, 'Revolts under the Ptolemies', 154–71.
29 For a discussion of intercommunal boundaries and social fragmentation in Roman Alexandria, placing urban violence in the urban topography, see Haas, *Alexandria in Late Antiquity*. For a discussion focused on intercommunal clashes and their sociocultural roots, see Watts, *City and School* and *Riot in Alexandria*.
30 Ilbert, 'Une certaine citadinité', 28–9.
31 Jockey, 'Le Musée gréco-romain', 25–50.
32 See also Starr, *Remembering Cosmopolitan Egypt*, 1–10.
33 Chiti, 'Conflicting Histories of Alexandria', 71–97.
34 Breccia, *Alexandrea ad Ægyptum*, vii: 'Là où la ville des Ptolémées avait mené sa vie de magnificence, de splendeur et de gloire, la ruine et la mort régnaient en maîtresses depuis de longs siècles.'
35 Benoît, 'La Maison du Mex', 138–9.
36 Basch, 'Henri Thuile', 127–37. The text studied by Basch, dating back to 1921, has been republished with a preface by Jean-François Livi and a critical apparatus by Paul-André Claudel: Thuile, *Littérature et Orient*.
37 Jean-Léon is mentioned, alongside his brother, as a member of Giuseppe Ungaretti's entourage: Livi, *Ungaretti*; 'Ungaretti a Parigi', 23–49; 'Tra Alessandria d'Egitto e Parigi', 195–210; Basch, 'Le rendez-vous des étrangers', 89–98.
38 Experts of Egyptian francophone literature mention this novel as being lost. Cf. Basch, 'Henri Thuile', 127–37.
39 Thuile, *L'Eudémoniste*. The publisher is Basset and not Grasset as is asserted in several sources that take the novel as lost.
40 Ibid., 7–8.
41 Ibid., 3.
42 Nizza, 'Brindilles', 34.
43 The only references to Nizza that I could find are in: Moscatelli, *Poètes en Égypte*, 227–8, and Luthi, *Entretiens*, 136. Luthi recalls an interview with an Alexandrian Swiss poet, Jacques-René Fiechter, conducted in the 1960s in which Fiechter talked about Nizza as a promising Swiss poetess he had himself discovered and promoted, and whose production was scattered among Egyptian francophone magazines.
44 Gerteiny, *La gamme alexandrine*.
45 My sincere thanks to Sally, Alfred and Gilbert Gerteiny for their help in piecing together information on Émile, which they also strove to collect.
46 Gerteiny, *La gamme alexandrine*, 20–1: 'petites gens de commerce ou de banque, sans le sou, sans pudeur, d'origines mêlées, riches en brillantes bêtises, enflés de sot orgueil, dénués de vraie culture.'
47 Ibid., 1: 'brouhaha cosmopolite.'
48 Ibid., 22: 'parle toutes les langues, grâce à la vie cosmopolite des plages et la fusion des races.'
49 Ibid., 144 for all the quotes: 'Les représentantes de toutes les classes de la société cosmopolite alexandrine obéirent soit à ses caprices, chèrement payés, soit aux leurs, purement vicieux!'; 'jeunes filles déjà femmes dès l'âge de la puberté'; 'forment l'autre pendant d'une société aux ascendances louches.'
50 Ibid., 21 and 91.

51 Ibid., 21: 'ramassis de bourbe humaine sans cesse vomi par les autres ports de la Méditerranée.'
52 These data are taken from my PhD dissertation, Chiti, 'Écrire à Alexandrie'.
53 Breccia, *Alexandrea ad Ægyptum*, 28: 'Le caractère essentiel de l'art hellénistique serait le cosmopolitisme.'
54 Eldem, 'The Undesirables of Smyrna', 223–7.
55 On the circulation of persons, goods and ideas in the Mediterranean basin before the Great War, see Clancy-Smith, *Mediterraneans*; Khuri-Makdisi, *The Eastern Mediterranean*; Kozma, Schayegh and Wishnitzer, *A Global Middle East*.
56 For a broader discussion of this point, see Chiti, 'Écrire à Alexandrie'.
57 This is also true for Italian and English texts.
58 Details can be found in Chiti, 'Écrire à Alexandrie', 273–306.
59 For more images of Casino San Stefano, see: http://www.aaha.ch/photos/sanstefano.htm; for a brief historical overview: http://www.egy.com/landmarks/99-01-08.php.
60 Lagarenne, *L'Égypte fantaisiste*, 226:

> Magique ruche d'or, Babel en miniature, / Où bourdonne la joie, où dans l'air pur et sain / De chaque peuple vibre un généreux essaim. / Penseurs qui nous parlez de l'Unité Future, / N'en est-ce pas ici la vivante peinture? // Dans un même rayon le Ciel semble en effet baigner / Les fils de Cham, de Sem et de Japhet. / Le cœur s'ouvre, déborde, oublie et s'accoutume / À confondre, malgré la langue et le costume / Ceux qui suivent Jésus, Moïse et Mahomet.

61 Gerteiny, *La gamme alexandrine*, 21: 'dans les bas quartiers de la ville, au fond de ruelles aux émanations nauséabondes.'
62 Biographic details on Georges Orfali are very uncertain. Although I was able to find some members of the Orfali family who lived in Alexandria, none of them could provide information on him. Georges may have studied in the 1910s at the Francophone Collège de Sainte Catherine, since a 1913 issue of the school magazine – *Le Lotus* – lists a certain 'G. Orfali' among its best students, but this can only be a tentative suggestion.
63 Orfali, *Secret de Princesse*.
64 Ibid., 100: 'la torturante voix de la chair triomphait et étouffait en elle toute autre voix.'
65 Scouffi, *Navire à l'ancre*.
66 Ibid., 61: 'folle armée d'aventurières polyglottes.'
67 Ibid., 62: 'ce caravansérail international abrite couramment des races contraires, empressées de se nuire.'
68 See *L'Égyptienne* 29 (août 1927), 30; quotation: 'Europe aristocratique et cosmopolite.'
69 Mann, *Considérations d'un apolitique*, 148.
70 Paolo Terni was the grandson of the composer Enrico Terni, whose second wife, the writer Fausta Cialente (1898–1994), spent twenty years in Alexandria, from 1921 to 1947, and wrote several novels on the city.
71 Terni, *In tempo rubato*, 145.
72 Bourget, *Essais de psychologie contemporaine*, XXIV-XXV; 55–68; 308–319.
73 Blum, *Anthologie des écrivains d'Égypte d'expression française*, 35, my emphasis:

> Jeanne Arcache appartient, par son père, à une ancienne famille syrienne et, par sa mère, à une vieille famille provençale. Égyptienne de nationalité, elle est née et a été élevée à Alexandrie. Elle a souvent voyagé en Syrie, en France, en Italie, en Suisse, en Allemagne, en Hollande. Ce cosmopolitisme ne l'a pas empêchée

de poursuivre des études littéraires et musicales et de parfaire sa connaissance approfondie de cinq ou six langues étrangères.

Bibliography

'Photos d'Alexandrie. San Stefano'. *Amicale Alexandrie Hier et Aujourd'hui*: Accessed 1 September 2016. http://www.aaha.ch/photos/sanstefano.htm.

'La Presse Francophone d'Égypte numérisée'. *Centre d'Études Alexandrines*: Accessed 1 September 2016. http://www.cealex.org/pfe/index.php.

Amossy, Ruth, and Anne Herschberg-Pierrot. *Stéréotypes et clichés. Langue, discours, société*. Paris: Nathan, 1997.

Avon, Dominique. *Les Frères prêcheurs en Orient*. Paris: Éditions du Cerf, 2005.

Barry, W. D. 'The Crowd of Ptolemaic Alexandria and the Riot of 203 BC'. *Échos du Monde Classique* 37 (1993): 415–31.

Basch, Sophie. 'Henri Thuile. Lettres à Pargas ou Littérature et Orient'. In *Alexandria ad Europam*, edited by Sophie Basch and Jean-Yves Empereur, 127–37. Cairo: IFAO, 2007.

Basch, Sophie. 'Le rendez-vous des étrangers'. *La pensée de midi* 14 (Winter 2005): 89–98.

Benoît, Pierre. 'La Maison du Mex'. *La Réforme illustrée 1925–1950* (1 May 1925): 138–9.

Blum, Robert. *Anthologie des écrivains d'Égypte d'expression française*. Cairo: Lencioni, 1937.

Botti, Giuseppe. *Catalogue des monuments exposés au Musée gréco-romain d'Alexandrie*. Alexandria: Imprimerie générale A. Mourès, 1900.

Bourget, Paul. *Essais de psychologie contemporaine*. Paris: Alphonse Lemerre, 1883.

Breccia, Evaristo. *Alexandrea ad Ægyptum. Guide de la ville ancienne et moderne et du Musée Gréco-Romain*. Bergamo: Istituto Italiano d'Arti Grafiche, 1914.

Chiti, Elena. 'Conflicting Histories of Alexandria, or Alexandrians with no Museum (1892–2016)'. *Égypte/Monde Arabe* 17, no. 3 (2018): 71–97.

Chiti, Elena. 'Et si la Grande Guerre commençait en 1911? L'entrée en guerre vue d'Alexandrie'. *Revue des mondes musulmans et de la Méditerranée* 141 (2017): 153–71.

Chiti, Elena. 'Écrire à Alexandrie (1879–1940). Capital social, appartenances, mémoire'. PhD dissertation, IREMAM/Aix-Marseille Université, 2013.

Clancy-Smith, Julia. *Mediterraneans: North Africa and Europe in an Age of Migration, c. 1800–1900*. Berkeley: University of California Press, 2012.

Collins, John Joseph, and John Gilbert Manning. 'Revolts under the Ptolemies: A Paleoclimatological Perspective'. In *Revolt and Resistance in the Ancient Classical World and the Near East*, edited by Francis Ludlow and John Gilbert Manning, 154–71. Leiden: Brill, 2016.

Coulmas, Peter. *Les Citoyens du monde: Histoire du cosmopolitisme*. Paris: Albin Michel, 1995.

Durrell, Lawrence. 'Introduction'. In *Alexandria: A History and a Guide*, edited by Edward Morgan Forster, vi–x. London: Michael Haag, [1922] 1982.

Durrell, Lawrence. *The Alexandria Quartet*. London: Faber and Faber, 1962.

Eldem, Edhem. 'Istanbul as a Cosmopolitan City: Myths and Realities'. In *A Companion to Diaspora and Transnationalism*, edited by Ato Quayson and Girish Daswani, 212–30. Oxford: Blackwell, 2013.

Eldem, Edhem. 'Epilogue: The Undesirables of Smyrna, 1926'. *Mediterranean Historical Review* 24, no. 2 (December 2009): 223–7.

Empereur, Jean-Yves. 'Le rêve d'une ville cosmopolite'. *Les Cahiers durrelliens* 1 (2004): 23–33.

Fahmy, Khaled. 'For Cavafy, with Love and Squalor'. In *Alexandria Real and Imagined*, edited by Anthony Hirst and Michael Silk, 263–80. Aldershot: Ashgate, 2004.

Fahmy, Khaled. 'Towards a Social History of Modern Alexandria'. In *Alexandria Real and Imagined*, edited by Anthony Hirst and Michael Silk, 281–306. Aldershot: Ashgate, 2004.

Fischer-Bovet, Christelle. *Army and Society in Ptolemaic Egypt*. Cambridge: Cambridge University Press, 2014.

Forster, Edward Morgan. *Alexandria: A History and a Guide*. London: Michael Haag, [1922] 1982.

Forster, Edward Morgan. *Pharos and Pharillion*. London: Hogarth Press, 1923.

Gérard, Delphine. 'Le choix culturel de la langue en Égypte'. *Égypte Monde Arabe* 1, nos 27/28 (1996): 253–84.

Gerteiny, Émile J. *La gamme alexandrine*. Cairo: Imprimerie C. E. Albertiri, 1932.

Ghitani, Jamal. 'Mahraqat al-kutub'. *Al-Akhbār* 10 September 2012.

Haag, Michael. *Egypt*. London: Cadogan Guides, 2004.

Haas, Christopher. *Alexandria in Late Antiquity: Topography and Social Conflict*. Baltimore: Johns Hopkins University Press, 1997.

Halim, Hala. *Alexandrian Cosmopolitanism: An Archive*. New York: Fordham University Press, 2013.

Hanley, Will. 'Foreignness and Localness in Alexandria 1880–1914'. PhD dissertation, Princeton University, 2007.

Hanley, Will. *Identifying with Nationality: Europeans, Ottomans, and Egyptians in Alexandria*. New York: Columbia University Press, 2017.

Ilbert, Robert. *Alexandrie 1830–1930: Histoire d'une communauté citadine*. Cairo: IFAO, 1996.

Ilbert, Robert. 'Une certaine citadinité'. In *Alexandrie 1860–1960*, edited by Robert Ilbert and Ilios Yannakakis, 20–47. Paris: Autrement, 1992.

Ismail, Noha Shaath. *East of the Sun: A Memoir*. Bloomington, IN: AuthorHouse, 2011.

Jockey, Philippe. 'Le Musée gréco-romain d'Alexandrie ou les musées imaginaires d'Evaristo Breccia'. In *Alexandria ad Europam*, edited by Sophie Basch and Jean-Yves Empereur, 25–50. Cairo: IFAO, 2007.

Jouhaud, Christian, Dinah Ribard and Nicolas Schapira, eds. *Histoire Littérature Témoignage. Écrire les malheurs du temps*. Paris: Gallimard, 2009.

Khuri-Makdisi, Ilham. *The Eastern Mediterranean and the Making of Global Radicalism, 1860–1914*. Berkeley: California University Press, 2010.

Koselleck, Reinhart. *Futures Past: On the Semantics of Historical Time*. New York: Columbia University Press, [1979] 1985.

Kozma, Liat, Cyrus Schayegh and Avner Wishnitzer, eds. *A Global Middle East: Mobility, Materiality and Culture in the Modern Age, 1880–1940*. London: I.B. Tauris, 2015.

de Lagarenne, Édouard. *L'Égypte fantaisiste*. Alexandria: Imprimerie de la Correspondance égyptienne, 1897.

Livi, Jean-François. *Ungaretti, Pea e gli altri*. Naples: Edizioni Scientifiche Italiane, 1988.

Livi, Jean-François. 'Ungaretti a Parigi: nuove lettere a Jean-Léon Thuile'. In *Nouveau cahier de route*, edited by Alexandra Zingone, 23–49. Firenze: Pagliai, 2000

Livi, Jean-François. 'Tra Alessandria d'Egitto e Parigi: Ungaretti e i fratelli Thuile. Nuove prospettive'. In *Giuseppe Ungaretti. Identità e metamorfosi*, edited by Lia Fava

Guzzetta, Rosario Gennaro, Maria Luisi and Franco Musarra, 195–210. Lucca: Maria Pacini Fazzi, 2005.
Luthi, Jean-Jacques. *Entretiens avec des auteurs francophones d'Égypte*. Paris: L'Harmattan, 2008.
Mann, Thomas. *Considérations d'un apolitique*. Paris: Grasset et Fasquelle, [1918] 1975.
Moretti, Franco. *Graphs, Maps, Trees: Abstract Models for a Literary History*. London: Verso, 2007.
Moscatelli, Jean. *Poètes en Égypte*. Cairo: Les Éditions de l'Atelier, 1955.
Municipalité d'Alexandrie. *Guide de la ville et du Musée d'Alexandrie*. Alexandria: Imprimerie générale A. Mourès, 1907.
Nizza. 'Brindilles'. *La Semaine égyptienne* 27–28 (September 1927): 34.
Oksenberg Rorty, Amelie, and James Schmidt, eds. *Kant's Idea for a Universal History with a Cosmopolitan Aim: A Critical Guide*. Cambridge: Cambridge University Press, 2009.
Orfali, Georges. *Secret de Princesse*. Alexandria: Stabilimento Grafico Dante Alighieri, 1934.
Postel, Guillaume. *De la République des Turcs*. Poitiers: Enguibert de Marnef, 1560.
Poumarède, Géraud. 'Négocier près la Sublime Porte. Jalons pour une nouvelle histoire des capitulations franco-ottomanes'. In *L'invention de la diplomatie: Moyen Âge-Temps modernes*, edited by Lucien Bély, 71–85. Paris: Presses Universitaires de France, 1998.
Raafat, Samir. 'Adieu San Stefano'. *Cairo Times*, 1 January 1999. Accessed 1 September 2016. http://www.egy.com/landmarks/99-01-08.php.
Scouffi, Alec. *Navire à l'ancre*. Paris: Louis Querelle, 1932.
Starr, Deborah. *Remembering Cosmopolitan Egypt: Literature, Culture and Empire*. London: Routledge, 2009.
Temimi, Sonia. 'From Intellectual to Professional: The Move from 'Contributor' to 'Journalist' at Ruz al-Yusuf in the 1920s and 1930s'. In *The Press in the Middle East and North Africa, 1850–1950*, edited by Anthony Gorman and Didier Monciaud, 207–34. Edinburgh: Edinburgh University Press, 2018.
Terni, Paolo. *In tempo rubato*. Palermo: Sellerio, 1999.
Thuile, Henri. *Littérature et Orient. Préface de Jean-François Livi, notes et dossier par Paul-André Claudel*. Grenoble: Ellug, 2013.
Thuile, Henri et al. *Henri Thuile, L'homme, l'oeuvre, les témoignages. Numéro spécial de L'Égypte nouvelle*, 11 avril 1925.
Thuile, Jean-Léon. *L'Eudémoniste*. Paris: Basset et Cie., *1913*.
Watts, Edward. *City and School in Late Antique Athens and Alexandria*. Berkeley: University of California Press, 2006.
Watts, Edward. *Riot in Alexandria: Tradition and Group Dynamics in Late Antique Pagan and Christian Communities*. Berkeley: University of California Press, 2010.

5

Negotiating an entry to modernity through Marie al-Khazen's photographs (1920–30)

Yasmine Nachabe Taan

According to Linda Nochlin's discussion of the way women were depicted in nineteenth- and twentieth-century Western painting,

> Like the Orient, woman … cannot be seen as a fixed, pre-existing entity or frozen 'image', transformed by this or that historical circumstance, but as a complex, mercurial and problematic signifier, mixed in its messages, resisting fixed interpretation or positioning despite the numerous attempts made in visual representation literally to put 'woman' in her place.[1]

Ideas about the ways women are represented in photographs during the French Mandate era in Lebanon, with various dimensions of identity and power, provide insight into the role of women in society and the making of a nation.[2] This chapter analyses representations in the photographs of Marie al-Khazen of local women riding horses, sporting European dresses, driving cars and masquerading in Bedouin attire.[3] Such modes of representation point to women's inclusion within a larger project of modernity. At times, these portraits conform to and work with familiar visual codes; at other times, they challenge both local and Western conventions in order to redefine what it is to be a modern bourgeois Lebanese woman during the Mandate era.

This chapter is an examination of al-Khazen's engagement with photography to position herself and the women who appear in her photographs within the often-separated domains of nationalism, political reform, Orientalism and a feminist moment in Middle Eastern Arab women's history. By exploring how local photography in mandate-era Lebanon participated in, and departed from, photographic paradigms that take the 'Orient' as the primary site of historical research and interest, I seek to draw useful contrasts and comparisons following a body of scholarship that has investigated photography outside of the Western geographical purview in places like Lebanon, Syria, Egypt and Palestine.[4] I propose that al-Khazen's photographs not only served as historical artefacts but also contributed to particular constructions of class, gender and nation. In developing this analysis, I draw on debates on the role of women in education and nationalism that were of great concern in the popular press in Lebanon from the 1920s onwards. I argue that the behaviour, attitude, pose and attire of the women in al-Khazen's photographs appear as if negotiating their entry into modernity by their desire to appear dignified, determined and independent. Reading al-Khazen's photographs as a reconfiguration of Orientalist photographs of an earlier period, I draw on postcolonial theory in art history and photography, combined with concepts from social history, to look into al-Khazen's photographs, in which women appear actively engaged in the production of an aesthetically hybrid representation that challenges the values of Western cultures and preconceived attitudes towards images in the Middle East and especially those of women.[5]

Based on a close analysis of a selection of al-Khazen's photographs, I offer a new perspective in a developing global historiography of photography by considering how the representation of women in the photograph shaped our understanding of everyday and national life in Lebanon in the interwar period. First, I examine the Orientalist practices of photography and the way women were depicted through this lens, as a demonstration of colonial power to satisfy the Western consumer. Second, after offering an overview of the historical context of al-Khazen's photographs, and briefly looking into the limited information currently available on other women photographers in the region, I look at how local, indigenous photography operates within a predominant colonial and gender matrix. Finally, I examine the gendered dimensions of photography for a woman who not only took the wheel but also was keen on documenting her travel while traversing boundaries, both social and geographical.

Modernity as underpinned by colonial discourse

The term 'modern', in general, means of present or recent times, contemporary or in fashion. Yet a more complex understanding of the term is articulated depending on the social and geographical context. On the one hand, Jürgen Habermas explains that the term expresses the self-consciousness of an epoch that relates itself as the result of a transition from old to new or models itself on a classical past while rejecting tradition.[6] On the other, Johannes Fabian challenges the assumption that the idea of modernity is exclusive to Western cultures and that the 'other' exists in a time not contemporary with Western cultures.[7] While Habermas, like Enlightenment thinkers and practitioners before him, emphasizes the idea of social betterment through scientific progress, Fabian by contrast introduces the idea of alternative or multiple modernities. For Habermas, the idea of progress is future-oriented and not based on a relation to the past. With the escalation of industrial capitalism reaching the Levant, and the increasing movement of populations from rural communities into cities during the early twentieth century, the modern is characterized by the experience of upheaval and change, yet also of optimism and a belief in a better, more advanced future. The experience of modernity is thus that of increased urbanization, industrialization and technological change that results from industrial capitalism with its ideological faith in progress, but it must also relate to the demands and aspirations of local people. Thus, Fabian's model seems more compatible with al-Khazen's project since it pinpoints the emergence, transformation and differentiation of a variety of 'uses of time' in the history of separate particular cultures.

Fabian acknowledges the specific parameters between power and inequality that are set in categorizing interlocutors (people of other cultures studied) as modern or not modern. Terms such as 'alternative' or 'multiple modernities' used by postcolonial scholars challenge the role modernity has played in the historic construction of Western imperialism. Its political use is often intended to widen the gap between Western cultures and the colonized interlocutors. Modernity is underpinned by the colonial discourse, which is identified by Fabian as the denial of coevalness. Along the same line, Christopher Pinney sees modernity as the accelerated time that presents a thread to the organic growth of certain cultures.[8] It can be menacing in, for example, the development of a particular culture's artistic practices. Kirsten Scheid complicates the process of the cultivation of the 'modern' *hadatha* (novelty) and *muʿasira* (contemporaneity) during the Mandate era in Lebanon through her analysis of the nude in early Lebanese paintings, which raises questions of gender, identity and class.[9]

Like the representation of women in al-Khazen's photographs and the ways in which these articulate the relationship between modernity and femininity as made manifest through women's behaviour, position, gaze and attire in photographs, this shift does not happen without fear of the loss of tradition that produces a general cultural anxiety and an urge to protect the local culture. '*Tamaddun* brings with it positive as much as negative influences', an anonymous author writes in *Fatat al-Sharq*, expressing his or her concern over the influences of imported foreign cultures on the host culture in terms of new customs and behaviour.[10]

Historical background

The interwar period witnessed the growth of technology, machine industries and the development of modes of transportation in Lebanon as elsewhere. The railways and roads of Beirut and its surroundings were extended to accommodate modern life. This progress in transportation extended mobility and communication among Lebanese citizens, and rapid changes expanded the urban sphere and prompted conflicting attitudes towards the establishment of the French Mandate. With an urge to document the changes in the region, including the new competition among industrialists and manufacturers, professional and amateur photographers each sought the best type of photographic genre, the most practical camera and the most perfect lens. Experimentation with new techniques for manipulating the camera as well as printing photographs was fashionable at the time, as is evident in the numerous articles published in issues of the Arabic periodical *al-Muqtataf*.[11]

The fall of the Ottoman Empire and the establishment of the French Mandate in Lebanon created many conflicts and generated much social, political and cultural debate in the region. Conflicting views on women's activities and their status within their communities were discussed and argued over in journals circulating during this period, with initiatives emerging to establish a relationship between women's liberation and a nation's entry into modernity. In the early 1920s, 'Abd al-Rahman Shahbandar (1880–1940), a prominent Syrian nationalist and leading opponent of the French Mandate, argued,

> It is not education, nor knowledge, nor high-rise buildings, nor wider roads, nor faster vehicles, nor the other invented technologies that determine the nation's entry to the era of civilization and progress, it is rather the woman's awakening and her social status that will determine a nation's entry to modernity.[12]

Decades before Shahbandar and even Qasim Amin before him, women's emancipation was a centerpiece of reform in Lebanon when both Ahmad Faris al-Shidyaq and Butrus al-Bustani championed women's education in Syria and Lebanon and recognized women's increased role in society.[13]

During the 1920s and 1930s, people were divided into two camps on the issue of social change and identity: the proponents of change under the French Mandate and opponents who resisted the Mandate for fear of losing their Arab national identity. Supporters of the Mandate saw it as an opening to 'modernity' imported from Europe, whereas its opponents believed in the possibility of the production of their own 'modernity', one that might continue the Ottoman Empire's previous efforts to initiate technological advancement and progress in the region.[14] It is within this political, social and cultural context that Marie al-Khazen (1899–1983), a Lebanese amateur photographer, shot most of her photographs.[15]

Among her collection are a large number of photographs in which al-Khazen appears posing next to a car, gathering with her family and friends around her car, and driving with a group of people (Figure 5.1). These representations can be understood as indicative signs of al-Khazen's mobility, her independence in being in control of the steering wheel and choosing the destination of her trips, and her adventurous spirit in discovering new places and visiting tourist sites around the region. In these photographs, al-Khazen followed neither the supporters of the Mandate nor its opponents but negotiated her entry to modernity in her own way.

Whether driving a car or riding a horse, al-Khazen and her female friends seem to be leading the way in most of their endeavours. In Figure 5.2, a woman surrounded by men rides a horse astride, in contrast to the way women of the period generally used to ride horses, that is, side-saddle. The group of men and the woman look like they have just returned from a ride. Two women occupy this predominantly masculine space: the photographer and the woman riding the horse. Riding horses and accompanying men on their hunting trips counter our idea of the usual way in which women were portrayed during the 1920s and 1930s in Lebanon. The practice of photography provided a space for Marie al-Khazen to articulate her vision of *al-Mar'a al-Jadida*, or

Figure 5.1 0009ya00489, amateur photographer: Marie al-Khazen, El Khazen family, Lebanon/Zgharta, 1927 (Collection: Mohsen Yammine, © Arab Image Foundation).

Figure 5.2 0009ya00476, amateur photographer: Marie al-Khazen, Lebanon/Zgharta, 1929 (Collection: Mohsen Yammine, © Arab Image Foundation).

The New Woman, the title of a women's journal founded by Julia Dimashqiyya in Beirut in 1921.[16] For al-Khazen, the 'new woman' is one who disregards the roles of dutiful daughter, wife and mother, seeking sexual, economic and political emancipation. I suggest that al-Khazen's photographs can be read as expressions of her desire for liberty and independence within Mandate Lebanon.

Al-Khazen's photographs not only project how femininity is represented as a lived experience but also how female subjectivity is produced through new narratives. Since Linda Nochlin's groundbreaking essay, the first transposition of Edward Said's *Orientalism* into the domain of art history, Said's ideas have provided an important framework for the analysis and critique of Western images of the Orient.[17] More recently, scholars of photography such as Stephen Sheehi, Ali Behdad and Zeynep Çelik have taken up the challenge to reposition Western understanding of images in relation to photography and visual culture by practitioners from North Africa and the Middle East, and to rethink the forms of cultural encounter and exchange that took place between European and indigenous artists.[18] However, none of these recent writings address women photographers from the region. Only one book has been published in Arabic about a recently discovered Arab woman photographer, Karimeh 'Abbud, who lived in Palestine, where she took most of her photographs, between 1893 and 1940.[19] She appears in a photograph by C. Sawides, standing behind her camera, getting ready to capture one of her best shots at Sawides's studio in Nazareth where she worked as a photographer.[20] 'Abbud was a Palestinian professional photographer who specialized in portrait photography during British Mandate rule (1923–48). Her career as a professional photographer documented a rising Palestinian middle class who aspired to construct themselves as modern in building their nation.

Marie al-Khazen and Karimeh 'Abbud might both be considered the earliest local women photographers who depicted themselves and other women in a range of cultural and social contexts. 'Abbud established her own photographic studio in Haifa while al-Khazen documented her travels around tourist sites in Lebanon and sought creative experimentation with her camera by staging scenes, manipulating shadows and superimposing negatives to produce different effects in her prints. Unlike 'Abbud, al-Khazen did not practice photography as a profession, yet her photographs are evidence of significant creative experimentation and control over the image. 'Abbud and al-Khazen's photographs document the changing ideas about the politics of gender and social roles locally. This contrasts with the better-known work of Marie Lydie Bonfils, a French photographer who may have been the first professional woman photographer in the region but whose images highlighted the exotic and mysterious elements of the region's inhabitants and their surroundings through an outsider's eye.

Marie Lydie Bonfils's photographic practice

Marie Lydie Bonfils moved from France to Lebanon in 1867 when Felix Bonfils, her husband, opened Maison Bonfils, a photographic studio based in Beirut. Her practice

Figure 5.3 0010sa00083, professional photographer: Marie-Lydie Bonfils, Woman in traditional clothing, Lebanon, 1880–90 (Collection: Nawaf Salam, © Arab Image Foundation).

focused on producing Orientalist genre photography during the late nineteenth century. She joined forces with her husband, being mainly in charge of mixing the albumen to produce the photographs but later becoming involved in portraits and costume photography. She worked in the family's Beirut studio for some time after her son abandoned the trade in the early 1900s, specializing in pictures of Bedouin women posing in their traditional costumes (see Figures 5.3–5.5). Most of these photographs were taken in the Bonfils's Beirut studio around the mid-1890s.[21] As a woman, she was able to take pictures of Middle Eastern women who were more inclined to pose for a female photographer than for a man. Assembling signs of exotic and mysterious subjects, Bonfils developed an Oriental photographic genre for the costume series featuring women. Her Orientalist photographs were produced for commercial purposes to satisfy the expectations of a European clientèle. The Bonfils photographs were taken in a climate that widened the gap between what constituted the Orient and the Occident. This was a climate in which the portrait of the Orient as the Other – as the reflection, complement or opposite of the Occident – was being developed in the nineteenth-century European travel literature of the Comtesse De

Figure 5.4 0010sa00084, professional photographer: Marie-Lydie Bonfils, Woman in traditional clothing, Lebanon, 1880–90 (Collection: Nawaf Salam, © Arab Image Foundation).

Perthuis, Gerard De Nerval and Gustave Flaubert among other *Voyage en Orient* travel accounts.

Although not directly concerned with photography, Said's writing provided a model for thinking about how Western visual culture and early photographic practices participated in the discursive field of Orientalism. Flaubert's texts, heavily cited in Said's *Orientalism*, represent the Orient as erotic and feminine. Christopher Pinney's writings on alternative photographic practices in India provide a lens through which to extend Said's critique within the Orientalist discourse that is perceived as a discourse of power.[22] In Marie al-Khazen's photographic practice, the representation of the Orient and the Oriental subject reflect the changing historical circumstances and the shifts in power between the Western and the non-Western subject. Unlike the photographs by Bonfils, which reinforce the fictional Orient by portraying local women as mysterious and exotic subjects, al-Khazen's woman looks straight into the lens as if asking to be seen in the way she has chosen. In photographs of herself (Figures 5.6 and 5.7) al-Khazen seems actively engaged in the production of an aesthetically hybrid self-representation that challenges the values of Western cultures. Ideas about the ways

Figure 5.5 0010sa00089, professional photographer: Marie-Lydie Bonfils, Woman in traditional clothing, Lebanon, 1880–90 (Collection: Nawaf Salam, © Arab Image Foundation).

women are represented in photographs in this period thus engage various dimensions of identity and power.[23]

Marie al-Khazen and the practice of amateur photography

Marie al-Khazen's photographs were mostly taken during the 1920s and 1930s in the north of Lebanon. From a bourgeois family background, al-Khazen seized every opportunity to document her family and friends living their everyday life around the al-Khazen mansion in the villa of Zgharta.[24] However, Marie al-Khazen was equally interested in taking photographs of peasants, Bedouin, European friends and landlords. The al-Khazens did not really mingle with the Zghartawi villagers as they considered themselves to be upper-class *shuyukh*.[25]

The practice of amateur photography began in the 1880s, when the technology was being revolutionized by the widespread commercial success of the dry plate, which dramatically simplified it.[26] By the turn of the century, a period of unparalleled

Figure 5.6 0009ya00492, amateur photographer: Marie al-Khazen, Lebanon/Zgharta, 1920–30 (Collection: Mohsen Yammine, © Arab Image Foundation).

competition among industrialists, manufacturers, professional photographers and amateurs was in progress. In most research on amateur photography, the figure of the photographer is almost exclusively male.[27] Yet in recent studies of the emergence of the Kodak Eastman model and the introduction of the Brownie box camera and its commercialization through advertisements, Kodak and other photography companies appear to primarily address women.[28]

Like other serious amateur photographers, such as Hanna and Najib al-Alam and Abu ʻIzz al-Din, Marie al-Khazen was attracted to themes such as excursions, the seaside, children and animals.[29] She must have been in her mid-twenties when she was at the height of her photographic activity, by which time the act of photographing consisted of pulling the trigger, turning the key and pressing the button. Yet, she still faced the challenge of capturing the decisive moment: who to include and what to exclude in her photographs, how to arrange the scene and direct the subjects, and when to release the shutter speed. Her photographs are evidence of complex use of the device.

Figure 5.7 0009ya00495, amateur photographer: Marie al-Khazen, Marie el Khazen, Beirut port, Lebanon/Beirut, 1920–30 (Collection: Mohsen Yammine, © Arab Image Foundation).

Women and photography

Amidst the studies of local photography in Lebanon and its surroundings at the turn of the last century written from the mid-1980s, only one book focuses on women in the photographs of the Middle East, Sarah Graham-Brown's *Images of Women: The Portrayal of Women in Photography of the Middle East, 1860–1950.*[30] Although women had been practicing photography ever since the invention of the camera, they were not seen as photographers in their own right until scholars started writing on their practice. Recent studies of women photography are important as they depict women photographers not as mere assistants in the production of photography but as agents of their own work. No photograph was signed with a woman's name in the Middle East except for those credited to Marie Lydie Bonfils. The 1882 *Dalil Beirut* (*Guide to Beirut*) notes the existence of a photo studio entitled 'Studio Madame Philippe Sabunji', indicating that Philippe

Sabunji was assisted by his Danish wife, Rikke.[31] This is evidence that women were involved in the production of photography at that time in Beirut, even if they were not acknowledged or credited for this. Nor did they sign photographs as they did not often sign their texts and thus were denied authorship over their work.[32] This makes the task of tracing women photographers even more difficult. Only with further research do we discover that they were involved in the production of photographs.

A studio with a woman's name was established in the Gemmayzeh area in Beirut around the beginning of the twentieth century; on its sign is written, in upper-case Latin letters, 'Photographie Peintre Octavia Kova'.[33] Octavia Kova was most likely a descendant of the Kova brothers, Joseph (died *c.*1904) and Alexander (died 1911), originally from Latakia, Syria, who came to Beirut to establish their photographic studio. Under the 'photographer' pull-down menu in the Arab Image Foundation's (AIF) website, only nine female names are cited other than that of Marie al-Khazen, out of the hundreds of male photographers listed. One of them is identified as an amateur photographer, 'Aida 'Abdin. Two of the nine women photographers, Maria Zarur and Siham, have no photographs in the AIF archive but have their names listed. Six are cited as 'professional photographers', and the website's database search returns one photograph for each.[34]

Al-Khazen and early-twentieth-century visual culture

Born at the end of the last decade of the nineteenth century, al-Khazen was among the first generation to be exposed to printed photographs in periodicals through which women became increasingly visible. At the beginning of the twentieth century in Lebanon, widely circulating women's magazines such as *Minerva*, *Sawt al-Mar'a*, and *al-Mar'a al-Jadida* started publishing photographs of women to animate their pages; these are likely to have arrived by subscription at the al-Khazen house. We might wonder how the representation of women in these magazines influenced al-Khazen's own efforts at self-representation and portrayal of other women. Reading magazines emerged as the most modern of bourgeois women's *passe-temps* during the first decades of the twentieth century. In general, advertisements in Arabic magazines were mostly addressed to women. A significant number of the magazines were imported from Alexandria and Cairo and they advertised cigarettes, cars, nylon stockings, refrigerators and other electric appliances, Kodak films, radios and Eastman Brownie box cameras, all for women.[35]

Nevertheless, photographs of women in local journals did not appear without comment: In a letter addressed to Mayy Ziyada, a Lebanese poet and writer, Fatima al-Yusuf, editor of *Ruz al-Yusuf*, asked permission to publish the poet's photograph. The editor observed that after having previously encountered problems after publishing photographs of women without prior consent, she was now cautiously seeking permission prior to publishing their portraits in her journal.[36] Women's entry into the public sphere through their portraits, visible in the press, caused social concern and raised many questions about the ways women were allowed to appear, the frequency of their appearance in the circulating press and how this was perceived by the local social community.

The evolution of thought on the subject of Arab women during the twentieth century

The period after the First World War saw significant changes in Lebanon. The effect of the war was drastic and it impacted on women in different ways. Even though women did not achieve equal political rights, they still managed to acquire modest recognition on the basis of their intellectual and educational capabilities. Despite the rising mainstream nationalist movements, who felt threatened by women's ascendance, proponents of the women's liberation movement continued their efforts in organizing lectures and demonstrations. Determined, active women such as Nazik al-'Abid, 'Adila Beyhum, Anbara Salam and many others launched their own associations, each with a different goal to better women's circumstances.[37] All three women were activists and critics of Ottoman and French colonialism in Syria and Lebanon. Al-'Abid was the head of *Al-Najma al-Hamra* ('The Red Star') association for women in Damascus in 1920, and Anbara Salam publicly removed her veil in 1927 during a lecture at the American University of Beirut.[38]

In 1928, the same year in which a conference on women's rights was organized in Beirut, Nazira Zeineddin published her groundbreaking first book *Al-Sufur wa al hijab* (*Veiling and Unveiling*) followed by *Al Fatat wa al shuyukh* (*The Girl and the Sheikhs*).[39] Neither of Zeineddin's books circulated without causing turmoil. Zeineddin in both books fiercely contested religious laws on wearing the veil. The status of women proved to be a major source of dispute among religious, political and intellectual (patriarchal) authorities. The conservative community opposed the women's movement while a number of Lebanon's male intelligentsia strongly supported the women's cause. Muhammad J. Beyhum, and before him Butrus al-Bustani (1819–1883), one of the outstanding figures in the Arab renaissance and an advocate for women's education in the 1840s, and Jurji Niqula Baz (1881–1959), the founder of *al-Hasnaa*, the first women's magazine in Syria, were outspoken supporters of women's role in society. Following al-Bustani and Baz, Beyhum, 'Adila's husband, was the first Muslim intellectual to publicly advocate women's emancipation in Lebanon, urging them to seek knowledge not only to prepare themselves for the task of raising a new educated generation but also to attain a higher status in society.[40] 'Since the 1920s, Lebanese society is a social sphere in transformation, introducing reforms that included women's entry into the public sphere', he claimed.[41]

The archetypal Lebanese woman, who had been shy and reserved and whose domain had been restricted to the domestic sphere, now saw herself as an active citizen in society. This same woman, who had been passive and submissive, became, according to al-Khazen's representation, a determined modern woman, confident and daring. Al-Khazen's photographs were thus produced during a period when women contributed to education by organizing literary gatherings in Beirut and its surroundings. The interest in higher education and the increase in knowledge it brought about became popular among women, who would frequently hold books in their poses in photographs of this period in order to demonstrate their new interests. The messages thus evoked also found expression in writings such as those of Rose Ghurayyib who, like al-Khazen, rejected beauty as the only virtue of importance for women and stressed the significance of knowledge and strength as well.[42]

Marie al-Khazen, the cosmopolitan woman

Some decades after Marie Lydie Bonfils's photographs representing Oriental women were published and widely marketed in Europe, Marie al-Khazen produced a large number of photographs in which she appears with her friends and family members wearing the latest European fashion and travelling around the region (Figures 5.6 and 5.7). In Figure 5.7, al-Khazen appears sporting a European dress with a white embroidered bow, legs crossed, sitting on a tall column. The background, the dock at the port of Beirut with two boats leaving the jetty, symbolizes travel, mobility and an openness to the west.[43] Al-Khazen must have given directions for the photograph to be taken from below; she seems to know that when the camera is placed at a low angle it makes the subject appear more imposing. Her direct look conveys ease and confidence, indicating that she has taken command of her pose in the photograph. A determined woman addresses her viewer as an equal, and the photograph expresses the desire to communicate with them. Her sartorial choice is indicative of her position at the forefront of a trend towards fashionable European attire that emerged around the 1920s among women of the Lebanese elite. By the first decade of the twentieth century, stores catering to the social class that could afford shopping were spreading across the country's larger cities. One of these, located in Beirut, was the Bon Marché. Because it was harder to find similar stores with finished goods in the villages, bourgeois families would hire their own *franji* tailors, who advertized themselves as able to clothe men and women in the latest European fashions.[44] In Beirut and its surrounding villages, dressmaking workshops were organized to teach women new techniques in embroidery. Women produced their own dresses by mixing and matching local decorative patterns and European designs, creating a chic, graceful and convenient hybrid fashion.

After the Mandate, dress and manners became politically charged sites of cultural contestation where, for the first time, the very essence of the Lebanese traditional identity as part of the Arab nation – in the sense of a more general identity and sense of belonging – was at stake. Dress was becoming a signifier that occupied competing and sometimes conflicting temporalities, producing cultural tensions and anxieties that afforded new perspectives on the 'new woman'. Thus, wearing the latest Parisian fashion could be considered to embody a cosmopolitan attitude, reflecting an image of the cultivated, proud and confident woman who is committed to education and social reforms.[45]

However, embodying a cosmopolitan attitude was not, for al-Khazen, just about an outward emulation of Western attire. *Tamaddun*, or becoming cosmopolitan, was a much more complicated process than simply imitating foreign dress or rejecting local traditions. *Tamaddun* is a term that is derived from *medina* (Arabic: city). It refers to the transformation of a place whereby inhabitants reside together in a city or a town, or to dwelling together in public spaces. In al-Khazen's photographs, the mixed-gender socialization in public can be understood as signs of cosmopolitan identity in formation. Al-Khazen, as evident in the photograph (Figure 5.6), went together with friends and family on excursions to different historical sites; she also went on hunting trips and hosted friends and family members visiting the al-Khazen house. Al-Khazen, who was schooled at the Collège de la Sainte Famille Française in Junieh, was an avid reader of the circulating press of the time.[46] This tells us that she was aware of the debates in the press that reflected cross-gender anxiety about the influences of *franji* or Western culture.[47] The presence of men and women comfortably sharing the same space in the photographs of al-Khazen crystallizes a complex dynamic of an interdependent system of gender, mobility, consumption and knowledge that interacts with the meaning of cosmopolitanism within the context of industrialization and changing consumption habits. *Tamaddun* for al-Khazen as seen in her photographs meant not only sporting Western attire but also being mobile, experiencing different places within mixed-gender public spaces. This combination of local customs and imported ideas gave birth to local cosmopolitan subjects. An Oriental cosmopolitan model particular to the region required al-Khazen and her counterparts to become cosmopolitan, while still safeguarding a sense of authenticity in the face of westernization through new behaviour and consumption and a new aesthetics of order.

Al-Khazen dressed as a Bedouin

The Bedouin was a common subject and widespread in the late nineteenth century Orientalist paintings and postcards. In Figure 5.6, al-Khazen appears dressed up as a Bedouin, standing in front of a tent in the middle of the desert.[48] Photographs of the same woman taken in different places attests to her mobility. The desert background with a tribal tent signifies a closed mysterious space, or the reproduction of the unknown Oriental space. She stands in the foreground, her hands open wide, as if trying to strike a pose. The myth of the desert which found expression in the media and the circulation of postcards and photographs in early-twentieth-century Lebanon seemed to appeal to al-Khazen's taste. However, in this particular photograph, the idea of the exotic is no longer organized in spatial or temporal dimension as 'the lure of far-distant lands and peoples' or 'the pursuit of the historical "other" '.[49] Rather, it is precisely through the strategy of auto-Orientalizing her own culture, placing herself in the colonizer's camp, that al-Khazen reflects an image of herself as a modern subject.

In this photograph, al-Khazen has disguised herself as a Bedouin, mimicking the poses reminiscent of the circulating Orientalist postcards, yet her expression holds none of the passivity associated with the Oriental subjects seen in the work of Bonfils. Al-Khazen here is restaging a Western Oriental stereotype. This irreverent performativity is again a powerful testament to al-Khazen's agency. It profoundly challenges any notion of the silence or passivity of Ottoman Arab women implicit in the more familiar images that were so popular in Europe at the turn of the century. Al-Khazen seems to express her fascination with the idea of the exotic. In this way, she emerges as a figure of resistance to a dominant scopic regime: she presents herself as a sophisticated, visually literate instigator of the clichéd codes of Orientalist visual culture.[50] She rewrites these codes for a different purpose not to Orientalize her own culture but rather to show that she shares the sophisticated taste of doing so with European cultures. Such an interpretation highlights the cosmopolitan elites across cultures. Here, othering her own culture helps her situate herself at the very threshold within the binary between the modern and the traditional. She is divided between longing for a tribal past and fully participating in the modern culture that was rapidly taking shape during the second decade of the twentieth century. This is an example of the shift in colonial representation which occurs when mainstream notions about the Middle East are intercepted by local photographs. Western fantasy, in this case, can explain the constant aspiration to appropriate Orientalist behaviour.

Negotiating an entry into modernity

Through her photographs, al-Khazen partook of a cosmopolitan sensibility that reveals the region to have been far more international than is sometimes thought. After the second decade of the twentieth century, a number of Arabic, French and English dailies in Mandate Lebanon featured a weekly section dedicated to cultural events and reviews. Literary salons, cinema and theatre initially dominated these pages. Al-Khazen's photographs provide a glimpse of the women who began to engage with society and public spaces in new ways. She captures the new fusion of fashions that reached its climax at the beginning of the century with the imported garments from Paris which appear in most of her images. By depicting some women wearing traditional dress and others wearing the latest European fashion, Marie al-Khazen's photographs negotiate an entry into modernity, a 'modernity' that contains a number of logics which may work with and against each other simultaneously. This model of 'modernity' was particular to the colonial milieu in which the photographs were taken. Modernity and the different ways it was manifested through the transformation of appearances in the photograph might indicate social change and even social freedom, particularly in the case of women.[51] According to Graham-Brown, 'Western-style dress was used by some regimes as an indication of modernity and liberality in regard to women.'[52] As we have seen in the analysis of al-Khazen's photographs, dress was often used to ascribe modernity and progress to the subjects represented in the photographs. For example, a woman wearing a European dress might signify her belonging to a liberal well-to-do family or, conversely, it could gesture to her defiance of her class, gender, community and family. Caught between projecting a self-image as the cosmopolitan woman and as a traditional Bedouin simultaneously, al-Khazen's photographs provide a rich field for us to track ambiguous conceptions of modernity.

The parallel reading of Figures 5.6 and 5.7 is useful in analysing the way Marie al-Khazen wanted to be portrayed in them. In particular, it supports the thesis that through her photographs, al-Khazen projects unconventional representations of women that challenged their exclusion from the discourses and practices of leisure, community and individuality. From riding a horse astride to cross-dressing as a Bedouin to driving the latest model automobile, affirming her position in the front seat and holding the steering wheel, al-Khazen can be associated with being young in the pursuit of freedom and excitement, the embodiment of the figure of the New Woman. For wealthy people such as the al-Khazens, the automobile was a new way to occupy their leisure time. The automobile, among other innovative technologies of the era, radically changed al-Khazen's life (and that of her family and friends) by accelerating the outward expansion of her outings. The introduction of cars in Lebanon can be seen as a phenomenon that narrowed the gap between rural and urban life. The al-Khazens moved around easily, organizing excursions around different regions in Lebanon. We may speculate that by depicting herself as a driver, al-Khazen sought to celebrate her excitement at the accessibility that owning a car brought, even if driving was not an easy task given the poor state of roads, especially the bumpy track leading to her family's mansion.

By virtue of her mobility – travels and excursions – al-Khazen distanced herself from her own culture, and through her ability to perceive her culture from the outside, she partook of the west's impulse to exoticize it. The tension between the Orientalist representation of women in the Middle East and the changing attitudes to women's social, cultural and economic roles after the Mandate is made visible in the juxtaposition of Figures 5.6 and 5.7. This adds a twist to the old Orientalist debate. Instead of reinforcing the Orientalist perspective of the Middle East as a simple society, it complicates this relation by creating ambiguities. Representing herself across both sides simultaneously bridges the theoretical gap between Western and Middle Eastern women. This, in turn, contributes to a positioning of Woman as historically atemporal and modern at the same time.

Following Linda Nochlin's earlier claim that 'woman … cannot be seen as a fixed, pre-existing entity or frozen "image"', I have interpreted al-Khazen's photographs while raising questions as to whether Orientalist representations simply express the politics of Western domination or whether they can embody an exchange of ideas and representations. I have argued instead that Orientalism is often produced through cross-cultural interactions as a result of increased mobility and the circulation of images.[53] Although there are stylistic similarities between al-Khazen's stereotypical image of the Bedouin and Marie Lydie Bonfils's Orientalist photographs, these should not be understood as imitations; instead, they reveal a visual language of resistance to colonization. What is at stake in this representation is the fact that the Bedouin, who is not only a representative of traditionalism but also of a lower social class, *is* the cosmopolitan woman.

Notes

1 Nochlin, *Representing Women*, 7.
2 Baron, *Egypt as a Woman*, 83.
3 This chapter expands upon and refines discussion of al-Khazen's work first developed in my article 'Refracted Gazes'.
4 See Nassar, *Laqatat mughayira*; Behdad, *Camera Orientalis*; and Sheehi, *The Arab Imago*; among others.
5 Such as Çelik, 'Speaking Back to Orientalist Discourse'; Micklewright, 'Late Ottoman Photography'; Baron, *Egypt as a Woman*; and Roberts, 'Nazlı's Photographic Games'.
6 Habermas, *The Structural Transformation of the Public Sphere*, 56.
7 Fabian, *Time and the Other*, 12.
8 Pinney and Peterson, *Photography's Other Histories*, 51.
9 Scheid, 'Necessary Nudes', 210.
10 Anonymous author cited in Beyhum, *Fatat al-sharq fi hadarat al-gharb*, 15. *Tamaddun* is an Arabic term that means becoming cosmopolitan.
11 A scientific Arabic journal, *al-Muqtataf*, first published in the 1870s in Beirut, includes technical information and advice for improving camera technique. See, e.g., 'Al-Futugrafiyya al-Suriyya', 685; 'al-Futugrafiyya' in 'Bab al-sina'a', 291–3; 'Taswid al-suwar al-futugrafiyya', 366.
12 Shahbandar, 'The Answer', 33 (my translation).
13 See Anonymous, *Maqalat wa-khutub fi-l-tarbiyya*.
14 Exemplified in the albums of Sultan Abdul Hamid from the turn of the century which, by documenting the advance of technology, reflect his desire for a modernizing agenda. Allen, 'The Abdulhamid II Collection', 121.
15 In the mid-1970s, Marie al-Khazen handed a box of a hundred 9 cm × 6 cm negatives to Mohsen Yammine, a journalist and photo collector in Zgharta. The negatives remained part of Yammine's collection until they were donated to the Arab Image Foundation (AIF) archive in Beirut. Founded in 1997, the AIF launched a major project to collect, preserve and archive photographs from the region.
16 And following Amin's *The New Woman*.
17 Nochlin, 'The Imaginary Orient'.
18 Çelik, 'Speaking Back to Orientalist Discourse'; Behdad, *Camera Orientalis*; and Sheehi, *The Arab Imago*.
19 Rahib et al., *Karimeh 'Abbud*.
20 Ibid., 49.
21 Gavin, *The Image of the East*, 37.
22 Pinney, *Camera Indica*, 8.
23 Baron, *Women's Awakening*, 56.
24 The al-Khazen family, of whom Marie al-Khazen is a member, are not related to the Khazen family to whom Semaan Khazen (1898–1973) belongs. Marie's family were originally from Kisrwan. They migrated to Zgharta from Ghosta. The remains of the abandoned al-Khazen mansion, where Marie lived, with its high painted ceilings,

decorative arches and other interesting architectural details is situated on an isolated hill, now inaccessible by a proper road.

25 *Shuyukh*, plural for *sheikh*, is an honorific title in the Arabic language. It is commonly used to designate the front man of a tribe or feudal family who inherited this title from his father.
26 West, *Kodak and the Lens of Nostalgia*, 62.
27 Moore, *Jacques Henri Lartigue*, 28.
28 West, *Kodak and the Lens of Nostalgia*, 65.
29 Hanna and Najib al-Alam's and Salim Abu 'Izz al-Din's photographs are also part of Mohsen Yammine's collection of amateur photographers in North Lebanon.
30 Graham-Brown, *Images of Women*.
31 Debbas, *Des photographes à Beyrouth, 1840–1918*, 48.
32 Zeidan, *Arab Women Novelists*, 82.
33 A reproduction of this photograph can be seen in Debbas, *Beirut Our Memory*, 190.
34 The AIF website lists the following: a photograph of a baby boy with mother and grandmother in Jordan, 1925 (Karimeh 'Abbud); one photograph of what seems like a royal gathering in Egypt, 1951 (Widad Shoukair); a portrait of a young girl in Beirut, 1960 (Sonia Alemian); an identity card for Johannes Krikorian in Palestine, 1945 (Najla Krikorian); a photograph taken in Egypt, 1930s (Aida 'Abdin); and one photograph taken in Egypt, 1960 (Soeur Emmanuelle). Marie Lydie Bonfils has eight photographs of men and women in traditional clothing taken in the period between the 1880s and 1890s: http://arabimagefoundation.com/.
35 Russell, 'Marketing the Modern Egyptian Girl', 23.
36 al-Yusuf cited in Graham-Brown, *Images of Women*, 185.
37 Beyhum, *Fatat al-sharq fi hadarat al-gharb*, 119.
38 Khalidi, *Memoirs of an Early Arab Feminist*, 95.
39 Zeineddin, *Al-Fatat wa al-shuyukh*.
40 In 1921, Beyhum also wrote on women in history and laws, *al-Mar'a fi al-tarikh wa al-sharia*, followed by *Women in the New Civilization*, *al-Mar'a fi al-tamaddun al-hadith*.
41 Beyhum, *Fatat al-sharq fi hadarat al-gharb*, 109–13.
42 Nassar, 'Remembering Rose Ghurayyib', 104–5.
43 Nachabe, 'Refracted Gazes', 162–3. The French sociologist Pierre Bourdieu argues that a particular practice of photography can be associated with urban social practices, as a manifestation of the desire for social mobility. Bourdieu's ethnographical perspective is particularly useful to an examination of Marie al-Khazen's photographs in the Beirut port and the sense of cosmopolitanism deployed within them. Bourdieu, *Photography*.
44 *Franji* is an Arabic term used to designate the locals who are influenced in their dress and behaviour by Western culture, the French in particular. Khater, *Inventing Home*, 125.
45 For more on changing attire and how it reflected a cosmopolitan subject in formation in the Middle East and North Africa region during the second decade of the twentieth century, see Jacob, *Working out Egypt*.
46 According to Mohsen Yammine, when al-Khazen passed away, her abandoned house was full of journals, books and magazines. Interview with Mohsen Yammine, 12 July 2011.
47 The Collège de la Sainte Famille Française was founded in Junieh, Lebanon, in 1898 by the sisters of the Sainte Famille order from Villefranche de Rouergue, France.

48 More of these images in which Marie al-Khazen and other women masquerade as Bedouins before a tent appear as part of her photo collection in the AIF archive.
49 Graham-Brown, *Images of Women*, 5.
50 Nachabe, 'Refracted Gazes', 160–1.
51 Ibid., 155.
52 Graham-Brown, *Images of Women*, 249.
53 Nachabe, 'Refracted Gazes', 156.

Bibliography

Periodicals

Al-Muqtataf (Yaqub Sarruf and Faris Nimr (eds), Beirut, Cairo, 1876–1952).
Al-Hasna' (Jurji Niqula Baz (ed.), Beirut, 1909–12).
Al-'Arus (Marie 'Ajami (ed.), Damascus, 1910–18).
Fatat Lubnan (Salima Abi Rashed (ed.), Beirut, 1914).
Al-Mar'a al-Jadida (Julia Dimashqiyya (ed.), Beirut, 1921–28).
Minerva (Mary Yanni (ed.), Beirut, 1923–30).
Ruz al-Yusuf (Fatima al-Yusuf (ed.), Cairo, 1925–present).
Sawt al-Mar'a (Idvik Shaybub (ed.), Beirut, 1945–58).

Published works

Amin, Qasim. *The New Woman*. Cairo: American University in Cairo Press, 1992
Anonymous. *Maqalat wa-khutub fi-tarbiyya: 'asr al-nahda al-haditha*. Beirut: Dar al-Hamra, 1990.
Anonymous. 'Al-Futugrafiyya al-Suriyya'. *Al-Muqtataf* 1 (1876–7): 685.
Anonymous. 'Al-Futugrafiyya' in 'Bab al-sina'a'. *Al-Muqtataf* 19 (1895): 291–3.
Anonymous. 'Taswid al-suwar al-futugrafiyya'. *Al-Muqtataf* 24 (1899): 366.
Anonymous. 'Al-Sahafat al-nisa'iyyat fi Misr wa Surya'. *Minerva* 1 (1923): 103–8.
Anonymous. 'Al-Tamaddun'. In *Fatat al-sharq fi hadarat al-gharb*, edited by Muhammad J. Beyhum, 74–5. Beirut: Muhammad J. Beyhum, 1952.
Arab Image Foundation website: http://arabimagefoundation.com/.
Allen, William. 'The Abdulhamid II Collection'. *History of Photography* 8, no. 2 (1984): 119–45.
Baron, Beth. *The Women's Awakening in Egypt: Culture, Society, and the Press*. New Haven, CT: Yale University Press, 1994.
Baron, Beth. *Egypt as a Woman*. Berkeley: University of California Press, 2004.
Behdad, Ali. *Camera Orientalis: Reflections on Photography of the Middle East*. Chicago: University of Chicago Press, 2016.
Beaulieu, Jill, and Mary Roberts, eds. *Orientalism's Interlocutors: Painting, Architecture, Photography*. Durham, NC: Duke University Press, 2002.
Beyhum, Muhammad. *Al-Mar'a Fi Al-Tarikh Wa Al-Sharai*. Beirut: Muhammad Beyhum, 1921.
Beyhum, Muhammad. Al-Mar'a Fi Al-Tamaddun Al-Hadith. Beirut: Matbaat al-Salam, 1927.

Beyhum, Muhammad J., ed. *Fatat al-sharq fi hadarat al-gharb: tatawwur al-fikr al-'Arabi fi mawdu' al-mar'a khilal al-qarn al-ishrin* [The Eastern Girl in Western Civilization: The Evolution of Arab Thought on the Subject of Women during the Twentieth Century]. Beirut: Muhammad J. Beyhum, 1952.

Booth, Marilyn. *May Her Likes Be Multiplied: Biography and Gender Politics in Egypt.* Berkeley: University of California Press, 2001.

Bourdieu, Pierre. *Photography: A Middle-Brow Art.* Translated by Shaun Whiteside. Cambridge: Polity, 1990.

Çelik, Zeynep. 'Speaking Back to Orientalist Discourse'. In *Orientalism's Interlocutors: Painting, Architecture, Photography*, edited by Jill Beaulieu and Mary Roberts, 19–41. Durham, NC: Duke University Press, 2002.

Chadwick, Whitney, and Dawn Ades. *Mirror Images: Women, Surrealism, and Self-Representation.* Cambridge: MIT Press, 1998.

Cizgen, Engin. *Photography in the Ottoman Empire, 1839–1919.* Istanbul: Haset Kitabevi A. S., 1987.

Debbas, Fouad. *Beirut Our Memory: A Guided Tour Illustrated with Postcards from the Collection of Fouad Debbas.* Beirut: Naufal Group, 1986.

Debbas, Fouad. *Des photographes à Beyrouth, 1840–1918.* Paris: Marval, 2002.

Fabian, Johannes. *Time and the Other.* New York: Columbia University Press, 2002.

Fares Ibrahim, Emily. *Al-Harakat al-nisa'iyyat al-Lubnaniyyat.* Beirut: Dar al-Thaqafa, *c.*1970.

Fleischmann, Ellen L. 'The Other "Awakening": The Emergence of Women's Movements in the Modern Middle East, 1900–1940'. In *A Social History of Women and Gender in the Modern Middle East*, edited by Margaret L. Meriwether and Judith E. Tucker, 89–139. Boulder, CO: Westview Press, 1999.

Frierson, Elizabeth. 'Unimagined Communities: Woman and Education in the Late Ottoman Empire'. *Critical Matrix* 9, no. 2 (1995): 55–90.

Gavin, Carney E. S. *The Image of the East: Nineteenth Century Near Eastern Photographs by Bonfils, from the Collections of the Harvard Semitic Museum.* Chicago: University of Chicago Press, 1982.

Graham-Brown, Sarah. *Images of Women: The Portrayal of Women in Photography of the Middle East, 1860–1950.* London: Quartet, 1988.

Habermas, Jürgen. *The Structural Transformation of the Public Sphere.* Cambridge, MA: MIT Press, 1991.

Hanssen, Jens. *Fin de Siècle Beirut: the Making of an Ottoman Provincial Capital.* Oxford: Clarendon Press, 2006.

Hight, Eleanor M., and Gary D. Sampson. *Colonialist Photography: Imag(in)ing Race and Place.* London: Routledge, 2002.

Jacob, Wilson Chaco. *Working out Egypt: Effendi Masculinity and Subject Formation in Colonial Modernity, 1870-1940.* Durham, NC: Duke University Press, 2011.

Khalidi, Anbara Salam, and Tarif Khalidi. *Memoirs of an Early Arab Feminist: The Life and Activism of Anbara Salam Khalidi.* London: Pluto, 2013.

Khater, Akram F. *Inventing Home: Emigration, Gender, and the Middle Class in Lebanon, 1870–1920.* Berkeley: University of California Press, 2001.

Khazen, Semaan. *Tarikh Zgharta.* Ehden: Semaan Khazen, n.d.

Lewis, Reina. *Gendering Orientalism: Race, Femininity, and Representation.* New York: Routledge, 1995.

Lewis, Reina, and Nancy Micklewright. *Gender, Modernity and Liberty: Middle Eastern and Western Women's Writings: A Critical Sourcebook.* London: I.B. Tauris, 2006.

Maqdisi, Jean, ed. *Al-Nisa' al-'arabiyat fi al-'ishrinat hudur wa hawiyya*. Beirut: Women Researchers Association, 2001.
Micklewright, Nancy. 'Late Ottoman Photography: Family, Home, and New Identities'. In *Transitions in Domestic Consumption and Family Life in the Modern Middle East*, edited by Relli Shechter, 65–84. New York: Palgrave Macmillan, 2003.
Moore, Kevin D. *Jacques Henri Lartigue: The Invention of an Artist*. Princeton: Princeton University Press, 2004.
Nachabe, Yasmin. 'Refracted Gazes: A Woman Photographer during Mandate Lebanon'. *Altre Modernità* 8 (2012): 154–73.
Nachabe Taan, Yasmine. 'An Alternative Representation of Femininity in 1920s Lebanon: Through the Mise-en-abîme of a Masculine Space'. *New Middle Eastern Studies* 1, no.1 (2011). Retrieved from http://www.brismes.ac.uk/nmes/archives/219.
Nassar, Anita Farah.'Remembering Rose Ghurayyib, 1909-2006'. *Al-Raida* 23–4 no. 114–15 (summer/fall 2006): 102–6.
Nassar, Issam. *Laqatat mughayira: Palestine 1850–1948*. London: Qattan Foundation, 2005.
Nochlin, Linda. 'The Imaginary Orient'. *Art in America* 71, no. 5 (1983): 118–31.
Nochlin, Linda. *Representing Women*. New York: Thames and Hudson, 1999.
Pinney, Christopher. *Camera Indica: the Social Life of Indian Photographs*. London: Reaktion Books, 1997.
Pinney, Christopher, and Nicolas Peterson. *Photography's Other Histories*. Durham, NC: Duke University Press, 2003.
Rahib, Mitri, Ahmad Mrowat and Issam Nassar, eds. *Karimeh 'Abbud raidat al-taswir al-nasawi fi filastin 1893–1940* [Karimeh 'Abbud, A Pioneer Woman Photographer in Palestine 1893–1940]. Bethlehem: Diyar Press, 2011.
Roberts, Mary. 'Nazlı's Photographic Games: Said and Art History in a Contrapuntal Mode'. *Patterns of Prejudice* 48, no. 5 (2014): 460–78.
Russell, Mona. 'Marketing the Modern Egyptian Girl'. *Journal of Middle East Women's Studies* 6, no. 3 (2010): 19–57.
Said, Edward. *Orientalism*. London: Penguin, 1978.
Scheid, Kirsten, 'Necessary Nudes: *Hadatha* and *Mu'asira* in the Lives of Modern Lebanese'. *International Journal of Middle East Studies* 42, no. 2 (2010): 203–30.
Shahbandar, 'Abd al-Rahman. 'The Answer of Abdel Rahman Shahbandar'. In *Fatat al-sharq fi hadarat al-gharb*, edited by Muhammad J. Beyhum, 33–6. Beirut: Muhammad J. Beyhum, 1952.
Shaw, Wendy. 'Ottoman Photography of the Late Nineteenth Century: An 'Innocent' Modernism?' *History of Photography* 33, no. 1 (2009): 80–93.
Sheehi, Stephen. *The Arab Imago: A Social History of Portrait Photography, 1860–1910*. Princeton: Princeton University Press, 2016.
Thompson, Elizabeth. *Colonial Citizens: Republican Rights, Paternal Privilege, and Gender in French Syria and Lebanon*. New York: Columbia University Press, 2000.
Van Leeuwen, Richard. *Notables and Clergy in Mount Lebanon: the Khazin Sheikhs and the Maronite Church, 1736–1840*. Leiden: E.J. Brill, 1994.
Watenpaugh, Keith D. *Being Modern in the Middle East: Revolution, Nationalism, Colonialism, and the Arab Middle Class*. Princeton: Princeton University Press, 2006.
West, Nancy M. *Kodak and the Lens of Nostalgia*. Charlottesville: University Press of Virginia, 2000.
Woodward, Michelle L. 'Between Orientalist Clichés and Images of Modernization'. *History of Photography* 27, no. 4 (2003): 363–74.

Zeidan, Joseph T. *Arab Women Novelists: The Formative Years and Beyond*. Albany: State University of New York Press, 1995.
Zeineddin, Nazira. *Al-Sufur wa al hijab*. Edited by Buthayna Sha'ban. Damascus: Dar al-mada, [1929] 1998.
Zeineddin, Nazira. *Al-Fatat wa al-shuyukh*. Edited by Buthayna Sha'ban. Damascus: Dar Al-mada, [1928] 1998.

6

Porous boundaries: The 'local' and the 'foreign' in Cairo's vibrant francophone cultural scene (1919–39)

Hussam R. Ahmed

In his book *La Langue française dans le monde* (1936), Franck Schoell described the situation of the French language around the world. In a section devoted to the Levant, where he believed French occupied 'a special place', he devoted the larger part of the chapter to Egypt, noting, despite his general pessimism about the receding influence of the French language globally, how a set of circumstances 'hardly found anywhere else' rendered the situation of the French language in Egypt very favourable.[1] He concluded that 'among the countries of the Near East where French is used as a language of culture, Egypt undoubtedly occupies the first place'.[2] It is striking that Schoell's study gave such weight to Egypt at the height of the French Mandate in Lebanon and Syria, especially given France's legacy in Lebanon.[3]

Drawing on Egyptian francophone periodicals from the 1920s and 1930s and reports from the French Ministry of Foreign Affairs (AMAE), this chapter explores the 'special place' that the French language and culture occupied in Egypt prior to the country's full independence. It focuses on the French-speaking cultural scene during the interwar period, when Cairo saw a proliferation of francophone literary and artistic circles whose lectures and exhibitions quickly became fashionable society events. University professors, state officials, local artists and writers, and foreign intellectuals visiting the country gave talks and discussed topics of general interest. Photographs of these events, information on the speakers and sometimes full transcriptions of the lectures duly appeared in the city's French-language journals and magazines.

The crowd that animated this scene reflected the diversity of Egypt's urban centres before the 1960s. They were men and women of various ethnic origins: Egyptians, Greeks, Italians, Syro-Lebanese, French, Maltese and Armenians, usually born in Egypt and educated in its missionary and secular French schools or in community schools that paid special attention to teaching French, such as some Jewish schools. These French speakers regularly attended cultural gatherings and proudly referred to themselves, and were described in the city's French press, as the 'country's intellectual elite'.[4] They used this vibrant scene as a space not only to celebrate French culture and entertain visiting intellectuals but also to present and discuss their own artistic and literary work.

Yet, despite this scene's ethnic diversity and choice of language, scholars have struggled with categorizing its writers and their work as either 'local' or 'foreign'. Many of these francophone writers and artists were born to families that had lived in Egypt for two or three generations, and their work reflected on their lives and experiences in the country. They were most comfortable in an Egyptian dialect of French that had developed over several decades and were conscious that someone visiting from Metropolitan France would not understand many of the words and expressions that they used. To add to the complexity of this scene, it was animated and frequented by Egyptian officials, professors, students and other intellectuals who wrote primarily in Arabic but who were also fluent in French, like Taha Husayn, Khalil Mutran and Mustafa 'Abd al-Raziq.[5]

This chapter provides a survey of some of these francophone literary groups and salons, and an account of their gatherings, attendees and the topics they discussed. It then situates this local cultural scene within the larger history of the Egyptian francophonie, which remains, according to the French literary scholar Daniel Lançon, largely unknown (*mal connue*) to French and Egyptians alike.[6] In their meetings, articles and books, French speakers evoked an enduring Franco-Egyptian friendship which they traced back to Napoleon's campaign of 1798. In this well-known and now critiqued paradigm, contact with France inspired Muhammad Ali to hire French experts to help him create new, modern institutions.[7] French speakers in Egypt saw their thriving local francophone cultural scene as a product of this friendship and of their profound attachment to French language and culture, which they believed had played a major role in the creation of modern Egypt.

Deeper political and economic conditions were necessary to make this cultural scene possible, and this chapter shows that without fiscal and legal privileges granted to foreigners by the Capitulations, France could not have played such an important cultural role in Egypt. Under these extraterritorial privileges, European communities in Egypt were allowed to build and maintain their own schools. The French government actively supported the development of a large network of missionary and secular schools which taught French curricula without interference from the Egyptian government. Moreover, unlike other community schools in Egypt, French schools were keen to recruit students from various ethnic and religious backgrounds. The French authorities were particularly happy that most Egyptian decision makers and members of the royal family were graduates of their schools and professed a profound attachment to French culture.[8] Furthermore, the Capitulations made commerce, justice and the press important French-speaking spheres of influence. These developments took place against the backdrop of an ongoing British occupation and a traditional Franco-British rivalry, which rid the French language of suspicion of collaboration with the occupying power.

The French language in Egypt: A language of culture

Societies and institutions operating partially or entirely in French existed well before the francophone literary and artistic circles of the interwar period. The Institut d'Égypte (founded by Bonaparte in 1798), the Société de géographie d'Égypte (1875), the Institut français d'archéologie orientale (IFAO) (1880) and the Ecole française de droit (1891) were among the most famous. From 1920, these societies included the Union des professeurs français d'Égypte, created to develop French influence through teaching and to defend the interests of French teachers working in Egypt. In 1929, the Union published a yearbook, instructing French teachers in the country in the history of these organizations and asserting that they were the result of Napoleon's expedition and Muhammad Ali's reforms.[9] It highlighted the fact that, since Muhammad Ali's time, France had been the destination of choice for Egyptians who sought a modern European education: educational missions to France had started in 1826, and the Military Mission in Paris was founded in 1844. The yearbook mentioned many of those Egyptians who later returned to their country to occupy leading positions in politics and administration. French experts, too, made Egypt their home, such as Clot Bey, who created Egypt's first modern School of Medicine in 1827, which was run by French directors until 1883.[10]

While the yearbook reads like propaganda for French cultural influence in Egypt, some Egyptian officials at the time also gave considerable weight to cultural relations between Egypt and France. In 1931, the Egyptian Consul to Marseille spoke before the Committee for International Relations in the city: he emphasized the potential of Egypt's economy and how 'the intellectual ties' binding Egypt and France were important in solidifying commercial and economic links between the two countries. His examples included the increasing number of Egyptian students seeking education in France and the numerous French teachers in Egypt. Addressing the French audience, the consul stressed that 'almost all men who have distinguished themselves in our country have received their education in your faculties'.[11]

One important manifestation of this thriving French culture was the local French press. The yearbook referred to an interview with Henri de Jouvenel, former editor-in-chief of the Parisian daily *Le Matin* and French High Commissioner in Beirut in 1925–6, in which he expressed surprise at this flourishing media, saying that compared to other French journals outside France, those of Egypt 'are truly superior on every level: presentation, writing, information and circulation'.[12] Again, the yearbook traced this lively press back to Napoleon, who had brought a printing press to Egypt, and described *Le Courrier de l'Égypte* and *La Décade Égyptienne*, published in 1798, as 'the dean of all the Egyptian press, regardless of language'.[13] The yearbook's overall message not only emphasized France's cultural influence but also claimed that Egypt owed its modern progress to France.

At the time the yearbook was published, Cairo had five French dailies: *La Bourse égyptienne*, *Le Journal du Caire*, *La Liberté*, *L'Information* and *La Patrie*. There were also two in Alexandria: *La Bourse égyptienne* and *La Réforme*. These dailies had average circulation figures of between three thousand and ten thousand copies, and used the latest linotype printing machines. There were also prestigious reviews like *La Semaine égyptienne*, *Le Flambeau*, *Orient*, *Le Magazine égyptien*, *La Revue Médicale*, *La Gazette des Tribunaux Mixtes* and *L'Égypte Contemporaine*.[14] Equally important to the yearbook's authors and their claims to French cultural influence in Egypt was the Egyptian public, described as 'demanding, well-informed, and for whom French has become the language of culture and expression'.[15]

Francophone circles and salons

During the interwar period, many of these francophone dailies and magazines focussed their attention on a newly proliferating cultural scene that was gaining popularity among Egypt's French speakers. In 1931, for example, the journalist and literary critic Robert Blum wrote a series of articles in *Images* on the 'Mode des conférences', commenting on these new society events.[16] He stated that lectures had previously been rare in Cairo and while people discussed a lot, this usually took place in private salons:

> Now, we hardly talk in salons any more. As for lectures, there are so many that an amateur no longer knows which ones to choose. He is claimed left and right, in Heliopolis and in Giza, in the Continental Hotel and at al-Diafa, at the Union universelle de la jeunesse juive, at the Centre d'études hébraïque, and at the Société de Géographie. … In barely a week, the auditor who does not miss a lecture has had a chance to hear about the United States, the 'ransom of the machine age', young men and women, Jewish leaders, fictional biographies, French authors in Egypt, and psychoanalysis.[17]

Blum made an immediate connection between the talks offered by these new groups and the tradition of public lectures which the Egyptian University had started upon its inauguration in 1908.[18] University lectures were initially open to the general public, and between 1909 and 1912, the women's section of the university offered public lectures in Arabic and French that quickly became popular among society ladies.[19] The link between the university and these groups continued as faculty deans, university professors and students were regularly invited to give talks or attend the events organized by francophone circles.

With famous speakers, large turnouts and high society involved, periodicals like the popular francophone weekly *Images* (1929–69), published by the iconic house Dar al-Hilal, rushed to celebrate this new fashion.[20] It became customary for *Images* and other francophone journals to announce the start of the cultural season in the autumn and report on activities each week. Although some groups received more attention than others, *Images* usually announced the name of the speaker and the topic of discussion a week in advance, and then reported on the event, often with photographs, in the following issue. Certain clichés became standard in these laudatory reports. It was usually the 'intellectual elite', or 'all of Cairo's elite', or 'all the Egyptian and European elites', who celebrated the speaker, followed by a list of attendees. Words of praise for the lecturer and organizers were common: it was usually a 'brilliant gathering', 'so popular', 'the hall was full', 'some had to remain standing' and so on. Some lectures were transcribed in *Images* and other periodicals and were published more regularly from 1936 onwards in the *Revue des conférences françaises en Orient* (1936–51), which fully transcribed the four or five most successful lectures of the month.

Prominent literati *de passage* in Cairo were celebrated in these events, boasting modern Cairo's growing reputation on the intellectual map and reflecting positively on the city's intellectual elite, who were proud to receive important guests, engage with their ideas and introduce them to local thinkers and intellectuals. The list boasted French writers like André Maurois (1885–1967), Reynaldo Hahn (1874–1947) and Claude Aveline (1901–1992), but also included Thomas Mann (1875–1955), Filippo Marinetti (1876–1944) and Emil Ludwig (1881–1948). These literary groups included Les Amis de la culture française en Égypte (ACFE), al-Diafa, the Essayistes and the Association des écrivains d'Égypte d'expression française.

Under the patronage of Muhammad Ali's great grandson, Prince Haidar Fazil, and Henri Gaillard, the Minister of France in Cairo, ACFE was created in 1925 by Frenchman Morik Brin (1891–1951), who taught philosophy at the Egyptian University. The group started with seven members; twenty years later, membership was nearly four hundred.[21] In *Images*, Brin stressed what would resonate with his audience: he declared ACFE to be a society of elites, dedicated to developing friendship between France and all those living in Egypt, and claimed that the universality of French culture would help the association achieve this objective. According to Brin, French missionary and secular schools operating in Egypt, like the Jesuit schools and French Lycées, already demonstrated the success of that universality, attracting students from all communities. He referred to a 'work of bonding' to be carried out in the form of lectures dedicated to French culture and avoiding divisive political discussions. The association's objectives were

> to multiply between the elites of two people, who are already predisposed by all sorts of affinities to a mutual understanding, the opportunities to better know one another and to appreciate one another. Without direct propaganda for the French language and without political preoccupations, we simply want to develop the friendly relations between Egyptians and French of Egypt and to bring together, no matter the nationality, religious or political opinions, all those who live in this hospitable country and who mutually recognize these cultural affinities.[22]

In addition to lectures, the association organized exhibitions, film screenings and tea receptions. These events continued until Brin returned to France in 1945; the association ceased its activities a few years later.[23]

Another active group, the Essayistes, was founded in 1928 by young intellectuals Albert Saltiel, Jules Levi and Gabriel Boctor; its lectures, usually followed by musical recitals, seem to have been particularly popular.[24] The group published a bulletin, *Un Effort*, which in addition to articles by members also included the first writings of surrealist poet Georges Henein and the romantic poems of Ahmad Rassim.[25] In 1931, the Essayistes founded a library, which they opened to the public for a monthly subscription, using the funds raised to acquire new books.[26] Like ACFE, they received significant coverage from *Images*, another indication of their popularity. The group stopped its activities in 1939.[27]

Two society women particularly visible in this francophone cultural scene were Amy Kher and Nelly Zananiri. Born in 1897 in Mansura to a Lebanese father and an English mother, Kher received her education at the French missionary school before marrying Georges Kher and moving to Cairo. She wrote articles supportive of the feminist movement and published several novels – *Salma et son village*, *Remous à Bab Touma*, *Mes soeurs* and *Les Sycomores* – and poetry collections.[28] She regularly attended events organized by francophone literary circles, where she sometimes gave lectures.

Yet Amy Kher is perhaps best remembered for having held one of the most important private francophone salons in Cairo in the 1930s.[29] Starting in the late 1920s and continuing for about ten years, she hosted a salon, usually twice a month, for writers, artists and intellectuals.[30] Besides Egypt's francophone writers, like Jean Moscatelli and Robert Blum, who found in Kher's salon an opportunity to discuss and present their work, important regulars included Taha Husayn.[31] In one of Kher's gatherings, Edgard Gallad, editor-in-chief of the Egyptian *La Liberté*, recited verse by Fernand Leprette, the general inspector of French language in the Ministry of Public Instruction.[32] The poet Khalil Mutran was once invited to read some of his poems in Arabic, and *Images* described how 'the success of the sensitive poet became very lively, with roaring applause when he translated into French the beautiful Kabyle legend of love and war'.[33] Kher gave tea receptions in honour of writers visiting Cairo, like the French Claude Aveline, who was also received at al-Diafa and at the Essayistes.[34] The atmosphere in Kher's salon had 'a very particular charm', according to *Images*:

> With a cup of tea, around a table covered with nice things, a pleasant conversation with joyous laughs; Madame Kher receives her guests with tact and grace, putting everyone in such a good mood that it would be impossible to keep a morose face.[35]

Kher was also on the committee of the Société de musique d'Égypte, which organized musical afternoons for members of the group to perform in an intimate circle, with the self-declared goal of 'refining musical taste in the city'.[36]

Equally active in this francophone scene was the Alexandrian Nelly Zananiri. Born in 1897 to a family of Syrian origin established in Egypt since the eighteenth century,[37] Zananiri was educated in Alexandria at the prestigious Notre-Dame de Sion school, and the family used French at home.[38] She was active in feminist circles and was an intimate friend of Ceza Nabarawi, the well-known feminist.[39] In December 1945, she opened an art gallery, Aladin, in downtown Cairo, which she used for her salons.[40] She held another, more private, salon to discuss literature and politics until the regime change in 1952.[41] In addition to several poetry collections, she published a novel, *Vierges d'Orient*, in 1922.[42] In 1938, she was awarded the Prix Edgar Allan Poe in France for the best francophone book of the year, for her poetry collection *A midi sous le soleil torride*.[43]

Much of the information we have on Zananiri's involvement in the francophone scene comes from her participation in other associations, especially as secretary of al-Diafa, which she founded in 1929.[44] Over a period of four years, al-Diafa welcomed important literary figures visiting Cairo by putting them in touch with the country's intellectuals, and organized lectures and other activities. On 29 December 1929, *Images* reported the inauguration of the circle, using clichés such as a 'soirée of the highest elegance' that united the 'intellectual elite'.[45] Zananiri announced that she wanted al-Diafa to establish links between Egyptian and foreign intellectuals, a role she believed was the duty of a country's elite.[46]

Nelly Zananiri was also involved with l'Association des écrivains d'Égypte d'expression française, founded in 1929 by Robert Blum and Elian Finbert, with the goal of 'creating a link of solidarity between francophone writers living in Egypt and to make Egypt better known abroad'.[47] Feeling that Egyptian authors writing in French needed encouragement and support, the group created an annual literary prize for a work of verse or prose 'of Egyptian inspiration'.[48] They raised money to help young authors get their work published and created a literary review, *Le Flambeau*, devoted 'to the literary and artistic intellectual movement in the renewed (*renaissante*) Egypt'.[49] In 1931, the group organized the first book fair devoted to works by francophone Egyptian writers. The event was well received, and *Images* welcomed the richness of the francophone literary production and the quality of the publications.[50] In recognition of this vibrant francophone scene, a branch of the Association internationale des écrivains de langue française opened in Cairo in June 1936, with Nelly Zananiri as vice president.[51] Its mouthpiece was the prestigious *Revue du Caire*, established and edited by Muhammad Zulficar in 1938, which until 1961 published articles by prominent writers: Nelly Zananiri, Taha Husayn, Out el Kouloub, Ahmad Rassim, Marie Cavadia, Georges Anawati and others.[52]

The French government saw this lively scene as proof of its successful policy of funding secular and missionary schools in Egypt, as well as other schools in which French was the language of instruction.[53] Members of the French Legation attended the events, and reports to Paris spoke highly of the francophone intellectual activities taking place in Cairo and Alexandria. These reports indicate how closely the government was following these events, at times even fearing that the number of lectures and their growing popularity could trigger negative reactions from the British authorities.[54] The Franco-British rivalry over cultural influence in Egypt was not new. Well into the 1920s, Britain and France were considered to be the 'legitimate' providers of modern education in Egypt,[55] and this rivalry played out at the university, with European powers fighting over faculty deanships and chairs.[56]

Nevertheless, in general, official French reports reflected genuine pride in this cultural scene. In 1946, the Service d'information et de presse indicated that French was the second language in Egypt after Arabic, that it was the language of the Egyptian elite and the link that bound together the country's various communities.[57] That this elite included very few French nationals was further proof of the respect and prestige the French language and culture enjoyed:

> This is an elite composed of various nationalities, for whom French is endowed with all the attributes of a mother tongue. This elite, which occupies the highest positions in the country, has already provided a multitude of the most remarkable artists, thinkers and writers. They would be in the front row of any intellectual assembly in continental France.[58]

In line with its support for French education in Egypt, and to promote this cultural scene further, the French government honoured some of the key figures. In 1933, the French Republic awarded Amy Kher the décoration d'Officier d'Académie, and *Images* reported on an intimate ceremony at the French Legation at which Henri Gaillard, the

French Minister in Cairo, presented the award. The decoration, according to *Images*, recognized her role in promoting French literature in Egypt and her talents as a writer, poet and lecturer:

> As a lecturer, Madame Amy Kher has conquered her public with the elegance of her words and the lively interest in her topics of choice. The perfect society lady, she has formed a 'salon' where personalities from the literary and artistic world visiting Cairo could find themselves with the intellectual and literary world of our city.[59]

Kher was one of many of the francophone writers and poets who received decorations from France, such as the poet Ahmad Rassim, who received the Légion d'honneur in 1937, and Stavros Stavrinos, editor of the *La Semaine égyptienne,* who received the Médaille de la langue française from the Académie Française a year later.[60]

An insight into Cairo's cosmopolitan society

The press coverage of francophone cultural events, especially by *Images*, has left a detailed record of this social scene. The documentation reads like a *Who's Who* of Cairo's high society, including photographs and lists of names, professions and honorific titles of those constantly referred to as the city's elite. These lists give us a sense of the social networks extant within this society of elites. The same names appear at different events, sometimes on the same day. In 1932, for example, *Images* reported that guests left a tea reception and piano recital at Amy Kher's only to regroup at al-Diafa for a lecture.[61] The organizers of the different groups also knew each other. For example, the Association des écrivains d'Égypte d'expression française often organized its meetings or exhibitions at the premises of al-Diafa or the Essayistes.[62]

The existence of such detailed reports shows the importance of these events, enhanced by the presence of state officials from the Egyptian government and the foreign delegations in Cairo. Nonetheless, certain events seem to have attracted more official attention than others. When the ACFE organized a talk by the journalist Edgard Gallad on the works of the Prince of Poets, Ahmad Shawqi, the hall was full of local dignitaries, faculty deans and European ambassadors.[63] Similarly, a high-profile crowd attended the inauguration of al-Diafa in 1929 where

> the intellectual elite of Cairo found itself with the intellectual elite of several European nations in the presence of members of the *Association littéraire et artistique internationale*, in Egypt for their 37th congress.[64]

The list included the French, Greek, Italian, Dutch, Yugoslav and Swiss delegates in Cairo, the leader of the futurist movement Filippo Marinetti, Taha Husayn and his French wife, the founder of the Société des amis des beaux-arts du Caire and future President of the Egyptian Senate (1938–42) Muhammad Mahmud Khalil and his

French wife, Amy Kher and her husband, Emile and Shukry Zaydan (the sons of Jurji Zaydan and owners of Dar al-Hilal), Nabarawi, Stavrinos and others.[65]

Intellectuals were conscious of this new literary fashion, and some, like Robert Blum, commented on it. With humour, he praised the lecturers but stressed the importance of the art of performance necessary to capture the audience's attention. A good speaker, Blum insisted, must master the right oratorial skills and learn the correct formulas when addressing Cairo's dignitaries. While he praised those who paid attention to the lecturers and took assiduous notes, he scorned those who saw the lectures only as an occasion to see and be seen. Blum's account leaves no doubt that these were high-society events, which newcomers found intimidating. He described the young journalist sent by his magazine to cover these lectures and how unsure he was of himself at first. Only after he had perfected the right techniques and acquired the appropriate social graces could the journalist

> enter the hall with authority, instal himself in his *fauteuil* without asking anybody, greet this minister or that archbishop, and stand up to gently kiss the hand of a society lady who rebukes him for having missed her last *bridge dansant*.[66]

Intellectual interests

The majority of founders and organizers of these events were writers and journalists educated in French schools in Egypt, and the influence of French education was evident in their choice of topics.[67] Most lectures had to do with France, its history, literature and institutions, and general discussions of art, music, dance and travel. There were also lectures on ancient Egyptian history and an effort to celebrate some key Egyptian artists and intellectuals, especially local francophone writers. Those invited to speak were usually academics, local writers and journalists, or foreign intellectuals visiting Egypt.

The lectures organized by the ACFE between 1926 and 1943 give an indication of the intellectual interests of these groups. There were poetry readings by French and Egyptian poets and lectures on English literature, impressionism, cubism, futurism and even cosmetic surgery. Out of 158 talks given in this period, sixty-eight were on literary topics, fifteen on history, nineteen on philosophy and sociology, twenty on art, theatre and music, nine each on science and travel, and two on women.[68] French literature figured highly on the list, with talks on Anatole France, Collette, La Fontaine, Rimbaud, Molière, Lamartine, Baudelaire, Verlaine and others. Topics included 'La Décadence de l'hellénisme en Égypte', 'Les Voyageurs français en Égypte', 'La Sculpture et les arts mineurs de l'Égypte ancienne' and 'Hommage à Sarah Bernhardt'. The ACFE also organized over twenty art exhibitions showing works of Egyptian and non-Egyptian painters and sculptors.[69]

Despite a bias towards French topics, Egypt figured significantly with lectures on ancient Egypt, famous travellers who visited the country, Egyptian folklore, the relationship between Egypt and Europe, and contemporary Arabic literature. The

Essayistes dedicated an issue of *Un Effort* to Egypt's iconic sculptor Mahmud Mukhtar and organized a meeting in honour of his memory.[70] They also arranged a *grande soirée* for the poet Ahmed Shawqi, presided over by Hilmi 'Isa, the Minister of Public Instruction.[71] In May 1931, in what *Images* considered a 'poetic festival', al-Diafa organized a celebration and discussion of the works of 'the greatest three Arab poets' Ahmad Shawqi, Hafiz Ibrahim and Khalil Mutran.[72] Although there were frequent recitals of European classical music, Egyptian music was played as well. On a special occasion when al-Diafa hosted members of the 10th Congrès de la presse latine, Um Kulthum was 'a great and charming attraction'.[73]

In celebration of twenty years of continuous activity of the ACFE, the poet Joseph Ascar-Nahas delivered a lecture in which he reiterated the association's objectives and accomplishments, and celebrated the sociocultural tradition that it propagated. The Egyptian elite, according to Ascar-Nahas, went beyond a simple bonding with France to feel 'one with French culture'. He insisted that identification with French culture did not compromise one's relationship with one's own country; on the contrary, it doubled the possibilities. He praised the ACFE for having successfully forged a community of elites – journalists, professors and students, high society ladies and senior civil servants – who came to lectures and socialized at tea parties. Their faces, he went on, became familiar and they were missed when they did not show up. The association created an 'atmosphere of intimacy and solidarity', a 'great work of French culture'.[74] After Ascar-Nahas's lecture, two hundred guests attended a sumptuous banquet at Groppi's and then a gala at the Royal Opera House to mark the occasion.[75] With the recent liberation of France and the end of the Second World War, *Images* remarked how 'everywhere [at the banquet] was what seemed to be a hymn to a newly born France, home to all eclectics of the world'.[76]

A problematic 'Egyptianness'

According to Irène Fenoglio, Ascar-Nahas was one of three hundred francophone authors in Egypt who left around one thousand literary works between 1850 and 1950.[77] Recently, this literature has attracted scholarly attention, with many of its authors being rediscovered and their works studied and republished.[78] Some scholars have recognized the specificity of this Egyptian francophone literature and its resistance to easy classification. In her recent work on francophone literature of the Middle East, Zahida Darwiche Jabbour admits that defining Egyptian francophone literature is problematic. She argues that if such literature can be identified as the product of a francophonie that resulted from Egypt's cosmopolitanism, the identity of its authors remains paradoxical. Although many of these authors held non-Egyptian nationality, they were born in Egypt of families who had lived there for generations. They made their careers in Egypt, and even when they left, she believes, their writings remain 'strongly tied to Egypt's sociocultural reality'.[79] Jean-Jacques Luthi, who interviewed many of these authors, believes that the question of belonging and identity was not at the heart of their concerns, even when their writings evoke their Egyptian origins.[80] Of the literature itself and the ideas and feelings it expressed, Fenoglio concludes that it 'belongs in every respect to the Egyptian culture as a whole (*ensemble culturel égyptien*), which it enriched and on which it still has an effect'. These writers, she argues, wrote in French neither to break away from their original culture nor to express feelings of nostalgia or exile; they wrote simply to express themselves.[81] Like Ascar-Nahas in his lecture, the poet and novelist Andrée Chédid asserted that she never felt she *had* to adopt the French language: 'I never had the impression that I was turning myself away from an identity of birth, but on the contrary to have found it through another means of communication.'[82]

The Egyptian francophone authors and critics in question were aware of the particularity of their situation and debated some of the same questions. Were there specific criteria that defined who was Egyptian and who was not? When discussing literature, did the origin of the author matter? In the 1950s, Jean Moscatelli, editor-in-chief of *Images*, argued that the 'Egyptianness' of Egypt's francophone literature depended not on the origin of its authors but on its 'sensibility', defined as 'a certain vision of the world conditioned by Egypt; its land, its history, its culture'.[83] Even the Dean of Arabic Literature, Taha Husayn, seemed unsure what to think of this French output. In his review of *L'Égypte dans mon miroir*, by the Egyptian francophone writer Jeanne Arcache, Husayn complimented the writer on her command of the French language, which, according to him, made it hard to believe that French was not her mother tongue. There were many writers like Arcache in Egypt, Husayn went on, describing them as Egyptians who were totally proficient in French and used it in literary creation. 'I do not know if this is good or bad', he admitted, viewing these writers as honest translators of how Egyptians thought and felt, and 'successful Egyptian ambassadors'. Yet, by writing in French, they deprived their fellow Egyptians and the Arabic language itself of their creativity.[84] Indeed, he found Arcache's book so valuable and so full of admirable Egyptian imagery that he could not but feel sorry that most Egyptians would not be able to share his enjoyment of it.[85] Writing in 1935, Husayn blamed the state for not having protected the Arabic language, for not teaching it properly and for having failed to build schools, forcing parents to send their children to foreign schools.[86]

Adding to the specificity of this cultural scene and its literature were the changes the French language itself underwent in Egypt. In his study of Egyptian spoken French, Luthi argued that this was a dialect of its own, much like Algerian or Quebecois French, deeply marked by Egypt's polyglot urban society.[87] As a result of daily interaction, many words and expressions, mainly from Arabic and Turkish, but also Italian, Greek and Armenian, infiltrated the 'official' French which students learned at school.[88] He traced the features of this dialect in the francophone press and other written works to compile a list of approximately one thousand words, expressions and other lexical and grammatical innovations.[89] More importantly, he argued that one could speak of a French specific to Egypt, where local French speakers were conscious that they would not be fully understood except within their locale or social group and that their conversation would be obscure to someone from Metropolitan France.[90]

Writer Robert Solé distinguishes several levels of fluency in French. Between the refined French spoken in the closed circle of the Alexandrian Municipal Council and the impromptu French the man in the street had learned from his neighbours, Solé says there was the French of the French schools. Ethnic origin, he goes on, had some impact on the students' pronunciation – *u* became an *ou* with Italians and an *i* with Arabophones, while the *ch* tended to slip to an *s* with the Greeks – yet all students of the main French schools ended up having the same *Egyptian* accent:

> It is a charming talk, a bit musical. The stress is not on the same syllables as in France. When enumerating, the final vowels are elongated for more expressivity: 'Une femme riiche, qui a une autoo, une villaa, et cii et caa …' Gestures readily accompany the voice. The r's are rolled, as the grasseyement [the Parisian way of pronouncing the r from the back of the throat] is used as a sign of affection. *On* is often pronounced *en*; *ai* becomes *é*: 'en va boire du lé'.[91]

Visitors to big Egyptian cities, like Franck Schoell, would have met French speakers of various religions and ethnic origins. Yet this does not mean they formed a homogeneous group. Frédéric Abécassis highlights an important class dimension according to which elites from various ethnicities went to secular lycées or to the Jesuit schools, while the middle and lower-middle classes often sent their children to community schools such as the Jewish, Greek and Italian schools, in which French was also taught. Secondary Catholic schools, like the Frères des Ecoles chrétiennes, did not admit students on scholarships into 'paying' schools but to schools in poorer neighbourhoods financed by money from the paying schools. Likewise, as many Jews and Greek Orthodox preferred secular lycées to Catholic schools, he argues that different religions did not exactly mix in French schools either.[92]

France's 'special place'

Cairo's francophone cultural scene celebrated what francophone journals and magazines constantly referred to as 'the special relationship' that bound modern Egypt and France. Egyptian historian and editor of the *Cahier d'histoire égyptienne*, Jacques Tagher (1918–1952), for example, wrote in *Images* that 'it was by the mind and heart that France conquered Egypt'. This shifted focus from Napoleon's soldiers to his scientists; Tagher listed French doctors and engineers who had put their expertise at the service of Egypt and its rulers since 1798, such as Clot Bey and de Cérisy.[93] Even on the political level, ardent nationalists Sa'd Zaghlul and Mustafa Kamil repeatedly invoked the 'special relationship' between Egypt and France, especially when they appealed for French support against the British.[94]

Ironically, the British occupation of 1882 only increased French cultural influence as it spared France a direct colonial role in Egypt and allowed the French to focus their influence on economy and culture. This situation created a distinction between francophone Egyptian intellectuals and those from the French colonies, as the latter were condemned to 'invent the myth of a dual France, the colonizing, reactionary and racist France … and the noble France, mother of art and literature'.[95] The Egyptians, however, could seek 'Parisian recognition' without compromising their political demands. 'It was striking', Richard Jacquemond comments, 'to see the principal Egyptian writers of

French expression slip into the mould of that language, naturally, without remorse or ulterior motives.'[96] In a similar vein, Gilles Perrault, in his biography of Egyptian Jewish communist leader Henri Curiel, remarks that Francophilia in Egypt became a way of affirming one's Anglophobia.[97]

While France's long-standing legacy in Egypt and its traditional rivalry with the country's occupier legitimized the usage of French in certain circles and allowed this local cultural scene to thrive with a clear conscience, as Jacquemond implies, there was more to the story. Structural political and economic factors made such developments possible. At the fore were the extraterritorial fiscal and legal privileges granted to citizens of European countries in Egypt, known as the Capitulations, which boosted French influence in the country. These privileges, coupled with the strong French influence before 1882, allowed French investments to grow even after the British occupation, surpassing those of the occupier.[98] In his detailed study of economic relations between Egypt and France from 1882 to 1914, Samir Saul refers to an inquiry by the Quai d'Orsay in 1902 which revealed that out of sixty-two countries, Egypt ranked sixth in terms of French capital investments. The Suez Canal Company, the sugar refineries, the water and gas companies, banks, insurance companies and branches of Parisian department stores operating in Cairo and Alexandria all used French in their transactions.[99]

The Mixed Courts, established in 1875, were also tied to capitulatory privileges, making justice another French-language sphere of influence. Although Arabic, English, Italian and French were authorized languages in court, French dominated defence speeches and official documents, especially with the adoption of the Code Napoleon, simplified and adapted to Egypt.[100] Jacques d'Aumale, who represented France in Cairo between the wars, commented approvingly on a situation in which

> French codes and French law manuals had become the instruments of all judges, making knowledge of French indispensable. … A lawyer would be taking a risk if he did not make his case in French. French language, French thought and French law dominated.[101]

Lawyers and magistrates were trained at the École française de droit in Cairo, or at the Faculty of Law at the Egyptian University. The former, founded in 1890, was funded entirely by the Quai d'Orsay and dispensed degrees in law from the Sorbonne.[102]

The Capitulations gave the French and other communities the right to run their schools without interference from the Egyptian government. By the 1930s, there were 400 foreign schools in Egypt, with a population of about 75,000 pupils, or 25 per cent of all students in Egypt.[103] Almost half of these were French missionary and secular schools.[104] Such schools filled a significant void in educational facilities following the bankruptcy of the Egyptian state and the British occupation in 1882, which cut the annual education budget.[105] Even after nominal independence in 1922, when the Egyptian government started investing in schools again, the reputation and quality of French schools continued to attract Egyptian students. Until the beginning of the Second World War, the curricula in most French schools were the same as those taught in France.[106] Solé points out that boys were sometimes taught Arabic, but in the girls' schools, 'Arabic remained a foreign language, and simply ignored'.[107] At the time,

Ascar-Nahas found this alarming and warned that a situation in which francophone students knew more about France than their own country had to change.[108] The Ministry of Public Instruction continued to push for more government inspection of these schools and for the teaching of Arabic and Islam.[109] French Catholic schools were the most resistant to these changes, and it was not until 1948 that it became forbidden to teach students a religion that was not theirs – even if the parents agreed – while in 1953 teaching Islam to Muslim students became obligatory.[110]

With the impending end of the Capitulations, records from the Ministry of Foreign Affairs show the French clearly understood that the success of their school system depended almost entirely on the freedom their schools enjoyed. They were anxious over the fate of the schools and of the overall status of French cultural influence. Official reports indicate an awareness of escalating nationalist criticism of what one described as the 'excessive foreign character' of the French educational system in Egypt. In the late 1940s, the French Embassy repeatedly pushed for a new cultural agreement to guarantee the future of French schools in Egypt, admitting that with the expiry of the Capitulations in 1949, their mere existence depended entirely on the 'good will of the Egyptian government'.[111]

Conclusion

Until the end of the Capitulations, French language and culture occupied an exceptional place in Egypt. Unlike the more complex situation in French colonies, French-speaking circles in Egypt saw the language as a mark of distinction, as a choice not an imposition by an occupying power. They celebrated France as a friend whose culture and expertise had played an important role in the making of modern Egypt since 1798. The Franco-British rivalry encouraged French speakers to embrace the language and profess what often appears to have been an exaggerated attachment to France. Cairo's numerous francophone circles and salons in the interwar period developed as a space that brought a multi-ethnic community together to discuss works of art and literature, with local groups organizing lectures, exhibitions and tea receptions, and welcoming important foreign guests visiting the country.

Over several decades, Egypt's culturally rich francophonie developed its own dialect, sustained an active press and produced hundreds of literary works. The influence of French schools was not only evident in forging a powerful elite community but also in shaping the intellectual interests of francophone groups, which celebrated France and its culture. In their lectures, these French speakers discussed Egypt and its history and wrote about their local experiences and reflections in their literature. They did not necessarily see their francophonie as compromising their local culture or identity. As the first secretary general of the Organisation internationale de la Francophonie, Boutros Boutros-Ghali, explained, speaking French in Egypt at the time reflected a wish to be independent while remaining open to the world.[112] Despite the multi-ethnic background of these authors and their choice of language, it is difficult to ignore the local context that shaped their French acculturation. They described their literature as *littérature égyptienne d'expression française*, not as French literature.

Nevertheless, the celebration of French language and culture took place against the backdrop of capitulatory privileges that not only were legal and fiscal but also enabled the French to run their own schools and teach their own curricula without intervention from the Egyptian government. The French government and its representatives in Egypt actively supported this cultural influence and were particularly pleased with the francophone cultural scene of the interwar period. They saw it as testament to the success of their cultural diplomacy in Egypt, which reinforced their economic and legal influence and strengthened their ties to the country's elites. The French understood, however, that their influence in Egypt depended on the Capitulations, the end of which implied stronger Egyptian control over French educational establishments and the suspension of the Mixed Courts in 1949. French aggression against Egypt during the Suez Crisis a few years later dealt a heavy blow to the sense of moral superiority the French language enjoyed over English.[113] The special circumstances so favourable to the spread of French cultural influence in Egypt, which struck Schoell during his visit in the early 1930s, thus came to an end.

And yet the francophonie in Egypt continued beyond the era of the Capitulations and the departure of many of the country's French speakers in the 1950s and 1960s. In 1983, Egypt joined the Agence de coopération culturelle et technique, which later became the Organisation internationale de la Francophonie. At the time, Boutros-Ghali explained that even though French was now the third language in the country after Arabic and English, the 2 per cent of the population who spoke it made up more than a million people. Likewise, he claimed that the distribution figures of publications in French in Egypt were higher than in many francophone African countries.[114] Every year, thousands of Egyptian students go to French Catholic schools and to lycées that once belonged to the Mission laïque française. The IFAO attracts many researchers, and since 1968, the Centre d'études et de documentation économique, juridique et sociale (CEDEJ) has brought together scholars working on Egypt and the Near East. *Le Progrès Egyptien* has survived to this day, and *al-Ahram* created its French language weekly, *al-Ahram Hebdo*, in 1994. However, statistics and enduring institutions aside, when Boutros-Ghali evoked the memory of Egypt's former francophone writers, he immediately associated them with the 'special place' and 'vitality' that the French language and culture once enjoyed in Egypt.[115] The numerous francophone lectures, tea receptions and salons of the interwar period were an expression of that vitality, a vitality which does not yield easily to our present-day expectations of what is local and what is foreign.

Notes

1 Schoell, *La Langue française*, 228.
2 Ibid., 220.
3 For a recent work on the tension of writing Lebanese literature in French, see Hartman, *Native Tongue*.
4 E.g., *Images* 29 December 1929, 'Mondanités', 9.

5 Known as the 'Dean of Arabic Literature', Taha Husayn (1889–1973) was one of the most influential Egyptian intellectuals of the twentieth century and wrote dozens of literary classics and hundreds of articles. Khalil Mutran (1872–1949) was a Lebanese poet and journalist who spent most of his life in Egypt. Mustafa 'Abd al-Raziq (1885–1947) taught Islamic philosophy at the Egyptian University, was Minister of Religious Endowments and became Rector of al-Azhar in 1945.
6 Lançon, 'La France participée', 11.
7 Historians have refuted the idea of an Ottoman decline in Egypt to which the French expedition put an abrupt end, undermining the idea of a sharp rupture between the eighteenth and nineteenth centuries. See Raymond, *Artisans et commerçants*; Gran, *Islamic Roots*; and Hanna, *In Praise of Books*.
8 AMAE/Relations Culturelles 1945–1961/98. 1945–1947/ 'Note pour la Direction des Relations Culturelles a.s. influence française en Égypte', 24 January 1946.
9 Union des professeurs français d'Égypte, *L'Annuaire de l'enseignement français*, 9.
10 Ibid., 30–1.
11 The Egyptian National Archives/Abdin/0069-002327/ 'Aperçu sur les relations Franco-Égyptiennes: Conférence faite le 25 novembre 1931 au comité des relations internationales de Marseille par Mohamed Hamed, Consul de Sa Majesté le Roi d'Égypte à Marseille.'
12 Union des professeurs français d'Égypte, *L'Annuaire de l'enseignement français*, 57.
13 Ibid.
14 Ibid., 59. In 1938, there were two hundred Arabic periodicals published in Cairo and sixty-five in other languages, forty-four of them French. Fenoglio, 'Égyptianité et langue française', 21.
15 Union des professeurs français d'Égypte, *L'Annuaire de l'enseignement français*, 57.
16 Robert Blum (1903) was born in Tunis and moved to Egypt with his parents a year later; he was educated there and published several novels and plays. He immigrated to France in 1956, where he worked in commerce and literature until his death. See Luthi, *La Littérature d'expression française*, 244.
17 Blum, 'La Mode des conférences', *Images* 12 December 1931, 5.
18 Ibid.
19 Reid, *Cairo University*, 51–6.
20 Like its Arabic equivalent *al-Musawwar*, *Images* relied on illustrations, especially photographs, in its coverage. During the interwar period, its section Mondanités provided summaries of the booming cultural events and the social scene associated with them.
21 Brin, *L'Association des Amis*, 8.
22 Forzannes, 'Groupes intellectuels d'Égypte', *Images*, 28 May 1932, 10.
23 Luthi, *La Littérature d'expression française*, 35.
24 Gabriel Boctor (1909–1970) was a journalist and art critic. Besides the Essayistes, he was involved in the artistic group L'Atelier and worked for journals and magazines like *La Bourse égyptienne*, *La Semaine égyptienne* and *Images*. See Luthi, *La Littérature d'expression française*, 244.
25 Ibid.
26 *Images* 27 September 1931, 'Mondanités', 11.
27 Lançon, 'Fortune et infortune', 28.
28 Luthi, *La Littérature d'expression française*, 251–2.
29 Ibid., 252–3.
30 *Images* 22 November 1931, 'Mondanités', 11.

31 Moscatelli (1905–1965) was born and died in Cairo. He was a poet and one of the main figures of the Egyptian francophone scene. He held several editorial positions, including at *Images* and *La Semaine égyptienne*.
32 *Images* 22 November 1931, 'Mondanités', 11.
33 *Images* 22 December 1929, 'Mondanités', 42.
34 *Images* 26 March 1932, 'Mondanités', 12.
35 *Images* 10 December 1932, 'Mondanités', 9.
36 *Images* 12 December 1931, 'Mondanités', 10.
37 Nelly was the sister of poet and historian Gaston Zananiri (1904–1996) who studied at the École française de droit in Cairo and worked for the Ministry of Foreign Affairs in the 1940s. With Jean-Jacques Luthi and Auguste Viatte, he edited the *Dictionnaire général de la francophonie* and published his memoirs *Entre mer et désert*.
38 Luthi, *Entretiens*, 146.
39 *Images* 3 August 1930, 'Mondanités', 9. *L'Egyptienne*, the organ of the Egyptian Feminist Union, was also in French.
40 Luthi, *Entretiens*, 59.
41 Zananiri, *Entre mer et désert*, 28.
42 Luthi, *Entretiens*, 60.
43 Lançon, 'Fortune et infortune', 33–4.
44 Luthi, *Entretiens*, 59.
45 *Images*, 'L'Inauguration des nouveaux locaux du cercle al-Diafa: L'Intéressante conférence du Docteur Ali Pacha Ibrahim sur "Les Tapis d'Orient au XVII siècle" ', 23 November 1930, 4; *Images* 29 December 1929, 'Mondanités', 9.
46 *Images*, 'L'Inauguration du cercle al-Diafa', 29 December 1929, 17.
47 Luthi, *La Littérature d'expression française*, 36.
48 *Images*, 'La Vie littéraire', 12 December 1931, 7; and *Images* 19 December 1931, 'Mondanités', 10.
49 *Images* 28 May 1932, 'Mondanités', 14; and Lançon, 'Fortune et infortune', 25.
50 *Images*, 'La Vie littéraire', 12 December 1931, 7.
51 Lançon, 'Fortune et infortune', 34.
52 Other important groups continued to be active well into the fifties. These included: the Surrealist movement Art et liberté (1939), the Amitiés françaises (1944–56), the Société Anatole France (1949), the Société Romain Rolland (1951) and the Amis de René Guénon (1953). See Lançon, 'Fortune et infortune', 45–6.
53 Until 1936–7, the curricula, official exams and even the schedule of Jewish schools in Cairo were 'almost entirely French'. AMAE/Relation Culturelles/ 431/ 1948–1959/ 1948–51/'L'Enseignement du français dans les écoles de la communauté Israelite du Caire', 21 February 1948. For details of French funding of schools and educational institutions, see Abécassis, 'L'Enseignement étranger en Égypte et les élites locales', 234–41.
54 AMAE/K-Afrique-Égypte-1918–1940/ 34. Écoles et oeuvres françaises en Égypte-1925–1929/ 'Inconvénients des conférences trop nombreuses', 5 September 1929.
55 Abécassis, 'L'Enseignement étranger en Égypte et les élites locales', 231.
56 Reid, *Cairo University*, 37.
57 AMAE/Relations Culturelles 1945–1961/98. 1945–1947/ 'Note pour la Direction des Relations Culturelles a.s. influence française en Égypte', 24 January 1946.
58 Union des professeurs francais d'Égypte, *L'Annuaire de l'enseignement français*, 59.
59 *Images* 25 March 1933, 'Mondanités', 20.

60 Lançon, 'Fortune et infortune', 34. A poet who composed in French, Ahmad Rassim (1895–1958) studied at the École française de droit in Cairo and served as a diplomat and as Governor of Suez. See Luthi, *La Littérature d'expression française*, 256.
61 *Images* 9 January 1932, 'Mondanités', 11.
62 E.g. the association held its first book exhibition at al-Diafa's. *Images* 12 December 1931, 'La Vie littéraire', 7.
63 *Images* 17 December 1932, 'Mondanités', 8.
64 *Images* 29 December 1939, 'Mondanités', 9.
65 *Images* 29 December 1939, 'Mondanités', 9.
66 Blum, 'La Mode des conférences', *Images*, 19 December 1931, 17.
67 Luthi, *Entretiens*, 107.
68 Ascar-Nahas, 'Conférence sur les conférences', 14–5.
69 List from Brin, *L'Association des Amis*.
70 *Images* 31 March 1934, 'Mondanités', 8; and Images 28 April 1934, 'Mondanités', 6–7.
71 *Images* 31 December 1932, 'Mondanités', 8.
72 Lançon, 'Fortune et infortune', 28.
73 *Images* 9 January 1932, 'Mondanités', 11.
74 Ascar-Nahas, 'Conférence sur les conférences', 28.
75 Established in 1924, Groppi is a patisserie and tea room, once the place to be seen in Cairo. Ante Zielger describes it as 'a longtime center of attraction for the literati, which can almost lay claim to having embodied a piece of literary history': 'Arab Literary Salons', 244. The banquet and gala were listed in Brin, *L'Association des Amis*, 84.
76 *Images*, 'Vingtième anniversaire des A.C.F.E.', 20 March 1945, 'Mondanités'.
77 Fenoglio, 'Égyptianité et langue française', 21.
78 Zabbal, 'A Chacun son Égypte'. Several French language works from Egypt have been republished recently including the collected works of Georges Henein in 2005 and those of Ahmad Rassim in 2007.
79 Jabbour, *Littératures francophones*, 16.
80 Luthi, *La Littérature d'expression française*, 145.
81 Fenoglio, 'Égyptianité et langue française', 22.
82 Interview with Andrée Chédid in *La Quinzaine littéraire*, 436 (March 1985). Quoted in Daniel Lançon, 'Edmond Jabès l'égyptien', 185–6.
83 Quoted in Jabbour, *Littératures francophones*, 18–19.
84 Husayn, 'Kitab 'akhar 'an misr', 614.
85 Ibid., 615.
86 Ibid., 614–15.
87 Luthi, *En quête du français*, 237.
88 Luthi, *Égypte, qu'as-tu fait de ton français?*, 62.
89 Ibid., 63–127. Some of the Egyptianized expressions include: 'Il va couper les billets' instead of 'il va prendre' or 'il va acheter les billets', where to 'cut the ticket' in the Egyptian dialect refers to the tickets seller detaching the ticket from the ticket book. The Egyptian structure is also used when saying 'Il est entré dormir/se baigner', 'il est sorti travailler', 'il est parti manger'. See Luthi, *En quête du français*, 137–8. Luthi gives a long list of Arabic words used in French such as: *Baqqal* (grocer), *khaddam* (servant), and *pain baladi* (local bread), as well as words from Armenian, Italian and other languages.
90 Luthi, *En quête du français*, 240–1.

91 Solé, *L'Égypte passion française*, 313.
92 Abécassis, 'L'Enseignement étranger en Égypte et les élites locales', 247, 252–3. E.g., in 1929, the Frères des Ecoles chrétiennes ran three secondary schools in Alexandria which did not admit any non-paying students; four of their other schools provided free education for a thousand students, representing about a third of all their pupils in the city that year. Ibid., 252–3.
93 *Images*, 'Aux A.C.F.E.', 25 November 1945, 'Mondanités', 12.
94 Turkish was King Fuad's mother tongue; he never mastered Arabic or English but was fluent in French which he used it communications. See Reid, *Cairo University*, 28. His wife, Queen Nazli, studied at the Mère de Dieu in Cairo, while Queen Farida, Faruk's wife, went to the Notre-Dame de Sion in Alexandria. Sa'd Zaghlul addressed the French Parliament in 1919, highlighting the special relations that had existed between the two countries since Muhammad Ali and asking the French to help Egypt gain its independence. See Fahmi, *Mudhakkirat 'Abd al-Rahman Fahmi*, 50. For Kamil's similar appeals to France, see al-Rafi'i, *Mustafa Kamil*, 50.
95 Jacquemond, *Entre scribes et écrivains*, 142.
96 Ibid.
97 Perrault, *A Man Apart*, 41.
98 Saul, *La France et l'Égypte*, xv. For more on department stores, including Egyptian department stores, like Cicurel and Sednaoui, which used French (and Arabic) in their transactions, see Reynolds, *A City Consumed*.
99 Saul, *La France et l'Égypte*, xv.
100 Solé, *L'Égypte passion française*, 279.
101 d'Aumale, *Voix de l'Orient*, quoted in Solé, *L'Égypte passion française*, 279.
102 Abécassis, 'L'Enseignement du français dans les années 1920', 103–5.
103 Statistique scolaire de l'Égypte (1906–52), cited in Abécassis, 'L'Enseignement étranger (1930–1960)', 1.
104 Abécassis, 'L'Enseignement étranger et les élites locales', 814.
105 The education budget never exceeded 1 per cent of the annual budget between 1883 and 1901. See Abécassis, 'L'Enseignement du français dans les années 1920', 100–1.
106 Luthi, *La Littérature d'expression française*, 48.
107 Solé, *L'Égypte passion française*, 285.
108 Ascar-Nahas, *Égypte et culture française*, 8.
109 The Egyptian Secondary School Certificate was created in 1887; in 1913, it or an equivalent became obligatory to enter higher schools of education such as medicine or engineering; Abécassis, 'L'Enseignement étranger en Égypte (1930–1960)', 3. French schools had to respond to these changes, so in 1913 the Jesuit school introduced two programmes, a French section which prepared students for the French baccalauréat and another for the Egyptian Secondary Certificate. Even in the latter, most subjects were taught in French. Although Arabic was taught in both sections, it was as a 'foreign language' and students were not allowed to speak it during breaks; Abécassis, 'Une certaine idée', 250–2. In 1935, the Lycée français du Caire added an Egyptian section. Respecting the wishes of the Ministry of Public Instruction, history and geography were taught in Arabic. See ADN, série Le Caire Ambassade, volume n°5, revue de presse du 8 octobre 1935, quoted in Abécassis 'L'Enseignement français', 297–8. The Jesuit school was allegedly reluctant to cooperate with the Ministry of Public Instruction in the 'Arabization of education'; Abécassis, 'Une certaine idée', 252.

110 Abécassis, 'Ecole étrangère, école intercommunautaire', 227–8.
111 AMAE/Relations Culturelles 1945–1961/98. 1945–1947/ 'Secret: Monsieur Jean Lescuyer Ministre de France en Égypte à Son Excellence Monsieur Georges Bidault Ministre des Affaires Étrangères Paris', 29 April 1945.
112 Boutros-Ghali, preface to Luthi, *La Littérature d'expression française*, 9.
113 Despite his well-known family and cultural ties to France, Taha Husayn returned his Légion d'honneur to the French government in protest against what he considered to be a deep betrayal in 1956. Hussein, *Avec toi*, 216.
114 Cited in Solé, *L'Égypte passion française*, 441–2.
115 Boutros-Ghali, preface to Luthi, *La Littérature d'expression française*, 9.

Bibliography

Abécassis, Frédéric. 'Ecole étrangère, école intercommunautaire: Enjeux de formation d'une élite nationale'. In *Entre réforme sociale et mouvement national, identité et modernisation en Égypte (1882–1962)*, edited by Alain Roussillon, 215–34. Cairo: CEDEJ, 1995.

Abécassis, Frédéric. 'L'Enseignement du français dans les années 1920: Une nébuleuse à plusieurs degrés de francité'. *Documents pour l'histoire du français langue étrangère ou seconde*, no. 27 (December 2001): 97–115.

Abécassis, Frédéric. 'L'Enseignement étranger en Égypte et les élites locales 1920–1960, Francophonie et identités nationales'. PhD dissertation, Université D'Aix-Marseille, 2000. Accessed 15 June 2020. https://tel.archives-ouvertes.fr/tel-00331877.

Abécassis, Frédéric. 'L'Enseignement français en Égypte dans les années 1930: Les dévaluations contraintes d'un modèle'. In *Une France en Méditerranée: écoles, langue et culture françaises, XIXe-XXe siècles*, edited by Patrick Cabanel, 279–302. Grâne: Créaphis éditions, 2006.

Abécassis, Frédéric. 'L'Enseignement étranger en Égypte (1930–1960)'. *Aujourd'hui l'Égypte*, no. 30 (1995): 99–104. Accessed 15 Jun 2020. http://halshs.archives-ouvertes.fr/halshs-00159189.

Abécassis, Frédéric. 'Une certaine idée de la nation: Le collège de la Sainte Famille et l'Égypte nassérienne (1949–1962)'. In *Itinéraires d'Égypte: Mélanges offerts au père Maurice Martin, s.j.*, edited by Christian Décobert, 249–70. Cairo: Institut français d'archéologie orientale du Caire, 1992.

Ascar-Nahas, Joseph. 'Conférence sur les conférences'. In *L'Association des Amis de la culture française en Égypte (1925–1945)*, edited by Morik Brin, 9–46. Cairo: Éditions Horus, 1945.

Ascar-Nahas, Joseph. *Égypte et culture française*. Cairo: Éditions de la Société orientale de la publicité, 1953.

Brin, Morik, ed. *L'Association des Amis de la culture française en Égypte (1925–1945)*. Cairo: Éditions Horus, 1945.

Brin, Morik. 'Les A.C.F.E. et la presse'. In *Les Amis de la culture française en Égypte (1925–1945)*, edited by Morik Brin, 111–13. Cairo: Éditions Horus, 1945.

d'Aumale, Jacques. *Voix de l'Orient*. Montreal: Variétés, 1945.

Fahmi, 'Abd al-Rahman. *Mudhakkirat 'Abd al-Rahman Fahmi: yawmiyyat misr al-siyasiyya*, vol. 2, edited by Yunan Labib Rizq. Cairo: Al-Hay'a al-misria al-'ammah lil-kitab, 1993.

Fenoglio, Irène. 'Égyptianité et langue française: Un cosmopolitisme de bon aloi'. In *Entre Nil et sable: Écrivains d'Égypte d'expression française (1920–1960)*, edited by Marc Kober, Irène Fenoglio and Daniel Lançon, 15–25. Paris: Centre national de documentation pédagogique, 1999.

Fenoglio, Irène. 'L'Activité culturelle francophone au Caire durant l'entre-deux guerres: Du paradoxe à la contradiction'. In *D'un Orient l'autre*, vol. 1, 457–96. Paris: Éditions des CNRS, 1991.

Forzannes, Serge. 'Groupes intellectuels d'Égypte: Les Amis de la culture française'. *Images* (28 May 1932): 10.

Gran, Peter. *Islamic Roots of Capitalism: Egypt, 1760–1840*. Austin: University of Texas Press, 1998.

Hanna, Nelly. *In Praise of Books: A Cultural History of Cairo's Middle Class, Sixteenth to Eighteenth Century*. Syracuse, NY: Syracuse University Press, 2003.

Hartman, Michelle. *Native Tongue, Stranger Talk: The Arabic and French Literary Landscape of Lebanon*. Syracuse, NY: Syracuse University Press, 2014.

Henein, Georges. *Oeuvres: Georges Henein*. Paris: Denoel, 2005.

Husayn, Taha. 'Kitab 'akhar 'an misr'. *Majallati* 7 (1 March 1935): 613–20.

Hussein, Suzanne Taha. *Avec toi: De la France à l'Égypte: Un extraordinaire amour Suzanne et Taha Hussein (1915–1973)*. Paris: Les éditions du Cerf, 2011.

Jabbour, Zahida Darwiche. *Littératures francophones du Moyen-Orient: Égypte, Liban, Syrie*. Aix-en-Provence: Edisud, 2007.

Jacquemond, Richard. *Entre scribes et écrivains: Le champs littéraire dans l'Égypte contemporaine*. Paris: Sindbad, 2003.

Lançon, Daniel. 'Fortune et infortune du champ littéraire au Caire'. In *Entre Nil et Sable, Écrivains d'Égypte d'expression française (1920–1960)*, edited by Marc Klober, Irène Fenoglio and Daniel Lançon, 27–50. Paris: Centre national de documentation pédagogique, 1999.

Lançon, Daniel. 'Edmond Jabès l'égyptien'. In *Entre Nil et sable: Ecrivains d'Egypte d'expression française (1920–1960)*, edited by Marc Kober, Irène Fenoglio and Daniel Lançon, 173–89. Paris: Centre national de documentation pédagogique, 1999.

Lançon, Daniel. 'La France participée: Les grandes heures de la francophonie égyptienne'. *Bulletin of Francophone Africa*, no. 12–13 (July 1998): 11–40.

Luthi, Jean-Jacques. *Égypte qu'as-tu fait de ton français?* Paris: Synonym S.O.R, 1987.

Luthi, Jean-Jacques. *En quête du français d'Égypte*. Paris: L'Harmattan, 2005.

Luthi, Jean-Jacques. *Entretiens avec des auteurs francophones d'Égypte: et fragments de correspondances*. Paris: L'Harmattan, 2008.

Luthi, Jean-Jacques. *La Littérature d'expression française en Égypte (1798–1998)*. Paris: L'Harmattan, 2000.

Perrault, Gilles. *A Man Apart: The Life of Henri Curiel*. Translated by Bob Cumming. London: Zed Books, 1987.

al-Rafi'i, 'Abd al-Rahman. *Mustafa Kamil: ba'ith al-nahda al-wataniyya* Cairo: Dar al-Hilal, 1957.

Rassim, Ahmed. *Le Journal d'un pauvre fonctionnaire et autres textes*. Paris: Denoel, 2007.

Raymond, André. *Artisans et commerçants au caire au XVIIIe siècle*. Damas: Institut français de Damas, 1973–4.

Reid, Donald. *Cairo University and the Making of Modern Egypt*. Cambridge: Cambridge University Press, 1990.

Reynolds, Nancy. *A City Consumed: Urban Commerce, the Cairo Fire and the Politics of Decolonization in Egypt*. Stanford, CA: Stanford University Press, 2012.

Saul, Samir. *La France et L'Égypte de 1882 à 1914: Intérêts économiques et implications politiques*. Paris: Imprimerie nationale, 1997.
Schoell, Franck L. *La Langue française dans le monde*. Paris: Bibliothèque du 'Français Moderne', 1936.
Sfer, Abdallah. *Pour L'Union des syriens dans leurs intérêts sociaux*. Cairo: 1914.
Solé, Robert. *L'Égypte passion française*. Paris: Seuil, 1997.
Union des professeurs français d'Égypte. *L'Annuaire de l'enseignement français en Égypte*. Cairo: Imprimerie Paul Barbey, 1929.
Zabbal, Francois. 'A chacun son Égypte'. *Qantara* 27 (Spring 1998): 28–9.
Zananiri, Gaston. *Entre mer et désert: Mémoires*. Paris: Éditions du Cerf, 1996.
Zielger, Antje. 'Arab Literary Salons at the Turn of the 20th Century'. In *Understanding Near Eastern Literatures*, edited by Verena Klemm and Beatrice Gruendler, 241–53. Wiesbaden: Reichert, 2000.

7

The lost narratives of A. Z. Abushâdy, poet and bee master

Joy Amina Garnett

> In the stillness of the dark, in the desolate night,
> When mind and feelings are fraught with awe,
> I stand alone, a poet in self-communion,
> Thirsty for the Truth, wondering about the world
> While the world takes no heed of me,
> And all around me rushes swiftly past.[1]

A polymath who worked across several disciplines, Dr Ahmed Zaky Abushâdy (1892–1955)[2] is remembered for his Romantic poetry and as the man behind the influential poetry journal *Apollo* (1932–4).[3] In the period that stretched between the two world wars and the Egyptian revolutions of 1919 and 1952, Abushâdy cultivated his vision for a modern Egypt by enacting his ideals of liberal humanism through poetry and bee husbandry, and projects that invited cultural exchange.

This chapter focuses on aspects of Abushâdy's work that are not explored in the existing literature, which is mainly concerned with his literary contribution. It discusses little-known or lost narratives by excavating and examining some of the materials he left behind that bring his work into focus and offer insights into the creative, intellectual and political worlds in which he moved. My interest in these lost narratives of Abushâdy stems not from a scholarly agenda so much as the fact that Abushâdy was family, the grandfather I never met and for whom I continue to search. My sense of him continues to shift as I look through his papers, photographs and other belongings he managed to keep despite a series of disruptive moves from Egypt to England and back, and finally to the United States. These materials came to me through his children, my mother Hoda, uncle Ramzy and aunt Safeya, who salvaged what they could after his death and which I have since organized into an archive.

Abushâdy was the only son of Maître Muhammad Abushâdy Bey, a president of the Egyptian Bar Union and prominent supporter of the nationalist Wafd Party, who defended revolutionaries and assassins, and a wealthy and influential man (Figure 7.1). He owned lands in the Delta, mingled in the upper echelons of political and literary

Figure 7.1 Abushâdy and his father, Maître Muhammad Abushâdy Bey, *c.*1912 (Courtesy of the Abushâdy Archive).

society, and counted Sa'd Zaghlul and Ahmad Shawqi as close friends. His first wife, Amina Nagib, Abushâdy's mother, was an aspiring poet of Turkish descent; the family tree showed me how she was connected to her nephews, my 'uncles' the comedic film actor Sulayman Nagib and his brother Husni. Through Amina we are related to the celebrated Alexandrian artists, the brothers Seif and Edham Wanly, by her brother's marriage into Daghestani royalty.[4] She was said to have hosted a lively literary salon in Cairo where, as a youth, Abushâdy rubbed elbows with Shawqi and became a protegé of Mutran.[5] These men were not just mentors; eventually serving as editors of *Apollo*, they boosted its prestige with their names.

When Abushâdy was a teenager, his father took a second wife, a widow known in our family simply as 'al-Sitt'. Their marriage prompted Amina to decamp to another city; I never learned what became of her except that she died young. Al-Sitt brought along two daughters from her previous marriage and her young niece Zaynab. I grew up hearing the story that Abushâdy and Zaynab fell in love as teenagers, but al-Sitt forbade their marriage. It appears that Zaynab was the object of Abushâdy's youthful, anguished and most innovative poetry.[6]

In 1912, Abushâdy Bey sent his son to London to attend medical school rather than allow him to languish in Cairo writing dark love poetry. After completing his medical

Figure 7.2 Abushâdy with Annie and fox terrier Fahmy in the apiary at Benson, Oxfordshire, *c.*1922 (Courtesy of the Abushâdy Archive).

degree,[7] Abushâdy set himself up with a private practice in a rented house on Cairn Avenue in Ealing, where he lived with Annie Bamford, my future grandmother, until they moved to Benson, Oxfordshire, in 1919. Abushâdy had become interested in bees and bee pathology, and established a research institute and apiary there where he bred honeybees on a grand scale. He and Annie remained in Benson, marrying in 1922 just before returning to Cairo at the command of his ailing but ever forceful father, who died in 1925 (Figure 7.2).[8] I found a number of Abushâdy's medical residency logs, including one he kept for his rotation in obstetrics, laboratory notebooks with his drawings of test tubes and equations, and snapshots of him dissecting a cadaver, working in a laboratory and picnicking on the grounds of St. George's Hospital. In his letters and papers, there are mentions of societies and clubs that he joined. What I have yet to find is clear evidence of his literary activities over the course of the decade he spent in England, although, as I discuss below, we can gain a sense of his involvement with anti-colonial politics in London.

The Abushâdy archive

The materials in the archive span the years of Abushâdy's youth, his English education and marriage, his return to Egypt where he became a significant figure in modern Arabic poetry and bee husbandry, and his final years in the United States (1946–55) writing theatre and cultural broadcasts for the Voice of America's new Arabic radio programme. They include manuscripts, deeds, family trees, snapshots, large format photographs, significant artworks such as paintings, sketches, cartoons and calligraphy by artists in Abushâdy's circle, books and serials, audio recordings, small objects and ephemera, and a large amount of correspondence in English and Arabic between Abushâdy, his peers and family members. While most of these materials fit into rough categories, some items resist categorization such as ribbons entwined with wisps of a child's hair and seashells inscribed with coded messages of teenage love. In a velvet box lies a tangle of small kites fashioned from candy wrappers, while albums of pressed flowers tell us what Abushâdy planted in his garden for the delectation of his bees. Prior to writing this chapter, and with the help of a colleague well versed in tabulating the contents of family archives and private papers, I spent several years culling and organizing these materials. This process was tedious at times, but more often alchemical; it turned up unexpected fragments that impart a tactile sense of the world from which they came.

Hoda, Ramzy and Safeya were my last living connections to the Egypt of the ancien regime. As they aged, I feared their memories and first-hand knowledge would vanish with them. I spoke frequently with Safeya, who knew more about the family's history than anyone. We spent time together in her apartment, sifting through photo albums and documents. With her permission, I taped our conversations. In the years before her death at the age of 90, we discussed my grandfather's legacy in a battle of wills; she remained determined to control the narrative to the end, meting out to me select titbits by phone and by mail.

After Safeya's death, I discovered diaries and correspondence she never mentioned. For instance, I found a well-hidden bundle of nearly two hundred letters exchanged between Abushâdy and his wife, my grandmother Annie, during the summers from 1931 to 1934 when, to escape the heat of Cairo, Annie took the children to a hotel on the beach in Port Said while Abushâdy stayed behind to work. Their daily letters reveal

Figure 7.3 Rabindranath Tagore (centre) during his visit to Egypt in 1926. Far right: Dr Apostolos Skouphopoulos and A. Z. Abushâdy. Standing: Dr Muhammad Hamza. Port Said Casino, 31 December 1926 (Courtesy of the Abushâdy Archive).

the texture of their lives: Annie's wry sense of humour, disagreements over the care of their small children and the constant labour demanded by their bees and poultry. In one letter, Abushâdy emotes over the acquisition of their first radio; in others, Annie relates the rudeness of waiters, the size of water bugs, an acquaintance's dalliances with prostitutes and the calibre of the food served at the Marina Palace Hotel. Their constant money problems recur as a leitmotif as the two bicker over family finances against the backdrop of a politically turbulent Egypt, glimpses of which appear momentarily only to vanish under the weight of mundane matters. Tensions escalate to reveal the complexities of their marriage and the social and cultural gaps that remained between them.

Fragments of lost or forgotten narratives come to light through the many photographs in the archive. A group photo from 1926 marks the occasion of Bengali philosopher and poet Rabindranath Tagore's visit to Egypt (Figure 7.3).[9] The shot was staged outdoors in bright sunlight. Seven straight-back chairs are lined up on an ornate carpet with Tagore seated in the centre, flanked by two women in saris and three children who sit at his feet. Standing behind them is Abushâdy's friend and colleague, Dr Muhammad Hamza. Off to one side sits the journalist and trade unionist Dr Apostolos Skouphopoulos,[10] with Abushâdy, who seems a bit stiff in his tarbouche, next to him. Everyone looks straight at the camera while Tagore gazes into the middle distance. Tagore's personal connection to Abushâdy can be traced to their mutual

Figure 7.4 Left to right: K. Zeidan, Dusé Mohamed Ali, M. Omar and Abushâdy, 8 December 1913 (Courtesy of the Abushâdy Archive).

friend, Egypt's poet laureate Ahmad Shawqi, who hosted Tagore on his visit to Cairo.[11] A friend of his father, Shawqi had served as a mentor to the young Abushâdy. When he launched *Apollo* six years after this photograph was taken, Abushâdy invited Shawqi to be its editor and president of the group of poets he called the Apollo Society.

Abushâdy in England

Among the items that shed some light on Abushâdy's early days in England is a large mounted photograph that points to his activities while a medical student. It shows him posing with two young colleagues and the actor, playwright and pan-Africanist Dusé Mohamed Ali. On the wall behind them is a banner with Arabic calligraphy: 'Welcome to our lands … Freedom in our lands.' The photograph is dated 8 December 1913, about a year after Dusé Mohamed launched his *African Times and Orient Review* (ATOR), 'a monthly devoted to the interests of the coloured races of the world' (Figure 7.4).[12] I wonder what influence Dusé might have exerted on my young grandfather and if ATOR served as a model or inspiration for his future forays in publishing. Abushâdy makes several appearances as a 'nationalist friend and comrade' in Ian Duffield's doctoral thesis, quoting an MI5 file, where he was one of Dusé Mohamed Ali's 'closer Egyptian friends' and with whom he would continue to correspond after Abushâdy returned to Egypt. [13] At some point, Abushâdy apparently also helped the Sudanese-Egyptian nationalist obtain a copy of his own birth certificate. The MI5 file shows that Abushâdy himself was under some form of surveillance by the British authorities:

> An ex-employee of Dusé Mohamed says that 158 Fleet St was visited by Turks and Egyptians of all characters, some of whom were undesirable. He instanced Abushâdy, an Egyptian ... Ahmed Zaki Abushâdy is a student at St. George's Hospital. Apparently at some date early in January he sent a letter to his father in Cairo which was violently anti-English and in which he stated that although it was risky yet, Turkey's war with England was undoubtedly a source of hope for the Egyptians. Interviewed by the Police he said that he was very much disappointed when the proclamation of the Protectorate of Egypt was announced, but now that it appeared that Egypt was going to have home-rule, he considered that the position was better than before. Abushâdy recently wrote to Mrs Duse Mohamed and sent her an English translation of verses from the Arabic of Shawqi Bey. The verses were composed for school students and urged the young generation of Egyptians to cease to be slaves and by sacrificing themselves for the Motherland to restore the ancient glories of Egypt.[14]

It is worth noting that this idea of the youthful Abushâdy as 'violently anti-English' contradicts the widely held notion of him as an unapologetic anglophile. Considering his capacity for romantic idealism and romance itself, I imagine Abushâdy could have held these contradictory sentiments in his heart simultaneously.

Abushâdy met Annie on a London bus soon after he was photographed with Dusé. She was born in the town of Stalybridge in Greater Manchester, one of twelve children in a family of pub owners, Odd Fellows, and cotton weavers. She was a few years Abushâdy's senior and had a head of voluminous hair upon which she perched large feathered hats. As a teenager, she went to live in Germany where she worked as a governess. Annie liked to read the letters of Lucy, Lady Duff-Gordon and the novels of D. H. Lawrence. She chain-smoked. Together, they moved into the house on Cairn Avenue in Ealing (they were still several years away from getting married).

I wonder how Annie influenced Abushâdy. Perhaps she inspired him to implement the principles of the cooperative movement. The movement was also emerging in Egypt in late nineteenth and early twentieth centuries, but it is reasonable to imagine that Abushâdy became enamoured of the concept of cooperation through Annie and the sense of radicalism, historical depth and proximity which her family's past conferred. She grew up not far from its birthplace in Rochdale, where the Society of Equitable Pioneers established the first cooperative nearly twenty years earlier in 1844.[15] Also persuasive is the fact that Annie boasted Samuel Bamford (1788–1872), the famous labour organizer and voice for peaceful activism, as her forebear.[16] Bamford, who wrote poetry in Lancashire dialect, was present at the 1819 Peterloo Massacre, and authored several books, including *Passages in the Life of a Radical*, a chronicle of conditions among the working classes in the years after the Battle of Waterloo.[17]

Apollo Journal and the Apollo Society

In the years before my forays into the cupboards of my aunt Safeya's apartment, I worked as an assistant in a museum library in New York. I spent my spare time searching databases and scheduling interlibrary loans of journals and books on modern Arabic literature that included chapters on Abushâdy's poetry. I corresponded with close family friends who were either writers or scholars of modern Arabic literature who pointed me to the relevant literature.[18] There I learned that Abushâdy was a precocious young poet and that his influence on modern Arabic poetry began with his youthful love poems, which were fresh and wholly innovative.[19] I was able to confirm that in the landscape of modern Arabic poetry, Abushâdy's most notable achievement was *Apollo*, the first Arabic periodical devoted exclusively to poetry and poetry criticism. [20] *Apollo* provided a platform for experimental poetry that pushed beyond the conventions of content, rhyme and metre. Abushâdy brought together an ever-shifting group of men and women (including Nafisa al-Sayyid and Zaynab al-Rubi among the latter) to form what he called the Apollo Society (Jam'iyat Apullu), which welcomed poets that hailed from different schools and movements, and from beyond Egypt's borders (Figure 7.5).

Apollo was unusual on numerous levels. It was lavishly illustrated with drawings, colour plates and calligraphy that Abushâdy commissioned from local artists

Figure 7.5 The Apollo Society. Back row (left to right): 'Abd al-Ghani Hassan, Hassan Kamil al-Sayrafi, Muhammad 'Abd al-Ghafur, A. Z. Abushâdy, Salih Jawdat, Ramzy Maftah. Seated: 'Ali Mahmud Taha, Zaki Mubarak and Sayyid Ibrahim (Courtesy of the Abushâdy Archive).

Figure 7.6 Cover of *Apollo* (Courtesy of the Abushâdy Archive).

(Figure 7.6). Some of these artists had already made a name for themselves, such as the poet and calligrapher Sayyid Ibrahim (Figure 7.7),[21] while others were unknowns yet to be discovered, like the self-taught painter Sha'ban Zaki,[22] who wrote art criticism and ran advertisements on the back pages of the journal for his services 'in the art of

Figure 7.7 Drawing by calligrapher Sayyid Ibrahim for *Apollo* (Courtesy of the Abushâdy Archive).

advertising and decorative paintings of Egyptian scenes'. Another unusual aspect of *Apollo* is its use of author portraits. Many of these were reproduced from photos I had seen in the albums in Safeya's apartment, including group photographs of the members of the Apollo Society.

Among the publications represented in the archive is a single issue of *Apollo* and a reprint of the full set bound as six volumes in red buckram, the 1983 bootleg published by Dar Sadr in Beirut. Safeya had once mentioned to me that she threatened to sue the publisher after he reprinted the journal without her permission. In the end, they agreed to settle: she, Hoda and Ramzy would each receive a set. During its short but influential run, *Apollo* counted among its contributors well-known figures such as the Syro-Egyptian poet Khalil Mutran (who became its editor after the death of Shawqi), Mustafa Sadiq al-Rafiʿi,[23] ʿAbd al-Rahman Shukri,[24] Hasan Kamil al-Sayrafi[25] and the then unpublished Tunisian poet Abul-Qasim Al-Shabbi.[26] One of its early issues includes the poem 'Buried Light' (*al-Ashuʿa' al-khaba*) written by a young aspiring poet named Sayyid Qutb before he abandoned verse to write the works on Islam that now define him (Figure 7.8). It has been generally assumed that Qutb never published poetry in *Apollo* despite Abushâdy's repeated invitations because Qutb was a student of ʿAbbas al-ʿAqqad,[27] Abushâdy's chief antagonist, who viciously attacked the Apollo group over its aesthetics and politics.[28] Over the course of the ongoing literary spat, Qutb adopted the withering style of his mentor and dubbed the Apollo Society 'the procession of the handicapped' (*mawaqib al-ʿajaza*).[29] The presence of Qutb's poem in an early volume suggests that he may once have held a different opinion and attitude

سيد قطب

قلتُ : ماذا ؟ قال لى رجْعُ الصدَى : لا تقلْ : ماذا ، ولا تسأل علاماً ؟
هاهُنا وادى المنايا والردَى حيثُ يطوِى الضوءَ فيه والظلاما !

ها هنا تنوِى الأمانى ، ها هنا !
فى مَهاوى اليأسِ ، فى كهفِ الفنا
كلُّ شىءٍ هالكٌ ، حتى أنا ...

ثم ضاع الصوتُ يفنى بَدَدَا وتلاشَى ، تاركاً منه النساما
وإذا بى صِرتُ وحدى مُفرَدَا لا أرى شيئاً ولا أدْرِي إلاما !

سيد قطب

Figure 7.8 Portrait of Sayyid Qutb with the first page of his poem, 'Buried Light' (*al-Shuʿaʿ al-khaba*), *Apollo* 1, no. 3 (1932) (Courtesy of the Abushâdy Archive).

towards the group, or that he was willing to hold his nose and appear among them in order to see his work in print.

The vitriol levelled at Abushâdy by his literary adversaries was fuelled by a political misstep.[30] For years, he habitually approached government officials to request funding for projects. When money ran out for *Apollo*, Abushâdy turned to the widely despised Prime Minister Ismaʿil Ṣidqi. Abushâdy's opponents saw in this association the opportunity to tar his reputation despite the fact that Ṣidqi had refused to help him.[31] In 1935, a year after *Apollo*'s demise, Abushâdy quit the Cairo literary scene with its feuding factions and moved his family to Alexandria.

Abushâdy the apiarist

I am not sure how or why Abushâdy first became interested in bees, but it may have stemmed from his research in bacteriology and infectious diseases. Bee culture—the notion of the 'hive mind' and harmony through cooperation—seems to have inspired Abushâdy and provided a metaphor for his work. But since the range of his many varied enterprises lies beyond the scope of modern Arabic literature, even the very literal connections he drew between the arts, biology, sociology and bee culture have not been explored.

I became interested in Abushâdy the Bee Master[32] and was struck by the ubiquitous presence of the honeybee across his writings and letterheads as literal figure and decorative symbol. I began to set up research appointments in various libraries that held Abushâdy's papers and publications to see if I could locate his writings on bees. My first stop was the Aziz S. Atiya Middle East Library at the University of Utah, which contains private papers that Safeya had donated in 1975 at the behest of the library's founder, Aziz Atiya, a close family friend.[33] There I found a reprint of a public address that Abushâdy delivered in 1922 under the auspices of the Apis Club promoting the standardization of bee husbandry.[34]

The Apis Club was a cooperative apiary with educational and research programmes that Abushâdy established in 1919 in Benson, a small village in the countryside near Oxford. He did so with the help of an investment from the Egyptian cotton magnate, 'Ali al-Manzalawi.[35] With this financial infusion, Abushâdy started a parent company called Adminson that financed the Apis Club until it could sustain itself through the contributions of its members. In its first year, the co-op attracted over thirteen thousand members and grew to over six hundred hives, an auspicious beginning of Abushâdy's lifelong venture in beekeeping.[36] In the same year, he launched his first scientific journal, *The Bee World*, and obtained a number of patents for beehive inventions. The most radical of these was a removable aluminium honeycomb, an improvement upon an existing removable comb whereby beekeepers can extract honey without destroying the colony, a method that remains standard practice today.[37] Abushâdy later adapted these and other practices for use in Egyptian apiaries where the traditional skep made from twisted straw or wicker baskets and mud was still prevalent.

The Apis Club and *The Bee World* provided Abushâdy with a platform by which he could implement his deeply felt humanist ideals. He had practised medicine during the influenza pandemic, dealt with cholera outbreaks, treated children suffering from malnutrition and witnessed the effects of extreme poverty across England and Scotland. A physician who provided care in the most basic sense, he also had a vision. The Apis Club became a way for him to disseminate his views while putting them into practice. He envisaged his headquarters in Benson as an educational centre for experts and amateur beekeepers alike, and he encouraged knowledge-sharing among beekeepers from different social strata and backgrounds. He promoted best practices through *The Bee World* and demonstrated to farmers how they could dramatically increase honey yields, and thus improve their standard of living.

My next appointment was at the archive of the Apis Club in Aberystwyth, in the special collections of the National Library of Wales.[38] The Apis Club archive offers a glimpse of the inner workings of the cooperative and early plans and designs for *The Bee World*,[39] now published as *Bee World* by the International Bee Research Association (IBRA).[40] There I learned that Abushâdy continued to edit *The Bee World* after he returned to Cairo in 1922 but soon resigned in order to focus his attention closer to home. In 1930, he launched another scientific journal, *The Bee Kingdom* (*Mamlakat al-naḥl*), which accepted contributions in both Arabic and English and took in advertising from around the world.[41] Next, he launched the Bee Kingdom League, an Egyptian bee husbandry cooperative, in the Matariyya suburb of Cairo where he and Annie were raising their family. Under its auspices, Abushâdy published papers and monographs on aspects of bee botany, bee diseases and different methods of bee breeding. With support from the Egyptian Ministry of Education, he taught classes in beekeeping to grammar school and high school students. With sponsorship from the Ministry of Agriculture, he organized the first international bee conference and honey fair in Cairo, and established the Royal Apiaries at the request of King Fu'ad.[42] *The Bee Kingdom* remained in print for a decade, while members of the Bee Kingdom League continued to hold meetings and conferences as recently as 1978.[43]

Abushâdy kept bees his entire life. Photos show him posing with his hives in every place he called home: the back garden in Ealing and the apiary at Benson, the rooftop in Matariyya and in backyards in Alexandria, Jamaica, Queens and Washington, DC. A photograph dated 11 August 1946, just a few months after his arrival in New York, shows him brandishing a cigar while posing with Safeya and Hoda among the predominantly female members of the Bronx Beekeepers Association. What Abushâdy found in bee culture provided a model that could be applied across disciplines. One could make the case that he drew on the concepts of hybridity and cross-pollination – concepts essential to botany and to bee breeding – while mining modern Western poetry for his experiments developing Arabic blank verse.[44]

Biography and the archive

Abushâdy's output in the literary, scientific and journalistic realms was formidable.[45] Indispensable to these pursuits were his skills as a publisher. In his letters to Annie, we learn that he was always on the lookout for cheap, second-hand accessories for his printing press. By the late 1920s, he was able to print and publish under his own imprint, Maṭba'at al-Ta'awun – Cooperation Press – from his home in Matariyya and later from his office on Rue de France in Alexandria.[46] In the 1930s, Abushâdy surreptitiously self-published two biographies, each focusing on different aspects of his work, and arranged to have them distributed. Taking into consideration his bitter experiences with the Cairo literary community, it seems that he tried to generate and control the narratives around his work. He commissioned the first biography from a young associate, an Alexandrian Turk with literary aspirations, named Ismail Ahmed Edham.[47] *Abushâdy the Poet: A Critical Study* offers a short and somewhat grandiose biographical sketch in English that includes an analysis of Abushâdy's modern Arabic poetry.[48] An earlier draft of the text had appeared in his self-published journal *Adabi* ('My Literature'), with Edham's by-line and a lengthy postscript by Abushâdy. It has been suggested that by providing this biographical text in English, Abushâdy was attempting to broaden his audience and better position himself in the wake of the 1936 Anglo-Egyptian Treaty.[49] When the biography first appeared, at least one of Abushâdy's detractors suggested that he wrote it himself,[50] but it is likely to be the work of Edham with considerable input and editing by Abushâdy. While its title page displays the name of a publisher in Leipzig, a centre for Middle East scholarship, on close inspection, with its telltale blue wrappers and quirky typography the book was obviously printed in Alexandria by the Cooperation Press.

Two years later, Abushâdy commissioned another biography from his long-time ally and colleague at Benson, Leonard Harker, which is a more substantial study and focuses on Abushâdy's contributions to bee science and husbandry.[51] *Blazing the Trail* seeks to do justice to these contributions by contextualizing them within the history of modern beekeeping and its major figures. The book is replete with photographs, many of which I recognize, yet again, from family photo albums. *Blazing the Trail* excerpts approximately a dozen pages of biographical material from Edham's biography and bears all the marks of having been printed in Alexandria by the Cooperation Press.[52]

Abushâdy clearly had a hand in constructing his own narratives; family members also contributed to the construct, omitting key facts and burnishing others, often inadvertently and sometimes by design. I recently discovered a sheaf of family trees and, separately, photographs of a woman named Wafiyya al-Rubi, Abushâdy's older sister. No one in my family ever mentioned her to me, and I always assumed that Abushâdy was an only child. But I grew up knowing several of Wafiya's children, and called them aunt and uncle when I stayed with them in Cairo. I never had a clear sense of how we were related, and I had no idea that they were my mother's first cousins. Nor did anyone give me straight answers when I asked.

Artworks in the archive

The archive contains original artworks, logos and designs that Abushâdy commissioned to illustrate his journals. Among these are a caricature of him by Edham Wanly that is reproduced as the frontispiece for *Abushâdy the Poet* (Figure 7.9), a pair of oil portraits of him and Annie painted by Muhammad Hassan when he was studying at London's Central School of Arts and Crafts,[53] and a pencil sketch of young Safeya by Sha'ban Zaki. There are also small paintings by Seif Wanly and original fine-line drawings by the poet and calligrapher Sayyid Ibrahim. When I first saw them reproduced in the pages of *Apollo* and in *The Bee Kingdom*, I assumed they were unsigned elements of graphic design produced by an anonymous hand. However, upon close inspection of the original drawings, which are larger than their reproductions, I found that each piece contained Ibrahim's minuscule signature.

Figure 7.9 Edham Wanly's portrait of Abushâdy reproduced in *Abushâdy the Poet* (1936) (Courtesy of the Abushâdy Archive).

Figure 7.10 Masthead of *The Bee Kingdom* by Paul Beer (Courtesy of the Abushâdy Archive).

Chief among the emblems that Abushâdy employed to represent his bee-related initiatives is the masthead and logo of *The Bee Kingdom*. Signed by the artist Paul Beer (who is identified on the back of one sketch as '*al-Nimsawi*' – 'The Austrian' – but is otherwise unknown), the illustration depicts a crowned queen bee sitting astride a throne, her arms embracing both Eastern and Western hemispheres (Figure 7.10). The image appears on letterheads and envelopes, gummed labels, lapel pins and enamel-inlaid medallions commissioned by Abushâdy from the preeminent silver workshop Mappin & Webb in London, as well as from craftsmen in Cairo.

A fine ink caricature by the Alexandrian cartoonist Mohamed Fridon best sums up Abushâdy's multicultural and interdisciplinary tendencies (Figure 7.11).[54] Originally featured in Abushâdy's *Mukhtarat al-wahy al-'am 1928*, it was widely reproduced by Abushâdy in the 1930s to illustrate the advertisements he placed to promote his own projects on the back pages of his magazines.[55] The drawing may well have been a commission; I found the original framed on a wall in Safeya's study. It depicts a bespectacled Abushâdy with his signature toothbrush moustache. His torso is a detailed rendering of a microscope from which extends elongated arms and legs; his bare feet cradle an inkwell and his right hand brandishes a quill pen. He composes a line of text in an open notebook that floats in the air before him, writing from right to left (hence, in Arabic). Between the thumb and forefinger of his left hand, he holds a gigantic honeybee; above the bee, flanked by cherubs, is a treble clef and bar of music. It shows Abushâdy as a many-faceted creature, a romantic idealist that bridged mediums and disciplines, who lived by the credo that neither poetry nor art nor science – nor nations and cultures – can develop and blossom in isolation.

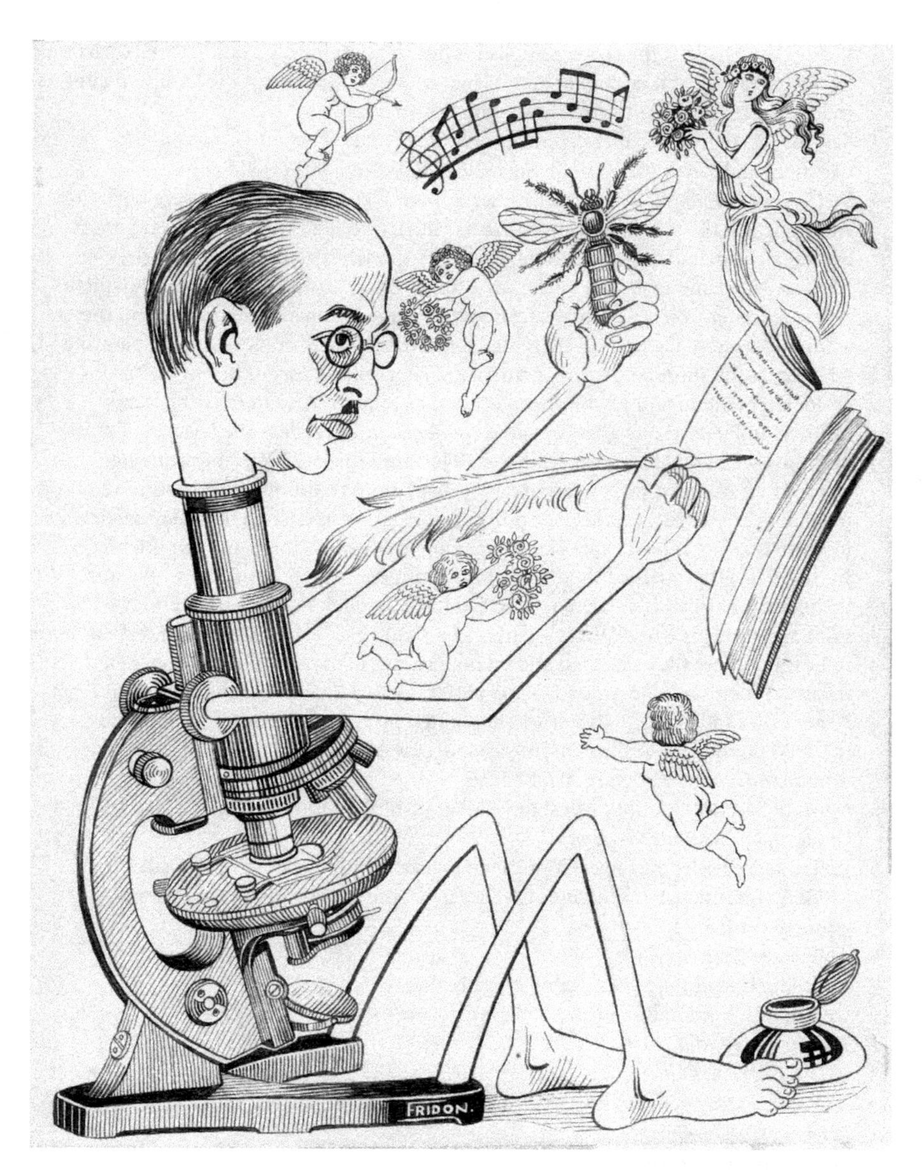

Figure 7.11 Caricature of Abushâdy by Mohamed Fridon, *c.*1928 (Courtesy of the Abushâdy Archive).

Notes

1 Opening lines from Abushâdy's poem 'In the Stillness of the Dark,' translated by Badawi, *Critical Introduction*, 120.

2 While 'Abu Shadi' is the correct English transliteration for my grandfather's surname, for the purposes of this chapter and related writings, I have kept the family spelling as well as the Ottoman 'â' that my grandfather favoured.
3 See, for instance, Kendall, *Literature, Journalism and the Avant-Garde*, 48–51; Gershoni and Jankowski, *Redefining the Egyptian Nation*, 131–2.
4 Seif Wanly (1906–1979) and his brother Edham Wanly (1908–1959) were born in Alexandria at the palace of Irfan Pasha in Muharram Bey. Their uncles were the brothers Husni and Sulayman Najib (1892–1955), whose father was the writer Mustafa Najib and maternal uncle was Ahmad Ziwar Pasha (1864–1945), Egyptian prime minister from 1924 to 1926. Sulayman was a famous comedic film and theatre actor and head of Cairo's Royal Opera House. The Wanly brothers studied painting together at the studio of Arturo Zanieri and later with Ottorino Bicchi (1878–1949), an Italian painter from Livorno who opened a studio in Alexandria. The Wanly brothers influenced one another and developed similar styles. They became fixtures of the art scene in Alexandria from the 1940s until the late 1960s, introducing European modernist tropes and breaking away from traditional folk motifs. They painted everyday life, cafe scenes, portraits and landscapes. Together they participated in more than seventeen exhibitions, including the Venice and Sao-Paolo Biennales. In the 1940s, they opened their own studio with the help of Muhammad Bayumi, the pioneer of Egyptian cinema. Seif used his first name to sign his paintings while Edham signed his work 'Wanly'. During the 1950s, the brothers travelled regularly to Europe where they sketched and painted scenes of ballet, the circus, opera and theatre. When sculptor Ahmad Osman (1907–1970) established the Faculty of Fine Arts in Alexandria in 1957, Seif was appointed Professor of Painting. An entire floor of the Mahmoud Said Museum in Alexandria is dedicated to their work. Abaza, *Twentieth-Century Egyptian Art*, 215–16.
5 Mustafa Badawi describes Abushâdy's relationship to Mutran as that of 'disciple' (Badawi, *Critical Introduction*, 115).
6 Pieced together from conversations with Safeya Abushady and Robin Ostle.
7 LMSSA (Licentiate in Medicine and Surgery of the Society of Apothecaries), graduated 1915.
8 Abushady, 'Obituary', 44.
9 Marashi, 'Imagining Hafez: Rabindranath Tagore in Iran, 1932'.
10 Dalachanis, 'Internationalism vs. Nationalism', 332.
11 *The Times of India*, 2016.
12 Grant, *Negro with a Hat*, 40.
13 Duffield, 'Dusé Mohamed Ali and the Development of Pan-Africanism, 1866–1945', 478–9.
14 The National Archives, FO 371/2355/15047, February 1915, 'Dusé Mohamed Ali and the Development of Pan-Africanism, 1866–1945'. My thanks to Robert Vitalis for bringing this to my attention which clarifies the authorship of the verses, a point which Duffield misread.
15 Birchall, *Co-op*, 1994.
16 Harker, *Blazing the Trail*, 38.
17 Gardner, 'The Suppression of Samuel Bamford's Peterloo Poems'.
18 Wadei Philistin and Mohamed Mustafa Badawi attended Alexandria University (then Faruq University) with Safeya Abushady, with whom they remained lifelong friends. Philistin went on to become a well-connected journalist and editor, working for *al-Muqtataf* and *al-Muqattam*, and author and translator of over forty books in

literature, economics, biography, politics and journalism. Between 1948 and 1957, he taught journalism at the American University in Cairo. Badawi became a scholar of English and Arabic literature and a Fellow of St. Antony's College (1967–2012) at Oxford University, where he was the first lecturer in Modern Arabic at the Middle East Centre.

19 From correspondence and conversations with Robin Ostle, 2008–13.

20 Jam'iyat Apullu. *Apullu = Apollo*. Cairo, s.n., 1932–34; see also Badawi, *Critical Introduction*, 127 *passim*.

21 A pioneer in the art Arabic calligraphy, Sayyid Ibrahim (1897–1994) was known as a particular innovator of the art who was well known as a teacher to many students throughout the Arab world. See Bibliotheca Alexandrina (https://www.bibalex.org/en/News/Details?DocumentID=4959&Keywords=).

22 Sha'ban Zaki (1899–1968) was a self-taught Egyptian artist known for his paintings of Egyptian everyday life. From a lower middle-class family of government employees, he worked in a railway station and studied art by correspondence with an institution in Chicago. He became involved in the local art scene in the 1920–40s and was a close friend to many luminaries of his time like the poet Hafiz Ibrahim. Abaza, *Twentieth-Century Egyptian Art*, 216.

23 Mustafa Sadiq al-Rafi'i (1880–1937) was a Syro-Egyptian born in Bahtim, Egypt, and was one of the most important Arab poets of the early twentieth century. He played an important role in the literary and intellectual transformation of Arabic literature, promoting a return to a classical Arabic style and working to strengthen the Islamic identity of Egypt. He composed the words to the Egyptian national anthem, 'Islami ya Misr', adopted between 1923 and 1936, and co-wrote the Tunisian national anthem. Badawi, *Modern Arabic Literature*, 277, 412, 428.

24 'Abd al-Rahman Shukri (1886–1958) was born in Alexandria and studied in England at the University of Sheffield where he received his BA degree. He co-founded the Diwan school of poets with 'Abbas Mahmud al-'Aqqad and 'Abd al-Qadir al-Mazini but abandoned poetry after a dispute with them. Ostle, 'Three Egyptian Poets'.

25 Born in Damietta, Hasan Kamil al-Sayrafi (1908–1984) worked as an editor of the Egyptian journal *al-Majalla*. A member of the Apollo Society, frequent contributor to *Apollo* and one of Abushâdy's staunchest allies, his poetry has been characterized as melancholic and romantic. Interest in his poetry was rekindled in Egyptian literary circles in the 1980s. Meisami and Starkey, *Encyclopedia*, 696.

26 Abul-Qasim Al-Shabbi (1909–1934) was a Tunisian poet best known for 'The Will to Live', the poem he wrote in opposition to French colonial rule, which became the final verses of the National Anthem of Tunisia, 'Humat al-Hima' ('Defenders of the Homeland'). *Apollo* was the first literary journal to publish his poetry (Speight, 'A Modern Tunisian Poet'). During the 2011 Arab Spring, his poem 'To the Tyrants of the World' was circulated and chanted at demonstrations in Tunisia and later in Egypt.

27 'Abbas Mahmud al-'Aqqad (1889–1964) was a prolific Egyptian writer, journalist, poet, literary critic and polymath. Founder of the Diwan school of poetry with 'Abd al-Qadir al-Mazini and 'Abd al-Rahman Shukri, al-'Aqqad positioned himself as the intellectual and creative leader of the modern Arabic poetry movement and was a vigorous critic of Abushâdy and the Apollo Society (Badawi, *Modern Arabic Literature*, 88–95).

28 Badawi, *Critical Introduction*, 66–71.

29 Calvert, *Sayyid Qutb*, 71.

30 Toth, *Sayyid Qutb*, 23–4.
31 Calvert, *Sayyid Qutb*, 70.
32 The term applied to Abushâdy in the biography by Harker, *Blazing the Trail.*
33 Aziz Suryal Atiya (1898–1988) was an Egyptian scholar of Coptic history and Islamic and Crusades studies. He founded the Institute of Coptic Studies in Cairo in 1954, and in 1960 he founded the Middle East Center at the University of Utah, which houses the Aziz Atiya Library for Middle East Studies, the fifth-largest such collection in North America. Atiya was a close friend of Abushâdy, and he and his wife remained close to Safeya. See 'Biography of Dr. Aziz Atiya' (https://lib.utah.edu/collections/middle-east/atiya.php).
34 Shadi and Zaki, *International Standardisation.*
35 Al-Manzalawi would later serve as a Minister of Agriculture in 1933.
36 Harker, *Blazing the Trail.*
37 Abushady, *Improvements in and Relating to Combs for Beehives.*
38 I was initially drawn to the collection in Aberystwyth because it held the lanternslides Abushâdy used to teach bee husbandry. There, I was given access to the Apis Club archive, which holds a wealth of documentation, including shareholders' agreements, press clippings and photographs of famous beekeepers who became involved with the apiary. It contains fine anatomical drawings of bees, a series of botanical drawings of enlarged pollen grains and mock-ups for different *Bee World* covers. There are a few exceptionally evocative items, such as a diagram in Abushâdy's hand that maps out his plan (unrealized) for a public bee library. Unfortunately, I never got to see the lanternslides. After repeated cancellations and vague excuses, I was forced to give up. I still wonder if the boxes are lost, or locked in a dark cupboard in that vast neoclassical building.
39 Joy Garnett, 'Blazing the Trail'.
40 At time of writing, IBRA is celebrating its centenary with a special issue of the journal that charts its development since it was founded: see Brodschneider, 'Around the Bee World in 100 Years', 33-33; Richard Jones et al., 'Bee World – The First Hundred Years', 34–9.
41 *Mamlakat al-nahl*, 1930–40.
42 Ibid.
43 A renowned writer on bees and beekeeping, Eva Crane (1912–2007) established the Bee Research Association (BRA) in 1949 (later IBRA) and served as editor of *Bee World* from 1949 until 1984. In 1954, one year before Abushâdy's death, Crane visited him in his Upper East Side apartment where he gave her a menu from a recent dinner in his honour at the Waldorf Astoria celebrating the publication of his diwan *Min as-sama'* ('From the Heavens', 1949). Crane later reported that during a visit to Egypt to meet beekeepers in 1978, she learned that the Bee Kingdom League was still active and met several members who took her to their former headquarters, Abushâdy's old house in Rue Menasce in Alexandria. Later, in Cairo, she attended one of their meetings. It was quite an extraordinary experience, she said, for these old men treated her, the editor of *Bee World*, as if she were the living incarnation of Abushâdy: 'In Egypt, you know, the living and the dead are almost equally present.' (Letter of David Blair to Safeya Abushâdy, 30 January 1987).
44 Ostle, 'Modern Egyptian Renaissance Man', 184–92.
45 Jayyusi, 'A Short Account of Abu Shadi's Life in the United States.', 36–47.
46 Ibid.

47 Born in Turkey, 1911, of Turkish and German parentage, Adham spent part of his life in Egypt, where he invented for himself doctorates in physics and philosophy from Russian universities and elevated positions in Russian academia. On moving to Egypt, he became a prolific writer of literary and pseudoscientific works and gained considerable notoriety as an avowed atheist. He committed suicide in 1940, aged 29 (Juynboll, 'Ismail Ahmad Adham', 54–6, 63).
48 Edham, *Abushâdy the Poet.*
49 Juynboll, 'Ismail Ahmad Adham'.
50 Ibid.
51 Harker, *Blazing the Trail.*
52 Copies of both books can be found in major public and university libraries, including the New York Public Library, the British Library, National Library of Wales, Bibliothèque Nationale, National Library of Israel, Harvard Library and, of course, the Deutsche Nationalbibliothek in Leipzig. All copies seen have been inscribed with 'compliments of' and seem to have been donated to these libraries either by Edham or Abushâdy himself.
53 Muhammad Hassan (1892–1961) taught at the School of Arts and Crafts in Bulaq before being awarded a two-year scholarship from the Egyptian government to study painting and design at London's Central School of Arts and Crafts (1917–18), during which time he met Abushâdy and Annie Bamford and painted their portraits in oil. He returned to Egypt in 1919 after earning his certificate and taught at the School of Egyptian Arts and Decoration in Cairo. Later appointed Director of the Egyptian Academy of Arts in Rome, he returned to Egypt to become the Director of the Fine Arts Museum in Alexandria until his death in December 1961.
54 A friend of Abushâdy's, Fridon is otherwise unknown (conversation with Safeya, 2008).
55 Ostle, 'Modern Egyptian Renaissance Man', 190–2.

Bibliography

Anonymous. 'Egypt to Mark Tagore's Birth Anniversary'. *Times of India*, 9 May 2016. Accessed 15 June 2020. https://timesofindia.indiatimes.com/india/Egypt-to-mark-Tagores-birth-anniversary/articleshow/52185319.cms.

Abaza, Mona. *Twentieth-Century Egyptian Art: The Private Collection of Sherwet Shafei.* Cairo: American University in Cairo Press, 2011.

Abushady, Ahmed Zaki. *International Standardisation, etc.* (reprinted from *The Bee World*). Benson, Oxon: Apis Club, 1922.

Abushady, Ahmed Zaki. *Improvements in and Relating to Combs for Beehives.* Patent Specification 150,502, 24 July 1919. Application No. 18,419/19. Completed 30 December 1919. Accepted 9 September 1920. Kings Patent Agency Ltd, Queen Victoria St, London, E.C.4.

Abushady, Maitre M. 'Obituary'. *Bee World* 7, no. 3 (1925): 44.

Badawi, Mohamed Mustafa. *A Critical Introduction to Modern Arabic Poetry.* Cambridge: Cambridge University Press, 1975.

Badawi, Mohamed Mustafa. *Modern Arabic Literature.* Cambridge: Cambridge University Press, 2006.

Bamford, Samuel. *Passages in the Life of a Radical.* Heywood: J. Heywood, 1842.

Berque, Jacques. *Egypt: Imperialism & Revolution*. Translated by Jean Stewart. London: Faber & Faber, 1972.

Bibliotheca Alexandrina. https://www.bibalex.org/en/News/Details?DocumentID=4959&Keywords=.

'Biography of Dr. Aziz Atiya'. https://lib.utah.edu/collections/middle-east/atiya.php.

Birchall, Johnston. *Co-op: The People's Business*. Manchester: Manchester University Press, 1994.

Brodschneider, Robert. 'Around the Bee World in 100 Years'. *Bee World* 96, no. 2 (2019): 33.

Calvert, John. *Sayyid Qutb and the Origins of Radical Islamism*. London: Hurst, 2010.

Dalachanis, Angelos. 'Internationalism vs. Nationalism? The Suez Canal Company Strike of 1919 and the Formation of the International Workers' Union of the Isthmus of Suez'. In *Social Transformation and Mass Mobilization in the Balkan and Eastern Mediterranean Cities 1900–1923*, edited by Andreas Lyberatos, 323–35. Heraklion: Crete University Press, 2013.

Duffield, Ian. 'Dusé Mohamed Ali and the Development of Pan-Africanism, 1866–1945'. PhD dissertation, University of Edinburgh, 1971.

Edham, Ismail Ahmed. *Abushâdy the Poet: A Critical Study*. Leipzig: Gustav Fischer, 1936.

Gardner, John. 'The Suppression of Samuel Bamford's Peterloo Poems'. *Romanticism* 13, no. 2 (2007): 145–55.

Garnett, Joy. 'Blazing the Trail: A.Z. Abushâdy and The Apis Club'. *Bee World* 91, no. 3 (2014): 65–7.

Gershoni, Israel, and James Jankowski. *Redefining the Egyptian Nation, 1930–1945*. Cambridge: Cambridge University Press, 2002.

Grant, Colin. *Negro with a Hat: The Rise and Fall of Marcus Garvey*. Oxford: Oxford University Press, 2008.

Harker, Leonard S. *Blazing the Trail, Reminiscences of A.Z. Abushády, Poet--Bee-Master--Humanist*. London: C.W. Daniel, 1938.

Jam'iyat Apullu. *Apullu = Apollo*. Cairo: s.n., 1932–4.

Jayyusi, Salma Khadra. 'A Short Account of Abu Shadi's Life in the United States'. In *Mundus Arabicus*, vol. 1: Arab Writers in America: Critical Essays and Annotated Bibliography, 36–47. Cambridge, MA: Dar Mahjar, 1981.

Jones, Richard, Karl Showler and Robert Brodschneider (editor of *Bee World*). 'Bee World – The First Hundred Years'. *Bee World* 96, no. 2 (2019): 34–9.

Juynboll, G. H. A. 'Ismail Ahmad Adham (1911–1940), the Atheist'. *Journal of Arabic Literature* 3, no.1 (1972): 54–71.

Kendall, Elisabeth. *Literature, Journalism and the Avant-Garde: Intersection in Egypt*. Abingdon: Routledge, 2006.

Mamlakat al-naḥl: majallah shahriyya fi al-naḥḥalah al-ʻaṣriyya = The Bee Kingdom / li-sahibiha wa-muharririha Ahmad Zaki Abu Shadi. Maṭariyya, Cairo: A.Z. Abu Shadi, 1930–40.

Marashi, Afshin. 'Imagining Hafez: Rabindranath Tagore in Iran, 1932'. *Journal of Persianate Studies* 3, no. 1 (2010): 46–77.

Meisami, Julie Scott, and Paul Starkey. *Encyclopedia of Arabic Literature*, vol. 2. London: Routledge, 1998.

Ostle, Robin. 'Modern Egyptian Renaissance Man'. *Bulletin of the School of Oriental and African Studies* 57 (1994): 184–92.

Ostle, Robin C. 'Three Egyptian Poets of "Westernization": 'Abd al-Rahman Shukri, Ibrahim 'Abd al-Qadir al-Mazini, and Mahmud 'Abbas al-'Aqqad'. *Comparative Literature Studies* 7, no. 3 (1970): 354–73.
Speight, R. Marston. 'A Modern Tunisian Poet: Abu al-Qasim al-Shabbi (1909–1934)'. *International Journal of Middle East Studies* 4, no. 2 (1973): 178–89.
Toth, James. *Sayyid Qutb The Life and Legacy of a Radical Islamic Intellectual.* Oxford: Oxford University Press, 2013.

8

Political caricatures in colonial Egypt: Visual representations of the people and the nation

Sarah H. Awad

Images are not just a particular kind of sign, but something like an actor on the historical stage, a presence or character endowed with legendary status, a history that parallels and participates in the stories we tell ourselves.[1]

In issue number 347 of *al-Kashkul*, published in Egypt in January 1928, a caricature (Figure 8.1) depicts on the right a government official, a pasha in a suit and a fez, excessively overweight and persistently arguing with the police sergeant (*shawish*). At the back, a British official with sharp features stands confidently, smoking a cigar, looking on firmly as the pasha demands, 'We have to protect her and not let anyone come her way' (Ya basha ehhna lazem nedafe' 'anha wala nkhallish hhad yigi nahhyet-ha).[2] The *shawiish* stands in defence of 'her', keeping the *pasha* away by his hand gesture: 'You both stay away from her, you are after her jewellery' (eṭla' ya hhanash enta w howwa, 'intom 'enkom men sighet-ha), he says. The woman in the western-style green dress, with attractive and delicate features, wearing heavy accessories symbolizing her wealth, stands at the back in a seductive posture, overhearing the conversation. She waits passively for her fate after the negotiation. The woman in the green dress is Egypt.

This political caricature is typical of many others published in *al-Kashkul* and *al-Siyasa al-Usbu'iyya* during this time. The image positions each actor from the contemporary political scene: the European powers targeting corrupt government officials to benefit from Egypt, the corrupt pashas in turn seek their own gains and the *shawish* is the 'local' voice – and possibly the voice of the caricaturist – defending Egypt and the Egyptians from these transgressors. Egypt, the subject of the negotiation, watches the situation passively.

This chapter looks at images found in political caricatures published between 1926 and 1931 in two Egyptian journals: *al-Kashkul* and *al-Siyasa al-Usbu'iyya*. This marks a unique time in Egyptian national discourse when political movements were seeking to secure complete independence from British occupation. This period falls between the world wars and follows the 1919 revolution against British occupation, which had led to Egypt's nominal independence in 1922 and the implementation of a new constitution. And following this period was the 1952 revolution, which overthrew

Figure 8.1 *al-Kashkul* no. 347 (6 January 1928).

the Egyptian monarchy and completed independence from Britain. The social and historical context of the period offers an opportunity to look at the interplay between foreign and local cultures as they manifest themselves in visual culture, specifically the construction of national identity in journal caricatures.

My analysis of the caricatures which appeared in these publications during this period interprets the meanings embodied in the images in relation to the nation. The lens of social and cultural psychology is used to understand the politics of the images in visually constructing national identity, positioning different social actors in social and political context, and feeding into an enduring national discourse about the agency of the people and the nation. The analysis reflects on concepts of visibility, national identity, agency and the representation of the nation as a woman. It also sheds light on the dynamics of creating a local identity that is distinct from foreign culture, yet borrows certain foreign tools and symbols in that process, as will be seen especially in the origins of the art of caricature in Egypt and how it was appropriated and invested with local characterizations.

The significance of the image

We use images as tools for social action, and in turn, images we see around us act back upon us. They constitute signs in our shared environment that are endowed with symbolic power, with a privileged influence over the human mind. They solidify ideas and modes of meaning-making in tangible forms that are open to perception and analysis. This empowers images with the potential to perform different political functions.[3] First, they create visibility, as they are capable of making absent objects present, giving shape to abstract entities and creating characters that embody generalizations.[4] They can thus provide the figurative nuclei of social representations,[5] where they borrow from existing common knowledge, reinstating some, while also reconstructing others. Second, they are affective symbols that can shape emotions, motivate action and mobilize people around common goals or ideas. Third, they position their producers and audience in relation to different social issues, ascribing various rights and duties to different social actors.[6] They suggest and convey arguments by representing the existing social realities of the time, while simultaneously communicating something new that may violate those realities.[7] And fourth, they commemorate: images surround us that constitute our collective memory and are capable of reinforcing certain memories while concealing others. Thus, the political power of images lies in their privileged potential to create visibility, to mobilize, to position and to commemorate.[8]

Political caricatures are a special form of image that visually present social commentary, communicate opinions and attitudes, and subjectively summarize events. They are specific in that they depend on the reader's recognition of the characters, subjects and events depicted; the caricature is thus used to aid identification, with occasional use of exaggerated features and stereotypes.[9] Political caricatures can use humour, satire or irony to differentiate what happened from what ought to happen, according to the artist's view. Thus caricatures could be seen as the outcome of a dialectical struggle between the ideal and the real.[10] The images analysed from both journals here could be classified as political opinion cartoons using the art of caricature.[11]

Researching images can provide a lens into human subjectivity. We see through them dialogues happening within a community in a tangible form, and tensions within these dialogues. The political caricatures discussed in this chapter are used as historical data to view the visualization of national debates and production of meanings in relation to the Egyptian people and nation. The analysis will look into the multiple meanings embodied in the images within the political and social contexts of the time. It examines the images, not as static representations from the past, but as endowed with a social life and enduring effect, and carrying condensed symbols of a national discourse.

In the next section, I present some context in relation to nationalist discourse in Egypt at the time, the art of political caricature in Egypt and the two journals analysed. I then elaborate on the *social life* of these images; looking at the social actors involved, as well as the process the images lived through from production, circulation, reception and censorship.[12] Following this, I analyse the images through four main themes: visibility, national identity, agency and representation of the nation as a woman. This leads to a final discussion of the potential of images in constructing meaning in relation to the nation, their political function in social reform to affirm or deny a sense of agency for the people and the nation after independence, and the endurance of some image symbols in contemporary Egypt.

Egypt and the nationalist discourse, 1800s–1950s

Throughout the nineteenth century, the Egyptian collective identity was closely associated with the Ottoman Empire. The Empire promoted itself as the representative and protector of the Muslim world.[13] This identity association was negotiated during the 1860s–1870s by a growing nationalist movement led by Egyptian elites and intellectuals. They challenged the position of the Ottoman ruling elite as well as European influence in Egypt. Egyptian thinker Rifa'a Rafi' al-Tahtawi was perhaps the first modern Egyptian writer to formulate an embryonic theory of an Egyptian national character that stems from ancient Egyptian civilization rather than the Ottoman Empire.[14]

The discussion of nationalism resurfaced in the early twentieth century as intellectuals in Egypt negotiated their political allegiance. Egyptian nationalist thinking during this period was mostly influenced by Mustafa Kamil and his Watani party and Ahmad Lutfi Al Sayyid and his Umma Party. Kamil and his journal *al-Liwa'* advocated Egyptian territorial nationalism, and even though Kamil saw the Egyptian bond with the Ottoman Empire as the means of liberation from the British occupation, his Ottoman orientation was not unconditional and he did not support the renewal of Ottoman political authority over Egypt.[15] Al-Sayyid and his journal *al-Jarida* rejected a continuing political bond with the Ottomans and saw religiously based solidarity as contradictory to a territorial and secular nationalism of 'Egypt for Egyptians'. They also expanded the idea of a 'homogenous' Egyptian identity extending back to ancient Egypt. Following in his footsteps was Muhammad Husayn Haykal (the editor of one of the journals discussed here).[16]

It was not until 1919 that the leaders of the revolution and the Wafd publically promoted an exclusive territorial nationalist orientation that was secular and completely separate from the Ottoman-Islamic orientation, calling for complete independence and self-determination for Egypt.[17] However, these nationalist movements were by no means homogeneous or representative of the full spectrum of Egyptian society. The Muslim Brotherhood, for example, established in 1928, believed that national independence could only be achieved through moral reform and strict adherence to Islam.[18]

The timeframe of the caricatures discussed in this chapter (1926–31) is of certain significance. First, internationally it falls in the interwar period. Second, it follows the national movement of 1919 that aimed to mobilize a bottom-up national and anti-colonial consciousness drawing on an 'indigenous' Egyptian identity, independent from Arab, Ottoman or British influence. Third, it follows the nominal independence of Egypt from British occupation in 1922 and the implementation of a new constitution, which further developed national identity. Caricatures were used by editors not only as humorous sketches or gap fillers but also to play an active role in the discourse of this nationalistic period,[19] which might be seen as a time of reconstruction for visions of an independent Egyptian state and what it meant for Egyptians to take charge of their own affairs.

Political caricature in Egypt from the 1870s to the 1930s

The Arabic language press was introduced in Egypt by Muhammad Ali who ordered an official government gazette to be published in 1828.[20] The beginning of political graphic caricature in Egypt, meanwhile, is commonly accredited to Ya'qub Sannu''s *Abu Naddara*, a satirical journal first published in 1877.[21] Sannu', an Egyptian Jew of Italian origin, studied in Italy and was inspired by the European press. His caricatures were critical of the British and French Controllers, and of the Khedive and Sultan, and were meant to be visually elaborate so that they would reach a wide, even illiterate, audience. The common theme of his caricatures was that Egyptians were victims not only of European bankers but also of their own corrupt government; his images communicated ideals of independence, freedom and national self-government. After initially encouraging him, when the Khedive Ismail realized the satire was aimed at him, he forced Sannu' into exile in 1878.[22] Sannu' continued to publish *Abu Naddara* from France until 1911, smuggling issues into Egypt where they circulated secretly.[23]

In the late nineteenth and early twentieth centuries, newspapers grew in influence as a result of the political contestations of the 1881 'Urabi Revolt and the arrival of British forces in 1882, which galvanized a new class of journalists writing about a wide range of political and social causes.[24] During this period, journalism became an integral part of the public discourse of modern Egyptian life, debating issues such as the British colonial presence, the nature of religious and secular authority and how to create a national community that was both authentically Egyptian and modern at the same time.[25]

Early in the twentieth century, in this atmosphere of nationalist anti-colonial politics, Egypt witnessed the founding of political parties alongside the launch of new satirical journals that used visuals, among them *Cairo Punch*, *al-Siyasa al-Musawwara*, *al-Arghul* and *Khayal al-Zill – HaHaHa*.[26] *Cairo Punch*'s editor 'Abd al-Hamid Zaki stated that the purpose of his brightly coloured journal of political caricatures was to insist on remembering events people had forgotten, to culturally reclaim visual art as an Eastern art and to serve 'the sons of the East'.[27] It has been argued, however, that still only a few journals featured political caricatures due to the relative novelty of this art form and the censorship of the nationalist press by the British occupation.[28]

During the interwar period there was a revival of the nationalist press.[29] By 1938, there were nearly two hundred Arabic newspapers and journals published in Egypt, even though the literacy rate was only around 30 per cent for males and 10 per cent for females.[30] This literary revival reintroduced political caricature and it continued to flourish whether in official or opposition journals. Political caricatures continued with not only similar targets of criticism but also similar consequences: censorship, imprisonment and exile. The common themes of caricatures were criticism of the government, the European powers, the British occupation and the military. They also commonly represented the Egyptian citizen as helpless and exploited by everyone above them in the hierarchy.[31] It is during this time period that the journals *al-Kashkul* and *al-Siyasa al-Usbu'iyya* were published, and they will be the focus of discussion thereafter.

The two journals: *Al-Kashkul* (1927–31) and *al-Siyasa al-Usbu'iyya* (1926–30)

Al-Kashkul ('The Scrapbook') was a weekly first published in May 1921 by journalist Sulayman Fawzi. The newspaper was among a wave of revived political journalism that started after the Great War.[32] Each issue included four full-page colour caricatures, the subjects of which targeted the government, criticizing its weakness in the face of the British and condemning its corruption.[33] Fawzi presented the newspaper as 'an independent journal that freely expresses its opinions for the sake of serving Egypt and promoting its complete independence. Not in favour of any political party or person … hated by backward thinkers … financially independent, refusing any generous offers that would affect its neutrality.'[34] He also explicitly stated its political opposition stance as 'in opposition to the government in general, the Wafd Party, and in particular Mustafa al-Nahas Pasha'.[35] The last issue appeared in 1934.

Al-Siyasa al-Usbu'iyya was founded in 1926 by the Liberal Constitutionalist Party (al-Aḥrar al-Dusturiyyin). Muhammad Husayn Haykal was editor-in-chief.[36] The journal included editorial pieces by Haykal and other writers, commentary on local and international news, advertisements and coloured and black-and-white caricatures. The newspaper stopped publication between 1931 and 1937, for reasons which are unclear and were not mentioned explicitly on the journal's relaunch. Upon its relaunch in 1937, Haykal wrote an editorial, reinstating the journal's aim to 'advocate for freedom of expression and to form knowledge sharing between East and West and spread the Eastern, Arabic, and Islamic Culture in a new scientific way'.[37]

Censorship: Journal editors and government

The process by which caricatures were created and decisions about what images to use were taken at the editorial level to communicate the journals' main messages. The political content of the two journals may have triggered government censorship, and this may be the reason for the closure of *al-Kashkul* in 1934 and the temporary cessation of *al-Siyasa al-Usbu'iyya* between 1931 and 1937, although no firm evidence was found for the actual reasons for the hiatus. There is one record, however, of *al-Kashkul*'s editor's arrest for insulting public officials, after the journal published a caricature showing the then prime minister, Sa'd Zaghlul, as an organ-grinder in June 1924.[38]

Social actors

To analyse the caricature images in the two journals, consideration is given first to the different social actors involved in the production, reception and censorship of the images. This methodological approach builds on the understanding that once images emerge in the public space they become interdependent between the agency of producers, audience and authority. This highlights the interactive dialogue and interdependence of the social life of the images on the triadic actors as they negotiate different issues in public discourse.[39] To analyse images as meaning-embodied non-static symbols, attention needs to be paid to the different moments in the cycle of their production, circulation and consumption. It is in these moments that meanings accumulate and transform.[40]

Production: The caricature artist

When *al-Kashkul* was founded, it hired Juan Sintes to draw the caricatures.[41] Sintes was a Spanish teacher at the new Royal School of Arts. He had a unique influence on Egyptian caricatures, being (together with Alexander Saroukhan and Ahmet Rifqi) among the foreign fathers who taught many famous modern Egyptian caricaturists such as Muhammad Rakha, 'Abd al-Sami, Salah Jahin and George Bahgouri.[42] This cultural exchange and foreign history of the art of caricaturing in Egypt highlights an interesting dynamic. While the caricature images represented the national ideology of the journals, they were in many instances drawn by non-Egyptians.

Other than Sintes, it is difficult to identify other artists in the two journals. However, in the data set, one artist's signature occurs regularly in both journals, suggesting that many of the caricatures in them were drawn by the same artist. This explains the similar style and representations and may suggest a common genre between the two journals, which makes analysing them together meaningful. Whether the caricatures were signed or not, it is difficult to know who the artist was as their name was not written anywhere in the journal, a common trait at this time. It is fair to argue, however, that the caricatures were largely influenced by their editor's ideology and used to promote the political agenda of the journal.

Reception: Journal audience

Circulation figures for each publication are difficult to establish. However, one record states that between 1927 and 1928 *al-Kashkul* had a circulation estimated at ten thousand.[43] This was considered significant at a time of high illiteracy rates, with 76 per cent illiteracy for males and 95 per cent for females in 1927. Also, the journal's relatively high cost (ten milliemes per issue or just over fifty piasters a year) could have limited its mass distribution.[44]

It is important, however, to look at patterns of literacy and distribution with caution. As Yousef argues, reading and writing practices were a central medium of public exchange for Egyptians, in spite of the many who were illiterate or never had formal schooling. For a largely illiterate and semiliterate society in the beginning of the twentieth century, the skills of reading and writing were deeply communal. Any individual who had learned to read could be called upon to read the news aloud, thus becoming mediators of the written word for the largely oral community around them.[45] Audience reach was therefore beyond a traditionally male urban and highly visible textual public. In terms of distribution rates, the collective impact of a single printed journal may have been more significant than circulation numbers would imply since journals were passed from one hand to another, read aloud, reused and rented from sellers.[46]

The caricatures also used familiar themes and well-known figures, and the captions were written in colloquial Arabic, which made them comprehensible to many Egyptians and could have been read aloud to people gathering to hear and see sections of the paper.[47] This suggests a much wider distribution, especially with the graphic image offering greater accessibility than written text. Unlike Sannu''s *Abu Naddara* and *Cairo Punch*, in which English and French were used, *al-Kashkul* and *al-Siyasa al-Usbu'iyya* were entirely in Arabic, which frames their target audience as local Egyptians. A look at the contents of the articles in the journals, their style of writing and the advertisements placed in their pages would also suggest a more specific Egyptian elite male target audience. This description of producers and audience of the journals' caricatures suggests certain imbalances, particularly as print became more pervasive in the new visual spaces. Print technology privileged certain interactions by certain actors as it was used almost exclusively by the literate to reach the illiterate and literate alike.[48]

The data and visual analysis method

The data set for this chapter constituted all the caricatures produced in *al-Kashkul*'s issues from 1927 to 1931 and in *al-Siyasa al-Usbu'iyya*' from 1926 to 1930. The analysis focused only on the visual images of the caricatures in both journals. However, to understand these images in context, captions, articles surrounding the caricatures and advertisements displayed on the same pages as the caricatures were also considered. The total number of caricature images from both journals is 322 images (107 from *al-Siyasa al-Usbu'iyya'* and 215 from *al-Kashkul*). The hard copies of these issues were obtained through the archive of the American University in Cairo; the one-year difference in the timeframe of the two titles is due to archive availability.

The visual analysis was carried out in three steps: First, image content analysis[49] was used to classify and provide a general quantifiable understanding of the main contents of the images and the frequency of their occurrence to check for their significance in relation to the total number of images under study. This provided the data's essential character and will be discussed in the first theme of analysis. The second step moved from the denotative visual elements of the picture to the connotative social and historical meanings embodied in the symbols of the visual image.[50] Finally, the third step was to identify the main overarching themes that summed up the patterns emerging from the whole data set. Selecting these themes depended on those that responded the most to the chapter's focus of the meanings related to the perception of the nation. The themes are national identity, agency of the people and the image of the nation as a woman. These will be discussed in themes two, three, and four.

Visibility: Representing whom and how

Content analysis of the data set aimed to give an overview of who is represented in the images, how they are depicted and how frequently they are presented. Images were coded for the actors involved in each image, how they are portrayed (e.g. body shape, dress, posture, explicit traits) and the setting and ambiance of the image (e.g. government office, capital city). Those features helped to formulate the overall image presented of each actor (such as an Egyptian peasant) and each concept (such as the Egyptian nation). The text of the caricatures was used to supplement the understanding and analysis of the visual content and to identify the different characters and their voices.

The explicit overall message of the majority of the caricatures in both journals is political opposition to authority, resisting foreign presence, taxes and government corruption. The majority of the caricatures explicitly showed the corrupt government as the main reason for the suffering of Egyptians, with a significantly higher depiction of Pashas in government than British or foreign officials. This is further emphasized in one caricature where a Pasha (as an official) is represented as more corrupt than the British,[51] and in another, a Pasha official is seen as unfit to join the newly established Muslim Brotherhood because he lacks honesty.[52]

Out of 322 caricatures, 122 depicted government officials. Most were drawn wearing suits and a fez, typical dress of government bureaucrats at the time. In 114 of these 122 images, the official is portrayed visually as corrupt and greedy, using exaggeratedly overweight bodies (Figure 8.2). Their facial features were also depicted as evil-looking, typically conspiring at the backdoor with each other or with British officials against each other and against the general Egyptian public. Only in 8 images out of the 122

Figure 8.2 *al-Kashkul* no. 358 (23 March 1928).

were brave national Pashas depicted, portrayed as resisting the British presence and working for Egyptians.

The second-most represented figure is that of the Egyptian, in most instances as a peasant in the village or an urban worker. Of forty-nine images, they are represented as helpless and passive through facial features, posture and dress forty-three times (Figure 8.3). Only six images out of forty-nine depict informed, well-dressed citizens in upright postures stating their opinions and discussing politics. The portrayal of the

Figure 8.3 *al-Kashkul* no. 538 (4 September 1931).

Egyptian citizen is predominantly male, although twelve images show female peasants or upper-class women in Cairo streets with western dresses.

British officials still serving in Egypt were the third-most represented group in the caricatures. They were presented in twenty-four images with evil facial features, mostly dressed in suits and in office environments (Figure 8.4). They were portrayed visually and in text as intrusive 'unwelcome guests' (*ḍuyuf to'aal*) conspiring against the interests of the Egyptian public. With one exception, they were presented as relatively less corrupt than the Egyptian pashas and government ministers who were depicted as harming their own people.

Characters appearing in the caricatures fewer than ten times were sheikhs, priests, police, military officers, actresses, members of the Society of the Muslim Brothers[53] and citizens of other Arab countries. Other than these few occurrences, the diversity of Egyptian society in terms of gender or class was not explored beyond the two

Figure 8.4 *al-Kashkul* no. 344 (16 December 1927).

categories described above, of the disempowered citizen – mostly a peasant – and the corrupt government official.

Visually constructing national identity

Looking at the images in the context of the discourses around national identity at the time, the focus is on what these caricatures say in relation to identity negotiation. The explicit visual message that recurs throughout the caricatures is the search for a national identity that is authentically Egyptian, not borrowing from Western or Ottoman dress and traditions. Figure 8.5 is a clear example, using a full page to lay out the different outfits found in Egypt, explicitly asking, 'The chaos of fashion customs in Egypt, where is the national custom then?'

Resorting to the past for a distinct Egyptian identity was clear in the use of icons from ancient Egypt to refer to the glorified past in contrast to the disempowered situation of the present. For example, some caricatures used ancient Egyptian symbols such as the Sphinx or the faces of ancient Egyptian kings as they looked ashamedly at the current state of Egyptian society. There was no emphasis on an Arab identity. The

Figure 8.5 *al-Siyasa al-Usbuʿiyya* no. 22 (4 December 1926).

images did not communicate a significant Egyptian national identity that is attached to its Arab neighbours. There was only one caricature that mentioned nearby Arab nations, in the context of the need to connect with 'our Arab brothers' to support an independent Egyptian entity.

There was a prevailing contradiction, however, in terms of the search for an independent national identity. The images mentioned looked for a unique independent national character and referred to ancient Egypt as the source for resurrection of a glorified nation, but this message was contradicted by a different kind of image on the same pages of the journals, that of advertising and fashion articles. While the caricatures distanced the orientation of the journals from everything foreign, the advertisements reflected a yearning for an upper-class western lifestyle, in fashion, eating and drinking (Figure 8.6).

From one side, advertisements in those journals could be seen as a reflection of and an understanding from the advertisers as to what their mainly upper-class readership was looking for in terms of lifestyle and identity associations. But advertisements could be also endeavouring to create a yearning to sell their foreign products. It is hard to find evidence to put more weight on one assumption over the other, and it is probably an interplay between both: a need from the educated upper class to associate with the 'modern' world standards in dress and lifestyles, as well as an advertising strategy to associate the product with a distinct and high status for its consumers.

Agency of the Egyptian citizen

In spite of the ancient Egyptian imagery communicating a distinct national identity, and the mission of the two journals for a strong independent nation, the representation of the Egyptian citizen in the majority of the caricatures communicated a different message. This figure was far from being an independent, dignified agent but was most often represented as a helpless peasant, with faceless features, poor clothes and a bent forward posture, passively awaiting his destiny (Figure 8.7a). The popular masses were portrayed in the background of several caricatures as children, immature in size and features, compared to government officials (Figure 8.7b). The pattern of the citizen in 43 out of 49 images was of one who is exploited, ignorant, passive, lazy, lacking political engagement and unqualified to take a government position. The Egyptian peasant character was represented as oppressed by poverty and debts, following orders blindly for lack of agency and commonly accompanied by a donkey, which signifies being far behind in terms of modernity. Only in six instances were they represented as 'actors': twice in memory of the 1919 revolution, which highlights a period of active citizenship and agency against British occupation, and four times as actively discussing politics in the field, voicing opinions and being politically aware. Unlike the faces of government officials and notables, peasants in most instances lacked any distinctive facial features, drawn with anonymous shaded faces, positioned in the background and in many instances with their backs to the main action of the image.

This sense of denied agency was evident in text as well as imagery. Examples of the passive connotations accompanying the images included statements such as 'they will leave us to the British to abuse us',[54] 'who will dress us, feed us, and fix our lives?'[55] and 'I am afraid they will make us sell our own cloth'.[56]

Figure 8.6 Black and white whisky: The drink of the British and international aristocratic class, *al-Siyasa al-Usbuʿiyya* no. 226 (5 July 1930).

Neither journal developed a distinct stock character of the 'average' Egyptian citizen, whether a city worker or a peasant. This differed from other publications such as *Ruz al-Yusuf*, founded in 1925, whose caricaturists created *al-Masri Efendi* (Mr Average Egyptian), a short, middle-class citizen, wearing a fez and glasses, a character

Figure 8.7a *al-Kashkul* no. 524 (29 May 1931).

known for his sense of humour and intelligent sarcasm and not for the arrogance of the aristocratic class.[57] Later in 1941, Muhammad Rakha decided that al-Masri Efendi no longer represented the Egyptian character and instead developed the character of *ibn al-balad* (the son of the people), who is a more independent and emancipated personality, one which more accurately represented Egypt, according to the artist.[58]

This lack of a distinct visual character in the caricatures and the disempowered, anonymous representation of citizens can be explained through the ideology of Haykal, the editor of *al-Siyasa al-Usbuʿiyya*. For Haykal, the natural environment of the Nile Valley, with its remarkable stability, formed the national character of Egyptians. He portrayed his countrymen's behaviour as inclined towards acceptance, submissiveness and stability. He described the Egyptian people as immortalizing the past, having no wish for change or progress, prioritizing continuity between generations and submitting blindly to customs and habits. He saw them as having the patience to wait passively for change, apathetic and dislocated from politics, never thinking they had a share in any regime or obligation in political struggles.[59] This portrayal of the Egyptian character contradicts his own ideas of modernism and social reform, as according to his own argument there was little that could be done about it.[60]

Figure 8.7b *al-Siyasa al-Usbuʿiyya* no. 228 (19 July 1930).

The woman in green

As mentioned above, women were rarely depicted in the caricatures. Only twelve images out of the total showed female Egyptian citizens; eight of these showed helpless female peasants similar to the general representation of citizens, with women mostly part of the background rather than main characters. The remaining examples depict upper-class women in Cairo streets, wearing western dresses, and cinema actresses such as Ruz (Fatima) al-Yusuf (by this time also the owner of a journal) and feminists such as Nabawiyya Musa.

However, of particular interest here is a recurring female character that differs from these. She wears a green dress, sometimes decorated with a white crescent and three white stars, resembling the Egyptian flag of the time. Sometimes a girl, at other times she is a woman in contemporary dress and high heels, or a woman in peasant clothing (Figures 8.8a–d and 8.9). In all eight instances, she symbolized Egypt as a nation.

In *al-Kashkul*, she appears seven times. The visual is not fixed: in some instances, she is an elegant woman in a green western-style dress with high heels and a black

Figure 8.8a *al-Kashkul* no. 321 (8 July 1927).

Figure 8.8b *al-Kashkul* no. 345 (23 December 1927).

head scarf (Figures 8.1 and 8.8a). In others, she is a young girl wearing bows, small and naïve in comparison to other figures, such as politicians holding her by the arm (Figure 8.8b), serving her on a tray as a gift to European officials (Figure 8.8c) or standing in front of other European countries as a diminutive figure (see Figure 8.8d). The common meaning, whether she is an attractive woman or a vulnerable girl, is that of passivity, powerlessness and lack of self-ownership; she is always controlled and occupied by others, whether Egyptian government officials or foreigners.

Al-Siyasa al-Usbuʿiyya offered a different kind of representation. There is only one occurrence of the nation as a woman in this journal (Figure 8.9) and it is that of a peasant conservatively covered. Standing firmly, and unlike the *al-Kashkul* character that has no voice, this woman is the only voice narrated in the caricature, standing with the background of the pyramids and sphinx in defiance of the government official who has his back to her and the British official sitting oblivious to her. The police officer to the left is ready to do his job, though the Egyptian and British officials seem to object

Figure 8.8c *al-Kashkul* no. 526 (12 June 1931).

to his role. She is complaining about chaos breaking out in Egypt: 'The police are trying to control the chaos, while government officials are causing more chaos, and the British government with its ships are hindering my efforts … who will be responsible then for the consequences of this chaos for my children?' In this image, the nation as woman has a quite different significance to those in *al-Kashkul*. Here she is endowed with the status of an ancient civilization behind her, the rootedness of the peasant character through her dress and power in her posture and voice in defiance of the

Figure 8.8d *al-Kashkul* no. 317 (10 June 1927).

Figure 8.9 *al-Siyasa al-Usbu'iyya* no. 229 (26 July 1930).

other actors as she represents the 'mother nation' protecting her 'children'. The choice of the nation as a peasant could be understood as the territorial nationalist perception of peasants as 'culturally authentic', with an indigenous, concrete tie to the land unlike foreigners or the urban elite.[61]

The image of Egypt as a woman in a green dress is not restricted to these two titles. The representation of the nation as an abstract concept in visual form is a common practice used to reaffirm unity and create a strong icon for collective identity. Looking at the selection and attributes of the chosen icon is useful in understanding meanings relating to particular nationalist sentiments and, in this case, also illuminating gender roles. Also, the idea of the nation as a woman is not unique to the case of Egypt; it is also seen in European examples, such as the French 'Marianne',[62] who was a predecessor of the Egyptian figure and might have inspired the locally adapted representation.

A study of visual representations of the Egyptian nation from the 1870s to the 1930s shows that since Sannu''s caricatures (1877), Egypt was represented as a woman.[63] The image of the woman changed over time, differing in age, size and attributes. From the 1920s and early 1930s, the nation was represented increasingly in contemporary European dress, moving away from using a face veil or headscarf, in a process that coincided with the unveiling of Egyptian women. Thus, the perception of Egyptian womanhood and the nation of Egypt as a woman were tied together.[64] Images of women representing the nation multiplied in the 1920s as Egypt gained quasi-independence. This trend can be particularly attributed to the proliferation of one specific image: Mahmud Mukhtar's sculpture Nahdat Misr ('The Awakening of Egypt'), which depicted the sphinx rising and a peasant woman unveiling. Both the sphinx and the woman represent Egypt: one the ancient civilization, the other the modern nation with the peasant woman lifting her veil symbolizing liberation.[65]

The portrayal of Egypt as a woman can be seen as part of the construction of the new nation state, characterizing through this woman the entire population. The portrayal fits with the 1890s' domestic ideology of women's role as 'mothers of the nation' whose job was to teach their children patriotism.[66] The representation of the nation as a woman also touched upon notions of honour and instilled the viewer with a sense of duty to protect her,[67] as seen in the vulnerable images of *al-Kashkul* (Figure 8.8b–d), or perhaps generating a romantic attachment to the nation as a precious woman (Figures 8.1 and 8.8a).

The potential of visual images

Political caricatures may be less effective than the printed word for communicating reasoned criticism and detailed argument, but they have a significant role in disseminating representations.[68] While it is arguable how the audience comprehended the political commentary of the caricatures and whether the illiterate had the visual literacy to interact with them,[69] the representations in the images gave visibility to and positioned different actors in society: the powerful corrupt government elite, the interfering foreign powers and the passive actors of the citizen and the nation as an entity.

The effect of caricatures goes beyond the direct audience of these two journals. The art of political caricature in Egypt was revived during the 1920–30s, and it is fair to assume that the images in these journals, along with others, provided the references and visual clues for later caricaturists in journals that had much wider distribution, especially as these caricaturists became mentors or points of reference for later generations. Some reproduced similar representations of the social actors, and some reconstructed a more distinct and empowered vision of the 'average' Egyptian, such as the caricaturist Rakha in the 1940s. Thus, the social life of these images lived on as visual resources for later artists as well as visual evidence in archives representing the image of the nation and the people at a specific point in time.

This highlights the transformative social life of images and their effect on a community. Images in caricatures can be used by the literate elite to construct an 'imagined community',[70] give shape to the developing meaning of the newly independent nation and feed into the collective memory[71] of the community. The images analysed contributed to a helpless and passive image of the people, reaffirming a sense of denied agency with regards to taking control of their own affairs and forming an independent, grassroots, empowered nation.

Political use of visual images

The two editors of these two journals communicated a vision of Egypt as an independent nation moving towards modernization and development. They positioned their journals as oppositional, defending Egyptian interests, promoting an independent Egyptian identity and advocating for the development of the society. However, the portrayal of the people in the caricatures show little in support of the journal's stated social role.

One explanation could be that the visuals were meant as a descriptive tool to present reality from the editors' or caricaturists' perspectives: the people and the nation are disempowered and have little agency to change their destiny. Using those portrayals, they highlight their social critique of the power (or lack of power) of the people vis-à-vis the elite and foreign powers. Thus, the images described the present rather than reconstructing this present to orient a different future.

Another explanation could be that the editors' vision for the autonomous independent identity of the nation was a top-down one that had little faith in the potential of the people, especially the peasants, as active participants in this stage of social reform. This can be further seen in Haykal's ideas about the static and passive nature of the Egyptian character, especially the peasant. This elitist approach to political engagement and distrust of 'politics from below' is not unique to these journals but was common among the intellectual class of 1930s Egypt, seeing social change as only possible from top-down or foreign-led modernization.[72]

The style of the journal articles, language use and advertisements show that the target audience of the journals was a narrow, elite, literate portion of society. According to the second explanation, the images could be part of this elite-to-elite dialogue, talking *about* rather than *to* the 'average' citizen. It is unlikely that the images were meant by such reformists to disempower the people; rather, they were talking to a narrow elite audience, possibly oblivious to the fact that those disempowering images were also seen by the masses. Still, the representation reflects an upper-class mentality that – just like the government – sees the mass of Egyptians as illiterate and unfit to manage their own affairs, let alone lead the reform of the nation.

The visual representation not only contradicted the journals' claimed reformist aims but also the aspiration of what the peasant character and women mean in Egyptian culture. The portrayal of the disempowered peasant contrasts with celebrations of the Egyptian peasant that began in the 1890s, which saw them as the soul of Egypt representing all that was virtuous and noble in the nation.[73] The lack of representation of the female citizen contrasted with the reformist ideas of the editors. Even though the nation is represented as a woman, Egyptian women were rarely represented in caricatures or in political life but were kept to the perimeters of public life.[74]

A further contradiction in the political purpose of the journals and the images within can be seen in the advertisements. The journals claimed an Egyptian identity that is independent and indigenous and sought to move away from British, Ottoman and foreign influences. Yet the advertisements on the same page as the caricatures run counter to this: they were aimed at an elite class who aspired to a European lifestyle. This shows the often turbulent negotiations between a locally inspired tradition and the aspirational foreign culture in constructing an Egyptian national identity.

In a critical time of intellectuals negotiating the national discourse to reconstruct the nation and the Egyptian people's independent identity, images would have had the political and social potential to give visibility to the new nation, representing and positioning its key social actors for reform, and mobilizing the people around a future nationalist vision. Political caricatures specifically could have created a reflexive platform for the reconstruction of meaning. However, the caricature images provided a minimal renegotiation of national identity. The visual representations – even if they in part communicated a reality – failed to reflect on this reality or reconstruct it in a way to orient it to an imagined future to which the journals claimed to aspire. It rather fed into the existing dominant discourse of helplessness, conformity and powerlessness.

An enduring discourse

The images discussed here are not an isolated example but part of a larger national discourse that extended to other media (press articles, political speeches and television) and persisted over time. That is the discourse of authority as the guardian of the people, the leader as the father and protector of the nation, and the masses who lack the agency to manage their own matters or to have an informed voice in politics.

The images' political power in positioning the Egyptian citizen as helpless and incapable of change has its own ethical and practical consequences. The sense of denied agency repeated in the images had its effect on the audience's self-perception of helplessness. Learned helplessness explains how when people over time are shown that they are incapable and lack control over their environment, they suspend further efforts to reach their potential even when they have the necessary capacity.[75] Individuals can thus learn to attribute national failures to foreign powers and conspiracy theories because they have learned they have no control over their own society.

Looking at Egypt today, we see this conspiracy discourse still prevalent and propagated by the official media. Certain meanings and aspects of the symbols found in the caricatures endure in public discourse today; the general Egyptian public is

Figure 8.10a *Akhbar al-Yawm* 10 October 2013.

portrayed in a similar light by the elite class, and the current regime uses images to communicate a patriarchal protective role of Egyptians. One example is a widespread poster that was produced by the Egyptian army after the 2011 revolution, portraying an officer, symbolizing the army, holding a small baby that symbolizes the Egyptian people. The text reads, 'The army and the people are one hand.'[76] In an even closer parallel, a caricature published in *al-Akhbar al-Yawm* in October 2013 (Figure 8.10a) again represents Egypt as the woman in a green dress held helplessly in the embrace of her superhero saviour, President al-Sisi. The caption reads: 'Do not be surprised, this is not an American movie, this is 'El-Sisi-man' rescuing Egypt before its fall.' In a later caricature in *al-Yawm al-Sabi'a*, published in July 2018 (Figure 8.10b) titled 'Five years since al Sisi's 3rd of July declaration', Egypt, symbolized by the woman, holds tight to her saviour, who is rescuing her from 'the non-nation, chaos, dependency, loss of regional role, loss of identity' and taking her to the safety of 'nationhood, stability, independent decision making, return of regional role, and protected identity', while

Figure 8.10b *al-Yawm al-Sabi'a* 2 July 2018.

avoiding falling into the trap underneath of 'the terrorist brotherhood', a reference to the Muslim Brotherhood, which was declared a terrorist group after al-Sisi rose to power.

This discourse of the helpless nation in need of the father figure was briefly deconstructed by the 2011 revolution's visual production, which replaced the image of the leader with that of the people, introducing counter-images of empowered youth as agents of change leading the way. Revolutionary street art and caricatures portrayed protestors, especially women, as the heroes of their time (See Zeft's Nefertiti with the gas mask[77] and El Tenin's portrayal of the woman with the blue bra).[78] However these images were quickly overshadowed in public spaces following the military takeover in 2013, returning again to visuals such as those in Figures 8.10a and b that position the army (personified in the figure of al-Sisi) as the saviour of the helpless people and nation.

Examining these images, whether of the pre-independence caricatures or more recent examples, sheds light on the prevailing discourses and representations of the people and the nation in connection with different historical events and power transitions. The images communicate their producers' perceptions of agency and the power of the people in relation to the people in power. They also live on to tell stories to their audience about who they are and where they are positioned, and open up or exclude ways of seeing possibilities for change in the status quo.

Notes

I would like to express my gratitude to the editors for their thoughtful advice on this chapter and to Brady Wagoner, Cristina Dozio, Eman Maarek, Ivan Lind Christensen, Marina Assis Pinheiro and Shaimaa El Sadek who kindly reviewed it and provided helpful edits and comments.

1 Mitchell, 'What Is an Image?', 503–37.
2 Unless otherwise noted, all translations are by the author.
3 Awad and Wagoner, 'Image Politics', 197–210.
4 Lonchuk and Rosa, 'Voices of Graphic Art Images', 129–43.
5 Moscovici, 'Phenomenon of Social Representations', 3–68.
6 Harré and Langenhove, *Positioning Theory*, 14–30.
7 Marková, *Dialogicality and Social Representations*, 156.
8 Awad and Wagoner, 'Image Politics', 199.
9 Kemnitz, 'The Cartoon', 81–93.
10 Coupe, 'Theory of Political Caricature', 79–95.
11 Kemnitz, 'The Cartoon', 82.
12 Ibid.
13 Gershoni and Jankowski, *Egypt, Islam, and the Arabs*, 4–10.
14 Ibid., 11–15.
15 Ibid., 7–8.
16 Ibid.
17 Ibid.
18 Kandil, *Soldiers, Spies, and Statesmen*, 13.
19 ʿAbd al-Naʿim, *Hikayat fi al-fukaha*, 11.
20 Yousef, *Composing Egypt*, 2–4.
21 Gendzier, 'James Sanua', 25.
22 Marsot, 'Cartoon in Egypt', 2–15.
23 Gendzier, 'James Sanua', 26.
24 Yousef, *Composing Egypt*, 16–31.
25 Ibid.
26 Booth, 'What's in a Name?', 271–303.
27 Ibid.
28 Marsot, 'Cartoon in Egypt', 12.
29 Ibid.
30 UNESCO, *Progress of Literacy in Various Countries.*
31 Marsot, 'Cartoon in Egypt', 9.
32 Ibid.
33 Baron, 'Nationalist Iconography', 105–24.
34 *Al-Kashkul* no. 315 (27 May 1927).
35 *Al-Kashkul* no. 366 (18 May 1928).
36 A writer, journalist and politician, Haykal came from an upper-class landowning background. After studying law in Cairo, he graduated with a doctoral degree from the Sorbonne in 1912. He was a member of the committee which wrote the 1923 constitution and served as Minister of Education in 1938. He became Deputy President of the Liberal Constitutionalist Party in 1941 and President from 1943 to 1952, after which political parties were banned. Among the most influential

intellectuals in formulating a national orientation in the 1920s, Haykal developed an Egyptian territorial nationalism that linked national identity to the Egyptian environment in his writings, although he later took an Islamic turn. His many disciples carried forward his ideals and influenced Egyptian public opinion through their published works (Gershoni and Jankowski, *Egypt, Islam, and the Arabs*, 89).

37 *Al-Siyasa al-Usbu'iyya* no. 2-01 (16 January 1937) (author's translation).
38 Yousef, *Composing Egypt*.
39 Awad and Wagoner, 'Image Politics', 196–7.
40 Lister and Wells, 'Seeing Beyond belief', 61–91.
41 Ettmüller, 'Caricature and Egypt's Revolution of 25 January 2011', 138–48.
42 Ibid., 140.
43 National Archives (Great Britain), 149.
44 Baron, 'Nationalist Iconography', 116.
45 Yousef, *Composing Egypt*, 18.
46 Ibid., 31.
47 Baron, 'Nationalist Iconography', 116.
48 Yousef, *Composing Egypt*, 128.
49 Bell, 'Content Analysis of Visual Images', 10–34.
50 Barthes, *Image, Music, Text*.
51 *Al-Kashkul* no. 547 (6 November 1931), 1.
52 *Al-Kashkul* no. 550 (27 November 1931), 11.
53 The Society of Muslim Brothers, known also as Muslim Brotherhood, is a transnational Sunni Islamist organization established in 1928 by Hassan al-Banna.
54 *Al-Kashkul* no. 367 (25 May 1928).
55 *Al-Kashkul* no. 335 (14 October 1927).
56 *Al-Kashkul* no. 327 (19 August 1927).
57 Rizkallah, 'Visualization and Representation', 37.
58 Baron, 'Nationalist Iconography', 115–16.
59 Gershoni and Jankowski, *Egypt, Islam, and the Arabs*, 89.
60 Ibid.
61 Baron, 'Nationalist Iconography', 123.
62 Ibid., 122.
63 Ibid., 106.
64 Ibid., 116–17.
65 Ibid.
66 Baron, 'Nationalist Iconography', 122–4.
67 Baron, 'Construction of National Honour', 246–7.
68 Kemnitz, 'The Cartoon'.
69 Baron, 'Nationalist Iconography'.
70 Anderson, *Imagined Communities*.
71 Halbwachs, *On Collective Memory*.
72 Bayat, *Life as Politics*, 39.
73 Gershoni and Jankowski, *Egypt, Islam, and the Arabs*, 205.
74 Baron, 'Nationalist Iconography', 121–2.
75 Seligman, *Helplessness*.
76 Awad, 'Documenting a Contested Memory', 234–54.
77 Awad et al., 'The (Street) Art of Resistance', 175.
78 Awad, 'Documenting a Contested Memory', 241.

Bibliography

ʿAbd al-Naʿim, Ahmad. *Hikayat fi al-fukaha wa al-karikatir*. Cairo: Dar al-ʿUlum, 2009.
Anderson, Benedict. *Imagined Communities*. London: Verso, 1983.
Awad, Sarah H. 'Documenting a Contested Memory: Symbols in the Changing City Space of Cairo'. *Culture and Psychology* 23, no. 2 (2017): 234–54.
Awad, Sarah H., and Brady Wagoner. 'Image Politics of the Arab Uprisings'. In *The Psychology of Radical Social Change: From Rage to Revolution*, edited by Brady Wagoner, Fathali M. Moghaddam and Jaan Valsiner, 197–210. Cambridge: Cambridge University Press, 2018.
Awad, Sarah H., Brady Wagoner and Vlad Glaveanu. 'The (Street) Art of Resistance'. In *Resistance in everyday life: Constructing cultural experiences*, edited by N. Chaudhary, P. Hviid, G. Marsico, and J. Villadsen, 161–80. New York: Springer, 2017.
Baron, Beth. 'The Construction of National Honour in Egypt'. *Gender and History* 5, no. 2 (1993): 246–7.
Baron, Beth. 'Nationalist Iconography: Egypt as a Woman'. In *Rethinking Nationalism in the Arab Middle East*, edited by James Jankowski and Israel Gershoni, 105–24. New York: Columbia University Press, 1997.
Barthes, Roland. *Image, Music, Text* (essays selected and translated by Stephen Heath). London: Fontana, 1977.
Bayat, Asef. *Life as Politics: How Ordinary People Change the Middle East*. Amsterdam: Amsterdam University Press, 2010.
Bell, Philip. 'Content Analysis of Visual Images'. In *Handbook of Visual Analysis*, edited by Theo van Leeuwen and Carey Jewitt, 10–24. London: Sage, 2001.
Booth, Marilyn. 'What's in a Name? Branding *Punch* in Cairo, 1908'. In *Asian Punches, A Transcultural Affair*, edited by Hans Harder and Barbara Mittler, 271–303. Berlin: Springer-Verlag, 2013.
Coupe, William A. 'Observations on a Theory of Political Caricature'. *Comparative Studies in Society and History* 11, no. 1 (1969): 79–95.
Ettmüller, Eliane. 'Caricature and Egypt's Revolution of 25 January 2011'. *Studies in Contemporary History* 9, no. 1 (2012): 138–148.
Gendzier, Irene L. 'James Sanua and Egyptian Nationalism'. *Middle East Journal* 15, no. 1 (1961): 16–28.
Gershoni, Israel, and James P. Jankowski. *Egypt, Islam, and the Arabs: The Search for Egyptian Nationhood, 1900–1930*. New York: Oxford University Press, 1986.
Halbwachs, Maurice. *On Collective Memory*. Translated by F. J. Ditter Jr. and V. Y. Ditter. New York: Harper and Row, 1950/1980.
Harré, Rom, and Luk Van Langenhove, eds. *Positioning Theory: Moral Contexts of International Action*. Oxford: Wiley-Blackwell, 1998.
Kandil, Hazem. *Soldiers, Spies, and Statesmen: Egypt's Road to Revolt*. London: Verso, 2012.
Kemnitz, Thomas Milton. 'The Cartoon as a Historical Source'. *Journal of Interdisciplinary History* 4, no. 1 (1973): 81–93.
Lister, Martin, and Liz Wells. 'Seeing Beyond Belief: Cultural Studies as an Approach to Analysing the Visual'. In *Handbook of Visual Analysis*, edited by Theo van Leeuwen and Carey Jewitt, 61–91. London: Sage, 2001.
Lonchuk, Marcela, and Alberto Rosa. 'Voices of Graphic Art Images'. In *Dialogicality in Focus: Challenges to Theory, Method and Application*, edited by Mariann Märtsin,

Brady Wagoner, Emma-Louise Aveling, Irini Kadianaki and Lisa Whittaker, 129–43. New York: Nova Science, 2011.
Mitchell, William J. T. 'What Is an Image?' *New Literary History* 15, no. 3 (1984): 503–37.
Marková, Ivana. *Dialogicality and Social Representations: The Dynamics of Mind*. Cambridge: Cambridge University Press, 2003.
Marsot, Afaf. 'The Cartoon in Egypt'. *Comparative Studies in Society and History* 13, no. 1 (1971): 2–15.
Moscovici, Serge. 'The Phenomenon of Social Representations'. In *Social Representations*, edited by R. M. Farr and S. Moscovici, 3–68. Cambridge: Cambridge University Press, 1984.
The National Archives (Great Britain), Foreign Office (FO) 371/13880/8570, Annual Report for 1927–1928, Cairo, 26 August 1929, 149.
Rizkallah, Sara. 'The Visualization and Representation of Gender in Egyptian Comics, What Is the Fuss All About?'. MA dissertation, American University in Cairo, 2015.
Seligman, Martin E. P. *Helplessness: On Depression, Development, and Death. A Series of Books in Psychology*. New York: WH Freeman, 1975.
UNESCO. *Progress of Literacy in Various Countries: A preliminary Statistical Study of available census data since 1900*. Paris: Firmin-Didot, 1953. http://unesdoc.unesco.org/images/0000/000028/002898EB.pdf.
Yousef, Hoda A. *Composing Egypt: Reading, Writing, and the Emergence of a Modern Nation 1870–1930*. Stanford, CA: Stanford University Press, 2016.

9

Cultural communicators: The Greek Arabists of interwar Egypt

Anthony Gorman

At the beginning of the twentieth century, Egypt was composed of a majority Arabic-speaking population with numerous smaller groups of other Middle Eastern and Mediterranean peoples and colonial elites.[1] The multiplicity of local, regional and imperial languages it supported were configured unevenly in status, currency and functionality in a way that reflected the contemporary political, economic and social realities. A diverse education system of government schools, private foreign colleges and religious centres of learning served as primary sites for language acquisition and propagation while governmental and community bodies consolidated the authority and prestige of particular tongues. Mediated by various hierarchies, specific contexts and social boundaries, communication between different language communities nevertheless functioned as a vital organic part of a culturally pluralist society. Within the framework of economic and social life, for example, entrepreneurial men and women negotiated commercial transactions while social intercourse was pursued in personal conversations, neighbourhood relations and other communal activities. In the cultural field, journalists, commentators and other writers wrote in the press and elsewhere engaging in matters of intellectual debate and public interest. Such intercommunal exchanges represented creative sites of cultural production that reflected the dynamic nature of cross-cultural relations and the organic character of Egyptian multicultural society.

In exploring this multilingual environment, this chapter examines the role of Greek Arabists of Egypt as cultural communicators between the majority Arabophone culture and the local Greek population. Initially focused on Arabic as a language to learn, these scholars over time expanded their range and focus to produce a significant body of popular learning on Egyptian and Arab culture through translation, commentary and popularization. An informal circle rather than a tight coherent group, some would participate in a broader progressive movement during the interwar period that sought by educating the community to accommodate the changing political circumstances as Egypt moved towards an anticipated postcolonial future after a long period of British occupation. Their collective activity would capture an important manifestation of entangled culture and at the same time seek to facilitate its realignment. It would also contribute an important dimension to the development of Egyptian Hellenism (Αιγυπτιωτισμός), that is, the Egyptian Greek culture that was the product of the specific conditions of Greek life in Egypt in contrast to the metropolitan national culture promoted by the Greek state or mainland Greek society.[2]

In the modern Middle Eastern context, the phenomenon of translation has been a potent force, associated on an international scale with the Nahda and the rendering of European, chiefly French, works *into* Arabic, variously framed in terms of enlightenment, modernization and seduction.[3] Within the Arab world itself, the role of translators and translation *from* Arabic has been examined in specific ways that engage with economic, social and security activities, such as tourism, working relationships on archaeological sites[4] and the gathering of intelligence on minority communities.[5] In this discussion, Egyptian Greek Arabists are cast as cultural communicators whose activities were a function of the connection and concerns of their community within a majority Arabic culture.

Historical background

The Greek presence in modern Egypt derives principally from the mass migration encouraged by Muhammad Ali and his successors in the nineteenth century to attract those with desirable skills to settle in the country. The phenomenon was part of a political and economic reconfiguration of the region in which the pluralist character of Eastern Mediterranean society was transformed by expanding international trade and rising European political influence. Many Greeks, both from the new state of Greece and the Aegean islands and Anatolia that were still part of the Ottoman Empire, took up economic opportunities and at times political safe haven, or were drawn by family networks and community connections. By the beginning of the twentieth century, Greeks had already assumed a significant position in many aspects of Egyptian commercial, cultural and social life. Most familiar in the literature are the cotton merchants, bankers and industrialists,[6] but the socio-economic profile of the Egyptian Greek population was in fact much more diverse and included members of the professional classes, such as lawyers, doctors and pharmacists, as well as grocers, small shopkeepers and factory workers. By the late 1920s, the Greek population of Egypt would reach a peak of almost one hundred thousand, found principally in the cities but with a notable presence in the villages of the Delta and Upper Egypt.[7]

During this period, Egyptian Greeks created a vibrant cultural and intellectual life that not only expressed a Hellenic character but also the influence of the local Egyptian environment. This was created, disseminated and sustained in both formal and informal ways. The education system, including an extensive network of local Greek community institutions, and an extensive array of cultural clubs and organizations, such as the Alexandrian Library Association and the Endefkterion Cairo, constituted significant loci in the development of Egyptian Greek intellectual life. Less formally, workplaces, cafes and literary salons provided venues for social and cultural interaction.

The extensive record of Greek language publications in Egypt served as a vital medium for the expression of this cultural effervescence. From the mid-nineteenth until the mid-twentieth century, more than three thousand books were published on a great array of topics on history, literature, religion and poetry, both fiction and non-fiction.[8] The press, both newspapers and periodicals, demonstrated a similar diversity. In the century following the appearance of the first Greek language newspaper in Egypt, *I Egyptos* [Η Αίγυπτος], in 1862, over four hundred different newspaper and journal titles owned by Greeks were published in Egypt. They ranged greatly in character, orientation, circulation and longevity. Long-running dailies such as *Kairon* (Κάϊρον) (est. 1873) in Cairo and *Tachydromos* (Ταχυδρόμος) (est. 1880) in Alexandria, each with estimated circulations of about ten thousand in 1929, focused on a broad spectrum of local and world affairs.[9] Other more specialized periodicals dedicated to the arts and literature, satirical reviews, student publications and illustrated magazines had a more limited readership and sometimes fleeting existence.[10] The great majority of these were published in Greek but over fifty newspapers were bilingual, most often Greek with French or Arabic, or multilingual, such as *Dodekanessos* (1925–9, 1933–8), which employed four languages. A small number were in another language entirely, notably the French language *Le Phare d'Alexandrie* (1874–1912) and *La Semaine égyptienne* (Cairo, est. 1926–*c.*1952), the latter a review of record of elite Francophone society in Egypt and for a time the official organ of the Comité Egypte-Grèce.[11] This abundance of published material testified to a great cultural vitality both in the depth of talent of individual editors, journalists and commentators and in the appetite of the local readership, as well as a clear manifestation of the entangled polyglot character of Egyptian society at large.

Egyptian Greeks and the Arabic language

Egyptian Greeks enjoyed a relatively high literacy rate in Greek and often a good knowledge of other European languages, especially French.[12] Competence in Arabic is more difficult to ascertain. Many, if not most, Greeks had a certain familiarity with spoken Arabic but relatively few Greeks were able to read and write it at an advanced level. In general, Greeks who lived in Upper Egypt and in the Delta, or in particular urban neighbourhoods of Alexandria, Cairo and the cities of the Canal where there was greater everyday contact with Egyptians, possessed a better understanding of Arabic than other Greeks whose knowledge of it was rather limited at least until the late 1950s, when changes in the education system made its study compulsory.

In the period after the First World War and against the background of Egyptian self-government granted in 1922, discussions were held within the Greek community on how best to address this language deficit, particularly in relation to the community education system. In the absence of any quick institutional solution, some who knew Arabic well came to play an important role in disseminating knowledge of Egyptian history, culture and social life. In this way, Egyptian Greek Arabists (Αραβισταί or Αραβομαθείς) served as important cultural communicators in translating, interpreting and commenting on Arabic literature and Egyptian affairs for the Greek-reading public.[13] Relatively few in number and with no specifically defined identity,[14] they were nevertheless on occasion referred to in the local Greek-language press as the embodiment of a collective expertise on Arabic pedagogy, literature and culture.[15] While not the only means by which Egyptian Greeks could gain access to such knowledge – relevant literature in French, for example, being another – the work of Greek Arabists as translators and interpreters, both in the narrow linguistic sense and as a wider cultural commentary, served as an important channel of intercommunal communication.

Egyptian Greek Arabists came from a range of backgrounds but they were most often members of professions which required Arabic competence, such as teachers, interpreters, translators, editors and journalists. Foremost among them was Evgenios Michailidis (1885–1975), born Najib Mikhail Saʿati in Jerusalem and of Christian Arab background, who obtained a doctorate in Arabic philology at Zahle in Lebanon. In early 1912, Michailidis moved to Alexandria where he adopted a Greek persona and taught Arabic, religion and history in a series of Greek community, patriarchal, private and evening schools.[16] Over the next sixty years, he proved to be a prolific writer, authoring a great number of articles and books in both Greek and Arabic, as well as editing two periodicals of the Alexandrian Patriarchate, *Ekkliastikos Pharos* and *Kalos Poimin*, the latter an Arabic-Greek bilingual title. Other Arabists held government posts, such as Gerasimos Pentakis (1838–1899) and Andreas Petrocheilos, both interpreters at the Greek consulate in Alexandria, or were educators and teachers, such as Georgios Kokkinidis and Artemios Thalassinos. Panos Patrikios and Xenophon Paschalidis (the latter as translator of Greek newspapers) held positions in the Press Office, while lexicographer Socrates Spiro worked in the Ministries of Finance and of Public Works.[17] Prolific translator Nikitas Kladakis worked as a journalist in the 1930s and ultimately became editor of *Tachydromos*. A smaller group were amateur scholars pursuing their interests in Arabic culture alongside their professional careers. Nikolaos Zacharioudakis (*c.*1870–1938+) and Nikolaos Mavris (1899–1978) were doctors trained in Athens who had (probably) returned to Egypt to take up positions, the former in Manuf and the latter in Zagazig to work as an eye specialist. Their long-standing residence in the Delta may partly explain their facility in Arabic.[18]

The cumulative efforts of these Arabists over decades would produce a body of work, beginning with the first Greek-Arabic dictionaries and language textbooks and extending to translations, discussions and reviews of Arabic books and scholarly articles. From the 1920s, the press and periodical literature served as a principal forum for this work that contributed to an understanding of contemporary Egypt and of Arabic language, literature and culture. The collective result indicates something of the entangled character of cultural engagement in Egypt and of the different channels of communication between different language communities.

Dictionaries and language texts

The earliest published works of Egyptian Greek Arabists were largely dedicated to language learning, comprising a range of dictionaries, lexicons and phrasebooks. The first Greek-Arabic lexicon published in Egypt, at least in the modern period, was the

Greek-Arabic Lexicon [*Λεξικόν Ελληνο-Αραβικόν*] in 1867 by Gerasimos Pentakis.[19] Initially appearing in pocketbook format, it was subsequently doubled in 1885 to a larger edition of over three hundred pages that employed Greek characters to represent Arabic. By this time, Pentakis had left the employment of the consulate in Alexandria and been awarded the Order of the Mejidie by the Sultan, possibly in recognition of his Greek translation of the Quran that had been published in 1878.[20] Pentakis's work was the first in a series of dictionaries and lexicons, increasingly sophisticated in form: there followed a Greek-Arabic lexicon [*Λεξικόν Ελληνο-Αραβικόν*] by a priest, Ioannis Chazpoun, that was only part-published in 1913 but notably employed Arabic letters; *al-Farid, Arabic-Greek Lexicon* [*Ελ-Φαρίδ, Λεξικόν Αραβο-Ελληνικόν*] of Konstantinos Melas appeared in 1927; a Greek-Arabic lexicon by Panos Patrikios followed the next year.[21] Later dictionaries were notable for being collaborations between Greek and Arab, presumably Egyptian, authors. The Greek-Arabic lexicon of two teachers, Philippos G. Glitsis and Muhammad ʻAbd al-Rahman, was published in 1948 followed three years later by the *Arabic-Greek Lexicon* of Samwil Kamil and Artemios Thalassinos, the latter the Arabic teacher at Ambetios School in Cairo.[22] Bilingual dialogues and short stories supplemented these lexicographical works. The Greek-Arabic dialogues of Alexandros Parodis, published in 1875, seems to have been the first of this genre.[23] Those that followed – by Mouzé (1883), Zannoudakis (1905) and an anonymous work (1909) – sometimes brought a third or even a fourth language (Italian and/or French) into the dialogues but maintained the use of Greek characters to represent the Arabic.[24]

More sophisticated language textbooks were published after the First World War. An Arabic grammar by Andreas Petrocheilos in 1925 offered a 'quick and easy' means to learn the language.[25] The author explained his fuller purpose for the book in the prologue:

> The knowledge of Arabic today is more urgent for every foreigner living in Egypt. On the other hand the difficulty of this language and the lack of good instructive books make it inaccessible to all foreign speakers trying to learn it.[26]

A reprint published two years later suggests a significant demand for the volume. A teacher as well as an interpreter, Petrocheilos would produce two more textbooks designed for use in Greek community schools, the first a short Arabic-Greek vocabulary list,[27] followed by a collection of short stories in Greek and Arabic.[28]

In 1935, Odysseus Spanakidis offered a more systematic Arabic programme.[29] Set out in forty lessons, the *New Practical Method for the Learning of Spoken and Written Arabic Language* covered both spoken and written Arabic, a distinction that would have been a very familiar concept to Greek speakers (Spanakidis actually uses the term *katharevousa* for Arabic *fusha*) and comprised a section each on grammar, written script and vocabulary. Printed in 1,100 copies, the book received widespread praise and endorsement from local diplomatic, religious and pedagogical authorities, respectively the Greek Ambassador Vasilis Dendramis, the Alexandrian Patriarch Meletios Metaxakis and Arabic teachers in Greek community schools.[30] A second edition, again with a substantial print run, appeared in 1948 dedicated 'to Hellenism in

Egypt and in all Arabic-speaking countries', with pictures of the late King Fu'ad and his successor, Faruq. Spanakidis spelled out his aspirations for the work:

> We pray that it may contribute to a greater strengthening of the already happily existing most virtuous bonds of friendship and love between the two Egyptian and Greek brother peoples, through their even more whole-hearted approach of which the fundamental condition is knowledge of the native language.[31]

Interwar engagement

The work of Spanakidis and his predecessors that focused on Arabic language learning represents a significant phase and important tradition of local Greek Arabist scholarship. However, the interwar period would witness the emergence of a more sophisticated literature as a result of a maturing erudition and prompted by political exigencies. Following a sustained period of protest across Egypt against continuing British occupation, new constitutional arrangements were put in place that granted Egypt self-government under its own king and constitution in 1922. Britain retained certain reserve powers for itself, but the foundations of the colonial order were clearly shifting.[32]

These changes provoked a great deal of reflection within the Greek community at large on how best to react to the implications of the changing political order. Responses ranged from seeking support of the British government and the Greek state to safeguard the relative privilege of Greeks in the country, a view largely held by the community establishment, to the views of more progressive circles who called for the need to adapt to the new realities by pursuing greater engagement with indigenous Egyptian society.[33] Among a number of ideas proposed was the need for greater prominence of Arabic language study in the curriculum of Greek community schools.[34] More broadly, certain community figures and intellectuals recognized the need to foster a greater knowledge and awareness of Arabic and Egyptian culture within Egyptian Greek society through commentary, translation and discussion of both historical and contemporary issues.

One obvious forum in which to implement this programme was the daily press, where newspapers such as *Tachydromos* and *Kairon* carried regular reports, feature articles and opinion pieces on matters of culture. During the 1920s, certain cultural and literary journals were also strongly influenced by these ideas. Periodicals like *O Pharos* (1920–7), *Ermis* (1926–7) and *Panorama* (est. 1928–*c.*1944) carried articles, sometimes reprinted from the press, which gave greater space to Egyptian cultural issues. The editors of *O Pharos*, organ of the Alexandrian Library Association, made clear its focus: 'Our programme is to present … the intellectual and artistic expression of Egypt from the Greek as well as the native perspective.'[35] To this end it featured, for example, a series of biographical sketches of historical and contemporary thinkers, writers and artists of both local Greek and Egyptian communities, penned by Evgenios Michailidis, Panos Patrikios and others.[36] Among his other contributions, Michailidis was particularly active in reviewing articles published in *al-Muqtataf* and *al-Hilal*, two well-established Arabic language journals.[37]

In the 1930s, this focus on Arabic literature and Egyptian culture was taken up with particular commitment by two Alexandrian publications, *Panegyptia* (Παναιγύπτια) and *Egiptiotis Ellin* (Αιγυπτιώτης-Ελλην – *al-Yunani al-Mutamassir* ('The Egyptianised-Greek'), henceforth *AE*). Originally a children's magazine (1926–8), *Panegyptia* resumed publication in 1931 as a more substantial, sophisticated review. Its founder, Stephanos Pargas (real name Nikolas Zelitas) (*c.*1891–1938) had come to Egypt as a child and by the 1920s had established a reputation for himself as a progressive intellectual, based on his editorship of the Alexandrian literary journal *Grammata* (1911–21) and his association with *O Pharos*. Under his leadership, *Panegyptia* became an influential liberal voice of Egyptian Hellenism with a circulation of about one thousand copies and a readership of three thousand. In early 1938, following criticism of the Metaxas regime in Greece published in the journal, deportation proceedings were initiated against Pargas.[38] He died suddenly soon after, possibly under the stress caused by the affair, and *Panegyptia* folded later that year.

More modest in size – each issue was usually just four broadsheet pages – the bilingual *AE* was in some ways a more ambitious undertaking.[39] It was established by Angelos Kasigonis (1892–1975), a native of Adrianople (Edirne), who had served in the Greek army during the Asia Minor campaign and moved to Alexandria by June 1920. In 1922, Kasigonis set up a successful newsclipping service, Egiptiakos Argos, which would sustain his other activities financially. Notable among these was Erevna, a publishing house, launched in 1927, that produced a wide range of Greek language works, including a long-running series of booklets on religion, society, philosophy and Greek history. The launch of *AE* in June 1932 represented an attempt to engage both Greek and Arabic readers.[40] By 1934, the paper claimed six hundred subscribers, a creditable number for such a specialized title, and would appear regularly over a period of eight years in all. By the time of its last issue, published exceptionally in Cairo in January 1940, the increasingly difficult climate that included the heavy censorship of the authorities and problems in securing paper supplies had persuaded Kasigonis to cease publication.[41]

Both *Panegyptia* and *AE* pursued a programme dedicated to engagement with Egyptian Arabophone society albeit in somewhat different ways. In its January 1931 issue, *Panegyptia* outlined an ambitious agenda that included issues of Egyptian Hellenism, relations with the Greek state and support for Greek-Egyptian cooperation, as well as a focus on various international causes. To this end, it drew on a wide range of contributors, principally journalists, critics and other public intellectuals, from the local Greek community. These addressed political, economic, social and cultural matters relating to the affairs of the local, national and international community, the last particularly concerned with the rise of fascism, the peace movement and the women's movement.[42] *Panegyptia*'s cultural programme was more specific, proposing 'that Greeks should become familiar with Arabic and especially Egyptian literature, and that Arabic speakers, particularly Egyptians, should come to know modern Greek literature'.[43] For this it relied principally on the talents of local Arabists.

Both in its title and bilingual format, and with a masthead that proclaimed in both Greek and Arabic 'published in the service of fraternal links of two peoples',[44] *AE* proposed a more integrated conception of Egyptian Greek identity. Not knowing

Arabic himself, Kasigonis employed an Arabic-speaking collaborator who served as editor-in-chief, a post first held by Ibrahim al-Jawahari (1932–3), then by Ahmad al-Sidudi (1933–8).[45] *AE*'s contributors comprised a large number of local Greek and Arabophone Egyptian writers. Among the former were journalists Dinos Koutsoumis, Nikitas Kladakis and Loukia Marva, lawyers I. Meletios and Platon Valaskakis, and notable scholar Georgios Arvanitakis. The Arabic writers included journalists Mahmud Ibrahim of the Wafdist *al-Balagh* in Alexandria and Karim Bey Thabit of *al-Muqattam*, Niqula Hanna Ibrahim, teacher at the Berlitz School, who authored a series on Greek-Egyptian relations, and Muhammad ʿAbdalla Zayn al-Din, an Egyptian customs official. Contributions were published first in their original language and then translated from Arabic into Greek, or from Greek into Arabic, often in consecutive issues. For the task of translation into Arabic, Kasigonis relied on the skills of local Greek Arabists Nikitas Kladakis, Nikolaos Mavris, Nikolas Zacharioudakis, Xenophon Paschalidis, Odysseus Spanakidis and Panos Patrikios.

Arabic language and Egyptian culture

In pursuing their agendas, *Panegyptia* and *AE* stressed the pressing need for Egyptian Greeks to learn Arabic as an essential step in adapting to the changing economic and political circumstances in Egypt and avoiding the marginalisation of the Greek community. An early *Panegyptia* cover (see Figure 9.1) that featured a handwritten Arabic translation of the publication details that normally appeared only in Greek made the point clear.[46] Solicited for his view on knowledge of Arabic, one Arabist (Nicholas Mavris) asked why Greeks 'who had lived in Egypt for decades and spoke Arabic everyday did not know the basic grammatical rules of the language so that they used the present instead of the past tense, or the feminine instead of the masculine'.[47] To remedy this state of affairs, *Panegyptia* drew on the talents of local Arabists to promote Arabic and familiarize its readers on matters of Egyptian culture and history, on at least one occasion publishing an article from the Arabic press on the issue.[48] The journal did not confine itself to commentary. In December 1933, it announced the forthcoming publication of an Arabic textbook of Odysseus Spanakidis, introduced by an article from the author himself, and serialized the book over the following months.[49] The commitment of *AE* to Arabic was implicit in its bilingual format, but it also conducted a sustained campaign to promote the study of Arabic among Egyptian Greeks, soliciting the views of experts on the issue who suggested solutions ranging from reform of the Greek community education system to the placement of its students in Egyptian schools for a certain period.[50]

Arabic language competence was not the only concern. Both publications sought to keep their readers informed on Egyptian and Arab affairs. *Panegyptia* featured a weekly column, 'News of the Week' [Τα επίκαιρα της εβδομάδος], that offered short commentaries on topical matters of Egyptian politics (often drawing on the Arabic press to do so), as well as Greek community and national affairs. *AE* provided a running commentary on its articles that were republished by the Arabic press, reporting twelve

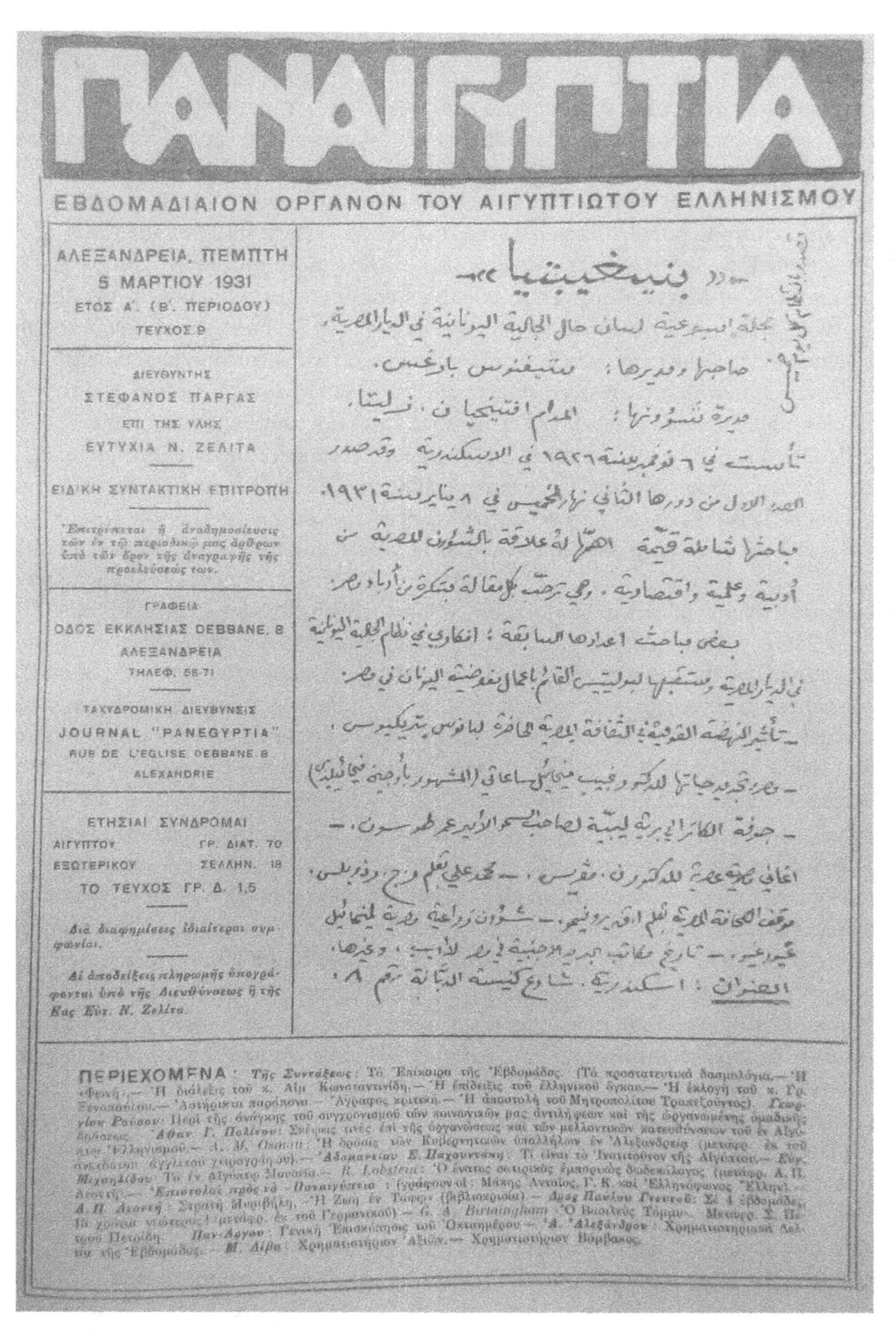

ΠΑΝΑΙΓΥΠΤΙΑ

ΕΒΔΟΜΑΔΙΑΙΟΝ ΟΡΓΑΝΟΝ ΤΟΥ ΑΙΓΥΠΤΙΩΤΟΥ ΕΛΛΗΝΙΣΜΟΥ

ΑΛΕΞΑΝΔΡΕΙΑ, ΠΕΜΠΤΗ
5 ΜΑΡΤΙΟΥ 1931
ΕΤΟΣ Α΄. (Β΄. ΠΕΡΙΟΔΟΥ)
ΤΕΥΧΟΣ 9

ΔΙΕΥΘΥΝΤΗΣ
ΣΤΕΦΑΝΟΣ ΠΑΡΓΑΣ
ΕΠΙ ΤΗΣ ΥΛΗΣ
ΕΥΤΥΧΙΑ Ν. ΖΕΛΙΤΑ

ΕΙΔΙΚΗ ΣΥΝΤΑΚΤΙΚΗ ΕΠΙΤΡΟΠΗ

Ἐπιτρέπεται ἡ ἀναδημοσίευσις τῶν ἐν τῷ περιοδικῷ μας ἄρθρων ὑπὸ τὸν ὅρον τῆς ἀναγραφῆς τῆς προελεύσεώς των.

ΓΡΑΦΕΙΑ
ΟΔΟΣ ΕΚΚΛΗΣΙΑΣ DEBBANE, 8
ΑΛΕΞΑΝΔΡΕΙΑ
ΤΗΛΕΦ. 58-71

ΤΑΧΥΔΡΟΜΙΚΗ ΔΙΕΥΘΥΝΣΙΣ
JOURNAL "PANEGYPTIA"
RUE DE L'EGLISE DEBBANE 8
ALEXANDRIE

ΕΤΗΣΙΑΙ ΣΥΝΔΡΟΜΑΙ
ΑΙΓΥΠΤΟΥ ΓΡ. ΔΙΑΤ. 70
ΕΞΩΤΕΡΙΚΟΥ ΣΕΛΛΗΝ. 18
ΤΟ ΤΕΥΧΟΣ ΓΡ. Δ. 1,5

Διὰ διαφημίσεις ἰδιαίτεραι συμφωνίαι.

Αἱ ἀποδείξεις πληρωμῆς ὑπογράφονται ὑπὸ τῆς Διευθύνσεως ἢ τῆς Κας Εὐτ. Ν. Ζελίτα.

«بنيغيبتيا»

مجلة اسبوعية لسان حال الجالية اليونانية في الديار المصرية.
صاحبها ومديرها: ستيفنوس بارغس.
مديرة شؤونها: المدام افتيخيا ن. زليتا.
تأسست في ٦ نوفمبر سنة ١٩٢٦ في الاسكندرية وقد صدر
العدد الاول من دورها الثاني نهار الخميس في ٨ يناير سنة ١٩٣١.
مباحثها شاملة قيمة اهمها له علاقة بالشؤون المصرية من
أدبية وعلمية واقتصادية. وهي ترحب بكل مقالة مبتكرة من أدباء مصر.
بعض مباحث اعدادها السابقة: افكاري في نظام الجالية اليونانية
في الديار المصرية ومستقبلها لبوليتيس القائم باعمال مفوضية اليونان في مصر.
- تأثير النهضة القومية في الثقافة المصرية الحاضرة لبافوس بتريكيوس.
- صور تجديد حياتها للدكتور وغيب ميخائيل ساعاتي (المشهور باوجين ميخائيليدس)
- جوقة الكلارينيت ليبية لصاحب السمو الأمير عمر طوسون. -
اغاني مصرية عصرية للدكتور ن. مقريس. - محمد علي بقلم ... ودبلس.
موقف الحكومة المصرية بقلم ... رونيمو. - شؤون زراعية مصرية لميخائيل
... - تاريخ مكاتب البريد الاجنبية في مصر للأديب ... وغيرها.
العنوان: اسكندرية. شارع كنيسة الدبانة رقم ٨.

ΠΕΡΙΕΧΟΜΕΝΑ: Τῆς Συντάξεως: Τὰ Ἐπίκαιρα τῆς Ἑβδομάδος. (Τὰ προστατευτικὰ δασμολόγια.— Ἡ «φωνή».— Ἡ διάλεξις τοῦ κ. Αἰμ. Κωνσταντινίδη.— Ἡ ἐπίδειξις τοῦ ἑλληνικοῦ ὄγκου.— Ἡ ἐκλογὴ τοῦ κ. Γρ. Ξενοπούλου.— Ἀστήρικτα παράπονα.— Ἄγραφος κριτική.— Ἡ ἀποστολὴ τοῦ Μητροπολίτου Τραπεζοῦντος). Γεωργίου Ρούσσου: Περὶ τῆς ἀνάγκης τοῦ συγχρονισμοῦ τῶν κοινωνικῶν μας ἀντιλήψεων καὶ τῆς ὠργανωμένης ὁμαδικῆς δράσεως. Ἀθαν. Γ. Πολίτου: Σκέψεις τινὲς ἐπὶ τῆς ὀργανώσεως καὶ τῶν μελλοντικῶν κατευθύνσεων τοῦ ἐν Αἰγύπτῳ Ἑλληνισμοῦ.— Α. Μ. Osman: Ἡ δρᾶσις τῶν Κυβερνητικῶν ὑπαλλήλων ἐν Ἀλεξανδρείᾳ (μετάφρ. ἐκ τοῦ ἀνεκδότου ἀγγλικοῦ χειρογράφου).— Ἀδαμαντίου Ε. Παχουντάκη: Τί εἶναι τὸ Ἰνστιτοῦτον τῆς Αἰγύπτου.— Εὐγ. Μιχαηλίδου: Τὰ ἐν Αἰγύπτῳ Μουσεῖα.— R. Lobstein: Ὁ ἔνατος σειριακὸς ἐμπορικὸς δωδεκάλογος (μετάφρ. Α. Π. Λεοντῆ).— Ἐπιστολαὶ πρὸς τὰ «Παναιγύπτια»: (γράφουν οἱ: Μάκης Ανταῖος, Γ. Κ. καὶ Ἑλληνόφωνος Ἕλλην).— Α. Π. Λεοντῆ: Στρατὴ Μυριβήλη, «Ἡ Ζωὴ ἐν Τάφῳ» (βιβλιοκρισία).— Δρος Παύλου Γνευτοῦ: Σὲ 4 ἑβδομάδες 16 χρόνια νεώτερος! (μετάφρ. ἐκ τοῦ Γερμανικοῦ).— G. A. Birmingham: Ὁ Βασιλεὺς Τόμμυ. Μετάφρ. Σ. Πετσούλη. Παν-Άργου: Γενικὴ Ἐπισκόπησις τοῦ Ὀχταημέρου.— Α. Ἀλεξάνδρου: Χρηματιστηριακὸν Δελτίον τῆς Ἑβδομάδος.— Μ. Λίβα: Χρηματιστήριον Ἀξιῶν.— Χρηματιστήριον Βάμβακος.

Figure 9.1 Cover page, *Panegyptia* 5 March 1931.

such cases in *al-Ahram*, *al-Jihad*, *al-Siyasa*, *al-Muqattam*, *al-Bashir* and *al-Balagh* during its first three months.[51]

Matters of traditional Arab culture and folklore was a particular interest of both titles. *Panegyptia* featured extracts translated by Mavris on the Sanusi of the Western Desert taken from the travel account of Egyptian explorer Ahmad Hasanayn Bey.[52] Elisabeth Psara, although not an Arabist herself, contributed a series of articles on Arabic poetry and popular Egyptian songs that relied on the translations of Mavris and Theodoros Kavour.[53] *AE* embraced Egyptian folklore more extensively, also drawing on the work of Mavris who was developing a considerable reputation in the field.[54] In 1931, Mavris had published a collection of popular Egyptian songs, *Contribution à l'étude de la chanson populaire égyptienne*, categorized according to the occasions or context in which they were sung, such as work, weddings, circumcisions and funerals, lullabies and love songs.[55] The subject was not new, but Mavris's method of collecting songs 'directly from the people without interpreters and writers intervening', and particularly by interviewing women (made possible by his Arabic and status as a doctor), distinguished it from earlier scholarly collections.[56] The following year, *AE* serialized a Greek translation of the work which subsequently appeared in book form.[57] Another long-running *AE* series featured the Arabic sayings of Ahmad Rassim, originally written in French, and translated into Greek by Socrates Petrou Petridis.[58]

AE took a particular interest in travel writing as a genre, something no doubt encouraged by the fact that Kasigonis's wife, Chrysa, a native of Smyrna, was herself a specialized travel writer and contributed a number of articles.[59] From its first issue, *AE* carried extracts in Greek and Arabic from the work of Herodotos, ancient historian and visitor to Egypt in the fifth century BCE, which emphasized the antiquity of travel across the region. More contemporary accounts followed. In March 1934, *AE* began serializing *Rasa'il sa'ir* ('Letters of a Wanderer'), an account by Shaykh Muhammad Sulayman of time spent in Greece, first in the original Arabic and subsequently in a Greek translation of Nikitas Kladakis.[60] Kladakis's translation skills were called upon again the following year when extracts from writings of an (unnamed) Coptic priest, again of travels in Greece, were featured.[61] This type of material provided a popular basis for highlighting the connections between Egypt and Greece. Indeed, when Muhammad Abu al-Fath, managing editor of *al-Ahram*, began a series of reports for his own newspaper on his tour of Greece in 1934, *AE* featured a prominent article covering the matter.[62]

AE's mission to inform both Arabic and Greek readers of the historical and contemporary relationship between Egypt and Greece remained a hallmark of the newspaper, but it also stressed local connections whenever possible. In May 1934, the visit by members of the Endefktirion Kairo, a celebrated progressive Greek cultural club in Cairo, to al-Azhar to meet the Grand Imam, Shaykh Muhammad Ahmadi al-Zawahiri, illustrated aspirations of shared respect between intellectuals of two distinct scholarly traditions.[63] The Endefktirion president, Xenophon Paschalidis, recited a poem in Arabic composed specially for the occasion that spoke of the close relationship between Greeks and Egyptians. Mutual sentiments were expressed and a photograph taken to mark the event (Figure 9.2).

Figure 9.2 The visit of Endefkterion Kairo members to al-Azhar; May 1934. Its President Xenophin Paschalidis stands to the right of the Grand Imam Shaykh Ahmadi al-Zawahiri (*AE* July 1934).

Panos Patrikios

The life and work of Panos Patrikios captures important aspects of the role of Egyptian Greek Arabists as cultural communicators on Egyptian intellectual and literary life to the local Greek community during the interwar period. Born on the Greek island of Kythera in 1899, Patrikios had migrated to Egypt as a child with his family and settled in Tanta in the Delta. There he was educated in the Egyptian state school system, rather unusual for a Greek in a city where a Greek community school operated, and surely the basis for his later proficiency in Arabic. (He was also fluent in French and English.) After finishing school, Patrikios worked briefly for a bank in Alexandria but by 1918 had taken up a position in the Press Office, part of the Egyptian Interior Ministry, where he would work for the next twenty years. In 1938, as a Greek national, Patrikios was required to resign his position as director of the Press Office under the terms of the Anglo-Egyptian treaty signed two years before. It was perhaps a measure of his status that his departure was announced in a wide range of local Arabic, Greek, French, English and Italian language newspapers.[64] Thereafter, Patrikios continued to draw on his language skills, working as an Arabic teacher in Greek community and patriarchal schools in Alexandria. After the war, he was employed for a time by the well-known commercial house of KM Salvagos and died in Alexandria in April 1948.

Figure 9.3 Caricature of Panos Patrikios by N. Panagou (*Panegyptia* 24 April–1 May 1937).

From the early 1920s, Patrikios had begun to establish himself as a significant public intellectual based on his knowledge of Egyptian affairs and his proficiency as an Arabist, displaying a breadth of knowledge and industry that placed him probably second only to Michailidis among Greek Arabists. He utilized his talents in a variety of forums, principally as a journalist, book reviewer and translator in the local Greek, French and Arabic language press and periodical literature. He also delivered public lectures in French and in Arabic, speaking on one occasion to the Union of Government Employees in Alexandria in 1929, an address subsequently published in *Wadi al-Nil*. Patrikios also compiled an Arabic-Greek lexicon, published by Kasigonis (by this time a relation by marriage), and penned a number of entries relating to Arabic culture for the *Encyclopedia Eleftheroudakis*.[65]

Patrikios's published work ranged over a broad spectrum of historical and literary topics relating to Egypt and the Arab world. The historical relationship between the Arabs and the West in the medieval period represented a favoured theme and something he addressed on a number of occasions in Greek, Arabic and French.[66] He was therefore well qualified to review the works of Christophoros Nomikos (1883–1951), one of the few Egyptian Greek historians who wrote on early Islamic history.[67] However, Patrikios also took a strong interest in contemporary intellectual issues. His 1924 article 'Intellectual Egypt' [Η διανούμενη Αίγυπτος] used the occasion of the publication of a translation of Aristotle's *Ethics* by Ahmad Lutfi al-Sayyid, then rector of the Egyptian (later Cairo) University, to provide readers with a roll call of Egyptian intellectuals over the previous half century.[68] Beginning with the work of Jamal al-Din al-Afghani and Muhammad 'Abduh, Patrikios referenced a succession of writers and thinkers including 'Abdalla Pasha Fikri, author of children's books, Qasim Amin, pioneer of feminist thought, Malak Hifni Nasif ('first Egyptian woman of letters') and a series of poets, and scholars including sociologist Muhammad Bey Farid Wajdi, Taha Husayn and Hebraist Dr Inani. In bringing his survey to a close, Patrikios observed,

> It is true that Egyptian youth have still not produced the philological and intellectual enthusiasm that characterizes the cultural centres of Europe; and the circulation of the Arabic book is not enviable, but there is no doubt that the core of cultural progress and development has been created and that Egypt, the greatest Arab state, with the reform of its political issues, will obtain a literary production worthy of the wonderful traditions of Arabic philology and arts.[69]

In another article, Patrikios addressed two causes célèbres that convulsed Egyptian public discourse in the mid-1920s. The first, the publication of *Islam and the Principles of Rule* [*al-Islam wa usul al-hukm*] by 'Ali 'Abd al-Raziq in 1925, concerned the sensitive question of the relationship between spiritual and political authority, which in the author's view should be separated. In assessing 'Abd al-Raziq's position, Patrikios remarked on its mixed reception across Egyptian society,

> Such a daring conclusion that is completely opposed to Muslim tradition has upset religious circles and conservative elements in the country. On the other hand the

> ideas of ʿAli ʿAbd al-Raziq are read with great interest by true intellectuals and the supporters of modern development.[70]

An even greater controversy arose with the 1926 publication of Taha Husayn's *Pre-Islamic Poetry* [*Fi al-shiʿr al-jahili*] that, in questioning the origins of pre-Islamic poetry and the Quranic account of the building of the Kaʿaba, again provoked the ire of religious conservatives. Pointing out its daring in scrutinizing matters that the Muslim world considered 'holy and inaccessible', particularly sensitive in relation to the divine inspiration of the Quran, Patrikios observed that criticism of the work was widespread: 'Even some more liberal thinkers were not able to support the ideas of the book publicly.' Yet, despite the acrimony surrounding both works, Patrikios took an optimistic view of the intellectual future in Egypt,

> Regardless of the correctness or not of the theories that these two Egyptian writers bring out, they characterize the tendencies of thinking Egyptians towards the horizons of philological research which will certainly guide Egypt one day to a cultural rebirth.[71]

Egyptian poetry was a central interest of Patrikios and one to which he dedicated a number of articles of both commentary and translation, particularly on the work of Ahmad Shawqi.[72] However, the work of Egyptian women of letters represented an arguably more sustained focus. His article on ʿAʾisha Taymur (1840–1902), first published in 1924 (and later to appear in *O Pharos*), introduced Greek readers to the 'first Egyptian female poet' and set her life and work in context. His translation of excerpts from her poetry included the poignant lines dealing with the death of Taymur's 10-year-old daughter: 'Heaven closed, the midday sun was hidden and the moon was lost. In the month of the fast were spread the magic cups of death and now are spread the cups of tears.'[73]

In the same series, Patrikios discussed Malak Hifni Nasif (1886–1918), dubbed 'the Mother of Egyptian Feminism', again setting her life in historical context. [74] In assessing her feminist activism, he drew on comparative developments in the West but also demonstrated a sensitivity to the specific Egyptian and Muslim context of Nasif's circumstances. In his sampling of her writings, he quoted both from her despairing thoughts on polygamy ('What a terrible word polygamy is. My hands tremble as I write this. It is a nightmare for women and the demon of their destruction.') as well as her more uplifting views on life outdoors,

> How sweet is life outdoors and how artificial it is in the cities. What is the noise of electricity before the ripple of the water and the smoke of the factory before the clear sky that covers the lofty palm trees and receives light-winged skylarks in its arms.[75]

Patrikios maintained his interest in the intellectual and public activities of women for the rest of his life. His translation of an article by Mayy Ziyada in 1936 recognized her status as an eminent writer,[76] while his obituary of feminist pioneer Huda Shaʿrawi appeared in the local Greek press in December 1947 only six months before his own death.[77]

The range and industry of the work of Panos Patrikios were not simply representative of the interests and concerns of an individual Arabist but also part of a broader movement of progressive scholars and their collaborators to promote an understanding of Egyptian culture and intellectual life within the local Greek community. In his more political pieces Patrikios showed himself to support strongly Egyptian claims for independence and in an early article called on foreign community leaders in the country to recognize them.[78] Many years later in July 1946, the month in which Prime Minister Isma'il Sidqi ordered a massive roundup of leftists, he was stressing the importance of respect for Egyptian liberty and legal rights in a short piece concerning a series of arrests.[79]

Arabists like Panos Patrikios operated as important channels of cultural communication between Arabophone and Hellenophone communities in Egypt, serving as a local source of collective expertise that facilitated some acquaintance with the majority culture and language. The translations of Arabic texts, poetry and songs they produced provided some entrée into Egyptian popular and high culture, local traditions, social and sometimes political issues. While not necessarily of high academic quality, these works were informed analyses of historical and contemporary topics, of literature, folklore, politics and the women's movement made accessible to a local Greek readership in the daily press and periodical literature. On various matters these Arabists no doubt held different views. On one occasion, for example, when *Panegyptia* sought advice from four Arabists (Michailidis, Spanakidis, Patrikios and Paschilidis) on the correct meaning of *jihad*, the ensuing discussion produced some disagreement surrounding its specific religious dimension (see Figure 9.4).[80] However, such contrasting views arguably created an appreciation of the genuine complexity of matters of Arabic and Muslim culture.

Conclusion

Understandings of the multicultural character of Egyptian society have ranged from idealized models of an integrated cosmopolitan society to one determined by the logic and categories of a colonial regime, characterized by segregation and hierarchy between the Arabic-speaking majority and privileged resident European communities. In its examination of the work of Egyptian Greek Arabists, this chapter has sought to challenge these views and suggest that the relationship between the Egyptian Greek community and the wider Egyptian society was a more complex configuration mediated by local social and cultural factors. One of these elements was the tradition of Greek Arabist scholarship which emerged in the last quarter of the nineteenth century, originally focused on lexicographical and language learning but which expanded its focus after the First World War in part as a response to calls from within the Greek community to engage more directly with Egyptian society. Through direct translation, commentary and discussion in the pages of journals such as *Panegyptia* and *AE*, these Arabists played a central role in informing a local Greek readership on matters of

Figure 9.4 Arabists Evgenios Michailidis (left) and Odysseas Spanakidis do battle over the meaning of the word *jihad*, by G. Chiotis (*Panegyptia* 2–23 October 1937, 19).

Arabic language and Egyptian popular culture and literature. Broader themes on a larger historical canvas that concerned connections between Arab civilization and the West and the more contemporary issues regarding the relationship between Egypt and Greece implied a common future in a modern Egypt. In this enterprise, their work was a distinctive feature of an Egyptian Greek culture that made manifest both the barriers and interconnections between Egyptian Greeks and the Arabic-speaking majority in a culturally pluralist Egypt.

Notes

1 The author wishes to thank Mathilde Pyrli at ELIA for her assistance in accessing research materials and Katerina Trimi-Kirou for her valuable comments on an earlier draft. All translations from the Greek language sources are his own.

2 The celebration of Greek culture in Egypt, and especially of Alexandria, as an outpost of mainland Hellenism has been a well-established theme in Greek language scholarship.

3 See Patel, *Arab Nahdah*; Tageldin, *Disarming Words*.
4 Irving, 'A Tale of Two Yusifs', 224–7, 229–32.
5 See e.g. the activities of Israeli Arabists, in Beinin, 'Knowing Your Enemy'. Occupation forces have also regularly employed translators and interpreters, see Baker, *Routledge Encyclopedia of Translation Studies*, 322 (re Napoleon in Egypt), and Colla, 'Dragomen and Checkpoints' (US forces in Iraq).
6 Among the more celebrated were the Choremis, Benakis, Salvagos and Tsanaklis (Gianaclis) families, see Kitroeff, *Greeks in Egypt*, 80–2, 114–15.
7 Ibid., 13.
8 For a detailed if not always accurate listing, see Michailidis, *Bibliography* (Greek).
9 Kitroeff, *Greeks in Egypt*, 190.
10 For a catalogue of Greek newspapers and periodicals published in Egypt, see Michailidis, *Panorama*, 300–15.
11 Michailidis, *Panorama*, 265–6; see also Chapter 6 in this volume.
12 In 1917, literacy among Greek nationals was reported as 70.8 per cent for men and 48.4 per cent for women; about 35 per cent of all Greek nationals knew either English, French or Italian, with French (approximately 20%) being the most widely known; literacy in Arabic is not recorded: Egyptian Government, *Census of Egypt Taken in 1917*, Tables XI and XXVI.
13 Some Arabists also published in Arabic and so connected with a readership outside the Greek community. The record and reception of modern Greek works translated into Arabic has been little discussed in the literature, but see Margolis [Marangoulis], 'From Ancient to Modern'.
14 In 1937, Xenophon Paschilidis proposed forming an Arabist Society (Σύλλογος των Αραβιστών), although it is unclear if this was acted on, *Panegyptia* 25 September 1937, 18.
15 See *Panegyptia* 16 November 1935, 19.
16 Ap. G. K[onstantinidis], 'Evgenios Michailidis', 179–80.
17 Spiro's most influential work was *An Arabic-English Vocabulary of the Colloquial Arabic of Egypt* (Cairo and London, 1895).
18 See comments by Mavris, *Egyptian Folk Songs* (Greek), 7. To this group might be added Theodoros Kavour, a doctor based in Mallawi in Upper Egypt who also wrote on Egyptian folklore.
19 Michailidis *Bibliography*, 316.
20 Subsequently republished in Athens in 1886 and again in 1921, see Michailidis, *Bibliography*, 23.
21 See Michailidis, *Bibliography*, 317. For the lexicon of Panos Patrikios, see below.
22 Phil. G. Glitsis and Muhammad 'Abd al-Rahman, *Greek-Arabic Lexicon* [*Λεξικόν Ελληνο-Αραβικόν*] (Cairo: L'Art Graphique, 1948); Samwil Kamel and Artemios Thalassinos, *Arabic-Greek Lexicon* [*Λεξικόν Αραβο-Ελληνικόν*] (Cairo, 1951). An earlier *Arabic Primer* [*Αραβικόν Αλφαβητάριον*] by two Arab teachers Naji Sayqali and Habib al-Khuri al-Antaki, published in Cairo in 1918 (?), appears to be for Arabic speakers wanting to learn Greek (titles listed in Michailidis, *Bibliography*, 86, 316–17).
23 Alex. G. Parodis, *Greek-Arabic Dialogues* [*Διάλογοι Ελληνο-Αραβικοί*] (Alexandria, 1875), see Michailidis, *Bibliography*, 21.
24 N. Mouzé, *Greek-Italian-Arabic Dialogues and Nouns of the Absolutely Most Essential Words, Composed Entirely in Greek Letters* [*Διάλογοι Ελληνο-Ιταλο-Αραβικοί και Ονομαστικόν των απολύτως αναγκαιοτέρων λέξεων, συνταχθέντες δια γραμμάτων καθόλου Ελληνικών*] (Alexandria, 1883); P. Zannoudakis, *Greek-Italian-French-Arabic*

Dialogues [*Ελληνο-Ιταλο-Γαλλο-Αραβικοί διάλογοι*] (Alexandria, 1905); Anon., *Greek-Italian-Arabic Dialogues in Greek Characters* [*Διάλογοι Ελληνο-Ιταλο-Αραβικοί μετά Ελληνικών χαρακτήρων*] (Alexandria, 1909), as cited in Michailidis, *Bibliography*, 26, 56, 63.

25 Petrocheilos, *Practical Method for the Quick and Easy Learning of the Arabic Language*, 1st edn 1925, 2nd edn 1927 (Greek).

26 Ibid., Prologue.

27 Apparently sponsored by the local Greek Chamber of Commerce, the *Arabic-Greek Vocabulary* [*Αραβο-Ελληνικόν Λεξιλόγιον*] (Alexandria, 1943) was designed specifically for 4th class students of Greek schools in Alexandria. See Michailidis, *Bibliography*, 193.

28 Andreas P. Petrocheilos, *Selection of Greek-Arabic Stories for the Use of Greek Schools* [*Συλλογή Ελληνο-Αραβικών Διηγημάτων δια την χρήσιν των Ελληνικών σχολείων*] (Alexandria, 1945 and 1948). The later edition contained fifteen pages of Greek and twenty pages of Arabic text. See Michailidis, *Bibliography*, 221.

29 Published by Vallinaki in Alexandria, 1935 (Greek).

30 See comments of Apostolos Lambros and Georgios Kokkinidis, Arabic teachers in Mansura and in Port Said, respectively: *Panegyptia* 7 April 1934, 14 August 1937.

31 Spanakidis, *New Practical Method*, xvi. A projected second volume intended to include sections on parts of speech, dialects, dialogues, sayings and the writing of letters seems not to have appeared.

32 For a fuller discussion of this period, see Kitroeff, *Greeks in Egypt*, 37–54. The interplay between Egyptian national politics and Greek community anxieties has some parallels with the period after the Second World War, see Gorman, 'The Failure of Readjustment (*Anaprosarmoge*)'.

33 Manolis Maragoulis, *'Time That We Modernized'* (Greek), 99–135.

34 Ekaterini Trimi-Kirou, '"Kinotis"', 621–25.

35 'Statement of the Editor' [Δήλωσις της συντάξεως], *O Pharos* 6, no. 6 (June 1926): 188.

36 See e.g. Michailidis, 'Egypt in Arabic Philology', 68–71, which surveys Arabic writers from 'Abd al-Latif al-Baghdadi in the twelfth century to Jurji Zaydan in the twentieth. For Patrikios see below.

37 See *O Pharos* 6, no. 2 (February 1926): 62.

38 'The Stephanos Pargas Case' [Η Υπόθεση Στεφανού Πάργα], *Panegyptia* 29 5 January–5 February 1938, 20–2.

39 *AE* is held in a number of collections, among them the Michailidis Library in Alexandria and the Dar al-Kutub (National Library) in Cairo. ELIA holds the most complete collection. For an earlier discussion, see Gorman, 'Egiptiotis Ellin'.

40 The majority of readers were probably Greeks, inferred from the fact that some issues carried the instruction 'Give the paper to Egyptians' [δίδετε το φύλλον εις Αιγύπτιους].

41 *AE* later resumed publication under the abbreviated title of *Ellin*, as organ of the pro-communist EAS (National Liberation League), with Kasigonis as editor until his departure for Greece at the end of 1944 (interview with Avgi and Agis Kasigonis).

42 Prominent among these were members of the new radical generation, and basis of the future local Greek communist movement, Theodosis Pieridis, Lambis Rappas, Giorgis Dimou and Stratis Tsirkas, along with their mentor Sakellaris Yannakakis. See Gorman, 'Egypt's Forgotten Communists', 3–4.

43 *Panegyptia* 8 January 1931, 2.

44 Thus: «εκδίδεται προς εξυπηρέτησιν της συναδελφώσεως των δυο λαών»; and in Arabic: *li-taqwiyya al-rawabit al-akhawiyya bayna al-sha'bayn*.
45 Interview with Avgi and Agis Kasigonis.
46 *Panegyptia* 5 March 1931.
47 Nikolas Mavris, 'The Use of Arabic' [Η χρησιμότης της αραβικής], *Panegyptia* 24 March 1934, 9.
48 'The Arabic Education of the Greeks' [Η Αραβική μόρφωσις των Ελλήνων], *Panegyptia* 26 May 1934, 15, was taken from *al-Sabah* and translated from Arabic by Spanakidis.
49 Od. Spanakidis, 'The Learning of the Arabic Language' [Η εκμάθηση της αραβικής γλώσσης], *Panegyptia* 30 December 1933, 8. The series began in *Panegyptia* 13 January 1934, 8–9, and continued for about thirty issues.
50 See Karim Bey Thabit, 'The Learning of Arabic' [Η εκμάθηση της αραβικής] *AE* July 1932 (translated from Arabic of an article in *al-Muqattam*); G. Kokkinidis, 'The Teaching of Arabic' [Η διδασκαλία της αραβικής] *AE* 1 March 1934 (letter); N. A. Kladakis, 'The Issue of Arabic' [Το ζήτημα της αραβικής] *AE* August 1937.
51 *AE* 5 October 1932; see also *AE* January and February 1934.
52 'About the Sanusi' [Περί των Σενούσσι], *Panegyptia* 21 January 1933, 5, and 28 January 1933, 3; Hasanayn's account had originally been published in Arabic as *Fi Sahara Libya* (1923).
53 Elisabeth Psara, 'Folk Songs of Egypt' [Τα δημοτικά τραγούδια της Αιγύπτου], *Panegyptia*, 25 August–3 November 1934. These articles were later collected and published as *Exotic Pipes* [*Ξωτικές φλογέρες*] (Alexandria, 1954). Psara also wrote on the Egyptian feminist movement, on one occasion translating an article of Huda Sha'rawi from the French-language *L'Égyptienne*, organ of the Egyptian Feminist Union. *Panegyptia* 12 October 1935.
54 For an early example, see Mavris, 'Egyptian Folklore' [Αιγυπτιακά λαογραφία] *Panorama* 9–10 (September–October 1928): 12.
55 The song lyrics were provided in French translation and transliterated Arabic with a separate appendix of Arabic script; the supporting text was in French.
56 Mavris, *Egyptian Folk Songs* (Greek), 6–7.
57 The series ran from *AE* 6 November 1932–1 July 1933. Mavris, *Egyptian Folk Songs* (Greek), 1934.
58 *AE* July 1934–December 1937. Also published in book form as *Arabic Sayings* [Αραβικαί Παροιμίαι] (Erevna, 1934) with an introduction and notes by Petridis.
59 See, e.g., a series covering Kavala, Smyrna and Ankara, *AE* September 1937–January 1938.
60 'Rasa'il sa'ir' *AE* 1 and 15 March 1934 (Arabic); 'Επιστολαί Περιηγητού' *AE* June–November 1934 (Greek).
61 'Coptic Priest', 'Trip to Greece' [Εκδρομή εις την Ελλάδα], *AE* February–December 1935; see also the travels in Greece of Engineer Ghalib first published in *al-Sabah*, then in *AE*, in Arabic as 'Mudhakkirat misri 'an ziyaratihi li-bilad al-yunan', *AE* November 1933, and in Greek as 'Impressions of an Egyptian from his trip to Greece' [Εντυπώσεις Αιγύπτιου εκ του ταξίδιου του ανά την Ελλάδα], *AE* December 1933.
62 *AE* September 1934.
63 'The Arabic Education of Greeks' [Η Αραβική μορφώσις των Ελληνών] *AE* June 1934, with photo in *AE* July 1934. Established in 1915 by G. Skliros, a celebrated Marxist thinker who had settled in Egypt, the Endefktirion lapsed following his death in 1919 but was revived in the late 1920s. Stavridi-Patrikiou, *G. Skliros in Egypt*, 87–8.

64 See ELIA, 'Panos Patrikios' (Orange file).
65 E.g. s.v. Arabs [Αραβες] *Εγκυκλοπαίδεια Ελευθερουδάκη* (Athens, 1927–32). Patrikios had married Antigoni Koletti, the sister-in-law of Angelos Kasigonis in Alexandria in June 1924.
66 E.g. 'Arabic Culture in Medieval Europe' [Ο Αραβικός Πολιτισμός στη Μεσαιωνική Ευρώπη] (I) and (II) *Ermis* 1–2 (December 1926–January 1927); 'A civilisation arabe à travers les siécles'.
67 See reviews of Nomikos's works, *Aravika Istorimata* and *I Eisagogi stin Istoria ton Aravon* in *Ermis* no. 3 (1 February 1927): 99–101. On Nomikos, see Gorman, *Historians, State and Politics in Twentieth Century Egypt*, 189.
68 Patrikios, *Tachydromos-Omonoia* 17 December 1924.
69 Ibid.
70 'PP', 'Egyptian Thought', *Ermis* 1 (1 December 1926): 31–2 (Greek).
71 Ibid., 32. Husayn's work was subsequently banned and republished in a revised form as *Fi al-adab al-jahili* the following year.
72 'The Poetry and Poets of Egypt', *O Pharos* 6, no. 2 (February 1926): 39–45 (Greek); see also *AE* 'Taqdir al-jaliyya al-yunaniyya li-amir al-shu'ara' Shawqi Bey', *AE* 31 December 1932 (Arabic). He also wrote on the Abbasid-era poet, 'Ali Ibn al-Rumi; see *Ermis* no. 6 (1 May 1927): 188–92 and no. 7 (1 June 1927): 225–30.
73 Patrikios, 'The First Egyptian Female Poet', *O Pharos* 6, no. 3 (March 1926): 77–8 (Greek), originally published in *Tachydromos* 25 December 1924. Patrikios's article may have been inspired by the series on Taymur by Mayy Ziyada that was appearing in *al-Muqtataf* during this period.
74 Patrikios, 'Malak Hefni Nasef, 'The Mother of Egyptian Feminism', *O Pharos* 4 (April 1926): 118–21 (Greek).
75 Ibid., 120–1.
76 Mayy Ziyada, 'Neo-Egyptian Philology', *Panegyptia* 11 April 1936, 21 (trans. Patrikios) (Greek).
77 Patrikios, 'Huda Sha'rawi, The Dead Pioneer of Feminism', newsclipping (*c.*14 December 1947, probably *Tachydromos*), ELIA, 'Panos Patrikios' (Orange file) (Greek).
78 Patrikios, 'Egyptian Independence and the Foreigners', [??] 14 August 1923 (Greek).
79 Patrikios, 'Free Men in Free Egypt', *Tachydromos* 21 July 1946 (Greek).
80 See *Panegyptia* 18 September, 20; 25 September 1937, 18–19.

Bibliography

Archives

'Panos Patrikios' (Orange file), ELIA (Greek Literary and Historical Archive), Athens

Periodicals

Egiptiotis-Ellin [Αιγυπτιώτης-Ελλην]–*al-Yunani al-Mutamassir* (Alexandria, Cairo) (1932–40)
Ermis [*Ερμής*] (Alexandria) (1926–7)
Panegyptia [*Παναιγύπτια*] (Alexandria) (1926–8, 1931–8)

Panorama [*Πανόραμα*] (Cairo-Alexandria) (1928–44?)
O Pharos [*Ο Φάρος*] (Alexandria) (1920–7)

Interview

Avgi and Agis Kasigonis (Children of Angelos Kasigonis), Athens, March 1994.

Published works

Baker, Mona, ed. *Routledge Encyclopedia of Translation Studies*. London: Routledge, 1998.
Beinin, Joel. 'Knowing Your Enemy, Knowing Your Ally: The Arabists of Hashomer Hatza'ir (MAPAM)'. *Social Text* 28 (1991): 100–21.
Colla, Elliot. 'Dragomen and Checkpoints'. *The Translator* 21, no. 2 (2015): 132–53.
Egyptian Government, Ministry of Finance, Statistical Department. *The Census of Egypt Taken in 1917*. 2 vols. Cairo: Government Press, 1921.
Gorman, Anthony. 'Egiptiotis Ellin' [Αιγυπτιώτης- Ελλην]. *Τα νέα του ΕΛΙΑ* 58 (Summer 2001): 13–18 (Greek).
Gorman, Anthony. *Historians, State and Politics in Twentieth Century Egypt: Contesting the Nation*. London: RoutledgeCurzon, 2003.
Gorman, Anthony. 'Egypt's Forgotten Communists: The Postwar Greek Left'. *Journal of Modern Greek Studies* 20, no. 1 (2002): 1–27.
Gorman, Anthony. 'The Failure of Readjustment (*Anaprosarmoge*): The Post-War Egyptian Greek Experience'. *Journal of the Hellenic Diaspora* 35, no. 2 (2009): 45–61.
Irving, Sarah. 'A Tale of Two Yusifs: Recovering Arab Agency in Palestine Exploration Fund Excavations 1890–1924'. *Palestine Exploration Quarterly* 149, no. 3 (2017): 223–36.
K[onstantinidis], Ap. G. 'Evgenios Michailidis'. *O Pharos* 6, no. 6 (June 1926): 179–80.
Kitroeff, Alexander. *The Greeks in Egypt 1919–1937, Ethnicity and Class*. London: Ithaca, 1989.
Maragoulis, Manolis. *'Time That We Modernized', Egypt and Greek Egyptian Thought (1919–1939) [Μαραγκούλης, Μανώλης. «Καιρός να συγχρονισθώμεν», Η Αιγύπτος και η αιγυπτιωτική διανόηση (1919–1939)]*. Athens: Panepistimiakes Ekdoseis Kiprou, Gutenberg, 2011.
Margolis [Maragoulis], Manolis, 'From Ancient to Modern: Greek Literature Translated to Arabic'. *Classical Papers Vol. IX: Proceedings of the International Symposium 'Translation and Cultural Interaction'*, 105–12. Cairo: Cairo University, 2009.
Mavris, Nikolaos G. *Contribution à l'étude de la chanson populaire égyptienne*. Alexandria: P. Castrounis & Z. Halkiadis, 1931.
Mavris, Nikolaos G. *Egyptian Folk Songs [Μαυρής, Νικολάος Γ. Τα Αιγυπτιακά δημοτικά τραγούδια]*. Alexandria: Erevna, 1934.
Mavris, Nikolas G. 'The Use of Arabic' [Η χρησιμότης της αραβικής], *Panegyptia* 24 March 1934, 9.
Michailidis, Evgenios. *Bibliography of the Egyptian Greeks [Μιχαηλίδης, Ευγένιος. βιβλιογραφία των Ελλήνων Αιγυπτιωτών]*. Alexandria: Kentron Ellinikon Spoudon, 1966.
Michailidis, Evgenios. 'Egypt in Arabic Philology' [η Αίγυπτος εν τη αραβική φιλολογία]. *O Pharos* 6, no. 3 (March 1926): 68–71.

Michailidis, Evgenios. *Panorama [Πανόραμα]*. Alexandria: Kentron Ellinikon Spoudon, 1972.

Patel, Abdulrazzak. *The Arab Nahdah: The Making of the Intellectual and Humanist Movement*. Edinburgh: Edinburgh University Press, 2013.

Patrikios, Panos [Π.] 'Egyptian Independence and the Foreigners' [Πατρίκιος, Πάνος. Η Αιγυπτιακή ανεξαρτησία και οι ξένοι]. *Tachydromos-Omonoia* [??] 14 August 1923.

Patrikios, Panos. 'Intellectual Egypt' [Η διανοούμενη Αίγυπτος]. *Tachydromos-Omonoia* 17 December 1924.

Patrikios, Panos. 'Poetry and Poets of Egypt' [Ποίησις και ποιηταί της Αιγύπτου]. *O Pharos* 6, no 2 (February 1926): 39–45.

Patrikios, Panos. 'The First Egyptian Female Poet' [Η πρώτη Αιγύπτια ποιητρία]. *O Pharos* 6, no. 3 (March 1926): 77–8.

Patrikios, Panos. 'Malak Hifni Nasif, the Mother of Egyptian Feminism' [Μάλακ Χέφνη Νάσεφ, Η μητέρα του αιγυπτιακού φεμινισμού]. *O Pharos* 6, no. 4 (April 1926): 118–21.

Patrikios, Panos. 'Egyptian Thought' [Αιγυπτιακή Σκέψη]. *Ermis* 1 (1 December 1926): 31–2.

Patrikios, Panos. 'Book Review' [Βιβλιοκρισία, Εισαγωγή στην ιστορία των Αραβών (Χ. Νομικός)]. *Ermis* 3 (1 February 1927): 99–101.

Patrikios, Panos. 'Neo-Egyptian Philology' [Νεο-Αιγυπτιακή φιλολογία]. *Panegyptia* 11 April 1936, 21.

Patrikios, Panos. 'A civilisation arabe à travers les siécles'. *Le Journal d'Alexandrie et La Bourse égyptienne* (29 April 1944).

Patrikios, Panos. 'Free Men in Free Egypt' [Ελεύθεροι άνθρωποι στην ελεύθερα Αίγυπτο]. *Tachydromos* 21 July 1946.

Patrikios, Panos. 'Huda Sha'rawi: the Dead Pioneer of Feminism' [Χόντα Σαραούϊ: Η αποθανούσα πρωτοπόρος του φεμινισμού], *Tachydromos* c.14 December 1947 [?].

Petrocheilos, Andreas P. *Practical Method for the Quick and Easy Learning of the Arabic Language* [Πετρόχειλος, Ανδρέας Π. *Πρακτική μέθοδος προς ταχείαν και εύκολον εκμάθησιν της αραβικής γλώσσας*]. Alexandria: Kasimati and Iona, 1925 (2nd edn 1927).

Psara, Elisabeth. *Exotic Pipes*. [Ψαρά, Ελισάβετ. *Ξωτικές φλογέρες*]. Alexandria, 1954.

Spanakidis, Odysseus. *New Practical Method to Learn Spoken and Written Arabic Language [Σπανακίδης, Οδυσσεύς. Νέα πρακτική μέθοδος προς εκμάθησιν της ομιλουμένης και γραφομένης αραβικής γλώσσας]*. 2nd edn. Alexandria: Vallinaki, 1948.

Stavridi-Patrikiou, Rena. *G. Skliros in Egypt, Socialism, demoticism and reform*. [Σταυρίδη-Πατρικίου, Ρένα. *Ο Γ. Σκληρός στην Αίγυπτο, Σοσιαλισμός, δημοτικισμός και μεταρρύθμιση]*. Athens: Themelio, 1988.

Tageldin, Shaden M. *Disarming Words, Empire and the Seductions of Translation in Egypt*. Berkeley: University of California Press, 2011.

Trimi-Kirou, Ekaterini. '"Kinotis", Grecque d'Alexandrie: Sa politique educative (1843–1932)'. PhD dissertation, University of Strasbourg, 1996, 621–5.

10

Stephan Hanna Stephan and Evliya Çelebi's Book of Travels: Tracing cooperation and conflict in Mandate Palestinian translations

Sarah Irving

Between 1935 and 1942, Stephan Hanna Stephan, a junior employee of the British Mandate government's Department of Antiquities, published a translation of passages from Evliya Çelebi's celebrated *Seyahatname*, or Book of Travels, which described the seventeenth-century Ottoman courtier's expeditions to Palestine. The six sections of translated work appeared in the *Quarterly of the Department of Antiquities of Palestine* (QDAP).[1] In the (continued) absence of a comprehensive, critical edition of Çelebi's work, Stephan's version remains a widely cited resource for scholars of the Levant and is often used to illustrate arguments about the richness of Palestinian society and culture in the seventeenth century (and to refute claims that the area was empty and/or primitive).[2] This chapter explores Stephan's translation as an act within its entangled historical context: as the work of a Christian Palestinian Arab, employed by the British Mandate administration of Palestine but with social and professional links to members of the nationalist movement, and the author of a range of ethnographic and language books and articles which delineate and defend a particular vision of Palestinian history and culture. It also situates Stephan and his work in a larger picture of Palestine under British Mandate rule. The act of translation is thus set in the context of political and social factors such as the rise in Jewish immigration in the mid-1930s and the 1936–9 Palestinian Uprising, and their influences on Arab-Jewish relations – including those between Stephan and his partner in the Evliya project, the Jewish orientalist scholar Leo Mayer.[3]

Many contemporary theories of translation focus not on the equivalence of the translated to the source text in strict linguistic terms but on the social and political environment in which a translated text is created and how this informs translation choices and strategies.[4] These ideas inform this chapter's understanding of the processes which led to Stephan's translation of the Palestine sections of Evliya's *Seyahatname* and Stephan and Mayer's paratextual additions. I argue that in Stephan's choice of text and act of translation, we witness the conscious articulation of a certain vision of Palestine, a function of the time and place of its production. On the one hand, the geographically bounded image of Palestine in Stephan's text reflects the enforcement of colonial limits on the region. Stephan's focus on the sections of Evliya's travels which correspond to the Mandate borders of Palestine suggests an acceptance of the League of Nations' colonial logic and the outlines of the Palestinian nationalist project once its leaders had realized that pan-Syrian or pan-Arab aspirations would never be attained. On the other hand, the social richness and fluidity portrayed in Evliya's text, chosen for translation by Stephan, signals a vision of Palestinian society which resists the British authorities' imposition of communal boundaries and the increasing politicization of difference.[5]

As well as a text which highlights Palestine's diversity, Stephan's translation is a useful case study because, as the reworking of a two-hundred-year-old Ottoman Turkish text by a mid-twentieth-century Christian Palestinian Arab, it represents a kind of cultural entanglement across time. It crosses the border between two languages – Ottoman Turkish, in which Evliya wrote his travelogue, and English, the language of the colonial power during Stephan's adulthood. But it also carries a promise of diversity which, ultimately, does not live up to its potential: this edition of the Travels was almost, but in the end not quite, an example of a joint Arab-Jewish enterprise. The first published sections of the translation were produced by Stephan and Leo Mayer, a recent Jewish immigrant and fellow employee of the Department of Antiquities. But they ceased working together around halfway through the project, a division which coincides with heightened tensions between Arabs and Jews in Palestine and in particular with the outbreak of the 1936–9 Revolt.

Stephan Hanna Stephan

Stephan was born in 1894 in the largely Christian town of Beit Jala, near Bethlehem, probably to a Syriac Orthodox family. Little else is known of his origins.[6] He was educated at the Syrian Orphanage ('Schneller School'), a large institution run by German Lutherans in Jerusalem which, by the time Stephan attended, was one of the city's leading schools.[7] His intellectual career begins in the early 1920s with the first of over two decades of articles on folkloric and ethnographic topics published in the *Journal of the Palestine Oriental Society* (*JPOS*)[8] and with a short piece in Arabic on the position of women in the Palestinian nation in the Syrian-Egyptian cultural magazine *Sarkis*.[9]

In the early 1920s, Stephan joined the British Mandate administration in Jerusalem as a civil servant, first in the Treasury[10] and then in the Department of Antiquities (and later the Palestine Archaeological Museum, where the Department was based from the 1930s).[11] As assistant librarian to the Museum, he translated historical documents from Jerusalem, mainly from Ottoman Turkish, and wrote reports for the Department's journal.[12] In some respects, therefore, the *Seyahatname* translation fits the pattern of Stephan's work at the Department; however, it is a vastly more ambitious task than any other document on which he worked. In addition to scholarly works, he wrote Arabic phrasebooks for speakers of German and English, published by Steimatzky in 1935,[13] and several tourist guides to Palestine and Syria, aimed at British and Commonwealth troops on leave from Egypt during the Second World War.[14]

As a subject of scholarly attention, Stephan has appeared only as one of the loose circle of Palestinian Arab nativist ethnographers identified principally with Tawfiq Canaan. This group, which also included Omar Salih al-Barghuti, Khalil Totah and Elias Nasrallah Haddad, is generally associated with functionalist anthropological studies of Palestinian rural society, mainly published in *JPOS*.[15] Like Stephan, all of these men actually authored much broader ranges of work, including literary translations, language manuals, memoirs and histories of Palestine or Jerusalem.[16] Although his translation of the *Seyahatname* is widely cited, little curiosity seems to have been aroused about Stephan as a translator or the circumstances under which this version of Evliya's writings emerged.

As the outline biography above shows, Stephan was educated but was not among the notables of Palestinian Arab society. As a Christian, he started out with a greater chance of accessing education and, after the First World War, of being employed by the Mandate administration.[17] He worked alongside both British and Jewish colleagues and was educated in a German missionary institution,[18] but he also mixed socially and professionally with figures such as Canaan who were associated with the Palestinian national movement.[19] His writings show a sense of national consciousness and of a desire to help better his country, within modernist paradigms of social and civilizational progress he had absorbed from his education.[20] It is with this understanding of his social, cultural and professional position that we must evaluate Stephan's translation of Çelebi's *Seyahatname*.

Evliya's *Seyahatname* and Stephan's translation

Evliya Çelebi (the pen name of Mehmed Zilli, 1611–*c.*1682) was a Turkish court employee and writer whose ten-volume account of his travels, the *Seyahatname* (Book of Travels), is an epic extending from the Netherlands to Persia and spanning over four decades. His travel writings have been compared in breadth and significance with those of Nasir-i Khusraw, Ibn Jubayr and Ibn Battuta, and he has been described as 'generally acknowledged as one of the greatest of Muslim travellers'.[21]

Stephan Hanna Stephan published his English translation of the Palestine passages from Evliya's *Seyahatname* in six instalments in *QDAP*, a journal of the British Mandate authorities to which Stephan regularly contributed. The area described in the passages translated by Stephan roughly corresponds to that ruled by the Mandate administration, with the omission of the Negev desert and Gaza, but adding a small area of what is now southern Lebanon. It begins in the city of Safad, describing a number of Jewish and Muslim sites there, before moving south to Jenin, now in the northern West Bank, and northwest to the port city of Acre (Akka). His itinerary then takes Evliya back inland, to Nablus, before heading along a well-known route through Sinjil and Nabi Samwil to Jerusalem.

The translation was based on a photostat of the original Topkapi Saray (autograph) manuscript of the *Seyahatname*, held in the library of the Palestine Archaeological Museum where Stephan worked.[22] The six sections of the translation were published from 1935 to 1942 and were accompanied by notes and commentaries on subjects such as place names, elaborations on stories Evliya mentions, connections to Arabic, Jewish, Turkish and other literature and traditions, and historical and religious background. However, these annotations were only written by Stephan himself for parts five and six of the series. For sections one to four, they were contributed by Leo Aryeh Mayer, Stephan's colleague at the Department of Antiquities and a distinguished European Jewish scholar of the Islamicate world, whose contribution is discussed below.

Attitudes towards the reliability of the information in Evliya's text vary. Many commentaries note his tendency towards myth-making and hyperbole; however, the *Seyahatname*'s value as historical evidence is shown by the many historians who use it as a source. Van Bruinessen, for instance, describes the *Seyahatname* as reliable on Baghdad, southern Iraq and Iraqi Kurdistan, but not further to the East.[23] For historians of the seventeenth-century Ottoman Empire, Evliya's work is a default reference, albeit one used with caution. Gisela Procházka-Eisl observes that 'no historian seriously dealing with guild or labour history in Ottoman Turkey has disregarded Evliyâ's account'.[24] For Singer's research on Ottoman public kitchens, the *Seyahatname* provided the foundational list of institutions.[25] Even when Evliya's descriptions do seem bizarre or far-fetched, Yeliz Özay argues convincingly that this is signposted in the text, under headings which declare them to be 'strange and wondrous' or via narrative styles which highlight the storytelling function of a passage.[26] Large parts of Evliya's descriptions of Palestine are of undisputed veracity; in those instances where events seem, to the modern reader, fantastic, Özay's suggestion that this is 'signposted' by Evliya holds true. By way of example, Evliya attributes a retaking of the citadel of Akka by Baybars to a miracle performed by a sheikh from Aleppo.[27] But he follows the fanciful account with a certain scepticism:

> It behoves one not to deny the hidden things, for our holy books of faith state themselves that the miracles of the saints are true. The noble eye of the Sheikh Abdin, which 'suffered martyrdom', is still kept in an 'etui' [ornamental case] profusely adorned with jewels in the treasury of the richly illuminated mausoleum of el Melik ez Zahir at Damascus. However, I have not seen it myself.[28]

Stephan's translations of Evliya are often cited in arguments about the settlement of Palestine before Zionist immigration, making their trustworthiness a live issue; his descriptions of urban environments, society and culture, as rendered by Stephan, are widely quoted by historians.[29] As there is still no definitive critical version of the *Seyahatname*, and no comprehensive translated edition,[30] Stephan's Mandate-era translation must be understood as influential in its own right, allowing later scholars access to a rare, comprehensive and detailed account of the region from a non-Western perspective.[31]

However, in some respects, Stephan's translation does diverge from its source. Evliya's *Seyahatname* did not just describe Palestine but was also the chronicle of incredibly wide travels. The sections presented by Stephan and Mayer as 'Travels in Palestine' were drawn from several different sections of the original text,[32] joined to create the appearance of a coherent whole which was not presented as such by Evliya himself. Palestine in Evliya's time was divided into several administrative units; the borders of Stephan's Palestine were administratively meaningless in Evliya's time.[33] In selecting the particular sections for his translations, Stephan effectively creates a new text which accords with a different version of Palestine, one of popular sentiment and of his own era's politics. Whilst in the early days of the Mandate many Palestinian intellectuals and nationalists saw the country's future as lying within Greater Syria or a Pan-Arab nation state, by the 1930s most were focusing on a circumscribed territory which conformed to the borders of Stephan's translation.[34]

Portraying Palestine

One of the most significant aspects of Evliya's writing on Palestine is his repeated use of this actual term to describe the territory through which he journeyed, in reference to both the classical Islamic and pre-Islamic eras and to his own period. The implication is that, even if the Ottoman state did not see Palestine as an administrative entity, its population regarded themselves as inhabiting a region by this name. Haim Gerber argues that his use of the term Palestine has 'the ring of something Evliya had heard from people in the area'.[35] Evliya also 'reproduces an Ayyubid inscription from Jerusalem, dated 619/1213–14, which situates the building in *arz Filastin*, thereby avoiding the formal *jund* and opting for the more popular "land"'.[36] Stephan's translation replicates this impression, using phrases such as 'the land of Palestine',[37] and repeats assertions from Evliya such as 'all chronicles call this country the Land of Palestine'.[38] The standard name for Palestine among Arabs in the 1930s is thus asserted in an Anglophone scholarly context and attributed with longevity.

Evliya's Palestine also conforms socially to aspects of Stephan's national vision. It is a place of towns and cities; the spaces between populated centres were feared as the home of bandits or malarial illness. The yardstick for comparison was always Istanbul,[39] and Evliya's Palestine was urban in character; in Stephan's day (as seen in his ethnographic writings), urban was routinely equated with modernity. This busy, populous territory is shown as home to Druze, Jews, Kurds, Christians and Muslims, and filled with bathhouses, schools, mosques, synagogues, churches, caravanserais and markets, many with impressive, beautiful architecture and decorations. A typical entry from Evliya's *Seyahatname*, describing Hittin in the Galilee,[40] calls it

> a flourishing little town, abounding with vineyards, orchards and gardens … a large fair is held there once a week, when ten thousand men would gather from the neighbourhood to sell and buy … There is a mosque, a public bath, and a caravanserai … A shrine, called the Teyké Mughraby, inhabited by over one hundred dervishes, lies amidst verdant gardens, like that of Iram, where lemons, citrus medica, olive and fig trees and date palms grow.[41]

Importantly, Evliya presents an image of Palestine, particularly Jerusalem, which acknowledges not just Islam but also the other Abrahamic faiths.[42] Evliya and his co-religionists[43] wrote about Jews and Christians, but 'at no point did they proclaim the need to convert them or to cleanse the land of "infidels"',[44] although they were at times scathing about their beliefs. Evliya more strongly condemned people he saw as dissenters from Islam, such as the Druze, whom he calls 'heretic', 'loathsome' and 'cursed'.[45] The Christian presence is greeted in various ways. Sometimes they are not worthy of significant comment,[46] and occasionally they are criticized as 'infidels' but only for specific acts such as the theft of the body of John the Baptist by Maltese pilgrims.[47] At other times they are respected, as in a description of the conquest of Jerusalem by Sultan Selim from the Mamluks and his confirmation of clerical tax exemptions derived from the Covenant of 'Umar (the famed, if historically disputed,[48] guarantee of protection to the 'peoples of the book' made by the Caliph 'Umar ibn al-Khattab on the conquest of Jerusalem).[49] This portrayal, and Stephan's choice of it, is particularly significant when viewed against the increasing communal divisions in Mandate Palestine – between Jews and Arabs under the pressure of Zionism, but also the institutional lines between Jews, Christians and Muslims imposed by British orientalism.[50] Evliya's text thus represents an opportunity for Stephan to emphasize his vision of Palestine as a diverse, mixed society, in opposition to the divisive nationalism and sectarianism into which it was being drawn by Zionism and Mandate policies.

Stephan's vision of Palestine, as we see from his early essay in Sarkis, is also one in which women play a prominent role in society.[51] It was common in Middle Eastern nationalist writings from the late nineteenth century onwards to link the status of women to 'progress' and 'modernness'.[52] Evliya was 'impressed' by women in Jerusalem in particular, recording that they possessed social status, freedom and education[53] centuries before European imperial or Zionist tutelage could claim credit for improving their status. This image, too, accords with how Stephan wanted to show his country.

Palestine and Islam

Two themes stand out when reading Stephan's translation of the *Seyahatname*: a sense of continuity between Jewish and Muslim beliefs, and the deep, organic relationship between Islam and the land of Palestine. As a religious Muslim, Evliya's narrative pays particular attention to Jerusalem and its links to the Abrahamic religions, but especially to Islam. Evliya established his own personal and religious links to the city by mentioning his grandfather's brother, who spent his life in service at the Haram al-Sharif. Evliya tracks down his great-uncle's grave and copies the inscription on it, making 'Jerusalem … part of his personal history and worship'.[54] As a loyal Ottoman official, Evliya highlights the Ottoman sultans' recognition of Jerusalem's special status. The city was designated a *hass-ı hümayun* (imperial domain), one of only three places, with Mecca and Medina, too holy for the Ottomans to make their own stylistic additions to the religious architecture. At the same time, Evliya traces Jerusalem's splendour and status to its Israelite past, mentioning King David and emphasizing that, whilst the city's initial eminence came from King Solomon, its renewed glory was conferred by the 'second Solomon', the Ottoman Sultan Sulayman the Magnificent. Evliya also wonders at the beauty of Christian icons and other paintings, and notes the special place granted to the city's Christian clergy since the Caliph 'Umar.[55]

Alongside its depiction of Palestine, I see this Islamic focus as key to Stephan's choice of document. Although Stephan translated texts for his employers at the Palestine Archaeological Museum, it was extramural work for which he received extra pay for labouring 'in his spare hours'.[56] This suggests that he had some independence in deciding whether to carry out translations and makes the choice of the *Seyahatname* among the many available texts significant, given its reflection of themes prominent in Arab and Palestinian nationalist thought at the time.[57] In combination with features such as Evliya's use of the term 'Palestine' and his depiction of a cultural and religious space corresponding geographically with the borders of Mandate-era Palestine, Stephan thus presents us with a text which strongly asserts a socially and geographically coherent Islamicate Palestine.[58]

From the beginning of his journey, in northern Palestine, Evliya describes shrines and holy places linked to Jewish, Christian and Muslim figures and tales from the Bible. But alongside recognition of Jewish and Christian histories in Palestine, Evliya emphasizes not just the historicity of Islamic rule over the region but also the strength of more organic Islamic connections. This focus on Islam as a key aspect of identity, whilst acknowledging a wider cultural and religious background, fits with mainstream Arab nationalist narratives of Stephan's time, and particularly into many manifestations of Palestinian nationalism during the Mandate.[59] Islam, in Evliya's account, is not just a faith which came to the Holy Land with the first Caliphs but one rooted in the land via people and miracles dating back to the very earliest days of Islam and even before. This vision of Palestine as a country characterized by a contemporary Islamicate, Arab culture but with a strong sense of myriad peoples adding to its richness is key to the idea of Palestine put forward by Stephan and other Palestinian nativist or nationalist ethnographers.[60] This view of Palestine, not specifically nationalist but with a particular national vision, also emerges in Stephan's tourist guides and Arabic phrasebooks.[61] In particular, the sense that there is a *strategic* portrayal of Palestine in these writings is paramount, with their common image of the country as Islamicate, diverse and distinctly Palestinian.[62]

The actual historicity of Evliya's stories is not important here. The point is that Stephan chose to represent Palestine in this manner rather than following the Ottoman administrative boundaries employed by Evliya or the Judaeo-Christian positionalities of many of his Mandate colleagues. He cements Palestine's connections to Islam through claims not only to historical presence but even the semi-magical, permanent imprint of religious figures' visits on the land itself. In Safad, the Sanctuary is depicted in miraculous terms, as the hiding place of Yaʿqub (Jacob) and 'a mosque, yet it is not built'. Its mihrab is said to point to Mecca but following a sightline passing through Jerusalem (a geographical impossibility; the two lie at quite different angles from Safad), thus tying together the two holy sites not only through human worship but through a 'mosque' self-shaped out of living rock, implying a divine hand. Evliya acknowledges Safad's importance for Jews and the presence of a community there but also takes care to call Sufi rites performed in the cave-mosque 'time-honoured', emphasising that Islamic traditions there are also strong,[63] and claims that another cave in the city holds the tomb of an unnamed wife of the Prophet.[64] In the northern Galilee, he describes a site said to have been visited by ʿAli, companion of the Prophet and future Caliph, when he was a boy and again as an adult. On both occasions he was said to have performed miracles and his horse Duldul to have left hoofmarks on the rock. Islam is thus firmly rooted in the land, leaving marks on the rocks themselves and claiming longevity for the link; a similar effect is created by the claim that there are sites in the Marj ibn Amir (Jezreel Valley) where Companions of the Prophet were buried.[65]

An intimate, mystical link between Islam and Palestinian land and water is found in descriptions of a spring which responds to the name of a Muslim holy man:

> Any one who wants to drink from this spring would go to the source and implore, 'O Sheikh Mas'ūd, I am thirsty' (*yā sheikh Mas'ūd, 'aṭshāni(!)*). By the order of Allah the spring would immediately overflow and the man would drink.[66]

Islam is also connected to Judaism in this aquatic evocation by linking Islamic figures and Jewish prophets, principally Yaʿqub.[67] Even a common Islamic tale – of the monk Bahira who, meeting the young Muhammad near Damascus, told him that he would become a prophet – is reworked to incorporate the Holy Land.[68] In Evliya's version, Bahira tells Muhammad to visit Acre and wash in a certain spring in which Moses and Jesus had previously bathed.[69] Evliya thus not only ties together the three faiths, giving Muhammad equal status with Moses and Jesus, but also takes this story to a Palestinian city, and in a text from which Stephan chose a series of dislocated segments to fuse together under the heading of 'Palestine'. Although the image is far from unusual in older Arabic Islamic literature, Stephan gives it new prominence in Mandate Palestine, at a time when ownership of the land was being disputed in the national, political and even military arenas.

Leo Aryeh Mayer

However much Evliya might have wanted to stamp an Islamic identity onto the land of Palestine, and however much Stephan may have seen in this an Arab-Islamic territorial identity, there is another strand which fits Stephan and Evliya's narrative (in that it highlights the potential for diversity within a Muslim-ruled Palestine) and diverges from it (in that the potential is only partly fulfilled). The story of the *Seyahatname* translation has another angle, the involvement of Leo Mayer, and the light it sheds on the complexity of intellectual life in Mandate Jerusalem.

Despite his academic importance at the time, little has been written on Leo Aryeh Mayer (1895–1959), Stephan's collaborator on four of the six sections of the *Seyahatname* translation. Born in Eastern Galicia in 1895 to a line of rabbis, with parents who were early Zionist sympathizers, Mayer became fascinated by Islamic art whilst studying at the Oriental Institute of the University of Vienna.[70] He helped to found the Hashomer Jewish youth movement which, under the influence of Martin Buber, was at this stage mostly concerned with cultural and spiritual revival.[71] This combination of respect for Islamic culture and a cultural brand of Zionism may suggest why Stephan and Mayer's collaboration was possible in the first place.

In 1921, Mayer made the decision to move to Palestine. Having studied at prestigious European universities including Vienna and Berlin, and with a doctorate, Mayer had career advantages that Stephan lacked. He rapidly found a job as an inspector in the Department of Antiquities, under director John Garstang, outranking Stephan, the minor bureaucrat on constant secondment to the Department of Antiquities. Mayer rose through the ranks of the department and apparently found the situation congenial:

> He ... found his place in the circles of English society, and became friendly with the educated Arabs who opened their libraries to him ... His work was fully appreciated by the Government, which made it possible for him to travel abroad and further his studies by visiting museums and libraries.[72]

Under the auspices of the Department of Antiquities, Mayer excavated in Jerusalem with Eleazar Lipa Sukenik and conducted research on the Hittites with Garstang.[73] Alongside his role in the Mandate administration, Mayer was involved in plans to establish the School of Islamic and Oriental Studies at the Hebrew University.[74] He started lecturing informally as soon as it was established and took up a post as lecturer in Islamic Art and Archaeology when it formally opened in September 1925. Mayer's historical research is notable for its focus on recovering the names and life stories of Arab artisans and craftsmen,[75] sifting through signatures on museum pieces to reconstruct the links between scattered objects. At the International Congress of Orientalists in Istanbul in 1951, he reported on the identification of hundreds of individual creators of Islamicate arts, attaching artists' names to formerly anonymous masterpieces.[76] He published volumes on Muslim architects, astrolabists and woodcarvers, with more on metalworkers, armourers and stonecarvers issued posthumously.[77]

Alongside his fascination with the Islamic world, its culture and with individual creative figures rather than an abstract notion of 'art', Mayer was described in obituaries as a 'proud and devoted'[78] and 'convinced and staunch' Zionist.[79] Whilst the two facets of Mayer's life are not inherently contradictory, they were unusual for the period: of work sponsored by the Jewish Exploration Society and the Hebrew University during the Mandate period, only Mayer and Moshe Stekelis (who excavated early hominid remains) did not work on 'Jewish' subjects such as synagogues.[80] Mayer's social and intellectual circles included mainstays of Zionist knowledge production like the Jewish Palestine Exploration Society (of which he was president from 1940 until his death in 1959),[81] but also Palestinian Arabs and Europeans. Early in his career Mayer apparently took up Arabic linguistics, working in the 1920s on a dictionary of Palestinian spoken Arabic (never published) with philologist Naftali Tur-Sinai.[82] Hirschberg remarks that Mayer 'knew how to cooperate with other scholars and publish results jointly. Other scholars acknowledged his helpfulness and were therefore always willing to help him in return';[83] his work with Stephan perhaps attests to this.

Mayer's obituaries are full of descriptors such as 'retiring' and 'secretive', emphasising that he 'did not encourage familiarity' and 'only the barest details of biographical interest are known'.[84] But the facts suggest that, along with other key figures from the Hebrew University, such as university president and leading advocate of a binational state Judah Magnes, his sympathies lay with a 'cultural' Zionism which saw Palestine as the centre of an artistic, linguistic and spiritual renaissance, rather than 'political' Zionism which demanded an ethnically exclusive, settler-colonial state. Rice's obituary notes that whilst he was 'unwavering in his strong Zionist convictions', Mayer 'had from the start supported all moves for an entente with the Arabs and counted many of them among his friends'.[85] He was 'close to members of the Brit Shalom association [which sought Arab-Jewish co-existence], but was not involved in its ongoing activities', placing him (like his early activities in Hashomer) among those who believed in a binational state.[86] Such ambiguities were not uncommon among the founding generation of the Hebrew University; many came from a European tradition in which Jews were at the forefront of Orientalist scholarship and were seen as having greater religious and linguistic affinities with Muslims and Islamic culture than was possible for Western European Christians.[87]

What does this suggest about Stephan and Mayer's collaboration on the first four instalments of the translated *Seyahatname*? The appeal of having Mayer's name on the articles seems clear for Stephan; although he had by this time published numerous articles in the *JPOS* and *QDAP*, in formal terms he was a junior member of staff, lacking job security or advanced academic qualifications. As such, the signature of a university lecturer and PhD on his articles would have given them additional weight. Mayer's incentives are less clear: intellectual curiosity? Friendliness between colleagues? Stephan was employed in the library of the Palestine Archaeological Museum, so he and Mayer would have worked closely together, and Stephan's other jointly credited texts (travel books with Boulos 'Afif; an annotated bibliography with Stuart Dodd of the American University of Beirut) bear the stamp of professional pragmatism. But despite Stephan's lack of formal qualifications, his breadth of knowledge and linguistic abilities were outstanding and perhaps bore an 'authenticity' attractive to a comparatively recent migrant to Palestine.

What is certain is that their cooperation did not last the length of the project; the annotations and footnotes of the final two pieces are all Stephan's work. The publication dates of the six sections offer a clue. Two of those annotated by Mayer appear in 1935, one in 1936 and one in 1938; all are short sections of the whole – five, ten, four and thirteen typed pages, respectively, perhaps suggesting a slow and cumbersome or meticulous writing process. Those annotated by Stephan alone came later. Three of the joint works were probably written, then, before the Palestinian Revolt of 1936–9 and the fourth soon after its start. Did the relationship break down under political pressure between the two men or from their colleagues and associates? The pattern seems to fit wider events. Tensions were rising between Jews and Arabs after the Fifth Aliyah increase in immigration from under five thousand Jews in 1931 to over thirty thousand in 1933,[88] leading to the general strike and outbreak of a nationwide uprising among Palestinian Arabs in 1936. Stephan continued to work at the Department of Antiquities, although some rebels, particularly rural military leaders, demanded that Arab staff resign from Mandate administration jobs.[89] But he never followed up his other notable collaboration with a Jewish partner, Arabic phrasebooks published by the Jewish stationery and publishing firm Steimatzky.

Reading Stephan and Mayer's paratexts

Although Leo Mayer contributed the annotations for sections I–IV of Stephan's published translations in the *QDAP*, and Stephan wrote his own footnotes for only the final two parts of the series, Stephan's translations and additions comprise forty-four pages of the total, to Mayer's thirty-six (including blanks and illustrations). The main type of paratextual material is footnotes, positioned below the translation text on each page. The layout derives a technical appearance from the folio and line numbers of the Ottoman original, listed on the outside margin. In addition to formal footnotes, Stephan added minor comments and markings throughout the text. Most common among these are exclamation marks in parentheses, used when Evliya's accounts overstep the merely fanciful and are simply incorrect; examples include the assertion that Hebron is 'near Jerusalem'[90] or in the description of the walls and gates of the Haram al-Sharif in Jerusalem, where Evliya repeatedly gets his cardinal points confused.[91] Oddly, Stephan seems not to have noticed Evliya's claim that Christ was born in Jerusalem.[92]

A small percentage of the footnotes written by both Mayer and Stephan deal directly with the text of the *Seyahatname*. This is not a 'critical edition' of Evliya's work, in the sense of comparing different editions and rectifying errors.[93] Both annotators, do, though, point out typographical errors and spaces where Evliya apparently planned to return to the manuscript to fill in information, or where the original text reads 'year' but no space or date follow.[94] In several places, Stephan notes that he is giving a 'conjectural translation' where the 'text … is corrupted' or the meaning is ambiguous, highlighting his active role as translator.[95] Stephan also comments on some of the choices he made in translating, as when he notes that

> the letters allow a double reading, though 'Kurd' [the option given precedence in the actual text] may be preferable over 'Georgian' in determining the meaning of a word describing the origins of a wrestler executed outside one of the gates of Jerusalem.[96]

The two writers' annotations show differences of emphasis and tone. Mayer, for example, displays a great depth of knowledge on Jewish history and sites in Palestine, as in this observation on Evliya's writings about the Lower Galilee:

> So far as I am aware no Muslim author before Evliya ever considered this part of Palestine specially fertile in tombs of prophets. But early in the sixteenth century J. Luria, the famous Jewish cabbalist of Safad, during his peripatetic lessons with his pupils, has indicated the sites of hundreds of holy tombs …, thus creating a special literature and a tomb-worship hitherto unknown, at least so far as his followers were concerned.[97]

Stephan's ability to cite events in Palestine's Jewish history is impressive but, in sheer numerical terms – and even allowing for different concentrations of Jewish shrines across the country – his attention to this issue is less than Mayer's (7 of the

68 references written by Mayer deal with subjects particularly relevant to Judaism or Jewish communities, as against 10 of Stephan's 212 references).[98]

Both men also display considerable erudition (citing works in English, Arabic, German, French and Ottoman Turkish) but vary in style and content. Mayer's information is more obviously academic, lacking the immediacy of some of Stephan's observations and his intimate knowledge of the contemporary people of Palestine. Stephan's notes, in general, contain more contemporary and ethnographic knowledge, often not credited to other sources and therefore presumably from his own research or from what he considered common knowledge in Palestinian society. Examples include his claim, in response to Evliya terming Nablus a 'Samaritan' *sanjaq*, that 'the present-day inhabitants of many former Samaritan villages would resent being considered of Samaritan origin'.[99] He also states that many of Nablus's Muslim families 'are known to have converted to Islam as recently as two generations ago, the foremost of whom are the Darwaza'[100] and that there 'are families in Hebron' who are 'of Turkish stock, yet have become Arabs'. These kind of unattributed assertions suggest that he is drawing on his own general knowledge.[101] Nowadays we would call this oral history, but the respectability of such techniques outside of folklore studies was only established in the 1970s.[102] The notion that a family of Turkish origins might 'become Arab', and his matter-of-fact attitude to the Samaritan origins of notable Nabulsi families, also situates Stephan's understanding of Arabness alongside thinkers such as Sati' al-Husri, who located Arab identity firmly in the realm of culture, especially language, and not 'race' or descent.[103] Stephan's sense of Palestinian identity is ecumenical, incorporating ethnic and religious shifts and conversions without comment.

Conclusion

The English-language version of Evliya Çelebi's *Seyahatname* prepared by Stephan Hanna Stephan and Leo A. Mayer presents us with an opportunity to witness how a translation, understood as the product of active translators and of their social and political environment, reveals the entanglement of the political and the intellectual. Functional ideas of translation give us a means to analyse how translation operates, showing how Stephan and Mayer's work is not simply an English-language version of the source but a text in its own right, with its own contextual logics. These logics correspond to a number of ideological and political trends current at the time, namely, the conception of Palestine as a bounded territorial unit along the borders of the British Mandate and the idea of it as a religiously and ethnically diverse society with an underlying Arab-Islamic character. As such, they highlight the extent to which both Palestinian Arab and Zionist Jewish views of relations between their communities, and the prospects for cooperation, changed and declined during the 1930s. While the textual imagining of such relations was to continue in pamphlets and editorials, the actual possibilities for such encounters were increasingly being eroded.

In one respect, the triad of Evliya the Turkish Muslim, Stephan the Christian Palestinian Arab and Mayer the Zionist European Jew embodies the vision (already crumbling by the time the resulting text was published) of a diverse Palestine in which the three faiths and diverse ethnicities could coexist. But Mayer's departure from the project seems to symbolize a darker trajectory; the Palestinian Uprising of 1936–9 broke out not long after the first publications, and the fatalities included scholars from Stephan and Mayer's social and professional circles.[104] The individual statuses of Stephan and Mayer and their social positions as Palestinian Arab junior clerk versus elite-educated Zionist Jewish immigrant were increasingly out of step with one another. If the clues left by the dates of publication of the translated *Seyahatname* are correct, they reveal a collaboration which collapsed under the pressure of the wider political environment.

As Zachary Lockman stresses in his study of Arab-Jewish labour relations under the British Mandate, there is little or no use in constructing 'if only?' tales about the ways in which Palestinian Arabs and Jews encountered one another before 1948.[105] Such discourses do, however, make possible a challenge to dominant narratives about separation and difference, and explorations of a richer and more complex picture of entangled relations in this period of Palestine's history. As we can see from the content and the context of Stephan and Mayer's work, the rising hostility between communities in Palestine in the late 1930s was contingent, the product of ethnic nationalism and colonial pressures. Within that environment, however, Stephan and Mayer's textual and personal example emphasizes that cooperation could and did exist, interwoven with wider events.

Notes

1 Tshelebi, 'Evliya Tshelebi's Travels in Palestine'.
2 Ben-Naeh, for instance, emphasizes the value of Evliya's information on roads, towns and buildings in Palestine ('Thousands Great Saints', 10–12). References to Evliya's work appear repeatedly in arguments on Palestine solidarity websites such as Mondoweiss, see e.g. comment dated 8 January 2015, 5:52 pm, on http://mondoweiss.net/2015/01/reporter-palestinians-concessions/ and comment dated 1 July 2017, 6:05 pm, on http://mondoweiss.net/2017/06/palestinian-dehumanize-subjugate/ (both accessed 21 July 2017).
3 Sheffer, 'Intentions and Results', 50–5; Edelheit, *Yishuv in the Shadow*, 120.
4 See Kadhim, '*Skopos* Theory', and Venuti, *The Translator's Invisibility*, for discussions of the translator as an active agent in the production of the new text.
5 Winder, '"Western Wall" Riots', 7–8, 13–15, 20; Roberts, 'Re-membering the Mandate', 221–4.
6 Stephan's life story is hard to reassemble and has been pieced together from disparate sources; he married an Armenian woman, Arasky Keshishian, and they had two sons; after his death in 1949, she and their children (already refugees in Lebanon from the 1948 foundation of the State of Israel) moved to Brazil. See Irving, 'A Young Man of Promise', 42–62.
7 Albright, 'Report of the Director', 15.
8 The Palestine Oriental Society was a rare example of a social and scholarly society in Mandate Palestine which included Arab, Jewish and Euro-American members, subscribers and attendees at its events. Stephan, along with Canaan and the nationalist

George Antonius, were among the Arab figures who published in the Society's journal and/or sat on its Board (see committee membership and officer lists, *JPOS*, e.g. v3 (1923): 207–12; v7 (1927): 218–24).

9 Stephan, 'Al-Mar'a', 63–4. Sadgrove, 'Sarkis Family', 692. *Sarkis* was a monthly cultural journal published in Egypt by Salim ibn Shahin of the Lebanese Sarkis family between 1905 and 1924. It was part of the *Nahda* intellectual environment, linked to the Lebanese writer Amin Rihani, debating questions of religion and politics with him in print. The fact that Stephan, in his mid-twenties, sent his article to *Sarkis* suggests both personal self-confidence and awareness of debates on gender happening in the Syrian-Egyptian press.

10 'Subscribers', *JPOS* 1 (1920/21), 225.

11 Stephan and Dodd, *Post-War Bibliography*; Whitcomb, 'Dimitri Baramki', 78 ('a Palestinian (the self-taught scholar Stephan H. Stephan) worked in the library').

12 E.g. Stephan, 'An Endowment Deed of Khasseki Sultan'; Baramki and Stephan, 'Nestorian Hermitage'.

13 The bookshop and stationer Steimatzky, established in 1920 by Russian Jewish half-brothers, was by this time a major enterprise, with shops across the Middle East, including Baghdad and Damascus.

14 Stephan and 'Afif, *This is Palestine*; *Palestine by Road and Rail*.

15 Furani and Rabinowitz, 'Ethnographic Arriving of Palestine', 475–91; Tamari, *Mountain against the Sea*, 93–110.

16 Irving, 'Intellectual Networks, Language and Knowledge', 68–111.

17 Haiduc-Dale, *Arab Christians*, 85.

18 For views on the work of Syrian Orphanage and its impacts, see: the admiring introductions by Elias Haddad (1910) and Ramzy Bisharah (2009) to Bisharah's translation of Johann Ludwig Schneller's biography of his father, the founder of the Syrian Orphanage; Kark, 'The Impact of Early Missionary Enterprises' (arguing that seeing missionary activities as entirely colonialist and negative is an over-generalization); Tibawi on the deep hostility of Palestinian nationalists towards missionaries and missionary education: 'missionary activities came to be viewed, not as philantropic [*sic*] and cultural activities, but as some kind of reconnaissance in advance of foreign domination' ('Religion and Educational Administration', 8).

19 Nashef, 'Tawfiq Canaan', 12–26.

20 Examples include his arguments for an enhanced status for women within the Palestinian nation ('Al-Mar'a', 63–4); less positive influences are seen in a letter to Finnish ethnographer Hilma Granqvist, in which Stephan suggests that Palestinians need to learn modernity from Europeans (letter dated 15 April 1932, Palestine Exploration Fund Granqvist file 369).

21 Crane, 'Pamphylian Plain', 157.

22 Gerber, 'Territorial Concepts', 572 n. 39.

23 van Bruinessen, 'Kurdistan', n.p.

24 Procházka-Eisl, 'İbrāhīm and the White Cow', 157.

25 Singer, 'Evliya Çelebi on ʿimarets', 123.

26 Özay, 'Strange and Wondrous Europe', 63–4.

27 In addition to the improbable reason for this Mamluk victory, Evliya incorrectly attributes it to Baybars. Crusader Acre (Akka) was conquered in 1290 by Sultan al-Ashraf Khalil, thirteen years after Baybars's death.

28 Tshelebi, *Travels in Palestine*, 40.

29 See e.g.: Prag, 'Defensive Ditches', 299–301; Galor and Bloedhorn, *Archaeology of Jerusalem*, 286, 290; Firro, *History of the Druzes*, 43; Noy et al., *Folktales of the Jews*, 486; Petersen, 'Two Medieval Castles', 387; St. Laurent and Riedlmayer, 'Restorations of Jerusalem', 83.
30 Crane, 'Pamphylian Plain', 157. Sections of Evliya's original covering areas such as Kurdistan remain completely unpublished, so that researchers can only work from the original manuscripts (van Bruinessen, 'Kurdistan', n.p.).
31 Among indications that we should take Stephan's scholarship seriously in its own right are 'Aref al-'Aref's listing of the translation itself as an 'event' in his monumental 1961 history of Jerusalem (al-'Aref, *Tarikh al-Quds*, 267) and Dankoff's use of Stephan's suggested amendments, mentioned above.
32 Tshelebi, *Travels in Palestine*, 9.
33 See, for instance, Crecelius, 'Damiette and Syrian-Egyptian Trade', 157, 171; Weber, 'Ottoman Harbour Town', 180.
34 Khalidi, *Palestinian Identity*, 165; Parsons, *The Commander*, 109, 112, 115, 122; Parsons, 'Rebels without Borders', 396, 400–1.
35 In Evliya's time, this consisted of the sanjaqs of Gaza, Jerusalem, Nablus, Lajjun and Safed, which fell within the vilayet of Damascus. Gerber, 'Territorial Concepts', 565–7.
36 Ibid., 572 n. 39.
37 Tshelebi, *Travels in Palestine*, 68.
38 Ibid., 63.
39 Dankoff, *Ottoman Mentality*, 54–6; Hüner, 'Travelling within the Empire', 78–9, 84
40 Evliya does not name the village, but a footnote by Mayer states, 'As can be inferred from the mention of the shrine of Nabi Shu'eib, a few lines further, it must be identical with Hattin. The shrine is still venerated there' (Tshelebi, *Travels in Palestine*, 30).
41 Ibid.
42 This was not unusual for Muslim writers (Hayden and Matar, 'Introduction', 12–13); Stephan's choice of text might be attributable to the fact that, unlike works by e.g. Ibn Battuta or al-Nabulusi, well known in the Arabic-speaking world and translated into European languages in the nineteenth/early twentieth centuries, the *Seyahatnâme* had been largely ignored until the mid-nineteenth century and only translated in fragments.
43 E.g. Syrian writer 'Abd al-Ghani al-Nabulusi (1641–1731, a scholar and Sufi from Damascus whose three hundred books include several *Rihlas* (travel accounts) throughout the Ottoman Empire). Ibid., 15.
44 Tshelebi, *Travels in Palestine*, 15.
45 Ibid., 10, 11, 16.
46 Ibid., 36.
47 Ibid., 37–8.
48 The Covenant of 'Umar, a 637 agreement between the Caliph and Patriarch Sophronius of Jerusalem, still forms the ideological underpinning of Muslim-Christian relations in the city (Koulouris, 'Greek Orthodox Church', 232). The historicity and nature of the Covenant is disputed by religious scholars and historians (Cohen, 'What Was the Pact of 'Umar?').
49 Tshelebi, *Travels in Palestine*, 60.
50 See, e.g., Simoni, 'At the Roots of Division'; Winder, '"Western Wall" Riots'.
51 Stephan, 'Al-Mar'a'.
52 Shakry, 'Schooled Mothers', 129–32.

53 Ze'evi, 'Women in 17th-Century Jerusalem', 159, 167–8.
54 Baktir, 'Holiness of Jerusalem', 114.
55 Ibid., 119–22.
56 Israeli State Archives B/28/34, letters dated 7 May 1934, approved 16 May 1934.
57 Khalidi, *Palestinian Identity*, 33, 45; Fishman, 'Haram al-Sharif Incident', 6–7, 14, 19.
58 The term 'Islamicate' highlights Stephan's vision of a Palestine in which Muslims comprised the majority of the population and cultural forms associated with Islam permeated society, but where there was scope for religious diversity. This would have fitted with major strands within Arab nationalism at the time.
59 Dawn, 'Origins of Arab Nationalism', 4,7,10–11; Budeiri, 'The Palestinians', 195–6; Fishman, 'Haram al-Sharif Incident',14, 19.
60 Tamari, *Mountain sgainst the Sea*, 93–110; Furani and Rabinowitz, 'Ethnographic Arriving of Palestine', 477–8.
61 See e.g. Stephan and 'Afif, *This is Palestine* and *Palestine by Road and Rail*; Stephan, *Arabic Self-Taught*.
62 Furani and Rabinowitz, 'Ethnographic Arriving of Palestine', 478.
63 Ibid., 25. The Mamluks under Baybars built several Sufi *zawiyas* in Safad. This places Sufi rituals in Safad as early as the fourteenth century, three hundred years before Evliya. Petersen, *Towns of Palestine*, 73.
64 Tshelebi, *Travels in Palestine*, 27.
65 Ibid., 11–12, 34.
66 Ibid., 12–13.
67 Ibid.
68 The Bahira legend appears in early *sira* accounts such as al-Tabari and Ibn Ishaq, and in rewritten forms as Christian propaganda against Islam. In none of the early manuscripts, however, does this Acre story appear. Roggema, *Legend of Sergius Bahira*, 37–9; Gottheil, 'Christian Bahira Legend', 215–16; Thomson, 'Armenian Variations', 886–7.
69 Tshelebi, *Travels in Palestine*, 44.
70 Hirschberg, 'In Memoriam', 11.
71 Margalit, 'Hashomer Hatzair Youth Movement', 28, 31–2. As Margalit outlines, Hashomer Hatzair was a significant leftist secular force in Israel until the 1980s, through the kibbutz movement and the MAPAM political party. It formed as a youth movement in Eastern Europe before the First World War, many of whose members went to Palestine after the war to form kibbutzim. During the Mandate, the movement's political party urged equal status for Arab and Jewish citizens in a binational state, seeing the Jewish presence in Palestine as a matter of cultural revival rather than ethnic political dominance.
72 Hirschberg, 'In Memoriam', 12.
73 Ibid.
74 Milson, 'Arabic and Islamic Studies', 171–2.
75 E.g. *Islamic Architects and Their Works*, 1956.
76 Hirschberg, 'In Memoriam', 12; Rice, 'Leo A. Mayer', 455.
77 Hirschberg, 'In Memoriam', 12. Examples of the volumes include *Islamic Astrolabists and Their Works* (1956), *Islamic Woodcarvers and Their Works* (1958) and *Islamic Metalworkers and Their Works* (1959), all published in Geneva by A. Kundig.
78 Ibid., 15.
79 Rice, 'Leo A. Mayer', 454.
80 Moorey, *A Century of Biblical Archaeology*, 50.

81 Later the Israel Exploration Society.
82 Tur-Sinai, 'Remembering a Fine Man', XVI.
83 Hirschberg, 'In Memoriam', XIV.
84 Rice, 'Leo A. Mayer', 454–5.
85 Rice, 'Leo A. Mayer', 454.
86 Selzer, 'Leon Ary Mayer, 1895–1959', 212.
87 Milson, 'Arabic and Islamic Studies', 170.
88 Matthews, *Confronting an Empire*, 200.
89 Feldman, *Governing Gaza*, 82–4; Abboushi, 'Road to Rebellion', 42; Cohen, *Army of Shadows*, 103–4.
90 Tshelebi, *Travels in Palestine*, 26.
91 Ibid., 70–8.
92 Ibid., 56.
93 Ben-Naeh, 'Thousands Great Saints', 5.
94 See e.g. (Mayer's notes) 14 n. 1, 16 n. 4, 18 n. 5 and n. 7, 35 n. 6, (Stephan's notes) 48 n. 1, 51 n. 1, 56 n. 3 and n. 4, 59 n. 2, 60 n. 3, 93 n. 1 (all in 1980 edition of *Evliya Tshelebi's Travels in Palestine*).
95 Tshelebi, *Travels in Palestine*, 65 n. 3, 85 n. 1.
96 Ibid., 64 n. 5.
97 Ibid., 33 n. 3.
98 Counted from 1980 edition.
99 Ibid., 47 n. 4.
100 Ibid., 50 n. 1.
101 Ibid., 67 n. 4.
102 Smith, 'Making History'.
103 Cleveland, *Making of an Arab Nationalist*, 83–126.
104 Brit Shalom member and Hebrew University Arabist Levi Billig was shot in August 1936; Avinoam Yellin, an Arabist and Mandate Government Inspector of Jewish Schools, was killed in 1937 (Milson, 'Arabic and Islamic Studies', 174, 181).
105 Lockman, *Comrades and Enemies*, 360–1.

Bibliography

Abboushi, W. F. 'The Road to Rebellion: Arab Palestine in the 1930s'. *Journal of Palestine Studies* 6, no. 3 (Spring 1977): 23–46.

Albright, W. F. 'Report of the Director of the School in Jerusalem, 1920–1921'. *Bulletin of the American Schools of Oriental Research* 5 (January 1922): 9–23.

al-'Aref, 'Aref. *Al-Mufassal fi tarikh al-Quds*. Jerusalem: Matba'at al-ma'arif, 1961/1999.

Baktir, Hassan. 'Evliya Çelebi's *Seyahatname* and the Holiness of Jerusalem'. In *Through the Eyes of the Beholder: The Holy Land, 1517–1713*, edited by Judy A. Hayden and Nabil I. Matar, 111–24. Leiden: Brill, 2013.

Baramki, D. C., and Stephan Hanna Stephan. 'A Nestorian Hermitage between Jericho and the Jordan'. *Quarterly of the Department of Antiquities of Palestine* 4 (1934): 81–6.

Behar, Moshe. '1911: The Birth of the Mizrahi–Ashkenazi Controversy'. *Journal of Modern Jewish Studies*, 16, no. 2 (2017): 312–31.

Ben-Naeh, Yaron. '"Thousands Great Saints": Evliya Çelebi in Ottoman Palestine'. *Quest: Issues in Contemporary Jewish History* 6 (December 2013): 1–18.

van Bruinessen, Martin. 'Kurdistan in the 16th and 17th centuries, as Reflected in Evliya Çelebi's *Seyahatname*'. *Journal of Kurdish Studies* 3 (2000): n.p.
Budeiri, Musa. 'The Palestinians: Tensions between Nationalist and Religious Identities'. In *Rethinking Nationalism in the Arab Middle East*, edited by James Jankowski and Israel Gershoni, 191–206. New York: Columbia University Press, 1997.
Cleveland, William. *The Making of an Arab Nationalist: Ottomanism and Arabism in the Life and Thought of Sati' al-Husri*. Princeton: Princeton University Press, 1972.
Cohen, Hillel. *Army of Shadows: Palestinian Collaboration with Zionism, 1917–1948*. Berkeley: University of California Press, 2008.
Cohen, Mark. 'What Was the Pact of 'Umar: A Literary-Historical Study'. *Jerusalem Studies in Arabic and Islam* 23 (1999): 100–57.
Crane, Howard. 'Evliya Çelebi's Journey through the Pamphylian Plain in 1671–72'. *Muqarnas* 10 (1993): 157–68.
Crecelius, Daniel. 'Damiette and Syrian-Egyptian Trade in the Second Half of the Eighteenth Century'. In *Syria and Bilad al-Sham under Ottoman Rule: Essays in Honour of Abdul-Karim Rafeq*, edited by Peter Sluglett with Stefan Weber, 155–75. Leiden: Brill, 2010.
Dankoff, Robert. *An Ottoman Mentality: The World of Evliya Celebi*. Leiden: Brill, 2006.
Dawn, C. Ernest. 'The Origins of Arab Nationalism'. In *The Origins of Arab Nationalism*, edited by Rashid Khalidi, Lisa Anderson, Muhammad Muslih and Reeva S. Simon, 3–20. New York: Columbia University Press, 1991.
Edelheit, Abraham. *The Yishuv in the Shadow of the Holocaust: Zionist Politics and Rescue Aliya, 1933–39*. Boulder, CO: Westview Press, 1996.
Feldman, Ilana. *Governing Gaza: Bureaucracy, Authority and the Work of Rule, 1917–67*. Durham, NC: Duke University Press, 2008.
Firro, Kais. *A History of the Druzes*. Leiden: Brill, 1992.
Fishman, Louis. 'The 1911 Haram al-Sharif Incident: Palestinian Notables Versus the Ottoman Administration'. *Journal of Palestine Studies* 34, no. 3 (Spring 2005): 6–22.
Furani, Khaled, and Dan Rabinowitz. 'The Ethnographic Arriving of Palestine'. *Annual Review of Anthropology* 40 (2011): 475–91.
Galor, Katharina, and Hanswulf Bloedhorn. *The Archaeology of Jerusalem: From the Origins to the Ottomans*. New Haven, CT: Yale University Press, 2013.
Gerber, Haim. '"Palestine" and Other Territorial Concepts in the 17th Century'. *International Journal of Middle East Studies* 30, no. 4 (November 1998): 563–72.
Gottheil, Richard. 'A Christian Bahira Legend'. *Zeitschrift fur Assyriologie* 14 (1899): 203–68.
Gribetz, Jonathan Marc. 'An Arabic-Zionist Talmud: Shimon Moyal's At-Talmud'. *Jewish Social Studies* 17, no. 1 (Fall 2010): 1–30.
Haiduc-Dale, Noah. *Arab Christians in British Mandate Palestine: Communalism and Nationalism, 1917–1948*. Edinburgh: Edinburgh University Press, 2013.
Hayden, Judy A., and Nabil I. Matar. 'Introduction'. In *Through the Eyes of the Beholder: The Holy Land, 1517–1713*, edited by Judy A. Hayden and Nabil I. Matar, 1–25. Leiden: Brill, 2013.
Hirschberg, H. Z. 'Professor Leon A. Mayer – In Memoriam'. In *Eretz-Israel: Archaeological, Historical and Geographical Studies*, 7th edn, edited by M. Avi-Yonah, HZ Hirschberg, B Mazar and Y. Yadin, 11–15. Jerusalem: Israel Exploration Society, 1964.
Hüner, N. Ipek. 'Travelling within the Empire: Perceptions of the East in the Historical narratives on Cairo by Mustafa Âli and Evliya Çelebi'. In *Venturing beyond*

Borders – Reflections on Genre, Function and Boundaries in Middle Eastern Travel Writing, edited by Bekim Agai, Olcay Akyıldız and Caspar Hillebrand, 77–100. Würzburg: Ergon Verlag Würzburg, 2013.

Irving, Sarah. 'A Young Man of Promise: Finding a Place for Stephan Hanna Stephan in the History of Mandate Palestine'. *Jerusalem Quarterly* 73 (Spring 2018): 42–62.

Irving, Sarah. 'Intellectual Networks, Language and Knowledge under Colonialism: The Work of Stephan Stephan, Elias Haddad and Tawfiq Canaan in Palestine, 1909–1948'. PhD dissertation, University of Edinburgh, 2018.

Kadhim, Jawad. 'Skopos Theory: Basic Principles and Deficiencies'. *Journal of the College of Arts, University of Basrah* 41 (2006): 37–46.

Kaplony, Andreas. *The Ḥaram of Jerusalem, 324–1099: Temple, Friday Mosque, Area of Spiritual Power*. Stuttgart: Franz Steiner Verlag, 2002.

Kark, Ruth. 'The Impact of Early Missionary Enterprises on Landscape and Identity Formation in Palestine, 1820–1914'. *Islam and Christian–Muslim Relations* 15, no. 2 (2004): 209–35.

Khalidi, Rashid. *Palestinian Identity: The Construction of Modern National Consciousness*. New York: Columbia University Press, 1997.

Koulouris, Anna. 'The Greek Orthodox Church and the Future of Jerusalem'. *Palestine-Israel Journal of Politics, Economics, and Culture* 17, no. 1/2 (2011): 230–6.

Levy, Lital. 'Historicizing the Concept of Arab Jews in the "Mashriq"'. *Jewish Quarterly Review* 98, no. 4 (Fall 2008): 452–69.

Lockman, Zachary. *Comrades and Enemies: Arab and Jewish Workers in Palestine, 1906–48*. Berkeley: University of California Press, 1996.

Margalit, Elkana. 'Social and Intellectual Origins of the Hashomer Hatzair Youth Movement'. *Journal of Contemporary History* 4, no. 2 (April 1969): 25–46.

Matthews, Weldon. *Confronting an Empire, Constructing a Nation: Arab Nationalists and Popular Politics in Mandate Palestine*. London: I.B. Tauris, 2006.

Mayer, L. A. *Islamic Architects and Their Works*. Geneva: Albert Kundig, 1956.

Milson, Menahem. 'The Beginnings of Arabic and Islamic Studies at the Hebrew University of Jerusalem'. *Judaism* 45, no. 2 (Spring 1996): 169–83.

Moorey, P. R. S. *A Century of Biblical Archaeology*. Cambridge: Lutterworth, 1991.

Nashef, Khaled. 'Tawfiq Canaan: His Life and Works'. *Jerusalem Quarterly* 16 (November 2002): 12–26.

Noy, Dov, Dan Ben-Amos and Ellen Frankel. *Folktales of the Jews, Volume 1: Tales from the Sephardic Dispersion*. Lincoln, NE: Jewish Publication Society, 2006.

Özay, Yeliz. 'Evliyâ Çelebi's Strange and Wondrous Europe'. *Cahiers balkaniques* 41 (2013): 61–9.

Parsons, Laila. *The Commander: Fawzi al-Qawuqji and the Fight for Arab Independence 1914–1948*. New York: Hill and Wang, 2016.

Parsons, Laila. 'Rebels without Borders: Southern Syria and Palestine, 1919–1936'. In *The Routledge Handbook of the History of the Middle East Mandates*, edited by Cyrus Schayegh and Andrew Arsan, 395–407. London: Routledge, 2015.

Petersen, Andrew. *The Towns of Palestine under Muslim Rule, 600–1600*. Oxford: British Archaeological Reports, 2005.

Petersen, A. 'Two Medieval Castles and Their Position in the Military Architecture of Muslim Palestine'. In *Egypt and Syria in the Fatimid, Ayyubid, and Mamluk Eras*, edited by Urbain Vermeulen and J. van Steenbergen, 383–406. Leuven: Katholieke Universiteit te Leuven / Peeters, 2001.

Prag, Kay. 'Defensive Ditches in Ottoman Fortifications in Bilad alSham'. In *Muslim Military Architecture in Greater Syria: From the Coming of Islam to the Ottoman Period*, edited by Hugh Kennedy, 295–306. Leiden: Brill, 2006.
Procházka-Eisl, Gisela. 'İbrāhīm and the White Cow – Guild Patrons in Evliyâ Çelebi's *Seyahatnâme*'. *Cahiers balkaniques* 41 (2013): 157–70.
Rice, D. S. 'Leo A. Mayer: In Memorium'. *Ars Orientalis* 4 (1961): 454–5.
Roberts, Nicholas. 'Re-membering the Mandate: Historiographical Debates and Revisionist History in the Study of British Palestine'. *History Compass* 9, no. 3 (2011): 215–30.
Roggema, Barbara. *The Legend of Sergius Bahira: Eastern Christian Apologetics and Apocalyptic in Response to Islam*. Leiden: Brill, 2009.
Sadgrove, P. C. 'Sarkis Family'. In *Encyclopedia of Arabic Literature*, vol. 2, edited by Julie Scott Meisami and Paul Starkey, 692. London: Routledge, 1998.
St. Laurent, Beatrice, and András Riedlmayer. 'Restorations of Jerusalem and the Dome of the Rock and Their Political Significance, 1537–1928'. *Muqarnas* 10 (1993): 76–84.
Schneller, Ludwig Johann. *The Life and Work of Father Johann Ludwig Schneller, Founding Father of the Syrian Orphanage*. Translated (from the Arabic by Elias Nasrallah Haddad, from the German original) into English by Ramsay Fawzie Bisharah. London, Melisende, 2009.
Selzer, Assaf. 'Leon Ary Mayer, 1895–1959'. In *The History of the Hebrew University of Jerusalem: Who's Who Prior to Statehood – Founders, Designers, Pioneers*. Jerusalem: Magnes Press, 2015.
Shakry, Omnia. 'Schooled Mothers and Structured Play: Child Rearing in Turn-of-the-Century Egypt'. In *Remaking Women: Feminism and Modernity in the Middle East*, edited by Lila Abu-Lughod, 126–70. Princeton: Princeton University Press, 1998.
Sheffer, G. 'Intentions and Results of British Policy in Palestine: Passfield's White Paper'. *Middle Eastern Studies* 9, no. 1 (1973): 43–60.
Simoni, Marcella. 'At the Roots of Division: A New Perspective on Arabs and Jews, 1930–39'. *Middle Eastern Studies* 36, no. 3 (July 2000): 52–92.
Singer, Amy. 'Evliya Çelebi on ʿimarets'. In *Mamluks and Ottomans: Studies in honour of Michael Winter*, edited by David J. Wasserstein and Ami Ayalon, 123–33. London: Routledge, 2006.
Smith, Graham. 'The Making of Oral History: Sections 1–2'. *Making History: The Changing Face of the Profession in Britain*. Accessed 15 May 2019. https://www.history.ac.uk/makinghistory/resources/articles/oral_history.html.
Stephan, Stephan Hanna. 'Al-Mar'a'. *Sarkis* 11, no. 1 (January 1922): 63–4.
Stephan, Stephan Hanna. *Arabic Self-Taught: A Primer*. Jerusalem: Steimatzky, 1935.
Stephan, Stephan Hanna. 'An Endowment Deed of Khasseki Sultan, Dated the 24th May 1552'. *Quarterly of the Department of Antiquities of Palestine* 10 (1944): 170–94.
Stephan, Stephan Hanna, and Stuart C. Dodd. *A Post-War Bibliography of the Eastern Mandates, 1919–1930: Miscellaneous Fascicle*. Beirut/Jerusalem: American University of Beirut/Franciscan Press, 1936.
Stephan, Stephan Hanna, and Boulos 'Afif. *This is Palestine: A Concise Guide to the Important Sites in Palestine, Transjordan and Syria*. Jerusalem: Bayt-ul-Makdes Press, 1942.
Stephan, Stephan Hanna, and Boulos 'Afif. *This is Palestine: A Concise Guide to the Important Sites in Palestine, Transjordan and Syria* (second edition). Jerusalem: The Modern Press, 1947.

Stephan, Stephan Hanna, and Boulos 'Afif. *Palestine by Road and Rail: A Concise Guide to the Important Sites in Palestine and Syria*. Jerusalem: Ahva Co-operative Printing Press, 1942.

Tamari, Salim. *Mountain against the Sea: Essays on Palestinian Society and Culture*. Berkeley: University of California Press, 2008.

Thomson, Robert W. 'Armenian Variations on the Baḥira Legend'. *Harvard Ukrainian Studies* 3/4, no. 2 (1979–80): 884–95.

Tibawi, A. L. 'Religion and Educational Administration in Palestine of the British Mandate'. *Die Welt des Islams* (New Series) 3, no. 1 (1953): 1–14.

Tshelebi, Evliya. *Evliya Tshelebi's Travels in Palestine 1648–1650*. Translated by Stephan H. Stephan – with annotations by L. A. Mayer: *Quarterly of the Department of Antiquities of Palestine* IV, nos 1–2 (1935): 103–8; IV, no. 3 (1935): 154–64; V, nos 1–2 (1936): 69–73; VI, no. 2 (1938): 84–97; and with annotations by S. H. Stephan: VIII, no. 4 (1939): 137–56; IX (1942): 81–104.

Tshelebi, Evliya. *Evliya Tshelebi's Travels in Palestine 1648–1650*. Translated by Stephan H. Stephan. Jerusalem: Ariel Publishing, 1980.

Tur-Sinai, N. H. 'Remembering a Fine Man'. In *Eretz-Israel: Archaeological, Historical and Geographical Studies volume Seven: L.A. Mayer Memorial Volume*, edited by M. Avi-Yonah, H. Z. Hirschberg, B. Mazar and Y. Yadin, 16–17. Jerusalem: Israel Exploration Society, 1964.

Venuti, Lawrence. *The Translator's Invisibility: A History of Translation*. London: Routledge, 1995.

Weber, Stefan. 'The Making of an Ottoman Harbour Town: Sidon/Saida from the Sixteenth to the Eighteenth Centuries'. In *Syria and Bilad al-Sham under Ottoman Rule: Essays in Honour of Abdul-Karim Rafeq*, edited by Peter Sluglett with Stefan Weber, 179–240. Leiden: Brill, 2010.

Whitcomb, Donald. 'Dimitri Baramki: Discovering Qasr Hisham'. *Jerusalem Quarterly* 55 (Autumn 2013): 78–82.

Winder, Alex. 'The "Western Wall" Riots of 1929: Religious Boundaries and Communal Violence'. *Journal of Palestine Studies* 42, no. 1 (Autumn 2012): 6–23.

Ze'evi, Dror. 'Women in 17th-Century Jerusalem: Western and Indigenous Perspectives'. *International Journal of Middle East Studies*, 27, no. 2 (May 1995): 157–73.

11

When Malek Bennabi recollected his colonial education: Cultural authenticity, nostalgia and renaissance in Algeria

Idriss Jebari

The Algerian thinker Malek Bennabi (1905–1973) represents a cautionary tale on the valiant but often unsuccessful attempts by solitary intellectuals to produce a critical discourse on culture that is disentangled from the forces of colonialism and nationalism in the Arab world. Bennabi's large body of writings dealt with the decline and renaissance of Islamic civilization.[1] While he is usually omitted from studies on contemporary Arab thought because he wrote most of his work in French (although it was subsequently translated into Arabic), he is enjoying a revival among proponents of a liberal reform of Islam and for his ideas on Afro-Asian solidarity in the 1950s.[2]

As a historical figure, Bennabi found himself at every important juncture of Algeria's resistance to French colonialism. Yet he failed to leave his mark on each of these stages and on the country after its independence. Born in Constantine in 1905, he studied in a Franco-Arab *medersa* (madrasa[3]), a reformed Islamic school overseen by the French colonial authorities. Education was the front line of the Algerian cultural struggle against France, especially by the ʿUlema Association in the 1920s and 1930s.[4] However, young Malek Bennabi was not part of the movement. He then travelled to France to carry out his higher education in Paris where he was denied a place at the Ecole des langues orientales. Instead, he trained to be an electrician, which led him to spend time with the community of Algerian workers in France. These constituted the main ranks of nationalist parties such as the Parti du peuple algérien or the Etoile Nord-Africaine. Once again, Bennabi does not figure in most histories of Algeria's political life from the 1930s and 1950s despite his intellectual activism. Instead, these accounts revolve around prominent figures such as Messali Hadj or Ferhat Abbas.[5] Bennabi spent the years of Nazi-occupied France held in a camp and took refuge in Cairo after the war. Once more, he found himself in the thick of the action: Nasser's support for liberation movements and pan-Arabism attracted North African nationalists, such as Moroccan members of Istiqlal, Tunisia's Bourguiba and several Algerian nationalist leaders who would constitute the Algerian Front de libération nationale. Bennabi would later write that he had poor relations with the Algerian nationalists and steered clear of their internal competition for power.[6]

Algeria's independence in 1962 seemed to signal that his hour had arrived. Algeria's new president, Ahmed Ben Bella, reputed for his Marxist and modernist views, named Bennabi head of the University of Algiers and placed him in charge of reforming higher education. However, the 1965 military coup that saw Houari Boumedienne replace Ben Bella proved costly for Bennabi. He was sidelined from the reform of higher education in 1967 as the country was engulfed by a national polemic over the Arabization of education. Bennabi passed away in 1973, in relative anonymity and marginalized from the centres of power. His greatest legacy was a large body of underexplored texts on Islamic civilization and several editorials published after independence in the state journal *Révolution-Africaine*.

Like many contemporary Arab intellectuals, Bennabi stands on the margins of Algerian history because of his poor political acumen and refusal to compromise his principles. However, in this chapter, I argue that Bennabi also failed to leave his mark because of the position he adopted after independence regarding the place of the French cultural legacy in Algeria's redefined national culture. In the euphoric atmosphere of early independence, the Algerian state anchored the nation-building discourse in the need to reactivate an 'authentic Algerian personality' around Arabism and Islam. The authorities strove to erase the 'sequels' of French colonialism, mostly the use of French, by calling for a total Arabization of school programmes.[7] Bennabi was among the extreme few who defended the richness of the interplay between the two languages and their cultural traditions.[8] As the author of powerful essays on Islamic civilization such as *Le phénomène coranique* (1947), *Les conditions de la renaissance* (1949) and *Vocation de l'Islam* (1954), he could not be dismissed as a 'denatured' Algerian or a colonial apologist. But in writing in French to defend Arab civilization, familiar and comfortable with both cultures, he occupied a unique space and was quite alone there.[9] Ultimately, Bennabi's positions were ignored because of their historical timing and because he lacked a powerful constituency to echo them.

In this chapter, I explore the first volume of his memoirs, titled *Mémoires d'un témoin du siècle* (Memories of a Witness of the [Twentieth] Century) and published in 1965. The book focuses in large part on his childhood and his education during the colonial era. He published the second volume in 1970, in Arabic, in Beirut as *Mudhakkirat shahid lil-qarn: al-talib* (Memories of a Witness of the Century: The Student). This instalment failed to receive the same level of interest and he died before completing the later volumes. Philip Naylor has remarked on the difficulties raised by these memoirs, especially in terms of their historical accuracy and the author's tendency to embellish his views and involvement in Algerian history in the twentieth century.[10] Rather than seeing these memoirs as a nostalgic remembrance, I analyse them as a political statement destined to impact on public debates on Algeria's cultural identity and its problematic colonial legacy. The book paints a different picture of the colonial past from the nationalist narrative, and insists that Algerians have a role in defining their national identity. As such, he rejects grand narratives such as the 'alienating French colonial experience' or the 'salvation of Islamic civilization'.

The memoirs were published during and in response to the divisive debate over Algerian education reform. Some saw education as a 'positive legacy' of French colonization,[11] especially because the French-educated elites had taken over the country's administration and its affairs continued to operate in French.[12] However, as Fanny Colonna has shown, French colonial education was not a uniform system but contained different 'tracks' for 'Muslims', meaning indigenous Algerians.[13] Omar Carlier highlights the role that colonial schools played in reshaping the 'indigenous' elite in Algeria, often leading to a 'cultural shock' for students who were uprooted from their conservative Muslim social environments and made to adopt French social codes.[14] Resistance to French education and its resulting cultural alienation came from the reformist ʿUlema Association (Jam'iyat al-ʿulama al-muslimin al-jaza'iriyyin) from the 1930s. Its principles were encapsulated by Sheikh Abdelhamid Ben Badis in the famous slogan: 'Islam is my religion, Arabic is my language and Algeria is my country.'[15] The association set up a network of schools to rival French colonial education and shape an emerging national consciousness, and after independence its influence on state policy remained significant. After the hard-fought eight-year war of independence, official Algerian historiography painted the colonial experience as a homogeneously unfavourable transformation.[16] The topic of colonial education in Algeria, and the image of the French presence as a whole, continue to be captured by nostalgia and political instrumentalization, preventing the emergence of more nuanced histories.[17]

Instead, Bennabi's 1965 memoirs should be read alongside a strand of francophone Algerian literature from authors who investigated how colonial education transformed them individually.[18] This literature dives into memory in order to offer more nuanced portrayals of bicultural education made conscious of the social context of the French colonial system. As a result, it offers more satisfying avenues than the polarized and ideological commentaries on French legacies. For example, Nick Harrison examines the autobiographies of Assia Djebar, an Algerian Muslim woman, and Albert Memmi, a Tunisian Jewish man of the same generation, who portray their passage through French schools in a positive light because it opened up new perspectives and liberated them from oppressive social environments.[19] We find similar portrayals in a number of self-narratives from francophone Maghribi writers.[20] Similarly, Bennabi portrays how bicultural schools allowed him to gain a rich and layered worldview and imagine a path for a true cultural renaissance.

This chapter retraces how Bennabi's memoirs present a dissenting position on Algeria's post-independence cultural orientation in the way he recollects his cultural experience under French colonization. The first half of the chapter relies on his memoirs and how they portray his enriching and harmonious bilingual childhood education, followed by his recollection of the Islamic reformist movement in Algeria and the state of Algerian society in the 1920s and 1930s. The second half of the chapter studies the passage to independent statehood and addresses the genesis of the country's cultural orientations and policies centring on Arabization, before closing with the distinctiveness of Bennabi's call for a more ambitious 'civilizational renaissance' based on critical intellectual debates.

Memories of French education in Algeria: The origin of a double-culture

Bennabi's memoirs depict the period from his early childhood to his departure to France as a 22-year-old, roughly the period from 1910 to 1930. As part of the author's self-attributed creative licence, the story follows a protagonist called Seddik (rather than Malek); the preface specifies that the book should be read as 'an Algerian speaking behind a veil, maintaining anonymity'.[21] Its value lies not in the historical accuracy of Bennabi's account or the aesthetics of its prose but as an alternative and subversive portrayal of French colonialism.

'Seddik' grew up in the southern rural town of Tebessa, close to the Tunisian border, and studied in Constantine, the picturesque fortified mountain city in the east that was successively occupied by Phoenicians, Romans, Muslim and Ottoman rulers. He came from a 'typical' family, meaning large, conservative and financially strained. Despite the family's attachment to conservative social traditions and their resentment towards the impact of French colonialism on their community, the young Malek/Seddik was placed in the colonial education system. By this time, and especially from 1920, France had successfully imposed its education structures on Algeria. After decades of resistance, a significant portion of the native Muslim Algerian population embraced these schools, and demand for places far outstripped what the colonial authorities offered.[22] Colonna explains this rush for places as the sign of Algeria as a 'vanquished society' and a 'crumbled [indigenous] education system'.[23] Others, such as Pierre Vermeren, talking about the comparable cases of the Moroccan and Tunisian protectorates, emphasize how colonial education offered social promotion and possibilities for employment in the colonial administration.[24] This branch of the colonial education system did not seek to 'assimilate' Muslim Algerians and turn them into French nationals. Instead, students were prepared for a life of service in the colonial administration as translators or as junior legal clerks for Algerians[25] and to serve France as a bridge between colonial and Muslim societies. They studied in both languages and acquired a solid religious education.[26]

Seddik attended the local Quranic school early in the morning and the French school during the day. His descriptions provide fascinating observations on how he remembered the two schools before being aware of their respective power structures:

> I would regularly flee from the *taleb* [Quranic teacher] and the hard mat, and I would receive regular beatings from him and my father, which increased my hatred for Quranic school. I became a bad student … and after four years, my parents let me quit because I was learning nothing.[27]

Conversely, the 7-year-old's recollections portray French school as an exciting opportunity: he mentions his first 'modern' (i.e. Western) outfit, his backpack and his stationery. He shared a classroom with non-Muslims and was proud to be praised as a 'model of hygiene' by his French teachers, Mademoiselle Buil and Mademoiselle Rafi, with whom he 'fell madly in love'. He worked diligently on his French and even managed to 'catch up'.[28]

The contrast between the dark and repetitive traditional school and the brighter and exciting modern one represents more than the aesthetic setting of two different education systems. Rather, it shows France's irresistibly attractive cultural power. This new setting encouraged Seddik to devote time and effort to reading in French and, implicitly, to form associations in his head linking French colonialism and 'modernity', and Algerian culture (and Islamic education) with 'backwardness'. This has been a constant feature of North African autobiographies during the colonial period, as one finds in Driss Chraibi's *Le Passé Simple* in Morocco,[29] or Albert Memmi's *La Statue de Sel*, in which he describes how French school allowed him to leave the Jewish 'ghetto' (referring to the Jewish quarter in Tunis) and his family's poverty behind.[30] The famous writer and film-maker Assia Djebar (1936–2015), author of the seminal Algerian novel in French *L'amour, la Fantasia* (1995), also describes how French education became a tool for her emancipation. As a child, she broke a glass ceiling in her school by coming top of her class, a first for an *indigene*, and then became the 'Muslim spokesperson'. In one telling episode, she used the colonizer's own arguments of French *laïcité* (secularism), learned in school, to demand equal treatment regarding breakfast options and to challenge the unfair system.[31]

Bennabi's memoirs contain another dimension not always evoked by writers like Djebar and Memmi: a favourable depiction of the Arabic component of bilingual education. As a young teenager, Seddik is sent to study in Constantine and to live with relatives. His French teacher Monsieur Martin introduces him to the important *oeuvres* of French literature, and Seddik works diligently on composition, literature and vocabulary. He adds that Monsieur Martin made him fall in love with books, such as the adventure novels of Jules Verne.[32] In parallel, he studied under Sheikh Abdelmajid who taught Arabic grammar at the mosque each morning at seven. Instead of the dreary and insipid religious lessons of his childhood, he remembered these classes fondly. Every morning, he sat with the other pupils in a circle around the Sheikh, holding interactive discussions that often touched on current topics:

> Early on we noticed in him a resistance against old customs in society, against maraboutism, and against the abuses of French administration, and the students often sought to engage him on social and political issues.[33]

The narrator never raises his dual education as a problem or a source of malaise. Instead, the two professors 'formed in my spirit the two folds who determined my intellectual orientation'.[34] This idyllic portrayal of his double-culture continues as he writes, 'Rabelais and Victor Hugo, 'Imru' al-Qays and Hafiz Ibrahim gave [me] both dimensions of French and Arabic.'[35]

At this point in Seddik's childhood, the memoirs start to contain an awareness of the practical outcome of education, namely, his career options. He first mentions how, early on, his parents 'decided for him' that he should join the *medersa* track in order to become a magistrate.[36] Other students foresaw careers as *instituteurs* (French teachers)[37] or medical auxiliaries (assistants to colonial doctors).[38] Seddik describes the children of settlers of his age crossing town in their smart outfits, remarking how they could become lawyers, doctors and professors, while his own perspective seemed restricted.[39]

This depiction of intra-school dynamics highlights Seddik/Malek's failure to fit in. He did not conform to the profile of other provincial students who aspired to a minor administrative position and a stable income. Instead, he portrays his inclination as a curious observer of social life outside the classroom during the late 1910s and early 1920s, or what French settlers called *la belle époque*. He describes evening strolls in the markets of Constantine and visits to Sufi brotherhoods during their mystical ceremonies, or in the old town and Moorish cafés listening to recitals from the *Thousand and One Nights*. There were also those who stayed at the mosque after the *ʿisha* ʾ prayer to listen to religious lectures and sometimes even politically charged discussions of distant conflicts and local issues.[40]

The story that Bennabi tells of his childhood acknowledges the importance of his bicultural colonial education in order to dispel the false dichotomy between French and Arabic, writing instead '[my] conscience was formed by this double-stream'.[41] The author also brings out Seddik's curiosity about his social surroundings as a significant factor of his development. The historical period in which he grew up was arguably as significant as the nature of his schooling: the sociocultural revival taking place in Constantine from the 1920s was an important factor in his broader education and of his memory of French colonization.

Cultural resistance in Algeria: From Islah to authenticity

Bennabi's memoirs tackled two other pillars of Algerian colonial historiography: first, the idea that Algeria's cultural decadence was caused by French colonialism and, second, that the Islamic reformist movement (Islah) was responsible for reawakening the Algerian nation.[42] Historians routinely focus on the Front de Libération Nationale's 1954–62 war against France as the catalyst for independence. However, this overshadows the prior work carried out by the Association of Algerian Muslim ʿUlema to shape an Algerian consciousness in opposition to French subjugation. The ʿUlema were active across the country and argued that the Arabic language was the central means to 'recover' Algeria's 'authentic personality' and resist French assimilationism. The association set up a network of Arabic schools as an alternative to French institutions and began winning the hearts and minds of the Algerian masses: they would later have a seminal role in shaping the independent state's cultural policy.[43]

Malek Bennabi's memoirs offer a subaltern perspective on this period of Algeria's history to counter the dominant narrative of the ʿUlema Association. His testimony revolves around his personal experience as a student in Constantine, where the movement developed, and in rural Algeria during the 1920s. Instead of discussing the role of 'enlightened reformists' such as Sheikh Ben Badis, his narrative talks about social transformations during this period. Thus, his story challenges the heroic portrayal of the Algerian ʿUlema, giving more credit and agency to the Algerian people themselves.

The city of Constantine was the theatre of the Algerian reformist movement in the 1920s and became an important cultural centre thanks to the activities of Sheikh Ben

Badis and his schools. However, in 1921, Seddik joined the colonially administered *medersa* – the reformed Islamic school teaching in French and Arabic to Algerian natives. The *medersa* prepared for a career track in the 'Muslim Magistrature' and Sharia courts. The French colonial administration operated an Islamic legal system for private law, which it supervised, but maintained an appearance of autonomy by having Algerian natives as 'magistrates' (known as *qadi* or *wakil*).[44] These were state functionaries and one of the few administrative jobs available to Algerian natives. These came with financial advantages and social status, but their power was mostly illusory, as the secular courts' jurisdiction extended over the Sharia courts from the late nineteenth century onwards.

Seddik's family's decision to send him to a *medersa* was motivated by professional and economic calculations rather than an embrace of the colonial system. As a *mederséen* his career track seemed predetermined in a 'respectable profession', even if his mind was set on travel and adventure. At the *medersa*, he lived as a boarder. The French maintained the appearance of traditionalism: students wore the *burnous*, the hooded cloak that signalled their learned religious credentials. The institution was managed by an Algerian *chaouch* (doorman, concierge and handyman) and a French director, less visible to the students.[45] Status as a *mederséen* conferred social prestige; to Bennabi, 'I was no longer a "pupil", I was [now] a "student" at the *medersa*' and 'words themselves have strength over one's vocation'. He continued to expand his knowledge of Arabic and French culture, adding that 'Cartesian culture cleared the fog in which brewed the mythological mind, corresponding to superstitions in Algeria'.[46] Otherwise, his four years at this institution were banal. His account includes repeated descriptions of his interactions with his friends, the annual ritual of stressful, gruelling examinations which would determine if he would keep his scholarship and the challenges of adapting to a tight budget by switching to fried food and chickpeas.[47]

Seddik and his circle of friends began adopting different social habits, including spending time at the neighbourhood café. The development of 'café culture' was an important consequence of French colonialism in Algeria,[48] alongside the introduction of the first musical record from Egypt, an 'important factor of psychological and political evolution in the country'. Seddik recounts with emotion hearing the *kanun* and Salama Hijazi's voice for the first time.[49] While 'Algerian taste was becoming Egyptian' and 'dissident', he notes how French settlers listened to jazz, emphasizing the contrast between the communities.[50] The coffee shop also gave him a privileged insight into the changes impacting Constantine and the growing importance of the 'Ulema Association. The Benyamina café was the 'headquarters of *medersa* students', located on the city's 'thinking artery' in the old town, 'with the café … on one end, the Shihab printers on the other, and between them Sheikh Ben Badis's office'.[51] From the café, Seddik saw the reformist leader on a daily basis, sometimes accompanied by foreign travellers, 'silhouettes with distinctive turbans, coming to procure new ideas'.[52]

With this physical proximity to the heart of the Algerian Islah came contact with 'Ben Badis's students', those who studied in Arabic in the network of nationalist schools which began in Constantine.[53] Seddik first encountered them at Constantine's Anglican mission, where he went regularly out of curiosity. These students came to 'cross swords in defence of Islam', and meeting them was 'a revelation'.[54] Seddik realized that 'we belonged to the same line of thought, his "spiritual family", a feeling I did not have toward my fellow *medersa* students'.[55] Further cultivating the narrative of his own specificity, Seddik writes that he took a keen interest in the liberal nationalist movements of the Muslim world, from Kemalism to Sa'd Zaghlul in Egypt, rebelling against European imperialism and calling it 'a lightning strike that changed my life'.[56] Inspired by their courage, he challenged the *medersa*'s rules by wearing a modern pair of trousers instead of the traditional *siroual* worn by the other students and was reprimanded by the French director and his lackey, the Algerian *chaouch*.[57] He also began to read about the current realities of the Islamic world, rather than Chateaubriand's 'romantic … nostalgia for the Orient':[58]

> I discovered at the *al-Nadjah* library two books I consider had the most determining impact on my intellectual vocation … Ahmad Riza's '*Faillite morale de la politique occidentale en Orient*' [Moral Bankruptcy of Western Policy toward the East, 1922] and '*Risalat al-tawhid*' [Exposé on Muslim Religion, 1925] by Sheikh Muhammad Abduh.[59]

Unlike in his earlier years, Seddik now no longer portrays the two cultures in harmony. Instead, he criticizes French colonial education's portrayal of Arab culture to its Muslim Algerian students as decadent and antiquated. This ensured that the *medersa*'s student body were politically apathetic, they 'still read the *Thousand and One Nights*' and were mainly interested in their future careers.[60] They ignored the 'greatness of the [Arab] past' and texts of the *Nahda*, and were unfussed by the cultural 'poverty of the present'. Islah and Ben Badis were the factors that shook his conviction in the mutual complementarity of his French and Arabic education under the colonial system.

Despite his solidarity with Ben Badis's aims, Seddik remained an outsider to the movement, and his testimony cannot inform us of its internal realities or political action.[61] Furthermore, after his political awakening, he could not go back to chasing a position in the colonial administration until his passions had settled. Instead, when he graduated at 20, he spent time exploring his hometown of Tebessa and engaging with its social realities. His memoirs describe how Algerian society began to break away from past practices and superstitions in favour of reformed ways. His account is tinted by nostalgia, but it also forces his readers to think differently about the 'authentic Algerian personality' and reinstate the people's role at the expense of its political leaders.

In Tebessa, in semi-rural Algeria, Seddik describes several important social shifts. His mother stopped turning to the local Imam's *Baraka* (blessing) to complement the French doctor's medicine;[62] instead, his whole family discussed reformist ideas and opposed obscurantist practices. He speaks of a 'new social order' and the 'social mobilization of Islah',[63] and the 'ordinary people' who organize themselves autonomously at the *nadi* (club) or independent mosques, rather than relying on old structures of authority. They even named and shamed those who drank alcohol during the Friday *khutba* at the mosque.[64] Seddik affirms these radical transformations as 'the manifestation of a social spirit' and the 'birth of Algerian society'.[65]

A few months later, Seddik began working for the colonial administration as a paralegal, travelling around the country. His postings provide contrasting accounts of

Algerian reality which we must pair with the high-brow Islah to help us understand his emerging understanding of authenticity. In Aflou, a small semi-nomadic locality on the fringe of the Western Algerian desert, the narrator encounters a 'virgin' and 'lost Algeria', 'a corner still unpenetrated by colonialism, where the country took refuge to safeguard its treasures of good manners, its loyalty, its hospitality and horsemanship, and its naivety'. Crime was absent, thanks to internal methods of dispute resolution. These traits stemmed from a 'nobility that nature maintained in the veins of Bedouins'.[66] Along with the pleasure he took from encountering these preserved values, he also became anxious that colonialism would lead to their dissipation, as it had elsewhere in Algeria.[67] When he is sent to Chateaudun-du-Rhumel (today Chelghoum-Laid), a mixed locality in the east, he is unforgiving of the European settlers' impact: 'the whole cultural life of Chateaudun could be summed up in *anis* drinkers, card players swearing and stories of ghosts', a 'dehumanized environment' where he never feels comfortable.[68] These two accounts allow us to identify Bennabi's conception of 'authenticity': the honesty and generosity of the Algerian herders, and the social autonomy and mobilization in Tebessa, contrasted with the social and cultural decadence in Chateaudun caused by French colonial transformation. Frustrated by his status in the colonial administration and his stifled ambitions, Seddik soon resigns his post. Bennabi left for Europe and higher education around 1930, opening a much more troubled and unclear period in his life, not covered in these memoirs.[69]

Seddik's ominous predictions regarding the 'decadence' of Muslims fit suspiciously well with subsequent historical developments, especially the poverty that spread throughout rural Muslim society after the 1930 depression, spurring a popular nationalist mobilization. Colonial control and French arrogance reached new heights during celebrations of the centenary of French presence in Algeria that year, which was a significant event in igniting Algerian nationalist consciousness.[70] This is a reminder that the memoirs were written for Bennabi's present rather than for pure historical value. Overall, the published memoirs displace the reader's attention from the ʿUlema Association's role in leading social change and nationalist consciousness to give credit to Algerian society in taking ownership of reformist principles and rejecting the alienating effects of French colonialism. To understand why Bennabi devoted so much of his book and its focus to the Algerian people and away from the ʿUlema Association's leaders, one must consider Algeria after independence and the tensions sparked by the state's cultural orientations.

Arabization and the 'recovery' of Algeria's 'personality' after independence

Algeria's independence in 1962 was celebrated as a spectacular achievement for colonized people everywhere, but this moment of national unity hid serious rifts within the nationalist movement. Ahmed Ben Bella, one of the Front de libération nationale (FLN) leaders and the country's first elected president, was overthrown in 1965 by the military, who accused him of being too authoritarian and radical in his

Marxist-inspired policies. Houari Boumedienne, part of the coup and an Algerian army general, succeeded him as president, ruling until 1978 and overseeing the consolidation of state authority and extensive postcolonial transformation.[71]

The independent state's cultural policy was largely inspired by the ʿUlema Association's call to 'recover' an 'authentic Algerian personality'. From 1963, its flagship policy was the Arabization of education, and this binding 'campaign promise' became an opportunity to assert unity It also provides us with an example of how independent states negotiate colonial legacies, illustrating the process of competition between various constituencies, insofar as culture was 'war by other means' in the national project, in which the 'neo-ʿUlema' were the victors.[72] Their language of 'recovery' appeared in the earliest texts of the Algerian nationalist movement. The final document of the 1962 Tripoli Congress, the roadmap of the independent nation-building program, envisaged a 'national, revolutionary and scientific' Algerian culture in assured terms:

> In the first instance, we will restore the Arabic language [as] the very expression of our country's cultural values, its dignity and efficiency as the language of a civilization [we] will aim to reconstitute and praise our national legacy and its humanist dimensions, classical and modern, in order to introduce into the intellectual life and education a popular sensibility [sic]. Thus [Algerian culture] will fight against cultural cosmopolitanism and the western impregnation that have contributed to inculcate a number of Algerians with a disdain for national values.[73]

These principles were echoed by Ben Bella in a 1963 speech, in which he affirmed (in French): 'We are Arabs, Arabs, ten million Arabs … and there is no future for this nation outside of Arabism.'[74] These sentiments capture how strongly a large part of the country felt after decades of French colonialism. French anthropologist Gilbert Grandguillaume reports on a 1962–3 controversy in the National Assembly over Algerian radio's decision to play a Berber song, seen as a painful reminder of France's support for Berbers as a divisive strategy.[75] Representatives squared off on what they perceived as an infringement of the Algerian personality and the need to play Arabic songs, a sign of the country's heightened sensibility over the cultural ideals of the revolution. On the policy front, representatives criticized the continued use of French in the administration and called for immediate Arabization.[76] Boumedienne, a staunch proponent of Arabic, named a close collaborator, Ahmed Taleb-Ibrahimi, as Minister of Education (1965–70) and Minister of Culture (1970–7). Taleb-Ibrahimi was a doctor by training but his father was Sheikh Bashir Ibrahimi who ran the ʿUlema Association after Ben Badis. The son was sympathetic to the notion of recovery and the Arabic language, which he took on as a leading project and often in conflict with other members of the government.[77]

This nomination sent a powerful signal in favour of the ʿUlema Association's conception of the Algerian nation. The state adopted a series of education reforms under two principles: universal access and Arabization.[78] Problems included an insufficiency of qualified teachers and the pedagogical challenge of devising new curricula.[79] The authorities recruited massively in Egypt and Syria, Arabizing classes from the bottom up while it trained Algerian teachers and adapted teacher-training courses. This policy risked impeding Algeria's economic development: Algeria's technocratic and bureaucratic elite was still largely educated in French and continued to be educated in France after independence, while industrial partnerships required modern training that was carried out in French.[80] Considering the state's development agenda and the importance given to industrialization, the authorities adopted a '*bilinguisme de circonstances*', a 'pragmatic bilingualism' justified as temporary.[81] For the sociologist Ahmed Moatassime, this formula created confusion in the education system, which he called 'savage bilingualism', the product of failed pedagogical policies and political and ideological concerns.[82]

The Algerian government still maintained its public adherence to Arabization by introducing a subtle calibration of terminology, emphasizing its modernization agenda.[83] Taleb-Ibrahimi's official speeches reiterated the idea of 'recovery', a more flexible and gradual goal than 'Arabization', which gave the authorities some space. He relied on a convenient confluence of 'Arabness' and the 'Arabic language'. Passages from Taleb-Ibrahimi's speeches reveal how the official doctrine combined 'reactivation' and 'going forward':

> Our *goal* is to become once again ourselves, to recover and extend our cultural legacy in which language is the fundamental element. It is also a *means* since we propose to acquire a tool in order to progressively substitute a foreign language with a national language as a means of communication (oral and written) in public and private relations.[84]

This new discursive orientation underlines how Algeria was different from its North African neighbours when it came to negotiating colonial legacies. In Tunisia, the authorities adopted bilingualism as official policy and celebrated cultural plurality.[85] The Sadiki College in Tunis, established in 1875, taught in French and Arabic, and most of Tunisia's nationalist political elite were its graduates. After independence, the authorities sought to replicate this model at the national level with little resistance.[86] In Algeria, by contrast, the bicultural state-elite (of which Bennabi and Taleb-Ibrahimi were both part) did not shape state policy in the direction of bilingualism. Algeria's colonial experience was different from Tunisia's, where France had not targeted Arabic and Islamic instruction. Furthermore, the ʿUlema Association spent years campaigning on this issue during the anti-colonial struggle, and the public would hold it accountable if it reversed position.

A few Algerian intellectual figures still spoke against Arabization. In an influential 1963 article in Parisian journal *Les Temps Modernes*, Mostefa Lacheraf portrayed Arabization as inefficient and misguided. The Algerian state should, according to Lacheraf, pursue cultural renewal and scientific progress, for which bilingualism was an acceptable solution.[87] Lacheraf served briefly as Minister of Education (1977–9) and tried to apply these principles but was dismissed from his post before implementing his vision. The case for bilingualism was also made by francophone writers such as Kateb Yacine, the influential author of *Nedjma* (1956), who argued that 'literature seeks dominion over language', which was merely a tool for the expression of ideas that could be appropriated for revolutionary and nationalist aims; he called French the *butin de guerre* (spoils of war).[88] Even though French remained widely used in Algeria, this position remained marginal and the official line was a steadfast commitment to Arabization.

To explain the refusal to acknowledge bilingualism and the persistent discourse of 'recovery', we can turn to Albert Memmi's essay *Portrait du colonisé* (1957) and his depiction of the sensitivity of the colonial experience and the legacy of deep-rooted anxieties. Memmi writes of how language tapped into the internalization of inferiority in the colonized subject's mind:

> For the colonized [subject] there happen to be other priorities besides mathematics and philosophy and even technology. ... The colonized [subject] will go so far as to forbid himself the additional benefits of the colonizer's language; he will replace it as fast as possible. Between popular expression and learned expression, he will choose the learned [one] at the expense of [easy] communication. The priority is to rebuild one's people, whatever its authentic nature, to reestablish unity.[89]

'Forbidding the usage of the colonizer's language' was an internalized inferiority, Memmi adds, manifesting itself in the smallest details by 'changing signs ... even if he is the first to be inconvenienced by it'.[90]

In this passage, Memmi foretells a situation that would prevail in neighbouring Algeria less than a decade later. He foresees the passionate nature of decolonization, portrayed as a break-up that prevented a serene conversation on the role of Arabic and French in Algerian society and the establishment of an independent national culture. This process was condemned from the start, for even after 'he will no longer owe the colonizer anything, he will have eternally broken with him'.[91]

Thus, the ʿUlema Association's conception of national identity (based on Arabism and Islam) became the Algerian state's position after independence regardless of the fundamental challenges it posed to state policy. Rather than acknowledge the call for bilingual education, the state persisted, as Memmi argued, because of the Algerian elite's sense of cultural inferiority inherited from French colonialism. Recognizing this stark situation, Bennabi lamented the limited vision of those in charge of providing ideological guidance. Instead, he sought to address the deeper causes of Islamic civilizational decadence and formulate the necessary terms for a renaissance in Algeria.

Renaissance beyond the 'recovery' in Bennabi's intellectual project

Bennabi wrote his major texts on Islamic civilizational decadence and renaissance after 1945. His fifteen years in France are difficult to reconstruct, and Bennabi's early death means we lack the relevant memoirs: they include his marriage to a French woman; poverty and police harassment because of his community-building among the diaspora; and even being accused of and briefly jailed for collaborating with Nazi Germany under the Vichy regime.[92] He returned to Algeria in 1946 and stayed until his 1956 departure for Cairo, where he found the exiled Algerian nationalist leadership. Bennabi's rapport with them was tenuous and he preferred his independence and the company of others in this capital of non-alignment. His Cairo years were some of the most fruitful of his career, especially in writings on the historical destiny of Afro-Asian solidarity and decolonization.

After Algerian independence, Bennabi was called back but remained marginalized. His intellectual vision was not put to good use, illustrating the subjugation of critical thought by the centralizing force of the state. He was briefly put in charge of reforming higher education until the 1965 coup shifted power dynamics, and his post as head of the University of Algiers was mostly ceremonial.[93] His fraught relationship with Ahmed Taleb-Ibrahimi would prove his undoing. The two men entertained a problematic relationship throughout the decade as the latter took over education reform.[94] Bennabi lashed out in public in a series of attacks in the press against the *intellectomanes*, a play on word between *intellectuels* and *mythomanes* (compulsive liars). His refusal to conform compounded his isolation and he died in 1973, leaving a rich but largely unexplored body of texts.[95] They include several critical commentaries on the country's post-independence cultural realities in the Algerian journal *Révolution-Africaine*. As the following reading of his texts argues, his aim was sound but Bennabi underestimated the public appeal of 'cultural recovery' and overestimated the ability of Algerian intellectuals to replace defensiveness with critical thinking.

Cultural renaissance drove his major works. Decadence, he writes, was centuries in the making and predated the French arrival. Echoing Ibn Khaldun's analysis of the rise and fall of civilizations, Bennabi saw the Umayyad Caliphate as the height of Islamic civilization. The natural energies of men flowered in scientific achievements, arts and culture after embracing rationality and the Islamic message. The Almohad Caliphate (1180–1212), which unified North Africa and al-Andalus, was the last period which fulfilled Islamic civilization's promise. After this, Islamic society gave in to 'natural instincts', including moral corruption and frailty (traits of the *Jahiliyya*), underlining the centrality of human values in the growth and decadence of civilization. Bennabi coined the term 'post-Almohad man' to characterize the decadence that culminated in French colonization.[96]

In *Discours sur les conditions de la renaissance algérienne* (1949), he introduced his readers to the notion of 'colonizability', explaining how Algeria's ills were self-inflicted but how there was hope for 'rebirth' after working to restore past greatness.[97] The manifestations of this cultural decadence lay at the heart of the debate over Algeria's 'authentic personality' and the place of Arabic in the twentieth century. This reinforced Bennabi's claim that a mere 'return' would be counterproductive, and that instead Arab and Islamic cultural legacies had to undergo true reform. His 1954 *Vocation de l'Islam* unpacked the notion of 'colonizability', identifying present-day practices that were portrayed as the fundamental means to recover Islamic cultural identity but in fact perpetuated this decadent dynamic. This includes the *mujadala* (debate, polemics), a key activity of learned circles:

> We did not look for truths but arguments. We did not listen to interlocutors, but drowned them in verbal deluge. The *mujadala* is all the more harmful in that it is based on an irrational love of words … every newspaper headline is edifying: recently, a Tunisian newspaper announced the return of a political leader after a stay abroad, preceding his name by 5 or six laudatory epithets: *karim* [generous], *ʿadhim* [great], *jalil* [dignified], *zaʿim* etc. …, Arabic language is sacralized and cannot evolve through the adoration of its adepts … it has become sacrilege to constitute new forms.[98]

Bennabi's remarks targeted the glorification of a 'pure' Arabic language, as the neo-ʿUlema wanted, and demonstrated how this practice perpetuated cultural stagnation rather than promoting cultural renaissance. The reason, he believed, was that they failed to look critically at the current state of Algerian culture and the roots of its stagnation:

> The gravest paralysis is the moral one. Its origin is known: '*Islam is a perfect religion*'. No one challenges this truth, but it flows from our post-Almohad consciousness as another proposition: '*we are Muslims, therefore we are perfect*' … which neutralizes the quest for perfection … The Islamic ideal … has succumbed to vanity and the self-sufficiency of the believer who believes themselves to have achieved perfection by praying five times a day without seeking to better himself … these beings are static in their mediocrity, and they become the society's elites.[99]

Thus, the problems of Algerian culture lay with its elite. Conservatives were unwilling to change while modernists entertained a problematic relationship with European culture and their own civilization's heritage:

> [In Paris] the Muslim student has goggles that prevent him from contemplating civilization otherwise from the abstract or the futile … The Muslim student has not *felt* Europe, he is content with having *read* it, which means to learn rather than to understand. In the meantime, he remains ignorant of the story of his civilization, he cannot know how it has been made or is being unmade, with its internal contradictions, its incompatibility with human laws, and because his culture is no longer that of a civilization but has been transformed by colonialism.[100]

Bennabi moves from a broad argument to an assessment more applicable to Algeria's present cultural predicament. In 1967, he wrote a scathing assessment of the state's Arabization policies as profoundly unsuitable because all they contained were 'cosmetic' changes, not deep social and cultural transformations:

> We can change the name on a land title, change posts in such a way as to replace a Dupont with a Ben Kebir … we can change Latin characters to Arabic ones on the cabaret signs … these changes are meaningless and in no way definitive if the individual has not changed … a revolution can only achieve a new order and guarantee its achievements by transforming man first. It is an issue of civilization,

> but often formulated in political terms and requires the decolonization of the individual as a necessary condition.[101]

As for bilingualism in Algeria, Bennabi disagreed with those for whom it was merely a matter of practicality that would be eradicated via policies. Instead, bilingualism illustrated a 'deep rift' between two societies which refused to acknowledge each other.[102] The inertia of the neo-ʿUlema movement faced the 'hollow agitation of the secular, military and revolutionary trend', and together they kept the country stagnant.[103] Thus, Bennabi concludes, a focus on bilingualism alone was a false and inefficient solution to Algeria's cultural predicament.[104]

Bennabi called for an ambitious epistemological operation: self-critique and the 'necessary decolonization of the individual'. Algerian intellectuals had to excavate the internalized elements of colonial domination in their modes of thought. This would be a painful exercise, and, realistically, few of his peers proved able to carry this process out:

> We must first get rid of an obscuring complex … the veto each time someone formulates a critique, under pretext that critique helps imperialism … In June 1946, when I suggested creating a unified national party … each one of my critiques was brushed away. Not the arguments, but merely a refusal to take them into account. It was not the only time I was met with this paralysis, I should add, which I now see as having been costly to the national cause.[105]

Bennabi's call illustrates how he valued high intellectualism, but it would be perceived as posturing which, one can easily imagine, alienated him from political figures who came from more humble backgrounds. There was rampant 'anti-intellectualism' in the two Algerian nationalist parties in France, the Etoile Nord-Africaine and the Mouvement pour le triomphe des libertés démocratiques.[106] He did not even find support among other leading Algerian intellectuals in his calls for self-critique. Instead, they adopted combative postures when writing about Algerian culture and the nation. As Colonna notes, culture was the battleground on which independence was fought, and none of Algeria's most renowned intellectuals – Mostefa Lacheraf, Mouloud Mammeri and Abu al-Qasim Saʿdallah – displayed any self-criticism, instead engaging in identitarian struggles based on post-independence linguistic and ideological labels.[107] This striking 'absence of contradictory and democratic debate' on the part of the Algerian intellectual elite was 'nothing more than pro-domo self-defence'.[108] To expect self-criticism from this generation of Algerian intellectuals, Colonna emphasizes, is to be unaware of the historical context which shaped their personal experience, especially French colonialism:

> [They] already have enough to do in self-defence without starting to beat themselves up on their own account. Self-defence against whom, or what? Against political reproof, no doubt, against excommunication … but above all, I think, against themselves, caught in a reflex of self-censorship, all the more powerful for being unconscious: never to give weapons to those one considers as the enemy.[109]

This last point relates to the debate over colonial legacies in Algeria which drove Bennabi to write and publish his memoirs in 1965. Algerian intellectuals unapologetically defended a certain representation of Algeria, but these embattled reflexes were hard to abandon after France had left, while those who held state offices and responsibilities could not afford the luxury of self-criticism. In this light, Bennabi was not excluded so much as he chose to safeguard his freedom of speech and opinion. The publication of his memoirs in 1965 was meant to signal that he had overcome the embattlement of ideologies regarding colonial legacies by carrying out his own self-critical assessment of the formative years in which his views on culture and language in Algeria were founded.

By the early 1970s, independence was bearing fruit and Algeria looked ahead to a radiant economic, social and diplomatic future. National consultations for the new constitution in 1974 sparked widespread discussion, especially on the question of Algeria's cultural orientation. The intelligentsia debated the issue in relative freedom in the pages of *Al-Moujahid* and *Révolution-Africaine*, in short essays and in round-tables. Ultimately the 1976 Charter reiterated this question in the usual unitary terms:

> The Algerian people is attached to the Algerian nation of which it is an inseparable element ... From the seventh century, other elements have progressively been added that shaped the Algerian Nation's cultural, linguistic and spiritual unity ... Islam and Arab culture were simultaneously a universal and a specifically national framework ... it is in this double framework ... that the choices of our people and its evolution will be determined.[110]

Malek Bennabi was absent from this national conversation. He passed away in 1973 and his failure to accommodate the militant intellectual field cost him the ability to invite the Algerian intelligentsia to think more ambitiously about the deeper causes of Algeria's cultural malaise. Instead, by the early 1980s, Arabization policies were extended to higher education, partly under pressure from the growing Islamist constituency. The conflict between Algeria's 'two societies' continued to shape competition between francophone and Arabophone constituencies in the job market and for control of the rentier state and political office.[111] In today's Algeria, there is broad agreement that the country's linguistic conundrum goes back to the colonial era. What lies in between, however, is a contentious terrain of conflicting memories, defensive narratives and neglected intellectual projects.

Conclusion: The reconfigurations of colonial legacies

Focusing on the trajectory and writings of Malek Bennabi, an Algerian thinker known for his rich intellectual project on the Islamic renaissance, this chapter asks why he decided to publish the memoirs of his childhood education in 1965, portraying his bicultural education in favourable terms. The answer lies in Algerian cultural developments after independence and the state's pursuit of total Arabization at the expense of more ambitious measures toward cultural renaissance. By choosing to express himself in childhood memoirs, Bennabi praised the benefits of his bicultural education in order to move the conversation away from the question of language and toward broader issues.

These memoirs shed light on the transformation of colonial legacies in Algeria and how these were reshaped in light of new struggles. The national debate over Arabization of school education shows how the independent state inherited this ideological model from the ʿUlema Association – that 'personality' needed to be 'recovered' in order to be 'authentic' – which they pursued actively and unequivocally after independence. However, this was also a bone of contention as competing constituencies appropriated the issue in their attempt to gain control over the state, and conflict over language policy became tied to legitimacy and inclusion in positions of power to this day.

This example shows how memory became a battleground, often at the expense of individual recollections. Bicultural intellectuals such as Assia Djebar or Mostefa Lacheraf were inevitably sucked into the whirlwind of competing memories of the colonial era. Like Bennabi, they sometimes experienced independence as a lingering malaise rather than personal liberation, because their memory was captured and subjugated to the demands of the present.

Notes

1 Belahcene, 'Malek Bennabi's Concept'; Walsh, 'Killing Post-Almohad Man'; Boukrouh, *L'Islam sans l'islamisme.*
2 Benali, 'Les ancêtres fondateurs', 201.
3 'Madrasa' in *Encyclopaedia of Islam*, 2nd edn (2012).
4 McDougall, *History and the Culture of Nationalism.*
5 Rahal, *L'UDMA et les Udmistes.*
6 Sellam, 'Le FLN'.
7 Entelis, *The Revolution Institutionalized*, 91–7; Ruedy, *Modern Algeria*, 200, 224.
8 Seniguer, 'La civilisation islamique'.
9 Benali, 'Les ancêtres fondateurs', 201.
10 Naylor, 'Formative Influence', 138 n. 4.
11 N.A., 'La polémique sur la loi relative au 'rôle positif' de la colonisation enfle'.
12 Berrady, *Formation des élites.*
13 Colonna, 'Le système d'enseignement'.
14 Carlier, *Entre nation et Jihad*, 142–7.
15 An Algerian religious scholar and reformer from Constantine (Eastern Algeria) who studied at the Zaytuna Mosque in Tunis, Ben Badis was a leading figure behind the creation of several independent schools, cultural clubs and newspapers to spread reformist ideas. In 1931, he was a founder of the Association of Algerian Muslim Ulama (Jam'iyat al-ʿulama al-muslimin al-jaza'iriyyin) and in 1936 the Algerian Muslim Congress which played an instrumental role in the independence movement. See McDougall, 'Ben Badis'.
16 Sahli, *Décoloniser l'histoire*; Ahmida, *Beyond Colonialism and Nationalism.*
17 Stora, *La grangrène de l'oubli*; Bras, 'Introduction: la mémoire'; Djerbal, 'Dissonances et discordances'.
18 Kaye and Zoubir, *The Ambiguous Compromise*, 72–90.

19 Harrison, 'Ce pouvoir me fut aussi funeste que sauveur'.
20 Kelly, *Autobiography and Independence*; Hiddleston, *Decolonising the Intellectual.*
21 Bennabi, *Memoirs d'un témoin du siècle*, preface (n.p.).
22 Colonna, 'Le système d'enseignement', 198–9.
23 Ibid., 200.
24 Vermeren, *Ecole, élite et pouvoir*, 9–11.
25 Carlier, *Entre nation et Jihad*, 140–51.
26 Colonna, 'Le système d'enseignement', 199.
27 Bennabi, *Mémoires d'un témoin du siècle*, 22.
28 Ibid., 39.
29 Kelly, *Autobiography and Independence.*
30 Harrison, 'Ce pouvoir me fut aussi funeste que sauveur', 126–7.
31 Ibid., 128–32.
32 Bennabi, *Mémoires d'un témoin du siècle*, 52–4.
33 Ibid., 53–4.
34 Ibid., 53.
35 Ibid., 109.
36 Ibid., 53.
37 Kadri, *Institutеurs et enseignants.*
38 Clark, 'Expressing Entitlement'.
39 Bennabi, *Mémoires d'un témoin du siècle*, 58.
40 Ibid., 34–42.
41 Ibid., 27.
42 *Islah*, meaning 'reform' or 'repairing', envisioned a renewed Islam opposed to obscurantist superstitions and practices that were common in rural Algeria, and believed to keep Algerian society in a state of backwardness. See 'Islah' in *Encyclopaedia of Islam*, 2nd edn (2012).
43 McDougall, *History and the Culture of Nationalism*, 22–5.
44 Christelow, *Muslim Law Courts.*
45 Bennabi, *Mémoires d'un témoin du siècle*, 64.
46 Ibid., 76.
47 Ibid., 88–91.
48 Carlier, 'Le café maure', 123–6.
49 Ibid., 123.
50 Scales, 'Subversive Sound', 390.
51 Bennabi, *Mémoires d'un témoin du siècle*, 130.
52 Ibid.
53 Merad, *Le réformisme musulman*, 337–51; Courreye, 'L'école musulmane'.
54 Bennabi, *Mémoires d'un témoin du siècle*, 86–7.
55 Ibid.
56 Ibid., 106.
57 Ibid., 118.
58 Ibid., 78.
59 Ibid., 77.
60 Ibid., 103, 135.
61 McDougall, 'Abdelhamid Ben Badis', 387; Merad, *Le réformisme musulman*, 13–9.
62 Bennabi, *Mémoires d'un témoin du siècle*, 93.
63 Ibid., 226–7.
64 Ibid., 204–5.

65 Ibid., 205.
66 Ibid., 210–12.
67 Ibid., 213.
68 Ibid., 233–5.
69 Boukrouh, *L'Islam sans l'islamisme*, 61–195.
70 Peyroulou et al., *Histoire de l'Algérie*, 324–31; Julien, *Une pensée anti-coloniale*, 87; Ageron, *Histoire de l'Algérie*, 77–86.
71 Ruedy, *Modern Algeria*, 196–207.
72 McDougall, 'War by Other Means'.
73 Tripoli Charter, 1962, Section 3D.
74 Mbanaso and Korieh, *Minorities*, 88.
75 Grandguillaume, *Arabisation et politique*, 30.
76 Ibid.
77 Taleb-Ibrahimi, *Mémoires d'un algérien*, 39.
78 Ibid., 26, 36, 47; Souriau, 'La politique algérienne', 375–97.
79 Entelis, *The Revolution Institutionalized*, 91.
80 Etienne, *Algerie. Culture et Révolution*, 169; Adam Granai, 'Algérie: Chronique', 543.
81 Mignot-Lefebvre, 'Bilinguisme et système', 673.
82 Moatassime, 'Le "bilinguisme sauvage"', 619.
83 Taleb-Ibrahimi, *Mémoires d'un algérien*, 38.
84 Taleb-Ibrahimi, *De la décolonisation*, 101; original emphases.
85 Abbassi, *Entre Bourguiba et Hannibal.*
86 Sraieb, *Le collège Sadiki de Tunis.*
87 Lacheraf, 'L'avenir de la culture algérienne', 745.
88 Kaye and Zoubir, *The Ambiguous Compromise*, 133.
89 Memmi, *Portrait du colonisé*, 149.
90 Ibid., 151.
91 Ibid., 152.
92 El-Hamri, *Malek Bennabi.*
93 Boukrouh, *L'Islam sans l'islamisme*, 231.
94 Ibid., 238.
95 Ibid., 267–75.
96 Walsh, 'Killing Post-Almohad Man', 236–7.
97 Bennabi, *Renaissance algérienne*, 22, 31.
98 Bennabi, *Vocation de l'Islam*, 53–4.
99 Ibid 76–7.
100 Ibid 60–1.
101 Bennabi, 'Changer l'homme'.
102 Ibid., 122–3.
103 Ibid., 125.
104 Ibid., 127.
105 Bennabi, 'Sociologie de l'indépendance'.
106 Colonna, *Les versets de l'invincibilité*, 361.
107 Colonna, 'Unknowing Other', 164–5.
108 Ibid., 166.
109 Ibid., 167.
110 National Charter, 1976, first title, 83.
111 Addi, *L'Algérie et la démocratie*, 211; Grandguillaume, *Arabisation et politique*, 141–65.

Bibliography

Abbassi, Driss. *Entre Bourguiba et Hannibal: Identité tunisienne et histoire depuis l'indépendance*. Paris: Karthala, 2005.

Adam, André, and Georges Granai. 'Chronique Sociale et Culturelle'. *L'Annuaire de l'Afrique du Nord* (1963): 535–91.

Addi, Lahouari. *L'Algérie et la démocratie*. Paris: La Découverte, 1994.

Ageron, Charles-Robert. *Histoire de l'Algérie contemporaine*, t.II, 1871–1954. Paris: Presse Universitaire de France, 1979.

Ahmida, Ali Abdulatif. *Beyond Colonialism and Nationalism in the Maghrib: History, Culture and Politics*. New York: Palgrave, 2000.

Ali Benali, Zineb. 'Les ancêtres fondateurs: Elaborations symboliques du champ intellectuel algérien (1945–1954)'. *Insaniyat* 25–6 (2004): 201–14.

Belahcene, Badrane. 'Malek Bennabi's Concept and Interdisciplinary Approach to Civilisation'. *International Journal of Arab Culture, Management and Sustainable Development* 2, no. 1 (2011): 55–71.

Bennabi, Malek. 'Changer l'homme'. *Révolution-Africaine* 221 (8 May 1967) : 8–14.

Bennabi, Malek. *Discours sur les conditions de la renaissance algérienne: Le problème d'une civilisation*. Alger: En-Nahda, 1949.

Bennabi, Malek. *Mémoires d'un témoin du siècle*. Alger: Editions Nationales Algériennes, 1965.

Bennabi, Malek. 'Sociologie de l'indépendance'. *Révolution-Africaine* 87 (26 September 1964): 111–15.

Bennabi, Malek. *Vocation de l'Islam*. Paris: Editions du Seuil, 1954.

Berrady, Lhachmi. *Formation des élites politiques maghrébines*. Paris: Centre de recherche et d'études sur les sociétés méditerranéennes, 1973.

Boukrouh, Nour-Eddine. *L'Islam sans l'islamisme: Vie et pensée de Malek Bennabi*. Alger: Samar, 2006.

Bras, Jean-Phillipe. 'Introduction: la mémoire, idiome du politique au Maghreb'. *L'Année du Maghreb IV* (2008): 5–26.

Carlier, Omar. 'Le café maure: Sociabilité masculine et effervescence citoyenne (Algérie XVIIe-XXe siècles)'. *Annales. Economies, sociétés, civilisations* 45, no. 4 (1990): 975–1003.

Carlier, Omar. *Entre nation et Jihad: Histoire sociale des radicalismes algériens*. Paris: Presses de la Fondation Nationale des Sciences Politiques, 1995.

Carlier, Omar. 'Scholars and Politicians: An Examination of the Algerian View of Algerian Nationalism'. In *The Maghrib in Question: Essays in History and Historiography*, edited by Michel Le Gall and Kenneth Perkins, 136–69. Austin: University of Texas Press, 1997.

Christelow, Allan. *Muslim Law Courts and the French Colonial State in Algeria*. Princeton: Princeton University Press, 1985.

Clark, Hannah-Louise. 'Expressing Entitlement in Colonial Algeria: Villagers, Medical Doctors and the State in Early 20th Century'. *International Journal of Middle East Studies* 48, no. 3 (2016): 445–72.

Colonna, Fanny. The Nation's 'Unknowing Other': Three Intellectuals and the Culture(s) of Being Algerian'. In *Nation, Society and Culture in North Africa*, edited by James McDougall, 155–70. London: Routledge, 2003.

Colonna, Fanny. 'Le système d'enseignement de l'Algérie coloniale'. *European Journal of Sociology* 13, no. 2 (1973): 195–220.
Colonna, Fanny. *Les versets de l'invincibilité: permanence et changements religieux dans l'Algérie contemporaine*. Paris: Presses de la Fondation Nationale des Sciences Politiques, 1995,
Courreye, Charlotte. 'L'école musulmane algérienne de Ibn Badis dans les années 1930, de l'alphabétisation de tous comme enjeu politique'. *Revue des mondes musulmans et de la Méditerranée* 136 (2014). Accessed 16 June 2020. http://journals.openedition.org/remmm/8500.
DeGeorges, Thomas. 'The Shifting Sands of Revolutionary Legitimacy: The Role of Former Mujahidin in the Shaping of Algeria's Collective Memory'. *Journal of North African Studies* 14, no. 2 (2009): 273–88.
Djerbal, Daho. 'Dissonances et discordances mémorielles. Le cas des Aurès (1930–1962)'. *L'Année du Maghreb* IV (2008): 171–190.
El-Hamri, Jamal. *Malek Bennabi: Une vie au service d'une pensée*. Paris: Abouraq, 2016.
Entelis, John P. *Algeria: The Revolution Institutionalized*. Boulder, CO: Westview Press, 1986.
Etienne, Bruno. *Algerie. Culture et Révolution*. Paris: Editions du Seuil, 1977.
Garon, Lise. *L'obsession unitaire de la nation trompée: La fin de l'Algérie socialiste*. Sainte-Foy: Presse de l'Université Laval, 1990.
Grandguillaume, Gilbert. *Arabisation et politique linguistique au Maghreb*. Paris: Editions Maisonneuve et Larose, 1983.
Harrison, Nick. 'Ce pouvoir me fut aussi funeste que sauveur … La littérature francophone et l'enseignement colonial'. In *L'école aux colonies. Les colonies à l'école*, edited by Gilles Boyer, Pascal Clerc and Michelle Zancarini-Fournel, 125–41. Lyon: ENS Editions, 2013.
Hiddleston, Jane. *Decolonising the Intellectual: Politics, Culture, and Humanism at the End of the French Empire*. Liverpool: Liverpool University Press, 2014.
Julien, Charles-André. *Une pensée anti-coloniale: Postitions 1914–1979*. Paris: Sindbad, 1979.
Kadri, Aïssa. *Instituteurs et enseignants en Algérie 1945–1975: Histoire et mémoires*. Paris: Karthala, 2014.
Kaye, Jacqueline, and Abdelhamid Zoubir. *The Ambiguous Compromise: Language, Literature and National Identity in Algeria and Morocco*. London: Routledge, 1990.
Kelly, Debra. *Autobiography and Independence: Selfhood and Creativity in North African Postcolonial Writing in French*. Liverpool: Liverpool University Press, 2005.
Lacheraf, Mostefa. 'L'avenir de la culture algérienne'. *Les Temps Modernes* 209 (October 1963): 720–45.
Mbanaso, Michael, and Chima J. Korieh. *Minorities and the State in Africa*. Amherst: Cambria Press, 2010.
McDougall, James. 'Abdelhamid Ben Badis et l'Association des oulémas'. In *Histoire de l'Algérie à la période coloniale*, edited by Abderrahmane Bouchène, Jean-Pierre Peyroulou, Ouanassa Siari Tengour and Sylvie Thénault, 387–92. Paris: La Découverte, 2012.
McDougall, James. 'Ben Badis'. In *Encyclopaedia of Islam 3rd Edition*, edited by Kate Fleet, Gudrun Krämer, Denis Matringe, John Nawas and Everett Rowson. Leiden: Brill, 2013.
McDougall, James. 'Culture as War by Other Means: Community, Conflict and Cultural Revolution, 1967–1981'. In *Algeria Revisited: Contested Identities in the Colonial and*

Postcolonial Periods, edited by Rabah Aissaoui and Claire Eldridge, 235–52. London: Bloomsbury, 2017.

McDougall, James. *History and the Culture of Nationalism in Algeria*. Cambridge: Cambridge University Press, 2002.

Memmi, Albert. *Portrait du colonisé précédé de Portrait du colonisateur*. Paris: Gallimard, [1957] 2002.

Merad, Ali. *Le réformisme musulman en Algérie de 1925 à 1940; essai d'histoire religieuse et sociale*. Paris: Mouton, 1967.

Mignot-Lefebvre, Yvonne. 'Bilinguisme et système scolaire en Algérie'. *Tiers-Monde* 59 (1974): 671–93.

Moatassime, Ahmed. 'Le "bilinguisme sauvage": L'exemple maghrébin'. *Tiers-Monde* 59 (1974): 619–70.

N.A. 'A: l'origine de la polémique, le 'rôle positif de la colonisation'. Le Monde (7 December 2005). Accessed 16 June 2020. https://www.lemonde.fr/societe/article/2005/12/07/a-l-origine-de-la-polemique-le-role-positif-de-la-colonisation_718356_3224.html.

Ottaway, David, and Marina Ottaway. *Algeria: The Politics of a Socialist Revolution*. Berkeley: University of California Press, 1970.

Peyroulou, Jean-Pierre, Abderrahmane Bouchène, Ouanassa Siari Tengour and Sylvie Thénault, eds. *Histoire de l'Algérie à la période coloniale*. Paris: La Découverte, 2012.

Rahal, Malika. *Rahal, L'UDMA et les Udmistes: Contribution à l'histoire du nationalisme*. Algiers: Barzakh, 2017.

Ruedy, John. *Modern Algeria: The Origins and Development of a Nation*. Bloomington: Indiana University Press, 2005.

Sahli, Mohamed C. *Décoloniser l'histoire. Introduction à l'histoire du Maghreb*. Paris: Francois Maspero, 1965.

Scales, Rebecca P. 'Subversive Sound: Transnational Radio, Arabic Recordings and the Dangers of Listening in French Colonial Algeria, 1934–1939'. *Comparative Studies in Society and History* 52, no. 2 (2010): 384–417.

Sellam, Sadek. 'Le FLN vu par l'écrivain Malek Bennabi (1905–1973): Les relations malaisées d'un penseur non-conformiste avec le pouvoir algérien naissant'. *Guerres Mondiales et Conflits Contemporains* 208 (2002): 133–50.

Seniguer, Haoues. 'La civilisation islamique et l'humanisme Arabo-Musulman: Le regard de Malek Bennabi'. *Confluences Méditerranée* 89, no. 2 (2014): 187–209.

Souriau, Christiane. 'La politique algérienne d'arabisation'. *L'Annuaire de l'Afrique du Nord* (1975): 363–401.

Sraieb, Noureddine. *Le collège Sadiki de Tunis 1875–1956: Enseignement et nationalisme*. Paris: CNRS, 1994.

Stora, Benjamin. *La grangrène de l'oubli: La mémoire de la guerre d'Algérie*. Paris: La Découverte, 1991.

Taleb-Ibrahimi, Ahmed. *De la décolonisation à la révolution culturelle, 1962–1972*. Alger: SNED, 1981.

Taleb-Ibrahimi, Ahmed. *Mémoires d'un algérien. Tome 2: La passion de batir (1965–1978)*. Alger: Casbah Editions, 2008.

Vermeren, Pierre. *Ecole, élite et pouvoir: Au Maroc et en Tunisie au XXe siècle*. Rabat: Alizés, 2002.

Walsh, Sebastian J. 'Killing Post-Almohad Man: Malek Bennabi, Algerian Islamism and the Search for a Liberal Governance'. *Journal of North African Studies* 12, no. 2 (2007): 235–54.

Index

CPSIA information can be obtained
at www.ICGtesting.com
Printed in the USA
LVHW080057051122
732390LV00004B/217